942. 062 GAUN

YALE COLLEGE
LEARNING RESOURCE CENTRE £ 10.99

The English Civil War

10/12

_____ sam / Coleg Cambria- Yale Wrexh

D1347599

Coleg Cambria

76992

Blackwell Essential Readings in History

This series comprises concise collections of key articles on important historical topics. Designed as a complement to standard survey histories, the volumes are intended to help introduce students to the range of scholarly debate in a subject area. Each collection includes a general introduction and brief contextual headnotes to each article, offering a coherent, critical framework for study.

Published

The German Reformation: The Essential Readings
C. Scott Dixon

The Counter-Reformation: The Essential Readings
David M. Luebke

The English Civil War: The Essential Readings
Peter Gaunt

The French Revolution: The Essential Readings
Ronald Schechter

The Russian Revolution: The Essential Readings
Martin Miller

The Third Reich: The Essential Readings
Christian Leitz

In Preparation

The Italian Renaissance: The Essential Readings
Paula Finden

The Enlightenment: The Essential Readings
Martin Fitzpatrick

The Cold War: The Essential Readings
Klaus Larres and Ann Lane

The English Civil War

The Essential Readings

Edited by Peter Gaunt

BLACKWELL
Publishers

Copyright © Blackwell Publishers Ltd 2000. Editorial selection and introduction copyright © Peter Gaunt 2000.

First published 2000

2 4 6 8 10 9 7 5 3 1

Blackwell Publishers Ltd
108 Cowley Road
Oxford OX4 1JF
UK

Blackwell Publishers Inc.
350 Main Street
Malden, Massachusetts 02148
USA

All rights reserved. Except for the quotation of short passages for the purposes of criticism and review, no part of this publication may be reproduced, stored in a retrieval system, or transmitted, in any form or by any means, electronic, mechanical, photocopying, recording or otherwise, without the prior permission of the publisher.

Except in the United States of America, this book is sold subject to the condition that it shall not, by way of trade or otherwise, be lent, resold, hired out, or otherwise circulated without the publisher's prior consent in any form of binding or cover other than that in which it is published and without a similar condition including this condition being imposed on the subsequent purchaser.

British Library Cataloguing in Publication Data

A CIP catalogue record for this book is available from the British Library.

Library of Congress Cataloging-in-Publication Data is available for this book.

ISBN   0 631 20808 9
        0 631 20809 7 (pbk)

Typeset in 10½ on 12 pt Photina
by Best-set Typesetter Ltd., Hong Kong
Printed in Great Britain by MPG Books Ltd, Bodmin, Cornwall

This book is printed on acid-free paper.

Contents

Acknowledgements

The authors and publishers gratefully acknowledge the following for permission to reproduce copyright material:

Bennett, Martyn: 'Between Scylla and Charybdis: the Creation of Rival Administrations at the Beginning of the English Civil War' in *The Local Historian* 22. Copyright © 1992 British Association for Local History, Salisbury;

Crawford, Patricia: 'Charles Stuart, That Man of Blood' in *Journal of British Studies* 16 (1977): 41–61. Copyright © by The North American Conference on British Studies. All rights reserved. Reproduced by permission of The University of Chicago Press;

Davis, J. Colin: 'The Levellers and Christianity' in B. Manning (ed.), *Politics, Religion and the English Civil War*. Copyright © 1973 Edward Arnold, London;

Fielding, John: 'Opposition to the Personal Rule of Charles I: the Diary of Robert Woodford, 1637–1641' in *Historical Journal* 31. Copyright © 1988 Cambridge University Press, Cambridge;

Fulbrook, Mary: 'The English Revolution and the Revisionist Revolt' in *Social History* 7. Copyright © 1982 Routledge, London. Reprinted with permission of Taylor & Francis Ltd, PO Box 25, Abingdon, Oxfordshire, OX14 3UE;

Hill, Christopher: 'A Bourgeois Revolution?' in J. G. A. Pocock (ed.), *Three British Revolutions*. Copyright © 1980 by Princeton University Press;

Hirst, Derek: 'The Defection of Sir Edward Dering 1640–41' in *Historical Journal* 15. Copyright © 1972 Cambridge University Press, Cambridge;

Morrill, John: 'Sir William Brereton and England's Wars of Religion' in *Journal of British Studies* 24 (July 85): 311–32. Copyright © 1985 by The North American Conference on British Studies. All rights reserved. Reproduced by permission of The University of Chicago Press;

Morrill, John, Manning, Brian and Underdown, David: 'What was the English Revolution?' in *History Today* 34. Copyright © 1984 History Today Ltd, London;

Osborne, Simon: 'The War, the People and the Absence of the Clubmen in the Midlands 1642–46' in *Midland History* 19. Copyright © 1994. Reprinted with permission of The University of Birmingham;

Roy, Ian: 'England Turned Germany? The Aftermath of the Civil War in its European Context' in *Transactions of the Royal Historical Society* 5th Series 28. Copyright © 1978 Royal Historical Society, London;

Russell, Conrad: 'Why did Charles I Fight the Civil War?' in *History Today* 34. Copyright © 1984 History Today Ltd, London;

Russell, Conrad; 'Why did Charles I Call the Long Parliament?' in *History* 69. Copyright © 1984 Blackwell Publishers, Oxford;

Russell, Conrad: 'The British Problem and the English Civil War' in *History* 72. Copyright © 1987 Blackwell Publishers, Oxford.

The publishers apologize for any errors or omissions in the above list and would be grateful to be notified of any corrections that should be incorporated in the next edition or reprint of this book.

Editor's Introduction

'Our Unnatural Wars'

> Thou wouldest think it strange if I should tell thee there was a time in England when brothers killed brothers, cousins cousins, and friends their friends. Nay, when they conceived it was no offence to commit murder. To murder a man held less offence than to kill a dog, and they would glory in their actions as if they had done a pious deed. When thou wentest to bed at night, thou knewest not whether thou shouldest be murdered afore day. To take away other men's goods was held as lawful as to sell thy own, although the former owners went by that means a-begging. Sacrilege was a virtue, and to rail against sovereignty esteemed a high piece of piety. Think nothing strange in this world, for I have seen such mutations, changes and alterations within the verge of my time as almost no mortal could believe or apprehend . . . I believe such times were never before seen in England . . .

Sir John Oglander, who recorded these impressions of the English civil war in his commonplace book, was not a typical Englishman of the mid-seventeenth century. He belonged to the literate, educated elite, he was a knight and a former MP and sheriff, although he did not take up arms (he was in his late fifties by the time war broke out) he was consistently and clearly sympathetic to one side in the civil war (the royalists) and he lived not on the mainland but on the Isle of Wight. Nonetheless, in stressing the violence and uncertainty of the civil wars – probably exaggerating them, in fact, for the Isle of Wight was far from the most intense theatre of the war – and the unprecedented division, bitterness and lawlessness which they engendered, he was typical of many at both elite and non-elite levels of society. It was, he wrote, 'a miserable distracted time', which saw him stripped of office, summoned to London on several occasions and imprisoned in the capital for suspected royalism. He recorded the death of his wife during the 1640s, allegedly brought on by worry at his own imprisonment, as well as those of several grandchildren, his alienation from members of his own extended family, and his jaundiced view of the Isle of Wight under military and parliamentarian control, a 'melancholy, dejected, sad place', visited (like the mainland) in the late 1640s with some of the worst weather in living memory, as if 'the heavens were offended with us for our offence committed to one another'. 'God mend all. First let us repent all our bloody sins, then we shall find His mercy, and the earth will be again propitious unto us', he concluded gloomily in 1648, sentiments shared by many on both sides by the closing years of the decade.[1]

Oglander was just one of many literate English men and women who, from royalist and parliamentarian viewpoints, and from various parts of the country, recorded in their letters, journals and memoirs their horror at the civil wars which were engulfing England and Wales, and their acute awareness that they were living through and witnessing unprecedented, unnatural and cataclysmic events. Oglander often emphasized social division and overturning, seeing the civil war as a conflict which ruined many gentlemen and advanced upstart social inferiors – 'I verily believe that, in the quarrel of the Two Roses, there were never half as many gentlemen slain, and so many base men, by the others' loss and slaughter, made gentlemen'. But he did not go on to present a class-based interpretation of the grounds of the civil war and instead professed to share what he claimed was a widespread uncertainty about the causes and nature of the civil war – 'no man understanding the true grounds' of 'our unnatural wars'.[2] It was an incomprehension held by many of his class, including, from the opposing parliamentarian perspective, Bulstrode Whitelocke, whose reflections on the outbreak of war are both fuller and better known:

> It is strange to note how we have insensibly slid into this beginning of a civil war by one unexpected accident after another, as waves of the sea which have brought us thus far and we scarce know how, but from paper combats, by declarations, remonstrances, protestations, votes, messages, answers and replies we are now come to the question of raising forces and naming a general and officers of an army . . . What the issue

1 F. Bamford (ed.), *A Royalist Notebook. The Commonplace Book of Sir John Oglander, Kt, of Nunwell* (London, 1936), pp. 102–22.
2 Ibid., p. 109.

of it will be no man alive can tell. Probably few of us now here may live
to see the end of it.[3]

No historian can ever hope to see the end of the continuing debates
about the causes, course and consequences of the civil war in which
Oglander, Whitelocke and several million of their compatriots participated, willingly or unwillingly, directly or indirectly, during the 1640s.
Tempting as Whitelocke's expressions of incomprehension might at
times appear, most historians of the mid-seventeenth century feel the
need to advance broader interpretations of civil war, to give shape and
meaning to the events of the 1640s, to explain and interpret at a level
deeper than 'one unexpected accident after another'. But the very complexity and magnitude of the events of the mid-seventeenth century, the
richness and diversity of the surviving source material for many aspects
of the civil war combined with a frustrating paucity in other areas, and
the diverse and changing biases, viewpoints and fashions of the large
number of historians drawn to the civil war have together generated a
multiplicity of often conflicting interpretations and ensure that unanimity and lasting historiographical consensus are unlikely ever to be
achieved. Few historians would deny that the conflicts of the mid-
seventeenth century were important and merit detailed study; acade-
mics and non-academics alike are drawn to the period as one that
matters, as a formative era which is still important to us. But attempts
to explain why the civil war was important, to interpret causes and consequences, to assess the meaning, impact and legacy of the war, quickly
reveal broad spectra of historical opinion and unresolved – probably
unresolvable – historical debates.

If, as is often claimed, the history of the English civil war is the
supreme example of the need for each generation to rewrite its own
past, then the lifespan of a generation appears to be shortening, for
the closing decades of the twentieth century saw an appreciable accel-
eration and intensification in the development of new and often conflicting views. A recent historiographical study of the differing
interpretations of the causes of the civil war surveyed the debate from
the mid-seventeenth century to the end of the nineteenth century in
four chapters, but required a further seven chapters to cover the wide
variety of explanations advanced during the twentieth century.[4] One
of the best general overviews of the causes of the war, first published
in 1991, appeared in a second and substantially revised edition just

3   Quoted by many historians, perhaps most accessibly in J. Adair, *By the Sword
Divided. Eyewitness Accounts of the English Civil War* (Stroud, 1998), p. 9.
4   R. C. Richardson, *The Debate on the English Revolution* (3rd edn, Manchester,
1998).

seven years later; as the introduction to the revised edition noted, the historiographical context in which it appeared had changed appreciably since the first edition had been prepared less than a decade earlier.[5] The intensification of research and writing means that it is now much easier to attack and undermine interpretations than to advance broad, over-arching theories about the causes, nature and consequences of the civil war. A student approaching the 1640s at the beginning of the third millennium might be forgiven for finding the clarity and simplicity of some of the nineteenth and early twentieth century interpretations far more appealing than the current complex and often apparently contradictory or inconclusive theories on offer; all too many seem to end up sharing the bafflement and uncertainty of Oglander and Whitelocke.

This *Reader* seeks to pull together and republish some of the best and most interesting articles which have appeared over the last thirty years. In a work of this length, it would clearly be impossible to cover all the major themes of the 1640s or to reprint more than a selection of papers, but the pieces included here introduce many of the important issues, highlight several of the key areas of historical research and debate of the past few decades, and give a reasonably balanced coverage of the 1640s, spanning causes, course and consequences of the civil war. No attempt has been made to extend the chronological coverage beyond 1649, for it is intended that another *Reader* in this series will focus on the period from 1649 to 1660 often referred to as the 'interregnum'. The introductions to the principal sections (Parts I–IV) do not seek to provide full syntheses of work on the period, nor do they take the form of analytical narratives of the early and mid-seventeenth century. Instead, they attempt to do two things. They place each article reprinted in the section within its own immediate context, highlighting its key arguments and importance and, where appropriate, showing how research and publication in that area have moved on. But much more broadly, they also review the recent and current state of play in civil war studies and explore some of the key trends and issues in historical research and writing on the causes, course and consequences of the civil war.

5   A. Hughes, *The Causes of the English Civil War* (2nd edn, Basingstoke, 1998).

Part I   Approaches to the 1640s

Introduction to Part I

That historians adopt very different approaches to the 1640s and interpret the events of that decade very differently are immediately revealed by the wide variety of labels which they apply to the mid-seventeenth century. Even the apparently neutral phrase 'the English civil war', chosen for this volume, is not above criticism. Some historians would argue that there were two or even three different, if linked, civil wars (plural) in England between 1642 and 1651 and most would acknowledge that this label ignores the undoubted involvement of Wales and the Welsh. Some historians, such as Conrad Russell, John Morrill and Jane Ohlmeyer, have recently stressed that the causes, course and consequences of the conflict in England (and Wales) repeatedly intertwined with, and can best be explained and interpreted in the broader context of, associated conflicts within and between Scotland and Ireland, too.[1] Accordingly, some historians have recently moved away from Anglo-centric labels and have preferred to see the English conflict as just one element of 'the British War(s)' or 'the War(s) of the Three Kingdoms'. Others, including at times J. H. Elliott, Eric Hobsbawm and Hugh Trevor-Roper, have gone further and seen the English (or British) conflict as just one manifestation of a 'General European Crisis' of the mid-seventeenth century, a series of revolts, rebellions, civil wars and wars between states which shared common causes.[2] Those causes are explained variously as wide-ranging socio-economic problems (often viewed in a Marxist context), political tensions springing from the centralizing aspirations of heads of state or (possibly an allied factor) pressure upon existing governmental systems caused by military expansion and the associated heavier fiscal and administrative burdens.

These debates over whether to see the conflict as English, British or European mirror longer-standing differences over what to call the events of the mid-seventeenth century. For the royalist politician and statesman Edward Hyde, Earl of Clarendon, the 1640s saw a 'Great Rebellion' against the king, a label chosen by Ivan Roots as the title of his narrative history of the period 1642–60, first published in the

1 See, for example, C. Russell, *The Fall of the British Monarchies, 1637–42* (Oxford, 1991); J. Morrill, 'The Britishness of the English Revolution' in R. Asch (ed.), *Three Nations – A Common History?* (Bochum, 1992); J. Ohlmeyer, *Civil War and Restoration in Three Kingdoms. The Career of Randall Macdonnell* (Cambridge, 1993).
2 T. Aston (ed.), *Crisis in Europe, 1560–1660* (London, 1965); G. Parker and L. M. Smith (eds), *The General Crisis of the Seventeenth Century* (2nd edn, London, 1997).

mid-1960s.[3] Others have felt that the word 'rebellion' does not capture the magnitude and diversity of the events of the 1640s and of the changes which they wrought, and prefer the label 'revolution'. Thus Gerald Aylmer chose the question *Rebellion or Revolution?* as the title of his narrative overview of the period 1640–60, first published in the mid-1980s. In the closing paragraph of the book, he agrees that a great rebellion occurred but feels that the phrase is too limited, concluding that, in the light of the deep impact made by the conflict and the 'drastic and thoroughgoing' changes which it brought about, there had – 'if only temporarily and partially' – been a revolution in mid-seventeenth century England.[4] But the use of the word 'revolution' can unhelpfully and anachronistically bring to mind much later and very different political and military events in France, Russia, China and elsewhere, as well as wider changes in the fields of science, agriculture and industry. At the very least, it calls for careful definition and almost invites rather tedious debates over semantics. Moreover, even those historians who feel that a revolution did occur in mid-seventeenth century England and are happy to use the word, often go on to disagree sharply about the essence and nature of that revolution. Thus while some prefer the relatively neutral term 'English revolution' (though as Wales, Scotland and Ireland were directly involved, this Anglo-centricity might be regretted), others, especially late Victorian historians such as S. R. Gardiner, saw a 'puritan revolution' occurring in the mid-seventeenth century, in which strong, radical and reformist Protestant beliefs were in the van of, and drove on, wider religious, political and constitutional aspirations and reforms. In contrast, many twentieth century Marxist and neo-Marxist historians, taking a socio-economic or class-based approach, have cast the civil war era in that mould, claiming to detect a 'bourgeois revolution' in the mid-seventeenth century, in which a new capitalist-minded class overthrew the outdated feudal establishment.[5]

Differences in nomenclature are underlain by fundamental differences in the approach to and the interpretation of the period. Most obviously, perhaps, while some historians have worked on Scotland, Ireland,

---

3 E. Hyde, lst Earl of Clarendon, *The History of the Rebellion and Civil Wars in England, Begun in 1641* (3 vols, Oxford, 1704); I. Roots, *The Great Rebellion, 1642–60* (London, 1966).
4 G. E. Aylmer, *Rebellion or Revolution? England 1640–60* (Oxford, 1987), especially pp. 204–5.
5 Compare the introduction of S. R. Gardiner, *Constitutional Documents of the Puritan Revolution, 1625–60* (3rd edn, Oxford, 1906) with the line taken by C. Hill, *The English Revolution, 1640* (London, 1940).

England or Wales more or less in isolation, others have recently sought to pull the stories together to produce a British-wide or three kingdoms account, and some have gone further still, placing the English or British conflict in the wider context of a general Europe-wide crisis. While some historians have continued to focus upon developments at the centre, the closing decades of the twentieth century saw a mushrooming of local studies by a broad array of civil war scholars, including Anthony Fletcher, Clive Holmes, Ann Hughes, John Lynch, John Morrill, Roy Sherwood, Mark Stoyle and David Underdown.[6] Most of them focus upon individual counties, though some examine specific towns and localities or take a regional approach, spanning part or all of several counties. There have also been less numerous but very important studies of the interplay between the localities and the centre, such as John Morrill's *The Revolt of the Provinces* and Anthony Fletcher's *The Outbreak of the English Civil War*.[7]

More fundamentally, some historians adopt a top-down interpretation, focusing on the role and position of the elite in examining the causes, course and consequences of the civil war. For some, this is the political elite, especially that part of it which ran central government – the king and his councillors and advisors, the MPs and peers in parliament, the world of Whitehall and Westminster. For example, Conrad Russell's detailed study of *The Fall of the British Monarchies, 1637–42* encompasses the Scottish and Irish dimensions as well as some developments in the provinces of England and Wales, but the work focuses quite sharply upon English high politics in its account of a war resulting from political problems, crises and breakdown in central government. For others, the elite is seen in a more overtly social context. Thus in the mid-1960s Lawrence Stone linked the war to *The Crisis of the Aristocracy*, that is to a decline in the social, economic, cultural and politi-

---

6 A. Fletcher, *A County Community in Peace and War: Sussex 1600–60* (Harlow, 1975); C. Holmes, *Seventeenth Century Lincolnshire* (Lincoln, 1980); C. Holmes, *The Eastern Association in the English Civil War* (Cambridge, 1974); A. Hughes, *Politics, Society and the Civil War in Warwickshire, 1620–60* (Cambridge, 1987); J. Lynch, *For King and Parliament. Bristol and the Civil War* (Stroud, 1999); J. Morrill, *Cheshire, 1630–60. County Government and Society during the English Revolution* (Oxford, 1974); R. Sherwood, *Civil War in the Midlands* (Stroud, 1992); M. Stoyle, *Loyalty and Locality: Popular Allegiances in Devon during the English Civil War* (Exeter, 1994); M. Stoyle, *From Deliverance to Destruction: Rebellion and Civil War in an English City* (Exeter, 1996); D. Underdown, *Revel, Riot and Rebellion. Popular Politics and Culture in England, 1603–60* (Oxford, 1985); D. Underdown, *Fire From Heaven. Life in an English Town in the Seventeenth Century* (London, 1992).
7 First published London, 1976 and 1981 respectively.

cal fortunes of the hereditary peerage in the century or so before the civil war.[8] More recently, John Adamson has argued that the civil war should be seen as a baronial conflict and has stressed the political and military power, influence and leadership of the hereditary peerage in the key developments of the 1640s.[9] Many of the local and county studies have also tended to focus on the political and social elite, the charmed circle of gentry families, plus the occasional hereditary peer, in whom the political, administrative and military leadership of a county was vested. But in sharp contrast to this approach, other historians adopt a bottom-up interpretation, focusing upon the role and position of those outside and below the traditional elite in their assessments of the causes, course and consequences of the civil war. This approach, which underpins Marxist and Marxist-influenced interpretations, can be seen in the work of historians as diverse as Christopher Hill, Brian Manning, Mark Stoyle and David Underdown. Some studies of this type examine the broad mass of the non-elite, such as the work of Underdown and Stoyle on popular allegiance, attempting to reconstruct and interpret divisions within the society of several south-western counties in the decades preceding the civil war and during the war itself.[10] Others stress the role of particular elements of the non-elite, such as Manning's study of a rising 'middling sort' of independent small producers and the emphasis in some of Hill's work upon the 'industrious sort'.[11]

It follows from all this that historians differ markedly in interpreting what lay at the heart of the civil war and in identifying the nature and essence of the conflict. Some see it as a conflict of high politics, whose central elements were problems and attempted solutions in central government and the constitution in England and Wales, often exacerbated by inter-relations with Scotland and Ireland. Although many stressed a religious component and favoured the label 'puritan revolution', the so-called Whig historians of the nineteenth century broadly took this

8   First published Oxford, 1965.
9   This interpretation underpins a string of articles which Adamson published during the 1990s, but is seen at its broadest in J. Adamson, 'The Baronial Context of the English Civil War', originally published in *Transactions of the Royal Historical Society*, 5th series, 40 (1990), and reprinted in R. Cust and A. Hughes (eds), *The English Civil War* (London, 1997).
10   Underdown, *Revel, Riot and Rebellion*; Stoyle, *Loyalty and Locality*.
11   B. Manning, *The English People and the English Revolution* (2nd edn, London, 1991); for C. Hill see, amongst others, *Change and Continuity in Seventeenth Century England* (2nd edn, London, 1991), *Puritanism and Revolution: Studies in the Interpretation of the English Revolution of the Seventeenth Century* (London, 1958), especially part 1, and *Society and Puritanism in Pre-Revolutionary England* (London, 1964), especially ch. 4.

approach. More recently, some historians have emphasized religion as the key element of the civil war, perhaps the one aspect of people's lives so deeply rooted and so fundamental to them that it could drive them into and through a civil war, only to dominate and complicate the attempts at post-war reconstruction. Indeed, in the mid-1980s John Morrill referred to the conflicts of the mid-seventeenth century as 'the last and greatest of Europe's Wars of Religion', though he has since qualified the phrase and stressed that he never favoured a monocausal explanation.[12] Some historians, Marxist and non-Marxist alike, have emphasized the socio-economic aspects of the civil war and the class-based tensions, conflicts and resolutions of the mid-seventeenth century, directly involving large and significant elements of society outside the traditional elite. In short, the story of the mid-seventeenth century can and has been told in different ways to place at its heart the struggle for and the (often incomplete or temporary) achievement of personal liberty, intellectual freedom, liberty of conscience, moral and Godly reformation, political rights, representation and accountability, governmental reform at the centre and in the localities, social justice and realignment, legal and judicial rights or economic freedom and change. It is a moot point how many active parliamentarians, let alone active royalists (whose perspectives are rather overlooked in some accounts), would have viewed the conflict in some of these ways. Conclusions about whether to see this period as revolutionary and, if so, where and when to place the heart of that successful or failed revolution, depend upon which element or elements the historian sees as central to the struggle of the 1640s. Different approaches and perspectives inevitably produce very different images of the civil war.

Some of these differences can be glimpsed in the responses of three historians to the question 'What was the English Revolution?' (Chapter 1). Their answers, originally published together in 1984 and reproduced here in the same manner, overlap and share some common assumptions. All three believe that the 'revolution' combined political, religious and social elements. However, very different emphases also emerge. In his essay, John Morrill explores both the centre and the localities, both high politics and more popular participation. But a core theme, repeat-

12   See the articles reproduced as chapters 1 (from which the quotation is taken) and 8 in this volume, together with Morrill, 'The Religious Context of the English Civil War', originally published in *Transactions of the Royal Historical Society*, 5th series, 34 (1984), and reprinted in Morrill, *The Nature of the English Revolution* (Harlow, 1993), ch. 3. For subsequent qualifications and clarifications see *ibid*, chapter 2, and Morrill, *Revolt in the Provinces. The People of England and the Tragedies of War, 1630–48* (2nd edn, Harlow, 1999), p. 19.

edly stressed, is the centrality of religion to the conflict. It was religion, far more than 'localist' or 'legal-constitutionalist' issues, 'which stood out as the decisive' issue, just as after the war had been won, continuing and strengthened religious aspirations spurred on part of the victorious party to regicide and the establishment of a new regime, only for that religious enthusiasm to be overthrown by the Restoration settlement. Thus 'out of England's wars of religion came the modern secular state'. While Morrill avoids the word 'class' and explicitly claims that 'the war was not the result of social divisions', Brian Manning's account is underpinned by a class-based interpretation, in which many of the key issues are seen in the light of divisions between different social groups. Thus many members of the elite were moved to defend the Caroline church when it was attacked by 'lower-class religious radicals', for they were motivated by fear of 'popular disorders' and of a possible 'attack on the principle of hierarchy in society'. More broadly, popular disorder is seen as a key factor in generating the divisions within the elite which led to civil war, with a substantial section of the elite rallying to the king as the 'guarantee of the existing social hierarchy'. Although religion is portrayed as important in determining allegiances and motivating the parliamentarians during the war, the religious differences which then divided the parliamentarian cause in the mid and late 1640s are seen as resting on and reflecting 'social differences and conflicts'. Post-war politics and the subsequent rise and fall of radical groups and aspirations are portrayed as shaped by the power and outlook of various social groups. The 'old ruling class' returned at the Restoration, though now with new ideas and outlooks which would in the long term facilitate 'the development of a fully capitalist economy'. In the third essay, David Underdown also looks at divisions within society, though in this case they are not delineated on such explicitly class-based lines, with one social group opposing another. Instead, he sees the civil war springing from and following a century or more of growing strains, polarities and divisions within society which provoked 'a crisis of order'. These divisions were reflected in and exacerbated by religious differences, between the godly and the ungodly, and together they produced a growing 'cultural conflict', embracing religious, political and social strands, between groups and communities in which custom, tradition and hierarchy predominated and those in which individualism, new ideas and support for moral reformation flourished. These clashes of culture, which surfaced at key moments during the 1640s, shaped the revolution as 'a conflict over the moral basis of English society'. Thus despite some common themes, these three historians view the essence of the English revolution very differently – as a war of religion which led on to the establishment of the modern, secular state, as a class-based conflict which led on to the establishment of a fully capitalist economy, and as a conflict within a fractured society fought over its moral basis.[13]

13 For a concise but forceful summary of an alternative interpretation – that the changes of the mid-seventeenth century were modest and largely reversed at the Restoration and that the major and that the real 'revolution' occurred in the aftermath of the Glorious Revolution and Revolution Settlement of 1688–9 – see A. McInnes, 'When was the English Revolution?', *History* 67 (1982).

1

What was the English Revolution?

John Morrill, Brian Manning and David Underdown

Originally appeared as John Morrill, Brian Manning and David Underdown, 'What was the English Revolution?' in *History Today* 34. Copyright
© 1984 History Today Ltd, London.

Those living through the period 1570–1640 would have felt themselves
much closer to civil war in the first two decades than in the last two. A
disputed succession, organised Catholic and Puritan religious parties (in
the Catholic case made the more menacing by a strong advocacy of
tyrannicide), and the willingness of foreign powers to intervene in the
internal affairs of England: all these were far more the hallmarks of the
mid-Elizabethan than of the Caroline period. Yet these were the classic
occasions of internal conflict in Reformation Europe. They were the
major but not the only signs of a country moving away from civil war.
The Crown had weathered the storm induced by a century of population growth and price inflation. By the 1630s, both these were blowing
themselves out; the economic and social outlook were rosier. The Crown
doubled its real income between 1603 and 1637 and had the lowest
national debt in Europe. Although the methods used were unpopular
and provoked some limited passive resistance, the Crown got its way. In
the later 1630s only one fiscal device – Ship Money – was openly (and
largely ineffectually) resisted, and the Crown could have abandoned it
and still balanced the budget in peacetime. Since no foreign power in the
foreseeable future would declare war on England, the Crown had
another twenty years in what would have been a favourable economic
climate to solve the problems of war finance.

Far from being a state sliding into civil war and anarchy, the early
Stuart state saw measurable decreases in levels of extra-legal violence:
fewer treason trials, no revolts, fewer riots concentrated in fewer areas

(the western forests, the fenland), the ubiquity and omnicompetence of royal justice, the ability of the Crown to insist on the arbitration of disputes at law or by royal officers.

It can thus be argued that the civil wars grew out of the policies and out of the particular failings of a particular king, Charles I. For despite its growing strength, the English political system remained a frail one which required skilful management. The state did lack the means to wage war, even to develop as a major colonial power; it lacked a bureaucracy dependent for its income and standing upon the Crown; it lacked coercive power. Government had to be by consent, above all by the willing co-operation of political élites in the forty counties and in the two hundred self-governing boroughs. By and large, material self-interest bound those élites to co-operation even in the 1630s, and there was far greater ideological cohesion and agreement within these élites and between them and the Court than in other western European states, but they did believe themselves to have rights and liberties which it was the Crown's duty to protect, and much of the necessary modernisation of finance and administration in the early seventeenth century had involved the erosion of those rights.

On balance, however, Elizabeth and James were skilful in permitting changes in the distribution of political and administrative power which reflected changes in the distribution of wealth and social power. As the peerage declined as social and political leaders, and as wealth became increasingly concentrated in the hands of the gentry and of wealthy craftsmen and farmers, so there was an enormous expansion of the responsibilities and powers of the county community and of parish government. Thus the number of gentry appointed to prominent local offices increased fourfold (through commissions of the peace, lieutenancy, etc.), and the powers and responsibilities they discharged were massively increased; and at the same time the wealthier members of village communities gained enormous influence over their poorer neighbours through the statutory expansion of the powers of parish officers (the poor law, administration of charitable funds, etc.).

This redistribution of power away from the Church and the peerage (and away from the poor) was achieved by the co-operation of Crown and political élites in Parliament. This system of government, in which the governors were not easily or directly subject to royal control, needed very sensitive management. It needed control by a monarch who could make the loaves and fishes of patronage feed a multitude of suitors. It could be done, but in the reign of Charles I it was not done. Charles was an incompetent King; inaccessible, glacial, self-righteous, deceitful. Within fifteen years of his accession he had forfeited the goodwill of most of the political élite, who viewed his actions with alarm, incomprehension or dismay. Yet few, if any, contemplated trying to bring down his personal rule by force. Emigration not underground resistance was the ultimate preference of men like John Pym and Oliver Cromwell in the later 1630s.

In 1640, however, Charles blundered away his initiative. He tried to impose his will upon his Scottish subjects twice, both times without adequate means. He could have made painful concessions, resumed his personal rule in England and looked to divide-and-rule tactics to regain his power in Scotland. But by attempting to impose his own brand of Protestantism on the Scots through an unco-ordinated force of Irish Catholics, Highland Catholics and an English army containing many Catholics, all to be paid for with cash to be provided from Rome and Madrid, he turned the anti-Catholic fears which his policies and his cultural values had already stimulated into a deep paranoia. The Scots' occupation of northeast England, and their demand for war reparations guaranteed by Parliament, created a wholly unanticipated and wholly unique situation: a meeting of Lords and Commons over whose determination he had no control. The MPs who gathered for the Long Parliament knew they had a once-for-all chance to put things right. They did not set out to organise for war but to restore the good old days.

There were three strands to the opposition to royal policies in 1640: they were, for many men, intertwined; but for many more they were discrete. There were those whose opposition can be called 'localist', whose experience of government in recent years had been of insensitive interventionism by central government in the affairs of their shires or boroughs, the imposition of national priorities at the expense of local preference and custom; there were those whose opposition can be termed 'legal-constitutionalist', a genuine belief that the Crown had been persuaded by evil counsellors to invade the liberty and take away the property of the subject, at best to serve the venal self-interest of the evil counsellors, at worst as part of a grand design to set up popery and tyranny; and there were those whose opposition was religious, who saw Protestantism under attack from an insidious popish conspiracy at court, and a less concealed but just as deadly and systematic challenge to the identity of the Church of England instigated by an innovative and heretical Archbishop of Canterbury and his henchmen.

The events of 1640–2 showed that neither the 'localist' nor the 'legal-constitutionalist' perceptions of misrule led men to take up arms. Those primarily concerned with the disruption to local government and autonomy occasioned by royal policies in the 1630s were overwhelmingly neutralist in 1642, well aware that war could not but bring on much worse disruptions. At most, such men followed the line of least resistance, following reluctantly the orders issued by others. Constitutional grievances were keenly felt by most of those who gathered at Westminster for the Long Parliament. But constitutional remedy was not speedily or rigorously pursued. Only the Triennial Act reached the statute book in the first eight months; the prosecution of evil counsellors took precedence, and what time was left over was spent more on debating religion than the rule of law. However, when the Houses did get round to constitutional grievances they quickly, and largely without rancour, rushed through a body of remedial legislation. Two points are obvious about the constitutional grievances of 1640–1; that they were, without exception, grievances which had arisen since 1625 (that is, they were grievances against Charles I and not against the early modern state), and that Parliament saw itself as engaged in a restorative, conservative programme. By the summer, there were no constitutional grievances left except those created by the King's manifest bad faith in conceding the remedies to those old grievances.

The constitutional programme of 1641–2 was not – unlike the religious programme – an end in itself; it was a means to an end. Fresh guarantees were sought that the King would honour his pledges and rule responsibily. Whether or not such guarantees were necessary really depended on whether or not the King could be trusted, and that was a matter intimately connected with the religious question. Although Parliament issued the Militia Ordinance and the Nineteen Propositions, neither was the subject of prolonged debate in the provinces. There were no county petitions for or against the Propositions, for example. In 1641 petitions called for constitutional reform; in 1642 the overwhelming majority of those concerned with constitutional issues called for accommodation, for negotiation, for settlement. Yet throughout 1642 petitions from across England debated, in ever more sharply distinguished ways, the case for and against episcopacy. No more than a dozen serious pamphlets debated the constitutional issues in the months before Edgehill; there were scores of pamphlets considering the future of the Church. In the four weeks after the Attempt on the Five Members, pamphlets on that outrage were outnumbered four to one by pamphlets on the impeachment of twelve bishops the previous week.

Many of those who felt that the guarantees being sought were legitimate and proper did not feel that it was right to fight to achieve them. One could believe in the Propositions but vote against the raising of an army to enforce them. The constitutional issues were the occasion of the civil war but not the actual cause. Men decided whether to obey the Militia Ordinance or the Commission of Array not on the merit of those measures themselves, but on other grounds. The great majority tried not

to have to decide, seeing good and evil on both sides. They went reluctantly to war. But minorities in most counties felt there was a cause
worth fighting for; that there was a glorious future to command. Those
who felt thus were those who felt strongly about religion.

In 1640, there was near unanimity in county petitions to the Houses
and in the rhetoric of the members that the Laudian church was innovative, grasping, a threat to 'the pure religion of Elizabeth and James I',
and that Charles had become the victim of a popish conspiracy. He had
cut himself off from his people, had surrendered himself to the wiles of
his courtiers and of counter-reformation culture. He had been brain-
washed. The war with the Scots, together with his alleged involvement
in the Army Plots, the Incident, the Attempt on the Five Members, and
even in the Irish Rebellion, were all seen as the irrational acts of a King
poisoned by popery, a man no longer responsible for his actions. In so
far as there was a civil war because of the way men acted on their own
perceptions of events, there was a civil war in 1642 because many of
Charles's subjects believed that they had to look to their own defence,
the King having become incapable of discharging his trust. Moderate
clergymen like Richard Baxter and official parliamentary apologists like
Henry Parker supported Parliament not because they feared royal
tyranny, but because they believed the King had ceased to rule. He had
become a zombie. In so far as that explanation made sense to the leaders
of Parliament like John Pym, it was a religious explanation.

But many others saw a different side of Charles. They saw a King who
had abandoned the counsellors of the 1630s; who had accepted the
remedial legislation of the Long Parliament; who had abandoned Laudianism, had appointed moderate calvinist bishops, had promised to
reform abuses but to defend the 'true reformed Protestant religion by
law established without any connivance of popery or innovation' (a
euphemism which acknowledged his abandonment of his faithful Archbishop whom he left to rot in the Tower). Such men saw a threat to order
and liberty less in the antics of the King's *ultra* supporters than in
the tolerance and leniency which the parliamentary leaderhip extended towards the demonstrations and mass picketing of the Houses
by crowds of Londoners, and of the iconoclasm and popular disturbances throughout England.

Yet as these two sides emerged in Parliament and in the provinces, it
was the religious issue which stood out as the decisive one. While the
events of 1640–2 narrowed the constitutional issues which came to
revolve around means and not ends, religious issues broadened and
deepened. From a general detestation of Laudian innovation and
popery, there emerged a passionate defence of the pre-Laudian Church:
of bishops, the prayer book, the rhythms of the Christian year (built

around the festivals of Christmas and Easter). This passionate defence was sustained by increasing numbers in both Houses and in petitions from a majority of the shires, attested by gentry, yeomen, craftsmen and clergy. But there also emerged an equally passionate call (such as had not been heard for decades) for godly reformation, for the sweeping away of a corruptible church order, so recently and so easily taken over by the enemies of true religion, and for the erection of a Church committed to preaching, to discipline, to a programme of moral rearmament. Such a Church could turn England from a nation full of ignorance and vice into a model godly commonwealth, into Zion. This cry too was heard in Parliament and throughout the country. As the impasse was reached in 1642, small groups in many counties thrust themselves forward to fight for Church and King, or to fight for reformation and liberty.

In almost every case, those who thrust themselves forward were those who had previously campaigned for episcopacy or against it. Many of those who had had 'legal-constitutionalist' objections to the Personal Rule now fought for Church and King. No-one who argued for a godly reformation came over to the King's side because they found the Commission of Array more agreeable than the Militia Ordinance.

These 'militants' brought on the war. Others were dragged in, following agonised and slight preferences or taking the line of least resistance. The war was not the result of social divisions. Gentry, yeoman, tradesmen fought in equal numbers (though not equal numbers in each region) for King and Parliament. If militant puritan middling sorts can be identified, so can militant Anglican middling sorts and neutral middling sorts in similar numbers. If there were more puritan yeomen than puritan gentlemen, there were more yeomen than gentlemen to be puritan: there were also more Anglican yeomen than Anglican gentry. The civil war was not a clash of social groups: it was the result of incompetent kingship which allowed religious militants to settle their disputes about the nature of the church, and therefore of different concepts of the moral order, to fight it out. It was the last and greatest of Europe's Wars of Religion.

After four years of civil war, the Parliamentarian minority defeated the royalist minority. But they had alienated the uncommitted, the neutrals and their own moderate supporters. In order to win the war, they had had to impose a crushing burden of taxation, to set up a civil authority with draconian powers (of arbitrary taxation, arbitrary imprisonment), and had created a standing army kept up to strength by impressment and maintained by compulsory billeting and quarter. The security problem required the maintenance of expensive security forces. The measures required to sustain this expensive army increased the security problem. At the same time, the attempt of puritan zealots to impose their new and mandatory church and religious order foundered amidst the passive resistance of the majority who remained loyal to the old services and to their old ministers. The puritans' hope of imposing their Church was further weakened by internal disunity, extending beyond natural differences of emphasis over correct church order as the strain of events and a heady atmosphere engendered by a free press and the questioning of all established values produced the disintegration of puritan intellectual unity.

The yearning for settlement grew, with widespread recognition that the war had resolved nothing, merely brought unprecedented misery and loss. There was a massive call for a return of the King on terms he might well have accepted in 1642. The second civil war in 1648 was in large part the consequence of that yearning. But for many in the puritan vanguard of 1642, the dream of the New Jerusalem remained vivid. The sufferings of civil war were not a check but a spur; they had a meaning. God was punishing, chastening, cleansing his people. Theirs were pains with a purpose. The war had made the wickedness of the old order all the clearer. An incorrigible King refused to accept and actively sought to overture the judgment of God. He was a 'man of blood', whose judicial execution was now demanded in atonement. On January 30th, 1649, the Regicide marked the triumph of that minority position.

Yet by executing the King and consciously proclaiming a godly republic, the puritan vanguard further isolated themselves. So long as their Army remained united they could cow the majority into acquiescence. But the puppet regimes set up and pulled down by the Army were caught in a pincer. If they sought to realise the vision of the New Jerusalem they found themselves frustrated by the passive resistance of the old social élites; if they temporised with the élites, they lost the support of the Army. And meanwhile the unacceptable face of puritanism alienated them yet further from the majority. When Army unity crumbled with the death of Oliver Cromwell, who strove to infuse the old social order with new religious values, the return of the King was inevitable.

Charles II came back to a changed world. Constitutionally, he had to bow to the will of the country gentry and to accept their hegemony in the counties and increasingly in the towns. The power of the state was humbled and the autonomy of local governors exalted. But even more important, the Restoration settlement saw the overthrow of religious enthusiasm. Charles I and Laud had shared with the puritan county bosses like William Brereton, Robert Harley, John Wray, and Army bosses like Oliver Cromwell and Thomas Harrison, the vision of using an alliance of Church and State to impose a new moral order. All such hopes of realising a godly and ordered commonwealth were discredited by the Revolution. Religion was relegated to the fringes. The Church was emasculated and put under lay control; economic, political, artistic thought was secularised; science ceased to be the means to create an ordered world ('a great instauration' in which disease and dearth were vanquished and man's fleshly wants satisfied so that the spiritual values could be cherished). Science became, as politics, accepted as the art of the possible, a process of piecemeal empirical enquiry and improvement unrelated to grand designs of social engineering. In the 1680s, pleading for religious toleration, John Locke, heir to the puritan tradition, defined a Church as a voluntary society of men, meeting together to worship God in such fashion as they deemed appropriate. Religion had been pushed to the edge of life, almost into becoming a hobby. Out of England's wars of religion came the modern secular state.

JOHN MORRILL

For further reading

Before the Civil War, ed. H. Tomlinson (Macmillan, 1984) is an excellent set of essays on key aspects of 1603–42; Anthony Fletcher, *The Outbreak of the English Civil War* (Arnold, 1981), the best recent study of 1640–2; Caroline Hibbard, *Charles and the Popish Plot* (University of North Carolina Press, 1983), the best study of the collapse of royal credibility; *Reactions to the English Civil War*, ed. J. S. Morrill (Macmillan, 1982), a collection of essays on 1642–9; William Hunt, *The Puritan Moment*, is an important recent regional study. The main argument of this essay is developed at greater length in J. S. Morrill, 'The religious context of the English civil war', *Transactions of the Royal Historical Society*, 5th series, 34 (1984).

The Parliament which Charles I was obliged to summon to meet at Westminster on November 3rd, 1640, did not intend to initiate a revolution. The two Houses of Parliament were composed of nobility and gentry – wealthy landlords – who represented the ruling class of England. Their intention was to reinstate the ancient constitution which in their view had been undermined by the actions of the King since 1629, and to restore the Church of England to the position established by the Elizabethan Religious Settlement which in their opinion had been subverted by the innovations of Archbishop Laud. Charles and his advisers had strained the natural alliance and normal harmony between the monarchy and the ruling class. The aim of the Parliament was to recover the working partnership of the nobility and gentry with the Crown.

The King's policies in Church and State during the 1630s were blamed upon evil advisers. The first objective of the leaders of the Parliament was to remove those bad councillors. The Earl of Strafford was executed and Archbishop Laud was imprisoned in the Tower of London. But when the leaders of the Parliament went beyond the removal of evil advisers and demanded that the King 'employ such councillors and ministers as shall be approved by his Parliament,' they raised an issue which caused division in the Parliament. Many of the more conservative members of both Houses supported the King in the defence of the 'ancient and undoubted right' of the monarch to choose his own advisers.

The second issue which caused division in the Parliament was religion. Laud and the bishops were accused of betraying the Protestant tradition of the Church of England by introducing ceremonies which in the eyes of most of the nobility and gentry savoured of Roman Catholicism. But this was an issue which troubled not only the ruling class. In some parishes in London and in the provinces crowds tore down the rails in the chancel and put the communion table back in the nave of the church where it had been before the Laudian innovations. They assaulted ministers for wearing the surplice and shouted out objections to the liturgy of the prayer-book for having too much in common with the Roman Catholic Mass. Petitions attacked the bishops and called for the abolition of episcopacy. Some Members of Parliament rallied to the defence of the bishops and the prayer-book. They feared that an attack on the principle of hierarchy in the church might open the way for an attack on the principle of hierarchy in society at large. They were concerned to preserve the existing liturgy as an expression of a traditional order against attack, on the one side, from a 'popish' faction of 'upstart' clergy led by Laud and, on the other side, from a 'fanatical' faction of lower-class religious radicals. But they were also worried by the popular disorders which accompanied the arguments about the bishops and the prayer-book.

Thus the third factor which produced division in the Parliament was popular disorder. Demonstrations at Westminster against bishops and the prayer-book in the autumn of 1641 led some Members of Parliament to demand action to disperse assemblies of the people and to prevent them from gathering at Westminster. They feared that Members would be intimidated and the Parliament overawed by popular pressure. But the leaders of the Parliament were more fearful that the King planned to use force against the Parliament, and they were reluctant to discountenance popular demonstrations because their only defence against a royal attack was popular support. They were right. When the King attempted a coup and tried to arrest leaders of the Parliament in January 1642, he was frustrated by popular demonstrations and forced to flee from the capital. A majority of the House of Lords and two-fifths of the House of Commons also withdrew from Westminster in the following months, either out of sympathy with the King or from unwillingness to be implicated in actions against him.

Both the King with his supporters and Members who remained in Parliament at Westminster raised armed forces, not with the intention of fighting, but each with the object of deterring the other from resorting to violence, and each with the aim of strengthening its position in negotiations with the other. The Members at Westminster demanded control over the King's choice of advisers and of commanders of the militia. Charles would not concede this and a substantial section of the nobility and gentry rallied to him as the defender of the established forms of government in the State and the Church, and as the symbol of order and the guarantee of the existing social hierarchy. But few of the men at Westminster were revolutionaries. They were driven to make their demands by distrust of the King and fear that his intention was to get rid of the Parliament by force and return to his ways of ruling in the 1630s.

A revolution involves the replacement by force or the threat of force of one political or social system by another. So far what had happened in England was not a revolution. By the summer of 1642 the old political system had broken down, and the mechanism for resolving conflicts had failed, but no new political system was visualised. The country drifted into civil war. Most people remained, or attempted to remain, neutral, deploring the conflict, seeking peace, and trying to avoid a commitment to either side. The ruling class was split into three – royalists, parliamentarians, and neutrals – though probably more were royalists than parliamentarians. While most of the lower classes were neutrals, the parliamentarians had significant popular support amongst the small traders, artisans and apprentices of London, and amongst the people engaged in the manufacture of cloth in the provinces.

Political and constitutional issues caused the breakdown into civil war, but religious issues became increasingly influential in determining allegiance to one side or the other, although never the only issues. Opponents of the King included a broad alliance of moderate Puritans, militant Presbyterians, and radical sectaries. The Puritans wanted to maintain the Established Church and to retain a reformed episcopacy: their aims were to purge the Church of 'the remnants of popery', to improve the quality of the clergy, to promote preaching, to raise moral standards and to establish a stricter moral discipline over the whole population. The Presbyterians had the same aims as the Puritans but did not think that those could be achieved so long as the Church was governed by bishops. They accepted the Established Church but sought to change its government from the Episcopalian to the Presbyterian form, which was based on a hierarchy of assemblies with representatives of the laity as well as the clergy, rising from the parish assembly to the National Assembly. The Presbyterians also sought the replacement of the prayer-book by a liturgy on more strictly Calvinist lines.

The sects rejected the idea of an Established Church to which everybody was compelled to belong. They regarded a true church as a gathering of 'true believers' – a voluntary association of like-minded people who agreed to form a church and to worship together according to their own lights. They separated from the Established Church, whether Episcopalian or Presbyterian, and formed their own independent, self-governing congregations. If there was to be an Established Church they asked to be allowed to worship outside its jurisdiction in their own autonomous congregations according to their own consciences. This broad alliance of moderate Puritans, militant Presbyterians, and radical sectaries gave the parliamentarians victory over the royalists in the civil war. But this alliance was inherently unstable and was breaking up even before the war ended in 1646. This instability was a reflection of social differences and conflicts. Parliamentarian gentry tended to be moderate Puritans, and when they could not prevent the abolition of episcopacy, they sought a form of Presbyterianism which would be controlled by Parliament and the gentry. They were opposed by the militant Presbyterians who had popular support amongst the middling and smaller merchants, shopkeepers and apprentices of London. Presbyterianism in either form was resisted by the sects, which had become during the war increasingly influential in the parliamentarian army, London and some provincial centres, and drew their strength from small traders and artisans in London and people engaged in the manufacture of cloth in the provinces.

The sects generated a radical political group, the Levellers, who sought not only toleration for the sects but also the abolition of the monarchy and the House of Lords, and the establishment of the supremacy of the House of Commons, which was to be made responsible to an expanded electorate. The Levellers exercised some influence amongst sections of the rank-and-file of the parliamentarian army and amongst sections of the lower classes in London during the period 1647–49. But popular discontent at increased taxes and rising food prices benefited the royalists more than the radicals. Nevertheless the revival of royalism was crushed by the parliamentarian army in the Second Civil War in 1648. In December 1648–January 1649 the same army carried out a military coup: it occupied the capital, purged the Parliament, tried and executed the King, abolished the monarchy and the House of Lords, and established a republic with a unicameral legislature which elected the executive government. This was a revolution in that it involved a change of the political system by force and it was not just the substitution of one set of rulers for another. But the constitution devised by the Levellers was not implemented nor was the political revolution followed by a social revolution.

Power had been slipping during and after the civil war from the hands of the pre-war governing élites – the greater gentry, that is the bigger landlords, in the counties, and the greater merchants in the towns. The defeat of the King and the royalists meant that in London, some provincial towns, and many counties, power passed to lesser gentry and smaller traders. But the greater gentry and larger merchants were not displaced totally from power and held on to it in some counties and towns. Although the lesser gentry did not form part of the old governing élites, and did not belong economically to the same class as the bigger landlords, they did share the status which differentiated all gentry, whether greater or lesser, from plebeians, and they had more in common with the greater gentry than with radical traders and artisans. They were determined to preserve the social hierarchy and the distribution of power according to social status.

Radicals failed to move the revolution further to the left after 1649. In part this was due to the fact that they split into three broad tendencies. Many religious radicals were satisfied with the defeat of Presbyterianism and with the establishment of a degree of toleration for the sects in the 1650s, and they sought little further political and social changes. The other radicals were divided between the secular radicalism represented by the Levellers and the millennarian radicalism represented by the Fifth Monarchists. Up to a point both the Levellers and the Fifth Monarchists advocated similar programmes of reform; both demanded the abolition of tithes and revolutionary changes in the legal system; both sought economic growth; both drew their support from small traders, artisans and apprentices, and both were essentially urban movements; both denounced the nobility and gentry and the rich in general, and both sought to displace the old ruling class. But here they split. The Levellers aimed to transfer power by means of a more democratic and decentralised political system, in which the qualification for political power would not be wealth or social status but merely being 'a free-born Englishman'. The Fifth Monarchists, however, sought to transfer power to the 'godly people' or 'saints', that is the members of the sectarian congregations, by making 'godliness rather than wealth or social status the qualification to exercise political power. They rejected the

Leveller constitutional programme because it gave political rights to the ungodly as well as to the godly.

The second reason why the revolution did not move further to the left was that the social base of the radicals was too narrow. Radicalism was confined largely to small numbers of traders and artisans, and the peasants – the great mass of the population – were unaffected. Occasionally during the revolution particular grievances erupted amongst the peasants in some localities but rarely rose to the level of a challenge to the existing social and economic system.

The third reason was that the old social order remained strong and fear of radicalism steadily reunited the gentry: the return of the monarchy, of the House of Lords, and even of the bishops increasingly seemed the safest guarantees of order, stability and the old social hierarchy.

The monarchy was restored in 1660 but not to the position it had held in the 1630s and it was to be a constitutional monarchy and not an absolute monarchy on Continental lines. The power of the central government was curbed and the greater gentry were strengthened in their control of the counties and the greater merchants in their control of the towns. The Church of England could not be restored to the position it had held in the 1630s and it ceased to be the church of the whole nation. The religious spirit of the revolution flowed into Dissent and Nonconformity and the split in English religious life became permanent. The old ruling class came back with new ideas and new outlooks which were attuned to economic growth and expansion and facilitated in the long run the development of a fully captialist economy. It would all have been very different if Charles I had not been obliged to summon that Parliament to meet at Westminster on November 3rd, 1640.

BRIAN MANNING

For further reading

Robert Ashton, *The English Civil War: conservatism and revolution 1603–1649* (Weidenfeld and Nicolson, 1978); Anthony Fletcher, *The Outbreak of the English Civil War* (Edward Arnold, 1981); Alan Everitt, *The Community of Kent and the Great Rebellion 1640–60* (Leicester University Press, 1966); J. T. Cliffe, *The Yorkshire Gentry from the Reformation to the Civil War* (Athlone Press, 1969); B. G. Blackwood, *The Lancashire Gentry and the Great Rebellion 1640–60* (Chetham Society, Manchester University Press, 1978); David Underdown, *Pride's Purge: politics in the Puritan Revolution* (Clarendon, Oxford, 1971); B. S. Capp, *The Fifth Monarchy Men; A study in seventeenth-century English millenarianism* (Faber, 1972).

What was the English Revolution? Was it, as participants in the debate over the gentry a generation ago variously argued, a revolution generated by social tensions, confirming a changed balance of power within the élite, with a rising (or declining) gentry temporarily replacing an aristocracy in crises at the centre of power? Was it part of a European 'general crisis', one of many seventeenth-century 'revolts of the provinces' against the extravagance and assertive centralism of the new state-building monarchies? Was that general crisis the outcome of structural economic changes, the final stage in the replacement of 'feudal' productive relations by capitalism, the 1640s thus being in some sense England's 'bourgeois revolution'? Or was it perhaps not really a revolution at all, but merely a conflation of local struggles, or even, as Conrad Russell and other revisionists have recently suggested, simply a bit of bad luck, the result of, at most, short-term governmental breakdown?

As always, each historian has his or her own solution. My own starts from two innocuous premises: first, that the revolution was *not* a mere accident (though the fortuitous and unpredictable certainly played a part in it); secondly, that to understand it we need to look back once more over the history of the previous century. When we do so we find, I suggest, a profound division emerging among the English people about the moral basis of their commonwealth, a division expressed in a cultural conflict that had both social and regional dimensions. The revolution was an unsuccessful attempt to resolve the conflict by imposing a particular notion of moral order, articulated in the culture of the Puritan 'middling sort', upon the rest of the kingdom.

The Tudor state rested on a theory of order incessantly reiterated by preachers, publicists and politicians. 'Almighty God hath appointed all things in heaven, earth, and waters in a most excellent and perfect order': the sonorous message of the Homily on Obedience was regularly dinned into the ears of English men and women throughout their lives. Society was a harmonious organism, held together by reciprocal obligations. 'Some are in high degree', the Homily continues, 'some in low, some kings and princes, some inferiors and subjects, priests and laymen, masters and servants, fathers and children, husbands and wives, rich and poor'. The patriarchal authority of the father of a family was the cornerstone of order, reinforcing the corresponding layers of authority of lords over tenants, monarchs over subjects. The theory presupposed the universal existence of stable families, stable local communities, as the bases of a stable state.

But in practice England was far from stable. Excessive population growth had led to land shortage, unemployment, and 'masterlessness' for increasing numbers of people. Rapid inflation spawned disastrously high food prices, especially in crisis periods like the 1590s and 1620s. Some people profited from the situation: the farmer big enough to produce a surplus for the market, who could often buy out less fortunate manorial tenants, for example. Economic and social values, too, were changing. People prospering in the marketplace had less time for the old constraints of the 'just price' or the co-operative ethos of the traditional open-field community. The ideal of the harmonious 'vertical' society in which people of different degrees worked together, was being challenged by a new world of competition. Villages became more polarised, as 'parish notables', minor gentry and yeomen, began to rise above the rest of their neighbours.

People like this, newcomers to wealth and status, often felt threatened by the soaring numbers of poor generated by the population explosion. They saw themselves as islands of godly virtue in a sea of sinful disorder – a disorder distressingly visible in the drinking and merrymaking that constantly undermined household discipline, particularly among the young. 'Was there ever seen less obedience in youth of all sorts . . . towards their superiors, parents, masters and governors?' asked Philip Stubbes in his *Anatomy of Abuses*, a vigorous attack on the festive culture. Protestantism, especially its Puritan variant, taught doctrines of discipline, work and responsibility, and it is not surprising that the emerging local élites found in it a convenient justification for their authority. They, after all, were God's elect, charged with the duty of advancing godly reformation by disciplining the reprobate majority. County magistrates strove to suppress the church ales and other disorderly village festivals; in some places (Dorchester is a conspicuous example) their urban counterparts systematically enforced a 'culture of discipline' aimed at realising their ideal of a reformed Christian 'city on a hill'. Puritanism was of course much more than a system of social control, but this aspect of it is of particular relevance to the revolution.

Of course Puritan discipline was not the only available response to the crisis of order. There were those at court and in the Anglican hierarchy who abhorred the divisive impact of Puritan preaching, who like James I feared that its insistence on the primacy of individual conscience threatened the whole system of order, even monarchy itself. Stability could best be maintained, they thought, by more traditional policies: by a paternalist monarchy, aristocracy and church protecting the lower orders from exploitation by the acquisitive 'middling sort'. So they tried, as Robert Dover did at the Cotswold Games, to revive the old festive culture – the May games and revel feasts, and all the other calendric and religious rituals in which the values of 'good neighbourhood' had been affirmed. William Fennor captured the spirit of the conservative ideal in his nostalgic lines:

Happy the age, and harmless were the days
(For then true love and amity were found)
When every village did a maypole raise,
And Whitsun-ales and May-games did abound.

The resulting cultural conflict became more intense after James I issued the Book of Sports in 1618, proclaiming the legality of innocent recreations even on the sabbath, and still more so when Charles I and Archbishop Laud reissued it in 1633. Disputes over maypoles and church ales may seem far removed from the English Revolution, but in fact their political implications were clear. When village revels were prohibited by the JPs people murmured, one of Laud's bishops reported, that it was hard 'if they could not entertain their friends once a year, to praise God for his blessings, and pray for the King, under whose government they enjoyed peace and quietness'. The hierarchy's policy of protecting traditional culture further encouraged the suspicions, aroused in numerous other ways, of the existence of a sinister plot to restore Catholicism.

This is not to dispute the importance of the more familiar religious and political aspects of the revolution, or of the crucial role played by localist resentment of 'Thorough' policies. But politics and religion are part of culture, and this was a cultural as well as a political revolution: an attempt by the Puritan gentry and middling sort to impose their conception of godly order on the rest of the nation. The cultural aspect is clearly apparent in the well-known autobiography of Richard Baxter. When he embarked on his ministry at Kidderminster in 1641, Baxter encountered a situation typical of many English parishes: 'an ignorant, rude and revelling people for the most part', but also 'a small company of converts, who were humble, godly, and of good conversation'. The ungodly majority resisted efforts to suppress their 'painted forms of giants and suchlike fooleries' and soon, Baxter recalls, 'if a stranger passed . . . that had short hair and a civil habit, the rabble presently cried, "Down with the Roundheads"'. The familiar stereotypes of Roundhead and Cavalier (cultural as well as political symbols) were already emerging. Some of the local alignments in the civil war were soon to reflect earlier cultural divisons. The Welsh border counties and the downlands of southern England, always strongholds of traditional culture, were royalist in the 1640s; regions like the Essex and Wiltshire clothing districts, where the parish notables had been more successful in imposing godly reformation, were correspondingly parliamentarian.

We have been using the term 'English Revolution', but 'English revolutions' might be more appropriate, for there were in fact three distinct revolutions: a moderate, reformist one in 1641, many of whose constitutional achievements were endorsed by the settlement of 1660; a violent, republican one in 1648–9, only temporarily successful; and a third 'revolution that failed', the abortive democratic revolution whose adherents were driven into the political underground in the 1650s.

The first, reformist phase reflected the virtually unanimous rejection by 'the Country' of Charles I's 'Thorough' government; in it the Long Parliament outlawed Ship Money, dismantled the Star Chamber and punished Strafford and other agents of absolutism, all in the name of the freedoms guaranteed by the mythical ancient constitution. The cultural conflict was not a primary factor during this period of relative unity, though it occasionally surfaced in attacks on Laudian clergy and demands for 'Root and Branch' reform. Orchestrated by John Pym, a propaganda campaign also reawakened the lurking fears of Catholic conspiracy.

Parliament's reaction to those fears – its appeal to the people and its revolutionary claim to the militia power – drove moderate elements over to the King's side and precipitated civil war. In that war there were, as we have been often reminded, many neutrals, many who gave the integrity of their local communities a higher priority than the national aims of either side. But even neutrals had preferences, and not everyone was neutral. The war was not fought solely by conscripts or troops imported from Scotland and Ireland: leadership and volunteers on both sides reflected the enduring cultural split. Parliament depended heavily on Puritan reformers, the King on people who had long struggled against the socially divisive impact of godly reformation. It was, among much else, a war between adherents of two competing concepts of order.

The convoluted political struggle that followed the war contained further echoes of the cultural conflict. The Puritan minority, entrenched in the army and in Parliament's county committees, demanded further reformation at any cost. But the moderate gentry and their allies and dependants in 'the Country', even in the hitherto parliamentarian counties of the south-east, had had enough of the military burdens, taxes and other violations of ancient rights that made Parliament a far worse centralising menace than ever the King had been. Most of the propertied political nation wanted only a return to the settlement of 1641. Thanks to the disciplined power of Fairfax's army, the conservative, localist reaction was beaten back in 1648, opening the way to the second revolution in which the House of Commons was purged, the House of Lords abolished, and the King executed. The militant minority which did these things was aided, and indeed pushed onward, by adherents of the potential 'third revolution', the popular elements politicised by the war, the middle-class London Levellers and the separatists inflamed by millennarian visions of a new Jerusalem in which the godly 'saints' would rule. This, of course, was not what the parliamentary leaders, even revolutionary leaders like Oliver Cromwell, intended. Suppression of the Levellers was to be the new republic's first order of business; constant foot-dragging to frustrate the more extreme of the sects' promised reforms (of Parliament, the law, the tithe system) was to be the second.

Even at its zenith after 1649 the English Revolution was a limited revolution, never approaching the thoroughgoing reformism of, for example, Jacobin France in 1793. The vast majority of people of all social levels retained most of an older, deeply ingrained value system – beliefs in the patriarchal family, the primacy of ancient law and custom, the virtues of the traditional, co-operative community. This is abundantly clear in the outlook of the Clubmen, the biggest mass movement of the entire period, in 1645. And even the leadership contained many who were ambivalent about the revolution. Oliver Cromwell, one half of him a zealous Puritan reformer, the other half a conservative country squire, himself personifies the ambiguities of the revolution. When, after the failure of the Commonwealth either to gain public acceptance or to retain the confidence of the army, Cromwell attained the supreme power as Protector, his regime exemplified these same contradictions: two periods of 'healing and settling', separated by the interlude of the Major-Generals, in which yet another blast of authoritarian Puritan reformation was inflicted on the nation. It is not surprising that even many of those who had yearned for godly discipline at last concluded that military rule was too high a price to pay for it, and welcomed the restoration of Charles II.

In the end, the revolution was a conflict over the moral basis of English society. Behind the clash of cultures we can detect two social ideals, even two societies, in conflict: one stressing custom, tradition, and the co-operative, 'vertical' community; the other moral reformation, individualism, the ethic of work and responsibility. The middling sort's campaign to impose theirs as the national culture failed because deep-rooted social forces were too strong for them. The great cosmic drama, the battle of good and evil, the journey towards the eternal city on the hill: all were internalised after 1660, worked out within the soul of each individual. Defeat compelled John Milton to locate paradise within, John Bunyan to allegorise the quest for a righteous society as an individual, not a national pilgrimage. The civil war had begun, says Baxter in a passage alluding to the cultural conflict, 'in our streets before king or Parliament had any armies'. It ended, for many, in disillusion. But in both its successes and its failures the revolution was as much a cultural as a constitutional or political one.

DAVID UNDERDOWN

For further reading

Christopher Hill, *Society and Puritanism in Pre-Revolutionary England* (Secker, 1964); and *The World Turned Upside Down: Radical Ideas during the English Revolution* (Temple Smith, 1972); William Hunt, *The Puritan Moment: The Coming of Revolution in an English County* (Harvard University Press, 1983); Brian Manning, *The English People and the English Revolution* (Heinemann, 1976); J. S. Morrill, *The Revolt of the Provinces: Conservatives and Radicals in the English Civil War 1630–1650* (Allen & Unwin, 1976); Lawrence Stone, *The Causes of the English Revolution 1529–1642* (Routledge & Kegan Paul, 1972).

Part II Causes of the Civil War

Introduction to Part II

The hunt for the causes of the English civil war has probably generated more research and writing than any other single issue in English history. The key variables in the debate were laid out in the writings of two men who lived through the war, Edward Hyde, Earl of Clarendon, and James Harrington. While Clarendon saw the war caused by political and constitutional issues (including the state church and religion), Harrington saw it resulting from social and economic problems. While Clarendon stressed short-term causes, Harrington emphasized long-term developments and increasing tension.[1] These key variables provide a matrix into which most subsequent explanations can be placed. Although almost all historians have seen a range or combination of political, religious, social and economic factors playing a role in causing the civil war, as preconditions, contributing elements or even 'necessary' causes, many have laid particular stress on one issue or element as the key problem which drove England into war, as the principal or 'sufficient' cause of the civil war. Because many historians have claimed that the civil war had long-term causes, which built up over may decades prior to the 1640s, and because those historians who see only short-term causes need to demonstrate the absence of serious problems and divisions before their chosen starting points, the debate on the causes of the war has also been very broad, involving a wide-ranging examination of the early Stuart period and even, in some cases, of the latter half of the sixteenth century. There have been clear trends and fashions in the debate, periods when the overwhelming majority of historians held to a particular line and something approaching consensus seemed to be emerging. However, no dominant thesis has survived for more than a generation or two before being challenged and apparently overthrown by a newly fashionable approach. The battle to determine the true causes of the civil war is continuing and is unlikely ever to be concluded; the battle-field is strewn with corpses, most of them selectively picked over by succeeding ranks of combatants, some of them unexpectedly capable of flickering back to life.

In the course of the nineteenth century literary, polemic and (party) political accounts of the (causes of the) civil war gave way to a more academic, archival- and document-based approach to the war and its causation. With it emerged what became known as the Whig approach or school, seen at its best in a civil war context in the writings of S. R.

---

1   E. Hyde, 1st Earl of Clarendon, *The History of the Rebellion and Civil Wars in England, Begun in 1641* (3 vols, Oxford, 1704); J. Harrington, *The Commonwealth of Oceana and A System of Politics*, ed J. G. A. Pocock (Cambridge, 1992).

Gardiner and of his student C. H. Firth.[2] For historians working in the Whig tradition, the civil war marked a key stage in the constitutional, political and religious development of England, part of a long, evolutionary struggle to achieve the liberal democracy and religious toleration which these historians found in Victorian and Edwardian England. The civil war was the almost inevitable result of conflict stretching back several decades between an authoritarian crown which had absolutist tendencies and ambitions, and a House of Commons which was seeking a greater or more secure share of power in order both to curb monarchical ambitions and to preserve and enhance the rights and liberties of the people. The origins of this particularly bitter and ultimately violent stage of a much longer process might be traced back to the 1530s and the enhanced role of parliament in the Reformation, or to the tensions of the Elizabethan period between the queen and some of her parliaments. But for many Whig historians, England embarked on the high road to civil war in the early seventeenth century, with the political and constitutional clashes between James I and his parliaments, a conflict which intensified under his successor and eventually led to breakdown and war. Religion formed a central plank of this interpretation, with growing conflict between reform-minded Protestants and a conservative, backward-looking, intolerant crown; accordingly, the result was as much a 'puritan revolution' as a political and constitutional resolution.

By the time of the Second World War the Whig approach was being challenged by historians who believed that to focus upon political and constitutional clashes was to study the consequences rather than the causes of the conflict, and that the mainspring of the civil war was to be found elsewhere, in the socio-economic developments of the pre-war decades. Some of these historians took a purely Marxist approach and told a story of class struggle between the old feudal order of crown and aristocracy and an emerging capitalist class, which culminated in the 'bourgeois revolution' of the mid-seventeenth century. Others who were not themselves Marxists never the less went some way down this path, portraying the civil war as a class-based conflict, the almost inevitable consequence of long-term and worsening

2   S. R. Gardiner, *A History of England from the Accession of James I to the Outbreak of the Civil War, 1603–42* (10 vols, London, 1883–4); Gardiner, *A History of the Great Civil War, 1642–9* (3 vols, London, 1888–9); Gardiner, *The First Two Stuarts and the Puritan Revolution, 1603–60* (London, 1888); C. H. Firth, *Oliver Cromwell and the Rule of the Puritans in England* (London, 1900); and, in the same tradition, G. M. Trevelyan, *England under the Stuarts* (London, 1904). See also J. Adamson, 'Eminent Victorians: S. R. Gardiner and the Liberal as Hero', *The Historical Journal* 33 (1990); T. Lang, *The Victorians and the Stuart Heritage* (Cambridge, 1995); R. C. Richardson, *The Debate on the English Revolution* (3rd edn, Manchester, 1998), chs 5–6.

tenisons between different social strata. Returning to James Harrington, some saw a socio-economic 'rise of the gentry', beginning perhaps in the immediate post-dissolution era with the redistribution of land, often mirrored by a decline in the independence and standing of the aristocracy, which in turn generated political and ultimately military conflict as the rising gentry struggled to attain political power and status commensurate with their new socio-economic status. Although they shared a general approach, historians who interpreted the causes of the war in this way often emphasized different elements, defined terms like 'feudalism' and 'capitalism' differently or vaguely, and identified in a variety of ways the class which rose to challenge the old elite – 'the middle class(es)', 'the middling sort', 'the industrious sort', 'progressive' entrepreneurs, the gentry as a whole, part of the gentry, lesser landholders, merchants, artisans or a combination of them. Despite ambiguities and differences, historians who saw the cause of the civil war resting principally in long-term socio-economic changes – figures such as R. H. Tawney, Lawrence Stone and Christopher Hill[3] – dominated the field in the mid-twentieth century.

By the early 1970s, however, many historians believed that the attempts to explain the civil war in terms of socio-economic patterns had failed and felt able to dismiss class-based interpretations out of hand in a sentence or two. Intensive research in the 1950s and 1960s into the socio-economic standing of individual families, groups of families and country-wide social strata – especially a fierce debate on the fortunes of the landed elite, dubbed the 'storm over the gentry' – often failed to reveal clear, broadly-based, socio-economic trends common to each class.[4] Equally, far from confirming class-based divisions between future royalists and parliamentarians in the run up to the civil war, and

3 R. H. Tawney, *Religion and the Rise of Capitalism* (London, 1926); Tawney, 'The Rise of the Gentry, 1558–1640', *Economic History Review* 11 (1941); Tawney, 'Harrington's Interpretation of his Age', *Proceedings of the British Academy* 27 (1941); L. Stone, 'The Anatomy of the Elizabethan Aristocracy', *Economic History Review* 18 (1948); Stone, *The Crisis of the Aristocracy, 1558–1641* (Oxford, 1965); Stone, *Social Change and Revolution in England, 1540–1640* (London, 1965); C. Hill, *The English Revolution, 1640* (London, 1940); C. Hill and E. Dell (eds), *The Good Old Cause: The English Revolution of 1640–60* (London, 1949); Hill, *Puritanism and Revolution: Studies in the Interpretation of the English Revolution of the Seventeenth Century* (London, 1958); Hill, *Society and Puritanism in Pre-Revolutionary England* (London, 1964). See also Richardson, *Debate on the English Revolution*, ch. 7.
4 See, for example, M. Finch, *The Wealth of Five Northamptonshire Families 1540–1640* (Northampton, 1956); A. Simpson, *The Wealth of the Gentry, 1540–1660: East Anglian Studies* (Cambridge, 1961); J. T. Cliffe, *The Yorkshire Gentry from the Reformation to the Civil War* (London, 1969). On the gentry controversy see the relevant sections or chapters of Hill, *Puritanism and Revolution*, J. H. Hexter, *Reappraisals in History* (London, 1961), and Stone, *Social Change and Revolution*.

between active royalists and parliamentarians in and after 1642, this research strongly indicated that each class and plausible socio-economic grouping was divided by the civil war. As Tawney, himself in the van of socio-economic interpretations but no Marxist, had reportedly remarked when asked if the civil war was a bourgeois revolution, 'Of course it was a bourgeois revolution. The trouble is the bourgeoisie were on both sides.'[5] Much the same could be said of the titled aristocracy, the gentry as a whole, those gentry who held office at court and those who did not, commercial and professional men and so forth. Some social strata may have split unequally between king and parliament, between active royalism and active parliamentarianism, and there were certainly some distinct geographical, regional trends. However, the absence of any nation-wide class-based patterns severely weakened – fatally wounded, many historians concluded – explanations of the war as a conflict between different classes. Moreover, from James Harrington onwards, historians who have interpreted the causes of the war in a socio-economic or class-based mould have struggled to demonstrate how problems and tensions in society directly connected to and caused the political confrontations which clearly did play some part in precipitating the civil war. Many historians have concluded that the civil war was caused at least in part by political events and developments, and it is very difficult fully to explain them in terms of social factors and to demonstrate a tangible link between society and politics.

With the apparent collapse of long-term socio-economic explanations for the English civil war, substantial elements of the older Whig thesis of long-term political, constitutional and religious causation again held the field. Thus in his major new study of 1640–2, Anthony Fletcher could still refer to Gardiner's as the 'authoritative account', a narrative which needed correction only 'on a few points of detail'.[6] The Whig account had indeed been modified in places and, partly responding to Sir Lewis Namier's work on eighteenth-century politics, there was now more emphasis upon the composition, backgrounds and outlooks of certain powerful groups, especially the membership of the House of Commons, and upon the search for patterns of clientage and common interest.[7] But the Whig approach had yet to endure a frontal assault. It

5   Quoted in Richardson, *Debate on the English Revolution*, p. 124.
6   A. Fletcher, *The Outbreak of the English Civil War* (London, 1981), p. viii, though by that date many historians were, in fact, disagreeing profoundly with the interpretations of Gardiner and other Whig historians.
7   Works seemingly influenced by Namier's approach include D. Brunton and D. H. Pennington, *Members of the Long Parliament* (London, 1954) and M. F. Keeler, *The Long Parliament 1640–41: A Biographical Study of its Members* (Philadelphia, 1954).

did so during the 1970s and 1980s, as so-called 'revisionism' challenged and appeared to overthrow many of the key assumptions and elements of the Whig thesis (as well as what survived of the Marxist approach).

Revisionism was a broad outlook rather than a coherent movement; it has been described as 'not a school but an amorphous generational trend'.[8] Historians often lumped together as revisionists, such as Conrad Russell, John Morrill and Kevin Sharpe, in reality always held some widely divergent views on the early Stuart period in general and the causes of the war in particular. However, broad and common themes emerged. Revisionists were sceptical of the long-term causation favoured by the Whigs and the Marxists, and of their assumption that the war was the inevitable consequence of deep-rooted problems. Moreover, they claimed that Whigs and Marxists alike were guilty of a teleological approach, of writing accounts with the ends firmly in mind and of fashioning their stories so that they read as evolutionary paths towards predetermined and desired goals. Claiming to approach the seventeenth century with no such preconceptions, in place of constitutional clashes, long-term religious strife and conflict between crown and Commons, the revisionists saw the early Stuart state as being united, consensual and sound. Parliament was a weak institution anxious to cooperate with the crown and to avoid confrontations; these did occur but they were very infrequent and atypical, serve only to highlight the overwhelming peace and unity of the period and indicate that there was no consistent or coherent opposition 'party' in parliament. The House of Commons was often overshadowed by the Lords, whose members had far more prestige and influence; indeed, the aristocracy continued to dominate an ordered, stable, conservative society. Most MPs had little interest in national affairs and policies and were more concerned to aid their localities and to promote local and private business, a reflection of their localist outlook and their membership of inward looking 'county communities', far removed from the concerns of central government and national politics. Just as there was no principled political or ideological division in the early Stuart state, so there was little or no religious division in the opening decades of the seventeenth century. Even reform-minded Protestants were broadly satisfied with the Jacobean Church of England and with the religious leadership of James I; there was no puritan 'opposition'. In this revisionist account, the breakdown occurred suddenly and rapidly, caused by the personal, political and

---

8   G. Burgess, 'On Revisionism: An Analysis of Early Stuart Historiography in the 1970s and 1980s', *The Historical Journal* 33 (1990), one of the subtlest and most thoughtful assessments of revisionism; the quotation is from p. 617.

religious impact of Charles I, an interventionary and innovatory monarch, and by a handful of avoidable blunders and mistakes made by both sides in the run up to a war which could, with greater skill and luck, have been avoided. Some revisionists saw the accession of Charles in 1625 as the key watershed when order, consensus and harmony gave way to error, discontent and division, exacerbated by the strains of waging war against France and Spain in the late 1620s and an associated 'functional breakdown' in the military and fiscal sinews of the state; others placed the turning point later, around 1629 with the onset of the Personal Rule, or not until the late 1630s, when war with Scotland upset a balanced and harmonious England. But whatever their starting point, the revisionists saw the causes of the civil war principally grounded in short-term political and religious problems.[9]

Mary Fulbrook's article (Chapter 2), questioning this approach, was first published in 1982, when the revisionist flood-tide was in full spate. One of the first major counter-attacks, a trio of articles by Christopher Hill, Derek Hirst and T. K. Rabb, had appeared just a few months before, in the August 1981 edition of the journal *Past & Present*.[10] Echoing their tone, Fulbrook adopts a generally sceptical approach towards revisionism, impatient with the short-term, high political line which many revisionists had adopted and arguing – more persuasively in some areas than in others, perhaps – that longer-term political, governmental and administrative factors and both long- and short-term socio-economic trends and tensions played important roles in causing the war. She criticizes revisionists for viewing the participants as motivated by rather narrow factionalism, patronage contests and power struggles fought out within an accepted conservative and hierarchical context rather than by wider concerns and aspirations built upon ideology, constitutional

---

9 Revisionist interpretations in this mould include C. Russell (ed), *The Origins of the English Civil War* (Basingstoke, 1973); Russell, 'Parliamentary History in Perspective, 1604–29', *History* 61 (1976); Russell, *Parliaments and English Politics, 1621–9* (Oxford, 1979); J. Morrill, *The Revolt of the Provinces. Conservatives and Radicals in the English Civil War, 1630–50* (London, 1976); K. Sharpe (ed.), *Faction and Parliament. Essays on Early Stuart History* (Oxford, 1978); A. M. Everitt, *The Community of Kent and the Great Rebellion, 1640–60* (Leicester, 1966); A. Fletcher, *A County Community in Peace and War: Sussex 1600–60* (Harlow, 1975); J. C. D. Clark, *Revolution and Rebellion: State and Society in England in the Seventeenth and Eighteenth Centuries* (Cambridge, 1987); M. Kishlansky, 'The Emergence of Adversary Politics in the Long Parliament', *Journal of Modern History* 49 (1977); Kishlansky, *Parliamentary Selection: Social and Political Choice in Early Modern England* (Cambridge, 1986).

10 C. Hill, 'Parliament and People in Seventeenth Century England', D. Hirst, 'Revisionism Revised: The Place of Principle', and T. K. Rabb, 'Revisionism Revised: The Role of the Commons', *Past & Present* 92 (1981).

principle or class interests. Many of these points have subsequently been taken further as criticism of revisionism has gathered pace. Although Fulbrook's closing point, that the 'most fruitful' line for future investigation lies in exploring the 'drive towards absolutism' and in comparing this aspect of Caroline England with contemporary Continental states, has in fact played only a limited role in anti- or post-revisionism writing, her call for a renewed focus on longer-term 'structural', socio-economic and intellectual (in a broad sense, encompassing the 'mental world of participants') factors has borne fruit.

A generation after the revisionists began reappraising the causes of the civil war, it is clear that they have not managed to establish a new lasting orthodoxy, for already large sections of their interpretation have been challenged and at least partly overturned. Most historians would accept that revisionism contained constructive, valuable elements and served as a corrective to some earlier dubious assumptions and fashions. For example, the increased attention give to the political role of the peerage and to the House of Lords has been broadly welcomed, as has the attempt to gain a more rounded picture of the role, work and achievements of early Stuart parliaments. Equally, some attacks on revisionism have themselves gone too far and have painted unfair images – caricatures – of revisionist arguments. For example, some revisionist historians have consistently emphasized the role of religion and religious divisions as a fundamental and deep-rooted cause of the war; it is thus incorrect to claim that revisionism entirely disregarded matters of principle and ideology or focused solely on narrow, short-term causes. However, large parts of the revisionist canon and of the assumptions which underpinned it have been severely shaken by recent work.[11]

The image of the English provinces dominated by 'county communities', inward-looking, enclosed, localist-minded 'cantons', whose inhabitants were divorced from, and little interested in, the affairs of central government and national policies, has been attacked by Clive Holmes, Ann Hughes, Richard Cust and others.[12] Instead, it is argued that the gentry elite had interests, outlooks and connections that were both local

---

11   For a good, if early, statement of post- or anti-revisionist views, see R. Cust and A. Hughes (eds), *Conflict in Early Stuart England. Studies in Religion and Politics, 1603–42* (Harlow, 1989), especially the editors' introduction 'After Revisionism'.
12   C. Holmes, 'The County Community in Stuart Historiography', *Journal of British Studies* 19 (1980); A. Hughes, *Politics, Society and Civil War: Warwickshire, 1620–60* (Cambridge, 1987); R. Cust, 'News and Politics in Early Seventeenth Century England', *Past & Present* 112 (1986). See also A. Fox, 'Rumour, News and Popular Political Opinion in Elizabethan and Stuart England', *Historical Journal* 40 (1997).

and national. Moreover, it is argued that at a non-elite level, provincial Englishmen also had a high level of participation in public processes – in the legal and judicial systems, in the application of religious policies at parish level, in electing MPs and so forth – and were capable of independent activity and informed judgements. A thirst for news, met by oral communications, hand-written 'separates', ballads and clandestine printed material, created a provincial population with a keen and informed interest in affairs of state, ranging from fiscal and religious matters to foreign policy and war. Thus their elected representatives in parliament were not hidebound by purely localist concerns but, reflecting broader public opinion, were actively interested in the formulation and application of public legislation and state policy. Furthermore, they worked within a context of differing political ideologies. In place of the revisionist emphasis upon consensus and an absence of ideological division, Johann Sommerville and others have argued for contrasting political ideas circulating in early Stuart England.[13] In particular, some historians have portrayed potentially deep divisions between royalist or absolutist views on the one hand, in which kings were ultimately answerable to God alone and not to mortal laws or parliaments, and constitutionalist or contract views on the other, in which kings were deemed to have been entrusted with power by the people and were not only required to rule according to established laws and customs but could also be resisted or circumscribed by the law and by parliament if they abused their power. Proponents of both views were reluctant to state their beliefs in a clear or stark manner, and it is conceded that early Stuart politicians and commentators tended to dress their views in traditionalist clothes and to stress respect for the rule of law. However, many historians now argue that beneath this veneer lurked divergent political ideologies.

Springing from these foundations, historians have recently portrayed early Stuart politics as much more deeply divided than revisionists would claim. In place of the image of consensus and harmony surviving until the 'functional breakdown' of the late 1620s or beyond, historians such as Thomas Cogswell, Michael Young, Richard Cust and L. J. Reeve have argued that the 1620s saw deep political divisions at the centre.[14] Repeatedly during the 1620s both Houses of Parliament but

13   J. Sommerville, *Royalists and Patriots: Politics and Ideology in England, 1603–40* (Basingstoke, 1999). A different line is taken by G. Burgess, *The Politics of the Ancient Constitution* (Basingstoke, 1992).
14   T. Cogswell, *The Blessed Revolution: English Politics and the Coming of War, 1621–4* (Cambridge, 1989); Cogswell, 'A Low Road to Extinction? Supply and Redress of Grievances in the Parliaments of the 1620s', *The Historical Journal* 33 (1990); M. Young, 'Buckingham, War and Parliament: Revisionism Gone Too

particularly the Commons – whose members are no longer represented as inferior to and in the thrall of members of the Lords – vigorously opposed the crown on matters of state policy, at times delaying or withholding supply in pursuit of redress of grievances. Far from being a weak and declining institution dominated by localist concerns, parliament proved able and willing to criticize and mount attacks on the personnel and policies of the crown, fuelled in part by an alternative view of how the constitution should work. MPs may not have enunciated clear and consistent political philosophies, taken out membership of an organized opposition party or sought to overthrow the existing political system, but they did actively oppose royal policies and worked to curb the executive. It is argued that conflict as much as consensus, division as much as harmony, marked early Stuart (parliamentary) politics. Commons petitions and protestations, impeachments and the Petition of Right, are restored to centre stage. Shorn of some of their partisan and anachronistic flourishes and the air of inevitability, elements of the Whigs' political and constitutional account, apparently buried by the revisionists, may be returning to life.

The revisionist stress upon harmony and consensus, upon a political system which was working well and which contained no fundamental flaws, had created its own problems. As John Morrill noted in the preface to the 1980 reprint of one of his early works, a colleague had accused him of 'explaining why no civil war broke out in England in 1642'.[15] Their critics claimed that, in stressing the absence of serious divisive issues in early Stuart England, the revisionists had painted themselves into a corner, for they had somehow to explain how and why civil war broke out in the 1640s. Many found the emphasis upon short-term mistakes and blunders in high politics unconvincing, feeling that the enormous chasm which opened up in 1642 and the bitter civil war which followed could not adequately be explained in this way. These criticisms were not entirely fair, for a number of historians labelled revisionists did in fact see deeper and longer-term causes of the war. For example, Conrad Russell detected a functional breakdown in the late 1620s, caused by the strains of waging war against states which had modern, expanding military machines. In stressing the problems created by the absence of a standing army and salaried bureaucracy and by the weak financial position of the crown, Russell and others were pointing to deep seated weaknesses. In highlighting the failure of royal income to keep

Far', *Parliamentary History* 4 (1985); Young, 'Revisionism and the Council of War', *Parliamentary History* 8 (1989); R. Cust, *The Forced Loan and English Politics, 1626–8* (Oxford, 1987); L. J. Reeve, *Charles I and the Road to Personal Rule* (Cambridge, 1989).

15   Morrill, *Revolt of the Provinces* (reprinted Harlow, 1980), p. x.

pace with inflation, the inefficiencies of many sources of royal revenue, the underassessment of taxes by the gentry and the unwillingness of parliament, especially the Commons, to grant the crown the taxes it needed in peacetime or wartime and to support a reorganization of royal finances, these historians were pointing to problems which had worsened over several decades and whose origins are to be found in the sixteenth, not the seventeenth, century. It should be noted, however, that not all historians are convinced by this 'functional breakdown' thesis, arguing instead that England's poor performance in the wars of the late 1620s owed more to the shortcomings of Buckingham and other military commanders than to the weaknesses of the fiscal-military machine.[16]

More importantly, many revisionists always stressed religion as a deeper if sometimes partly concealed fracture line running through the early Stuart state. In this area there were significant differences between historians often grouped together under the heading of revisionists, and the dividing lines between them and post-revisionists are not so clear. Certainly, a revisionist line of sorts emerged. Over the last few decades, many historians have shied away from notions of the Whigs' 'puritan revolution', from the idea that from the reign of Elizabeth I onwards there was a distinct grouping of radical Protestants dissatisfied with the Elizabethan settlement and at least semi-detached from the Church of England, whose opposition to the religious policies of the crown and the state church developed into, and gave them the lead in mounting, political and constitutional opposition, too. Instead, they suggested that there was a broad religious consensus in the late Tudor and early Stuart period, built around a common Calvinist faith and a broad if sometimes grudging acceptance of an episcopalian structure. Crown and church were able to accommodate a variety of shades and emphases of belief. Puritans were the 'hotter sort' of Protestants within the Church of England, not a religious, political or constitutional opposition party working outside or against church and crown. This consensus was shattered during the reign of Charles I by the king's promotion of a different brand of Protestantism, often labelled Laudianism or Arminianism, which opposed the Calvinist tenet of predestination and which imposed ritualistic, ceremonial, high church policies upon an often unwelcoming population, many of whom viewed the new policies as a drift towards Roman Catholicism and a much-feared 'popish plot'. In this

---

16   The case is put by Russell most clearly in *Parliaments and English Politics*; see also Russell, 'Parliament and the King's Finances' in Russell (ed.), *Origins of the English Civil War*. For sceptical evaluations of Russell's thesis see A. Hughes, *The Causes of the English Civil War* (2nd edn, Basingstoke, 1998), ch. 1, and M. B. Young, *Charles I* (Basingstoke, 1997), chapter 2.

account, then, religious harmony was shattered during the late 1620s and 1630s by Charles's promotion of an anti-Calvinist state religion.[17]

However, by no means all recent historians, even those seen as revisionists, accepted this interpretation. Some, such as Peter White and Kevin Sharpe, have suggested that, far from being a radical and unprecedented anti-Calvinist campaign, the policies of the late 1620s and 1630s merely marked a return to the Elizabethan stress on order, unity and conformity.[18] This interpretation has not been widely accepted and has been countered by strong arguments that the character and approach of the religious policies of Charles I did mark a significant break with those of the preceding decades. Other historians have questioned the image of Calvinist harmony and unity in the late Elizabethan and early Stuart church. Peter Lake and others have suggested that there were sharp distinctions between credal or conformist Calvinists, for whom predestination did not shape religious practices and should not create divisions in this world, and experimental or experiential Calvinists, who believed that it was possible to distinguish in this world between those whom God had predestined for salvation and those doomed to damnation. It is argued that experiential Calvinists believed that they could usefully demonstrate to themselves and to others their status as one of the elect, chosen for salvation, through strict adherence to religious forms and duties, through conspicuous zeal in countering sin and evil, and through seeking out and working with others who had been similarly chosen for salvation. This approach sees a religious cleavage in early Stuart England, well before the rise of Arminianism and the accession of Charles I, and restores the notion of active, oppositional puritanism in the early seventeenth century, of puritans working individually and together to promote their interpretation of the true faith and to counter error, superstition and popery.[19] Charles's religious

17 N. Tyacke, 'Puritanism, Arminianism and Counter-Revolution', in Russell (ed.), *Origins of the English Civil War*; Tyacke presented a modified version of this argument at far greater length in *Anti-Calvinists: The Rise of English Arminianism, c. 1590–1640* (Oxford, 1987); P. Collinson, *The Religion of the Protestants* (Oxford, 1983); Collinson, *English Puritanism* (London, 1983).

18 P. White, 'The Rise of Arminianism Reconsidered', *Past & Present* 101 (1983); White, *Predestination, Policy and Polemic: Conflict and Consensus in the English Church from the Reformation to the Civil War* (Cambridge, 1992); K. Sharpe, 'Archbishop Laud', *History Today* 33 (1983); Sharpe, *The Personal Rule of Charles I* (London, 1992).

19 P. Lake, 'Calvinism and the English Church, 1570–1635', *Past & Present* 114 (1987); K. Fincham and P. Lake, 'The Ecclesiastical Policies of James I and Charles I', in K. Fincham (ed.), *The Early Stuart Church, 1603–42* (Basingstoke, 1993), an excellent and important collection, the introduction to which (by Fincham) outlines the rival interpretations.

policies of the late 1620s and 1630s could thus be seen as an attempt to counter this activism, though in the process they sharpened the divisions and served to strengthen religious opposition. Puritanism remained the faith of a minority, and John Morrill and Judith Maltby amongst others have stressed that the less rigorous and more accessible religion of the established church and prayer book may have been more to the taste of the majority. But many historians, Morrill most conspicuously, have also emphasized the central role played by the religiously motivated minority, arguing that their radical, reformist faith shaped the conflicts of the 1640s and drove men to take up arms against the king in 1642.[20]

Many revisionists have recently adopted another line in seeking to explain the causes of the civil war, namely a renewed interest in the 'British' nature of the conflict. A century before, Gardiner and Firth had taken careful account of Scottish and Irish interconnections with the unfolding English crisis, from the mid-twentieth century J. H. Elliott and others had been exploring the problems associated with 'multiple kingdoms', where one monarch ruled over several different and disparate states,[21] and during the 1970s and early 1980s John Pocock argued for 'British history: a plea for a new subject', as he entitled one of his articles.[22] But the recent emphasis upon a British interpretation of (the causes of) the civil war really stems from Conrad Russell's 1987 article, reproduced in this collection, which led on to fuller and more detailed studies in the 1990s. For its proponents, this British approach permits a much fuller understanding of the conflicts which rocked all three kingdoms during the mid-seventeenth century and also serves to pull together and give firmer contexts to some of the other strands, such as religion and the fiscal and administrative strains caused or exacerbated by war. Critics have rather harshly suggested that this approach is a revisionist escape route, that having portrayed early Stuart England as consensual, united and free from fundamental problems and thus reduced the causes of the war to an unconvincing assemblage of short-term political mistakes and accidents, the British problem has been seized upon by revisionists to restore a more plausible, major, deep-seated

20   J. Morrill, *The Nature of the English Revolution* (Harlow, 1993), part 1; Morrill, *Revolt in the Provinces. The People of England and the Tragedies of War, 1630–48* (Harlow, 1999), passim; J. Maltby, ' "By This Book": Parishioners, the Prayer Book and the Established Church', in Fincham (ed.), *The Early Stuart Church*; Maltby, *Prayer Book and People in Elizabethan and Early Stuart England* (Cambridge, 1998).
21   J. H. Elliott, 'The King and the Catalans, 1621–40', *Cambridge Historical Journal* 2 (1955).
22   J. G. A. Pocock's article was published in the *Journal of Modern History* 4 (1975).

cause of the war while leaving their portrait of early Stuart England more or less in tact.

Russell's 1987 article (Chapter 3) on the 'British' interpretation of (the causes of) the civil war opens by addressing this point, quoting Professor Elton's criticism of the revisionist approach, which itself echoes that of John Morrill's colleague, already noted. Although Russell claims that existing explanations of the war based upon long-term constitutional conflict or social change 'appear to have suffered irretrievable breakdown', he denies that he had ever ruled out the possibility of long-term causation and feels that it is 'highly improbable' though not impossible that the war was solely the result of short-term political failures. He argues that historians had hitherto largely overlooked one such major cause, because they had focused on England rather than Britain. Pointing to the repeated interconnections of the conflicts which broke out in Scotland, Ireland and England over a five-year period, 1637–42, he suggests that they may have resulted from common causes. His search for such causes leads him to highlight not only the personal and policy failings of the man who ruled all three kingdoms, Charles I, but also the problems likely to result within and between component parts of a 'multiple kingdom'. In the case of Britain, Russell highlights Charles's attempts to impose greater religious uniformity throughout his religiously diverse inheritance, which had the effect of 'drop[ping] a match into this powder-keg'. It should be noted that Russell's stress here upon the shortcomings of Charles was far from new and was consistent with many other and older accounts. It is also noticeable that although Russell was pointing to deeper and longer-term causes of the civil war, in this article the real difficulties emerge only in the decade or so before the outbreak of the English military conflict. Although there was a potential British problem dating back decades, to the Tudor reconquest of and much tighter control over Ireland and to the Stuart inheritance of 1603, here it is suggested that that potential was not fully realized until the reign of Charles I. Much of Russell's article focuses upon, and gives an account of, difficulties and divisions which emerged after 1625 and which appear to have been created by Charles.

The British causation and context of the English civil war became major elements of much of the new work of the 1990s. Many of the themes of Russell's article were taken further in his 1990 study of *The Causes of the English Civil War*, which did explore problems within the multiple kingdom from the 1580s onwards as well as examining in more detail religious issues, religious unity in the three kingdoms under Charles I and the deficiencies of Charles as monarch. Russell's 1991 heavyweight *The Fall of the British Monarchies* provided a detailed three kingdom narrative, though the chronological span had shrunk to just 1637–42.[23] John Morrill, John Pocock, Sarah Barber and others have adopted a British perspective in some of their recent work.[24] Revised editions of broader surveys by Roger Lockyer, Barry Coward and Derek Hirst have appeared, expanded to take fuller notice of the British dimension, and new accounts of the civil war, such as those written by Martyn Bennett and edited by John Kenyon and Jane Ohlmeyer, have emphasized their three kingdoms outlook.[25] However, even though this approach is still in its infancy, some historians have already expressed significant reservations and doubt whether it will prove to be a durable and convincing interpretation of the nature and causes of the civil war.

Several criticisms have been levelled at the 'British' approach to the civil war.[26] As Russell conceded in his article, almost of necessity it focuses on politics, religion and the military, thereby once more effectively excluding or denying the importance of social and economic factors. A British approach may exaggerate the unity and integrity of the component kingdoms and underplay internal divisions, such as that between the centre and the provinces in England, between different English and Scottish provinces or between the highland and lowland zones of Scotland and of England and Wales. It is also suggested that a British approach may exaggerate the problems inherent in the 'Atlantic archipelago'; despite the rumblings over Anglo-Scottish union in the years after he succeeded Elizabeth, in reality the British problem seems not to have created enormous problems for James I. Some would argue that there is nothing inherently wrong or necessarily inadequate in maintaining a focus on England and Wales while attempting to explain

23   Published Oxford, 1990 and 1991 respectively.
24   As editors or contributors to four important collections on this theme published during the 1990s: R. Asch (ed.), *Three Nations – A Common History?* (Bochum, 1993); A. Grant and K. Stringer (eds), *Uniting the Kingdom?* (London, 1995); S. Ellis and S. Barber (eds), *Conquest and Union. Fashioning a British State 1485–1725* (Harlow, 1995); B. Bradshaw and J. Morrill (eds), *The British Problem c. 1534–1707. State Formation in the Atlantic Archipelago* (Basingstoke, 1996).
25   R. Lockyer, *The Early Stuarts. A Political History of England, 1603–42* (2nd edn, Harlow, 1999); B. Coward, *The Stuart Age. England, 1603–1714* (2nd edn, Harlow, 1994); D. Hirst, *England in Conflict, 1603–60. Kingdom, Community, Commonwealth* (London, 1999); M. Bennett, *The Civil Wars in Britain and Ireland, 1638–51* (Oxford, 1997); J. P. Kenyon and J. Ohlmeyer (eds), *The Civil Wars. A Military History of England, Scotland and Ireland, 1638–60* (Oxford, 1998); Ohlmeyer, 'The Wars of the Three Kingdoms', *History Today* 48 (1998).
26   P. Gaunt, *The British Wars, 1637–51* (London, 1997) expresses some scepticism about the British approach; J. Adamson, 'The English Context of the British Civil Wars', *History Today* 48 (1998) is very critical. See also the important reviews of Russell's work by Morrill, *The Nature of the English Revolution*, ch. 13, and P. Lake, 'Review Article', *Huntington Library Quarterly* 57 (1994).

and interpret the English civil war, provided that the involvement and impact of Scotland and Ireland are fully recognized and examined; this was the approach taken by the best of the nineteenth-century Whig historians, such as Gardiner. Thus, despite the resulting accusations of Anglo-centricity from some quarters, it is claimed that it is not necessary to produce an account which accords Scotland, Ireland, England and Wales equal coverage. Perhaps most importantly, while the contributions of Scotland and Ireland to the English conflict undoubtedly help to explain the form and timing of the descent into civil war, many historians feel that they do not provide a full or sufficient explanation of the causes of the English civil war. In essence it was an English civil war, albeit one with Scottish and Irish connections, which broke out in the wake of an unresolved English crisis, which began in 1642–3 as a conflict between two armies of Englishmen and Welshmen, and which could only have happened if there were deep divisions within England and Wales. Accordingly, for many historians the 'British problem' does not provide the answer in the continuing quest for the causes of the civil war.

At the beginning of the third millennium there is no clear consensus on what caused the civil war, and no clear indication where the search for the causes will next lead. Most historians currently working in the field favour a range or combination of factors rather than a single overriding cause, and most see religion as one of the important elements. The two most recent surveys of the causes, by Ann Hughes and Norah Carlin, both stress the importance of deep-seated issues which created the context for the immediate crisis of the early 1640s and so shaped the form and nature of that crisis and war. Both are dissatisfied with short-term or high political explanations alone.[27] Indeed, many historians make the point that, although it is easy enough to point to the (principally political and religious) causes of the tide of opposition which broke on the king when he was forced to meet and respond constructively to an English parliament in 1640, we must search much deeper fully to explain why there was no political resolution and why instead there was a spiralling crisis such that by summer 1642 sufficiently large elements of the elite and the non-elite both at the centre and in the provinces were so bitterly divided that they were prepared to resort to arms and begin a major civil war. Although the events and developments of 1640–2 precipitated the war and helped to determine the precise form and timing of the outbreak of conflict, it is argued that the origins of the war cannot be found in the early 1640s alone.

27   Hughes, *The Causes of the English Civil War*; N. Carlin, *The Causes of the English Civil War* (Oxford, 1999).

Hughes, Carlin and others point to a range of deeper English and Welsh causes which drove on and shaped the political and military crisis of the early 1640s. Most have already been highlighted. There has been a continuing and strengthening emphasis upon religious divisions, often now expressed in terms of a puritanism which was politicized and mobilized in the decades before the civil war by a polarization of beliefs and by the actions of the crown in upping the stakes and deepening the religious cleavage. Equally, many historians have returned to the image of profound political divisions, springing from issues of principle and divergent ideological foundations. The groupings may have been fluid, the language of the participants cautious or ambiguous, the outward appearance often lacking a conscious or consistent revolutionary style, but the political arena was, it is suggested, being rent by fracture lines much deeper and profound than could be brought about merely by a succession of mistakes and misfortunes in the wake of the Scottish rejection of the new prayer book. But over and above this, there has also been renewed interest in the social dimension of the war, in looking for social roots of the conflict which might mesh with religious and politics issues. Hughes, who professes 'a conviction' that the civil war had long-term origins, suggests that there were 'connections between social changes and relationships and conflicting views of religion, politics and "culture"'. Carlin detects 'the importance of the middling sort as a catalyst which polarized the divisions over religion, politics and government in 1640–2'.[28]

Much of the recent work on the social history of the seventeenth century or the early modern period, on gender, particular social groups or professions, and wider themes such as crime or education, has taken a broad chronological approach and has avoided making direct or explicit links with the (causes of the) civil war. Equally many historians have noted that the undoubted socio-economic changes of the sixteenth and early seventeenth centuries – rapid demographic expansion, price inflation, a decline in the real value of wages, changing patterns of agriculture, manufacturing and commerce, increasing poverty and a widening gap between rich and poor – were slackening off by the middle third of the seventeenth century and suggest that this makes it harder to link such developments with a war which broke out in 1642 rather than, say, 1622.[29] And the main thrust of the attack on Marxist-inspired interpretations mounted in the third quarter of the twentieth century – the difficulties of demonstrating a link between socio-economic trends

28 Hughes, *The Causes of the English Civil War*, p. 7; Carlin, *The Causes of the English Civil War*, p. 162.
29 A point made by Morrill in chapter 1 of this volume and in his *The Nature of the English Revolution*, ch. 1.

and tensions on the one hand and an apparently political and military conflict on the other and of proving that the former caused the latter, especially as the fracture lines of the 1640s do not seem to have been broadly class-based – still largely holds true a generation on.

Never the less, socio-economic interpretations have continued. Some have held faith with the concept of one class or social grouping opposing another. Brian Manning, for one, believes that 'the causes and outcome of the revolution were determined by fundamental changes taking place in English society' and portrays a conflict of the aristocracy and governing elites against elements of the peasantry, artisans and small traders, an urban and rural mix of independent small producers, sometimes labelled 'the middling sort'. Where other historians have detected little popular unrest in the pre-war years, Manning suggests that the middling sort contributed to a rising tide of protest and disorder, in the provinces but especially in and around London. Fuelled by a mixture of socio-economic, religious and political grievances, it drove forward the parliamentary opposition to the crown in 1640–2, while also provoking many of the elite to rally to the king to forestall disorder and social overturning.[30] In a somewhat similar mould, Robert Brenner has recently seen the war resulting, at least in part, from a conflict between economically advanced and forward looking groups, especially a new, emerging mercantile group which allied with the parliamentary opposition, and a crown which was backward looking, careless of property rights and inhibited economic progress, and which was supported by some traditional groupings, especially established merchant oligarchies.[31]

Other historians have sought more subtle links between changes and dislocations within society and a 'cultural' conflict, broadly defined. For some, this has taken the form of a cautious exhumation of the 'court' and 'country' line, propounded by Perez Zagorin in the late 1960s, which presented a dichotomy between those who held office at court or in central government and those members of the elite whose allegiances lay primarily with parliament and the local world, who were critical of the court and supported reform.[32] Although that pattern was widely seen as too simplistic, underplaying divisions within and connections between the two groupings, more recent work on the 'culture of politics' or 'political culture' has pointed in a similar direction, to a growing

30   B. Manning, *The English People and the English Revolution* (2nd edn, London, 1991); the quotation is from the new introduction, p. 46.
31   R. Brenner, *Merchants and Revolution: Commercial Change, Political Conflict and London's Overseas Traders, 1550–1653* (Cambridge, 1993).
32   P. Zagorin, *The Court and the Country: The Beginnings of the English Revolution* (New York, 1969).

divergence between the image of an elitist, reserved, authoritarian court and a 'country' ideology which stressed public service, independent upholding of local rights and of reformed religion, and a suspicion of alleged corruption and popish leanings at the centre.[33] Other historians, most notably David Underdown, have explored the links between culture and society at a local or provincial level. Underdown sees growing divisions within early Stuart provincial society between one element which was paternalistic, hierarchical and deferential, grounded in traditional religious, ritualistic and communal forms, and another which was more open, individualistic and distinctive, sympathetic to religious and moral reformation. These dichotomies, which underlay the often bitter disputes over church ales, Sunday sport, popular revels and so forth, led to the development of two very different and rival 'cultures', which in due course divided and supported king or parliament in the 1640s. Furthermore, Underdown suggests that there were distinct geographical patterns to these cultural divisions, which were determined by factors such as different settlement patterns, land use and occupations, to reveal an 'ecology' of rival cultures and allegiances – the inhabitants of arable, mixed farming, downland areas tended to support the king, while many in wood-pasture, cloth- and cheese-making areas tended to support parliament.[34] However, while this interpretation may work for (parts of) the three counties upon which Underdown focuses, namely Somerset, Dorset and Wiltshire, many historians have found that it does not work there or elsewhere – it is not fully supported by Mark Stoyle's detailed work on neighbouring Devon, for example[35] – and are sceptical that it can provide a broadly applicable explanation of the causes of the civil war or of the complex pattern of war-time allegiances.[36] Some would argue that while the work of Underdown and others has told us more about the context of the civil war and about war-time allegiances (a matter we

33   R. M. Smuts, *Court Culture and the Origins of a Royalist Tradition in Early Stuart England* (Philadelphia, 1987); Smuts (ed.), *The Stuart Court and Europe: Essays in Politics and Political Culture* (Cambridge, 1996); K. Sharpe, *Criticism and Compliment* (Cambridge, 1987); S. Amussen and M. Kishlansky (eds), *Political Culture and Cultural Politics in Early Modern England* (Manchester, 1995).

34   D. Underdown, *Revel, Riot and Rebellion. Popular Politics and Culture in England, 1603–60* (Oxford, 1985).

35   M. Stoyle, *Loyalty and Locality: Popular Allegiances in Devon during the English Civil War* (Exeter, 1994).

36   See especially the detailed review by Morrill reprinted in his *The Nature of the English Revolution*, ch. 11, and Underdown's reply in *Journal of British Studies* 26 (1987). Underdown's thesis is also discussed by A. Hughes, 'Local History and the Origins of the English Civil War', in Cust and Hughes (eds), *Conflict in Early Stuart England*.

will pursue further in Part III), it presents a limited and incomplete picture of the origins and causes of the civil war.

For many historian currently working in the field, so-called post-revisionists as well as revisionists, a medium- or short-term narrative of the events leading up to the outbreak of war provides a major plank in explaining and understanding the outbreak of the war. Although making clear their belief that the war had longer-term causes, it is noticeable that in their recent surveys, both Norah Carlin and Ann Hughes devote considerable space to analytical narratives of the pre-war years. Thus Carlin's first main chapter (after an introduction on 'the problem of causation') provides a detailed three-kingdoms account of the years 1637–42, while Hughes's final chapter surveys the key developments and trends of the broader period 1625–42. In common with most accounts of the 1620s and 1630s, Hughes lays considerable weight on the personal and political failings of Charles I, though point-ing out that they 'exacerbated' existing tensions within England and were often ('ham-fisted') reactions to social and political developments, and she again stresses that the events of these years and the actions of the king and his opponents 'have . . . to be understood within a pre-existing framework'.[37] In contrast to the revisionist emphasis on con-sensus and good government during the 1620s and to Russell's account of a functional breakdown in the latter part of the decade caused by the strains of war, the recent work of Hughes and others portrays the 1620s as a decade during which there were growing political and religious rifts built upon ideological differences and divergent views of the role of parliament, a period when cooperation was tempered by conflicts borne of deep and growing cleavages within the state.

Even more starkly, recent work has presented two strikingly different images of the 1630s. One is dominated by the writings of Kevin Sharpe, especially his massive 1992 study of *The Personal Rule of Charles I*. In Sharpe's account, Charles I, driven into the Personal Rule by the failings of parliament and genuinely believing that he could provide sounder and more stable government, launched an effective programme of reform in church and state. This stressed public good, order, efficiency and decency, a refined and cultural court, a return to traditional if non-parliamentary styles of royal government and of central and local administration, a reduction in state expenditure, a substantial expan-sion in income through the revival and efficient collection of a series of long-established levies, and a drive to reinvigorate and strengthen the Church of England, to repair, beautify and reorder churches, and to reimpose religious unity and harmony. For Sharpe, England during the

37 Hughes, *The Causes of the English Civil War*, p. 152.

1630s was a nation at peace not only internationally but also with itself. There was, it is conceded, a degree of resentment at some of the interventions and initiatives of central government and a few minor examples of open resistance broke the calm, but in the main Charles's policies were accepted and enforced. If some of the financial levies, especially Ship Money, created local squabbles and rating disputes, there was very little principled resistance and financially they were remarkably successful. There was no indication of any widespread non-cooperation, clandestine plotting or would-be rebellions. Thus for Sharpe and the few who have followed him, the 1630s was a decade of renewed and growing peace and harmony, good government and stability, contentment and an air of calm, shattered only by the external intervention of the Scots.

Most historians do not accept this interpretation of the 1630s.[38] They suggest that there was widespread and substantial discontent with the policies and the constitutional basis of the Personal Rule. They point both to the large numbers who were so alienated by Charles's government, especially his religious policies, that they emigrated to the New World during the 1630s, and to the wide-ranging criticism of the Personal Rule and the ferocious attacks launched upon its personnel and policies in 1640–1, in the Short and Long Parliaments. They also question the selection of primary source material. They agree that there was little open and public resistance to the Personal Rule during the 1630s and that few people were willing to put their heads above the parapet and face the severe punishment likely to follow. Therefore formal governmental records of the 1630s, especially those of the Privy Council, are unlikely to contain evidence of deep or principled opposition, and conclusions drawn from such sources alone are incomplete and one sided. Historians must dig deeper, to explore the sentiments which the literate felt able to record in personal and private records, such as diaries, commonplace books and correspondence with close and trusted friends. When such sources are located and explored – notes of discussions amongst a group of Kent gentry in the wake of the Hampden decision, the personal papers of Sir Simonds D'Ewes and Nehemiah Wallington, the diary of Thomas Dugard, and so forth[39] – they present a different

---

38 Ibid., chs 1 and 4; Young, *Charles I*, chs 3–4; Carlin, *The Causes of the English Civil War*, esp. ch. 2; E. S. Cope, *Politics Without Parliaments, 1629–40* (London, 1987).

39 K. Fincham, 'The Judges' Decision on Ship Money in February 1637: The Reaction in Kent', *Bulletin of the Institute of Historical Research* 57 (1984); S. P. Salt, 'Sir Simonds D'Ewes and the Levying of Ship Money, 1635–40', *The Historical Journal* 37 (1994); P. S. Seaver, *Wallington's World: A Puritan Artisan in Seventeenth Century London* (London, 1985); A. Hughes, 'Thomas Dugard and his Circle in the 1630s – A "Parliamentary-Puritan" Connexion?', *The Historical Journal* 29 (1986).

picture. The sources reveal that although, in common with the mass of the population, these figures generally conformed to royal government and policies, in D'Ewes's case even playing a leading role in enforcing and collecting Ship Money when he was sheriff of Suffolk, they were very worried about the drift of events during the 1630s and unhappy with some or all of the policies of the Personal Rule. If these reactions can be taken as representative of wider responses and attitudes, they point to substantial discontent existing beneath the veneer of acceptance, obedience and outward calm. Many historians therefore suggest that the Personal Rule collapsed so ignominiously in the wake of the Scottish intervention because it served as a catalyst, helping to unleash widespread feelings of alienation against Charles's government which already existed in England and Wales.

The diary of Robert Woodford, drawn upon and analysed by John Fielding (Chapter 4), fits into this mould. Fielding's article was originally published in 1988, before the appearance of Sharpe's full-length study of the 1630s, though his line had already become apparent in a series of strongly-argued papers.[40] It analyses the views, opinions and stances of Woodford, a provincial, Midlands lawyer, and long-serving steward of Northampton, as recorded in his surviving diary of 1637–41. A very personal and private document, the diary is in large part a 'puritan spiritual autobiography', and it clearly reflects the type of intense spiritual beliefs and distinctive outlook held by Woodford and many other puritans of that era. Woodford was part of a provincial 'godly group', and he also regularly visited London, where he sought friendship and company within godly circles. Fielding shows that Woodford's faith underscored his very negative views of the royal court and of the religious, fiscal and judicial policies of the latter half of the 1630s; for Woodford, religious and secular affairs were intertwined and inseparable. The diarist looked to godly ministers and magistrates to speak out against the corrupt, popish or illegal policies, and held an idealized view that, once summoned, a parliament could 'redress' the 'exhorbitancyes'. Yet for all this, Fielding makes the point that on the surface and in the public world Woodford was entirely conformist, passive and obedient, paying the levies required of him, running foul neither of the secular nor of the ecclesiastical authorities. While Woodford expected ministers and magistrates to defend their beliefs and was willing to give personal and professional support to those who had encountered difficulties on these grounds, the diarist himself was generally discreet and reticent and saw little point in personally resisting

---

40   Especially Sharpe, 'The Personal Rule of Charles I', in H. Tomlinson (ed.), *Before the English Civil War* (London, 1983).

royal authority. Woodford's surviving diary and Fielding's detailed work on it reveal a high level of provincial political consciousness and paint a picture of strong antipathy to the policies of the Personal Rule stemming from an intensely religious perspective and puritan faith – consistent with John Morrill's view that there was 'a build-up of tention, or internalized anger, among the godly in the years before 1642' creating a 'coiled spring' of godly zeal[41] – but they also highlight an apparently contradictory attitude of outward conformity and public obedience. Woodford's public face during the 1630s is consistent with and in its way might support Sharpe's interpretation of the Personal Rule. By looking deeper, however, Fielding has shown that, in this case at least, the less favourable interpretation of the Personal Rule is the correct one.

The sequence of events from the calling of the Short Parliament in spring 1640 to the outbreak of war in summer 1642 has been well-established and there are fewer serious disagreements over the major staging posts of a high political story recounting the overwhelming opposition to royal policies of 1640, the concrete reforms but also growing divisions of 1641, the impact upon the English political crisis of the aftermath of the Scottish wars and the outbreak of the Irish rebellion, and the division of the English political elite during 1642, creating rival royalist and parliamentarian groupings which in due course turned from seeking a political to a military solution. There are, however, very marked differences of emphasis and disagreements about the importance of deeper, underlying factors, stemming from the divergent approaches already explored in this introduction. Thus historians rank differently the various elements or combination of elements – religious, political, constitutional, legal and personal, the degree of trust/distrust of Charles I, the pressure exerted by Scottish and Irish developments and representatives, and so on – which caused some members of the elite to continue to oppose the king and to seek further reform and others to come out in support of the crown in 1641–2. While for some historians the involvement of broader elements of society, ranging from protest and disorder in London and the provinces to the more orderly process of the country-based petitioning of parliament, plays only a minor role in a political story, for others it is essential in driving forward and shaping the high political process or for explaining why so many people were prepared to take up arms and start a civil war. While some historians are happy to focus on the growing division of the political (parliamentary) elite as the cause or at least the trigger for war, others believe that broader forces must be identified

41   Morrill, *The Nature of the English Revolution*, p. 15.

and explored – Underdown's cultural divisions, Morrill's zealous puritanism, Manning's social dislocation, and so forth – to explain the polarization of a broader swathe of society and the division not only of the political elite in London but also of a substantial section of the urban and rural population of England and Wales into two warring parties. In other words, for some historians these forces form a central strand of the causes of the war, and not merely part of the explanation of allegiances once war had broken out.

In recent years, Conrad Russell has been at the forefront of exploring the high political drift to war in the late 1630s and early 1640s. We have already noted his role in promoting a 'British' interpretation of the causes of the war. In 1984 he published (in different journals) two brief papers addressing specific but central questions about the English political crisis of 1640–2. In the first (Chapter 5), he asks why Charles called the Long Parliament in autumn 1640 and, more specifically, what he was seeking from it. He argues that Charles did not see the parliament as part of a process of making peace with the Scots and so ending the disastrous and expensive Scottish wars, but rather as a means to continue and renew military conflict. Choosing to ignore or misinterpret the advice of the Council of Peers that peace be made with the Scots, Charles continued to expect the new parliament to support him in the war, a belief which Russell terms 'a flight from reality', showing 'a grievous misjudgement of the public mood'. In reality, the Long Parliament did not support continuing war against the Scots, viewing it either as unjust or – like the Council – as a just war which had irredeemably failed. Instead, most members wished to move towards concluding a full peace with Scotland while also addressing a range of English grievances. Russell portrays a king isolated and out of touch with reality, pursuing policies which 'had ceased to be viable', unable to see and to accept that concessions were necessary and so almost relegated to a 'back seat' in governmental processes by parliament and Privy Council. It is a stark and striking image. The emphasis upon Charles's personal and political shortcomings is a common feature of most recent accounts, even those which lay greater stress than Russell's upon longer-term or non-political tensions.

In the second article of 1984 (Chapter 6), Russell asks why in 1642 Charles chose to fight the English civil war. He notes that during 1641–2 a more active king repeatedly took the lead and 'raised the stakes by introducing threats of force', in the Army Plots, the attempt to arrest the five Members and the raising of the standard at Nottingham. But he was, Russell argues, responding to opposition tactics, seen in earlier, medieval attacks on the crown, of seeking to take royal powers out of the hands of the king's person and to place them in those of individuals and institutions answerable to parliament. Here Russell seems to be likening the English civil war to a 'baronial' war, an interpretation advanced more forcefully by John Adamson a few years later[42] but one which many historians feel exaggerates the role and influence of the hereditary peerage and fails to explain the breadth and complexity of the (causes of the) civil war. As in some of the earlier baronial contests, Russell argues, civil war resulted in the early 1640s when the parliamentary opposition pushed too far, allowed the crown to divide the political nation and thus win over a party sufficiently large to fight for it. For his part, Charles was eager to fight, hurt by the indignities he was suffering at parliament's hands and pushed into a corner by parliament's treatment of royal finances, removing many existing sources of income but unable or unwilling to make a new and realistic financial settlement which would cover royal expenditure in peacetime and wartime. The king also saw it as his duty to enforce religious uniformity throughout his confessionally diverse kingdoms. In conclusion, Russell portrays Charles as a monarch who had a problematic inheritance and a difficult role to fulfil, and who was being starved of power and almost pushed into war by the parliamentary opposition. Like many historians, therefore, Russell sees civil war resulting from the short-term exacerbation of a combination of deeper tensions – political, constitutional, religious and, emphasized in more recent writings, 'British'. However, here and elsewhere, Russell's focus on the high politics of the period immediately preceding the outbreak of war is unusually sharp and, some historians would claim, unduly narrow, and many argue that a broader perspective is needed fully to explain and understand the division of English and Welsh society into two warring factions in the early 1640s.

42   See particularly J. Adamson, 'The Baronial Context of the English Civil War', originally published in *Transactions of the Royal Historical Society*, 5th series, 40 (1990), and reprinted in R. Cust and A. Hughes (eds), *The English Civil War* (London, 1997). Morrill, for one, argues against a baronial interpretation of the (causes of the) civil war in *The Nature of the English Revolution*, pp. 11–13 and elsewhere.

2

The English Revolution and the Revisionist Revolt

Mary Fulbrook

Originally appeared as Mary Fulbrook, 'The English Revolution and the Revisionist Revolt' in *Social History* 7. Copyright © 1982 Routledge, London. Reprinted with permission of Taylor & Francis Ltd, PO Box 25, Abingdon, Oxfordshire, OX14 3UE.

One of the most contentious problems of English history is the English Revolution, or English Civil War, of the mid-seventeenth century. Even the very name, the most appropriate characterization of the phenomenon, is contested. Was it a major historical revolution, requiring analysis in terms of long-term political, ideological and socio-economic causes? Or was it rather a mere rebellion, of a familiar and recurrent type, developing by a series of mistakes and ineptitudes which require short-term analysis of power struggles, patronage and personalities? In recent years, a flurry of writings by scholars such as Conrad Russell, Paul Christianson, Kevin Sharpe and others, have sought to revise what they term the 'traditional' approaches to English seventeenth-century history: the so-called 'Whig', 'Marxist' and 'sociological' approaches which share a grand conception of the Revolution and a grand approach to explanation. These revisionist writings, revolting against major traditions of interpretation, have been met with a growing wealth of rebuttals from historians concerned to defend older approaches. It seems that the battle over the Civil War will continue.[1] In the meantime,

1 See generally for revisionist approaches, G. R. Elton, 'A high road to Civil War?' in Charles Carter (ed.), *From the Renaissance to the Counter-Reformation: Essays in Honour of Garrett Mattingley* (1966); Conrad Russell, 'Parliamentary history in perspective, 1604–1629', *History*, LXI, 201 (1976), 1–27; Conrad Russell (ed.), *The Origins of the English Civil War* (1973); Conrad Russell, *Parliaments and English Politics, 1621–1629* (Oxford, 1979); John Morrill, *The Revolt of the Provinces* (1980; orig. 1976); Kevin Sharpe (ed.), *Faction and Parliament* (Oxford, 1978); Paul Christianson, 'The causes of the English Revolution: a reappraisal', *Journal of British*

however, recent debates have involved issues of more general historiographical interest.

This article will consider some of the wider theoretical implications of the revisionist revolt against Whig, Marxist and sociological approaches. The researches of revisionist historians have contributed a wealth of empirical detail to our picture of England in the seventeenth century, but have their ambitious theoretical claims made an equal contribution? How valid is their assertion that they have developed a 'new paradigm' which successfully overthrows the Whig, Marxist and sociological traditions?

On closer examination, it appears that something very limited is in fact implied by these labels. Revisionists such as Russell, Christianson, Sharpe and Ashton highlight what they consider to be a shared characteristic of the 'traditional' approaches: a teleological approach to history. History, according to the revisionist characterization of these approaches, is viewed as an inevitable progression towards some desirable goal. The nature of this goal varies: for Whigs, the progressive path was the rise of Parliament, particularly the House of Commons; for Marxists, it was the rise of the bourgeoisie. The 'sociological' caption is designed to cover those historians, not Marxists, who share the Marxist concern with social change, and in particular posit some decline in the position of the aristocracy as a crucial feature of the socio-economic background to the Civil War. Having taken a relatively broad criterion for defining these 'traditional' approaches – that of a teleological approach, in varying combination with preferred substantive emphases – revisionists proceed by adopting a very narrow operational definition of each type of approach. The way to attack these traditions, for revisionists, is to show, empirically, that the historically privileged institution or group had no conscious desire to bring about a revolution and was, in fact, inherently conservative.[2]

Studies, XV, 2 (Spring 1976), 40–75; Paul Christianson, 'The peers, the people, and parliamentary management in the first six months of the Long Parliament', *Journal of Modern History*, IL (Dec. 1977), 575–99; see also Robert Ashton, *The English Civil War* (1978).

For responses to revisionism, see: J. H. Hexter, 'Power struggle, Parliament, and liberty in early Stuart England', *Journal of Modern History*, L, I (March 1978), 1–50; Derek Hirst, 'Unanimity in the Commons', *Journal of Modern History*, L, I (March 1978), 51–71; Christopher Hill, 'Parliament and people in seventeenth-century England', *Past and Present*, LXXXXII (August 1981), 100–24; and the articles by T. K. Rabb, 'The role of the Commons', and Derek Hirst, 'The place of principle', *Past and Present*, LXXXXII (August 1981), 55–78 and 79–99.

2   See for example Russell, *The Origins of the English Civil War*, 'Introduction', particularly 4–7; Christianson, *The causes of the English Revolution*; Sharpe *op. cit.*, 'Introduction'; Ashton, *op. cit.*, 16–17.

The mode of revisionist theoretical critique is an oblique one. Entire historiographical traditions are demolished in the first instance through an ascription of guilt by association. Alternative substantive hypotheses remain subordinate in the critique and largely untenable. By this means, classes and ideologies are thus expunged as legitimate contenders for a place in explanation for inadequate *theoretical* reasons. After analysing this mode of revisionist critique, I shall suggest that there is in fact nothing in the empirical findings of revisionist research which cannot readily be reincorporated in the type of theoretical framework which is concerned with wider causes of the English Revolution. In the concluding remarks, the outlines of a specific set of assumptions are sketched, suggesting possible ways to proceed in the aftermath of the revisionist revolt.

'Traditional' Views Under Attack

Three main areas of substantive explanation have come under criticism from revisionist historians. The notorious 'storm over the gentry' gave rise to vitriolic controversies, a by-product of which was a concern with socio-economic questions in the recent proliferation of local studies. These tended to indicate that, whatever the conceptual, methodological and practical difficulties involved in tracing the fortunes of different social and/or economic groups in the century prior to the Civil Wars, no clear-cut correlation could be established between social status, economic fortunes and eventual political allegiance.[3] Explanations in terms of the different fates of different classes or sections of classes (rising, declining, 'mere', and so on), whether in the Marxist, the non-Marxist, or the anti-Marxist versions, were held to be at the least unhelpful. Second, revisions of parliamentary history have attempted to indicate

3   See, for example, B. G. Blackwood, *The Lancashire Gentry and the Great Rebellion 1640–1660* (Manchester, 1978); J. T. Cliffe, *The Yorkshire Gentry from the Reformation to the Civil War* (1969); J. S. Morrill, *Cheshire 1630–1660: County Government and Society during the English Revolution* (1974); J. S. Morrill, 'The northern gentry and the great rebellion', *Northern History*, XV (1979), 66–87; Anthony Fletcher, *A County Community in Peace and War: Sussex 1600–1660* (1975); and see more generally Alan Everitt, *Change in the Provinces: the Seventeenth Century* (Leicester, 1969; Department of English Local History Occasional Papers, Second Series, no. 1). The original debates are reviewed in Lawrence Stone, *The Causes of the English Revolution 1529–1642* (1972), ch. 2; and in R. C. Richardson, *The Debate on the English Revolution* (1977); see also J. H. Hexter, 'Storm over the gentry' and 'The myth of the middle class in Tudor England' in Hexter, *Reappraisals in History* (1961) and Christopher Hill, 'Recent interpretations of the Civil War' in Hill, *Puritanism and Revolution* (1958).

that even in the conflicts of the 1620s (seen as comparable perhaps to the 1580s in degree of conflict, though less burdened with ideological causes), no coherent parties of 'government' and 'opposition', based on different party principles and programmes and with continuities of membership and organization, can be identified. Conflict is better explained in terms of clashes based on patronage and faction, personality and power struggles. Furthermore, parliament itself – and in particular the House of Commons – cannot be seen as representing 'Country' interests in opposition to the 'Crown'. Far from being a strong institution, eager to attain more power for itself, the House of Commons was, according to revisionists, a weak mediating institution, which was not prepared to use any potential bargaining power it might have possessed to obtain redress of grievances in return for supply.[4] More generally, at no time prior to the 1640s did English people seriously countenance the idea of making a revolution – a concept which was, in its modern sense, unavailable to them and which, given their fears of 'innovation', would have been an anathema. The English political nation was concerned to defend the traditional order of things, to maintain the balance of a hierarchical society. They might jostle for advantage within the structure; they had no intention of overthrowing the structure itself.[5]

In combating the 'traditional' hypotheses, revisionists seek for consciously revolutionary intentions and organizations. Failing to find them in the decades preceding the outbreak of Civil War, revisionists rightly conclude that there was no intentional revolution, whether by class, party or institution.

How then do the revisionists seek to explain the events of the 1640s? Here, while there are broad areas of (largely negative) agreement, certain differences appear. Some writers wish to re-emphasize the traditional politics of faction and aristocratic patronage, resurrecting the once shaken importance of the peerage. Others emphasize the strains of war; or the consequences of parliamentary mismanagement; or the implications of particular personality factors. Most agree that the 'revolutionary' protagonist, if there is to be one, was the Crown and not any element of the 'Country'; most emphasize the traditionalism of the 'county communities' who resented the encroachments of centralizing rule. More energy has been devoted to a rectification of detail, by revealing substantive inadequacies in previous interpretations, than to a coherent and comprehensive development of a new explanation; this will anyway, it is believed, emerge eventually from the mass of new evidence being collected. The negative emphasis of much of revisionist

4   See particularly Russell, *Parliaments and English Politics* and various contributions in Sharpe, *op. cit.*
5   See Ashton, *op. cit.*; and the general emphasis in many essays in Russell, *The Origins of the English Civil War*, and Sharpe, *op. cit.*

work so far has quite understandably provoked the sort of reaction quoted by John Morrill in the preface to the new edition of his book, *The Revolt of the Provinces*: 'One colleague and friend wrily accused me of "explaining why no civil war broke out in England in 1642" . . .'.[6] But revisionists feel no great compulsion to develop a comprehensive explanation since they consider that the object of explanation has itself been misinterpreted: the English Revolution was not a world-historically important event requiring a commensurate scale of explanation, but rather represents, at least in origins, a somewhat bloody tiff between a specific monarch and certain factions among his subjects. Nevertheless, implicit or explicit in many – but by no means all – revisionist accounts is a notion of the tensions between the decentralized and conservative local government of England and certain innovatory policies of the Crown, as well as – particularly in the writings of Russell – a reiteration of the financial and administrative weakness of the English state as a machine for waging war.[7] We shall return to these important points below.

Linked to the criticisms of particular hypotheses assumed to represent the 'traditional' approaches are certain theoretical stances. Critique of theses involving intentionally revolutionary classes, parties or institutions is associated with rejection of broader Whig, Marxist and sociological historiographical orientations. These are seen to share both an inflated concept of the object of explanation and a teleological, long-term form of attempt at explanation of this inflated object. Such approaches are held to imply an 'inevitability' in the historical process, and to entail a one-sided selection of those aspects appearing to prefigure revolutionary conflict, increasing gradually to an unquenchable crescendo at the outset of revolution. Recurrent refrains of revisionists, then, are admonitions to view events 'in perspective', and assertions that certain outcomes were 'not inevitable'. We are entreated to view the unfolding of events without the benefit of hindsight, foreknowledge of the dénouement: the mid-seventeenth-century crisis was in no way inevitable, and long-term analysis of its causes is inappropriate and misleading.[8]

The mode of the revisionists' attack is simple. By effectively demolishing certain substantive hypotheses, couched in terms of intentional action, revisionists obliquely suggest that the wider theoretical traditions from which these hypotheses derived may also be rejected. In proceeding thus, they have failed to confront in a serious manner attempts

6 Morrill, *The Revolt of the Provinces*, x.
7 See for example Russell, *Parliaments and English Politics*, 426 and 431.
8 See particularly Russell, 'Introduction' to Russell, *The Origins of the English Civil War*, and Sharpe, 'Introduction: Parliamentary history 1603–1629: in or out of perspective?' in Sharpe, *op. cit.*

at long-term explanation oriented at the level of structural analysis, in both the Marxist and non-Marxist sociological traditions.

The Revisionist Contribution: Some Theoretical Considerations

In considering the revisionists' work in more detail, it becomes clear that their empirical findings can be incorporated more easily in the historiographical traditions they wish to reject than might be apparent if one accepts the revisionists' own theoretical assertions, based on analysis of explanations in terms of motives. At the structural level, long-term explanations in terms of social class relations, strengths and alliances are perfectly tenable on the basis of the results of revisionist researches (although not necessarily in harmony with the revisionists' explicit conclusions).

Long-term explanation

In a seminal article for revisionists, 'A High Road to Civil War?', Geoffrey Elton cast doubts on the validity of investigations seeking long-term causes of the Civil War. Discussing a variety of such approaches, he asserted: 'What these views have in common is a sense of inevitability, a feeling that so profound a disturbance as a civil war must have had roots so deep, causes so fundamental, that analysis can be expected to discover them clearly enough.'[9] By contrast, according to Elton, no long-term conflicts could be discerned: 1640 revealed the essential *unity* of the nation. Although Elton did not himself carry the analysis further, limiting himself rather to a revision of accounts of the Commons' *Apology* of 1604, his fundamental theme has influenced recent revisionist writing. Thus Russell introduced his article on 'Parliamentary History in Perspective, 1604–29' with an attack on notions of the 'inevitability' of the Civil War, and a plea to reconsider early Stuart parliaments in a less teleological perspective.[10] Sharpe, introducing a recent book of essays on early Stuart parliaments, elaborated variations on the same theme.[11] Christianson, in 'The Causes of the English Revolution: a Reappraisal', argues against the search for long-term causes because of the essential continuities of English social and political structure.[12] Similar sentiments are expressed in other revisionist works.

9   Elton, *op. cit.*, 327.
10   Russell, 'Parliamentary history in perspective'.
11   Sharpe, *op. cit.*
12   Christianson, 'The causes of the English Revolution'.

At the level of participants' intentions, this emphasis is doubtless salutary. The conflicts of the 1640s were not the conflicts of earlier decades and cannot be read back in any simple manner into previous developments – partly because before the lifting of censorship more radical sentiments could not be expressed, although it is also the case that much of the development of radical ideas was itself a product of the events of the 1640s.[13] But at the level of structural causality, this denial of attempts at long-term explanation is less easily sustained. The Civil War may not have been 'inevitable' (we shall return to this question later), but it cannot be understood without the benefit of long-term analysis. Moreover, this analysis can be based on the revisionists' own empirical accounts, although they fail to draw the same theoretical conclusions. This will become clear if we re-examine the English pattern of development in the wider context of a comparison with continental European political developments in the early-modern period.

Let us accept, with the revisionists, that it was indeed the Crown that represented the innovatory force in early Stuart England. There was the possibility that, like many continental counterparts, the late mediaeval *Ständestaat* might, through monarchical rejection of co-rulership with Parliament, develop into a form of absolutist state.[14] The importance of the events of 1640–60, consolidated in 1688–9, was that such a possibility did not develop into reality. Charles I, for his pains, lost his head; certain continental European rulers were more successful. The problem then becomes, to explain the failure of attempts to establish absolutist rule in England in comparison with, say, France or Prussia.[15]

The causes of attempts to institute absolutist rule are beyond the scope of this paper. But certain comments can be made about those

---

13   Cf., for example, Christopher Hill, *The World Turned Upside Down* (Penguin, 1975; orig. 1972), for radical ideas in the English Revolution; B. Manning, *The English People and the English Revolution* (Penguin, 1978; orig. 1976), on the development of Leveller ideology.

14   There is considerable debate over the nature of 'absolutism' as a concept (in contemporary usage as well as for the purposes of historians) and over the extent to which it can usefully be employed in the analysis of pre-revolutionary England. See, for example, Fritz Hartung and Roland Mousnier, 'Quelques problèmes concernant la monarchie absolue', *X. Congresso Internazionale di Scienze Storiche, Relazione, vol. 4, Storia Moderna* (Rome, 1955); R. W. K. Hinton, 'The decline of parliamentary government under Elizabeth I and the early Stuarts', *Cambridge Historical Journal,* XIII, 2 (1957), 116–32; J. P. Cooper, 'Differences between English and continental governments in the early seventeenth century' in J. S. Bromley and E. H. Kossmann (eds), *Britain and the Netherlands,* (1960); James Daly, 'The idea of absolute monarchy in seventeenth-century England', *The Historical Journal,* XXI, 2 (June 1978), 227–50.

15   It is rather surprising that revisionists, publishing largely since the mid-1970s, have not attempted explicitly to grapple with the theoretical contribution of a recent

aspects – long-term structural aspects – of English society and polity that rendered attempts at absolutist rule unlikely to succeed in England. There is as yet no definitive analysis of elements vital to the successful establishment of absolutism; there is debate, for example, over whether such a feature as a standing army is a cause or a consequence of absolutist rule.[16] Nevertheless, for a number of reasons it can be said that should English monarchs make such an attempt they would under certain combinations of circumstances encounter considerable resistance. And these reasons precisely include those elements of English regional political structure emphasized in revisionist accounts.

Because of the relatively early centralization of rule in England, and the domestication of the feudal political nobility into a court-oriented aristocracy, English monarchs were able to dispense with the development of a separate state bureaucracy and to rule instead through a decentralized form of local government based on local unpaid officials such as the Justices of the Peace.[17] They also made use of the bureaucratic apparatus of the Church – with considerable consequences for the eventual politicization of Puritanism.[18] Enjoying one of the longest periods of domestic peace in English history in the century prior to the Civil War, English monarchs were able also to dispense with the maintenance of an efficient repressive apparatus (professional army or police force). On a number of counts, therefore, the rulers of England appeared to possess considerable advantages over the rulers of, for example, the scattered and impoverished possessions of Brandenburg-Prussia in the seventeenth century.[19] But their apparent strengths involved associated weaknesses.

Marxist dealing with this problem, Perry Anderson. Anderson's *Lineages of the Absolutist State* (1974) presents a sophisticated (if ultimately unsatisfactory) attempt to explain the different trajectories of development – or failed development – of European absolutisms. For another stimulating contribution in comparative perspective, see H. G. Koenigsberger, 'Dominium regale or dominium politicum et regale?' in Karl Bosl and Karl Möckl (eds), *Der moderne Parlamentarismus und seine Grundlagen in der ständischen Repräsentation* (Berlin, 1977). Why absolutism should be attempted at all – why it should have developed anywhere – is an important question to which no completely satisfactory answers have yet been developed.

16   See, for example, H. G. Koenigsberger, 'Revolutionary conclusions', *History*, LVII, 191 (October 1972), 394–8.

17   For an outstanding study of English local government in practice, see T. G. Barnes, *Somerset 1625–1640. A County's Government during the 'Personal Rule'* (1961).

18   See particularly Christopher Hill, *Economic Problems of the Church* (Oxford, 1956); Mary Fulbrook, 'Religion, revolution and absolutist rule', *European studies Review*, XII, 3 (1982).

19   On Prussia, see F. L. Carsten, *The Origins of Prussia* (Oxford, 1954); and Hans Rosenberg, *Bureaucracy, Aristocracy, and Autocracy* (Boston, 1966; orig. 1958).

One was that of ensuring that central orders were effected locally. Local governors could simply ignore, or fail to implement effectively, orders with which they did not agree. The power of local government to obstruct centrally determined policies became evident in certain counties in the last year of collection of Ship Money.[20] Another was the financial situation of English monarchs. There is some controversy among historians over the nature and causes of the financial problems of early Stuart kings, as well as over their implications; but by 1640 at any rate English monarchs, while potentially solvent in peacetime, had failed to discover and institute an effective means of raising the revenue necessary for conducting an independent foreign policy without first obtaining the consent of Parliament – a Parliament which represented those who would be responsible for raising any parliamentary supply.[21]

In peacetime, English monarchs could afford the cultural alienation of large numbers of their subjects without any serious consequences. But when unpopular religious and cultural policies were combined with a determined foreign policy that was also unpopular, considerable resistance could be expected. This combination occurred when the Scottish troubles of 1637–40 necessitated the calling of Parliament ending eleven years of attempted personal rule. The strength of resistance to Stuart attempts at absolutism is highlighted in revisionist accounts; what is made less explicit by revisionists is that this strength cannot be explained without reference to the long-term peculiarities of the English state.

Class analysis

Revisionists may so far accept this argument, regarding it in terms of a difference of emphasis rather than as a serious disagreement. However, underlying any form of long-term explanation in the Marxist and sociological traditions would be some type of class analysis; and this second rejected element of these historiographical traditions must now be considered.

It cannot be denied that there are considerable problems associated with the use of class analysis in pre-industrial societies. This became

20   Cf., for example, Barnes, *op. cit.*, ch. 8.
21   See Derek Hirst, *The Representative of the People?* (Cambridge, 1975), for the extent to which early Stuart Members of Parliament had to be responsive to public opinion at home as well as to the prerequisites of their standing at Court. On early Stuart finances, see Russell, 'Parliament and the King's finances' in Russell, *The Origins of the English Civil War.*

clear in the debate over the gentry, a category to be defined less in economic than in legal and social terms – although even these are not completely determinant. There is inevitably some tension in social analysis between employment of terms used and perceived as important by contemporaries, and terms derived from later conceptual and theoretical frameworks. The views of their own society held by contemporaries are not always mutually consistent across positions, nor are they necessarily more revealing than concealing of important aspects of social processes; but later theoretical concepts imposed by historical analysts may well provoke controversy over the extent to which they are appropriate and relevant to particular forms of social organization and social action. Furthermore, revisionists are undoubtedly right to stress the inadequacy of explanations couched in terms of material interests leading to consciously revolutionary intentions or ideologies causing organized political action at this time. And certain historians have performed a valuable service in undertaking detailed empirical analysis of the opposing sides in the Civil Wars, showing that these cannot simply be explained in terms of antagonistic economic interests. However, the theoretical point has been overextended by most revisionists, who fail to consider, at the structural level, the implications of the relative strengths and relations of different classes for the peculiar form and mode of development of the English state. It is this type of class analysis that is most important and prevalent in Marxist and sociological analyses of history; it is time that revisionist historians paid it more explicit attention.[22]

There are considerable controversies over the ways in which the state should be conceived in relation to social classes. Approaches range from the Rankean tradition in which the state takes primacy over economic development; through pluralist theories seeing a relatively autonomous state interacting, as a potentially neutral arbiter among conflicting interests, with different social groups; to the various theories in the Marxist tradition suggesting either that the state functions to perpetuate and recreate the conditions for a given mode of production, or that the state apparatus is staffed by, and used as an instrument for, elements of the ruling class. These controversies cannot be considered in detail here. Nevertheless, implicit even in revisionist analyses are assumptions about the ways in which the strengths and relations of social classes affect political action and the development of the state. These assumptions must be focused more directly and analysed

---

22   In the following discussion I shall be using the term 'class' in a loose sense to refer to salient social groups defined in terms of status as well as relationship to the means of production, and disregarding questions relating to 'class consciousness'.

explicitly if revisionists are to achieve a genuine theoretical confrontation with contemporary Marxist and sociological approaches, rather than merely maligning their names with references to outdated hypotheses.

The most explicit attempt by a revisionist – perhaps the most sophisticated and subtle revisionist, pointing the way for others – to deal with social class analysis is that of Conrad Russell. Russell concludes his chapter introducing *The Origins of the English Civil War* by asserting:

> The particular situation which produced the Civil War was the result of two coincidences. The first, in 1625, was the decision of the King to challenge the religious orthodoxy of the Parliamentary classes at the moment when the need to settle his finances had become desperate. The second, in 1640, was the alliance of discontent among the gentry with two separate social discontents, that of the poor and that of substantial merchants who were not members of the privileged group. Without these coincidences there would have been some form of political crisis during the century, but it would have been a very different crisis from the one which actually happened.[23]

These comments of Russell's are extremely suggestive; yet Russell, at least so far, has failed to pursue the full import and meaning of these 'coincidences'. The innovations in the Laudian church, following the analysis of Tyacke, are viewed largely as a theological question, a matter of private theological preferences in relation to Arminian or predestinarian beliefs, rather than in terms of a political and economic strategy in relation to the use by the state of the bureaucratic apparatus of the Church.[24] And after – rightly – arguing against explanations 'designed to explain a deliberate aim at revolution on the part of a class as a whole', by pointing out that 'when the crisis came in 1640–2, the gentry did not react as a whole: they were split down the middle in ways which economics cannot easily explain', Russell refrains from pursuing the potentially extremely fruitful analysis of the alliance of different classes and class fractions suggested in his concluding remarks.[25]

'Coincidence' is to some extent an ambiguous word. In so far as it implies a chance occurrence, not susceptible of systematic explanation

---

23   Russell, *The Origins of the English Civil War*, 31.
24   See Tyacke, 'Puritanism, Arminianism and Counter-Revolution', in Russell, *The Origins of the English Civil War*.
25   *Ibid.*, 7. I understand that Russell has a forthcoming volume in the New Oxford History of England which should provide a more positive indication of the direction in which his approach is developing.

within the terms of an explicit analytic framework, Russell's use of it is misleading. In so far as one can see 'coincidence' in the sense of a unique combination of circumstances, under which certain developments were possible or likely which would not otherwise have been so, it can represent a useful point of entry for the sociologically informed investigation of unique historical configurations. It was not simply 'coincidence', in the former sense of chance simultaneity, that Charles and Laud pursued specific religious policies that had particular political implications; nor was it a chance occurrence that the gentry, in 1640, were prepared to allow expression to the rumblings of discontent from below, as they had done in some areas in 1569 but had not been prepared to do in, say, the 1590s or the 1620s.[26] Both the use of the Church as part of the state bureaucracy – however complicated by questions of theological dispute – and the willingness of discontented gentry to regard threats of social revolt from below as a lesser risk than compliance with the policies of absolutism above are susceptible of systematic explanation in the context of English society and politics.[27] Let us look first at the ways in which class strengths and relations affected the nature of the development of the English state, using again empirical data produced by, or not contested by, revisionist historians.

In the writings of certain revisionists (notably Russell and local historians such as Morrill and Fletcher) there is an emphasis on the tensions between central and local government; and, as mentioned above, Russell in particular stresses the administrative and financial weakness of the English state as a machine for waging war. (Revisionists of the patronage thesis persuasion appear to be less aware of such factors.) In discussing the long-term structural determinants of the potential weakness of absolutism in England – the inability of the Crown to conduct an independent unpopular foreign policy, to wage war without the consent of the political nation – only passing mention was made of class factors influencing this situation. These must now be made explicit.

The domestication of the late feudal nobility of England was one factor relating to the decentralization of English local government, the lack of need for developing a separate state bureaucracy on, for example, the lines of that of Prussian absolutism.[28] Of further importance was the relative homogeneity of the English upper classes:

26 See, for example, Mervyn James, *Family, Lineage, and Civil Society* (Oxford, 1974); Peter Clark, *English Provincial Society from the Reformation to the Revolution* (Sussex, 1977), chs 7 and 8.
27 On the use of the Church, see particularly Hill, *Economic Problems of the Church*.
28 Cf. Rosenberg, *op. cit.*; Carsten, *op. cit.*; Anderson, *op. cit.*

while there were of course considerable distinctions of wealth and status among armigerous families (with wealth and status not always neatly overlapping), the lack of notions of aristocratic derogation as in France, the interpenetration of landed and mercantile wealth, the ties of kinship and common interests between Lords and Commons (a favourite theme of revisionists), were of considerable importance for English political structure and change.[29] In contrast to Prussia – and in common with Württemberg, which also managed to maintain functioning representative institutions through to the nineteenth century – rulers of England could not play separate estates off against each other.[30] There was, however, something of a polarization occurring at the lower end of the social scale, with the top yeomanry becoming increasingly distanced in wealth, status and interests from the poorer peasantry; and this was to have important consequences for the actual course taken by the English Revolution.[31] The increasing wealth of certain sections of the population in a time of expanding commerce and production was also important in affecting the strength of potential opposition to unpopular policies, as well as in expanding the extent of the political nation in pre-revolutionary England.[32]

Historians have recently argued that it cannot be said that the economic policies of the early Stuart kings acted as fetters on some emergent capitalist mode of production. James I and Charles I had, in fact, no very consistent economic policies one way or the other, except in so far as they supported anything that seemed likely to profit the Crown, forever in search of new, politically acceptable, sources of revenue.[33] Nevertheless, the Crown's inconsistently pursued policies on monopolies, patents, enclosures and the like managed to antagonize considerable numbers of its subjects; and it was important for later developments that those antagonized were influential and wealthy members of the population.

For – following up Russell's suggestive remark about the 'coincidence' of class discontents – an analysis of class relations and class forces can

---

29   Cf., for example, the suggestions made by Barrington Moore, *Social Origins of Dictatorship and Democracy* (Penguin, 1967; orig. 1966). chs I and II.
30   On Württemberg, see F. L. Carsten, *Princes and Parliaments in Germany* (Oxford, 1959), part I; and Hartmut Lehmann, 'Die Württembergischen Landstände im 17. und 18. Jahrhundert', in Dietrich Gerhard (ed.), *Ständische Vertretungen in Europa im 17. und 18. Jahrhundert* (Göttingen, 1969).
31   See the suggestive remarks of Theda Skocpol, *States and Social Revolutions* (Cambridge, 1979), 140–4.
32   Hirst, *op. cit.*
33   Cf. the essays by Hawkins and Corfield in Russell *The Origins of the English Civil War*.

help to illuminate not only the structure of the English state, but also two more specific questions of importance: the strength and relative unity of opposition to the Crown in 1640; and the emergence of a split between an increasingly radical parliamentarian cause on the one hand, and those defecting or rallying to the defence of the King, on the other hand, by 1642. For a number of reasons, including the King's attempts at raising extra-parliamentary revenues of dubious constitutional standing, the unpopularity of the social, political and economic as well as theological implications of the Laudian régime in the Church of England, and the unpopularity of the Scottish Wars which prompted the calling of the Short and Long Parliaments, there was a remarkable unity of opposition among the political nation to the government of Charles I in 1640. Thus popular discontents and grievances – which, it may be argued, are perennial, although they only occasionally experience conditions favourable to effective expression – were not suppressed in 1640; and disaffected gentry, merchants and unprivileged poor were prepared and able to join together, for different reasons, in forcing concessions on the King at a time of administrative weakness. But the very voicing of more radical demands from below, coupled with fears of counter-reforming moves from the King's side, forced a polarization of positions: with popular movements variously provoking either increasingly conservative fears of social revolution from below, and hence support for the King as the lesser of two evils, or increasingly radical programmes for reform in order to retain popular support.[34] The winning of the City of London for the parliamentarian cause, and the wealth of the City of London (which cannot be divorced from analysis of the socio-economic developments of the previous century) were also crucial to the course of subsequent developments.[35]

Having rightly rejected simplistic forms of class analysis focusing solely on single classes in isolation and seeking (non-existent) coherent class intentions and actions, revisionists should not conclude that all forms of analysis of class relations, strengths and alliances should be declared beyond the bounds of explicit theoretical focus.

34   Cf. Manning, *op. cit.*, and Ashton, *op. cit.*; and more generally on the role of popular movements in affecting the class struggle, from a sophisticated (if perhaps inadequately substantiated) Marxist viewpoint, B. Manning, 'The nobles, the people and the constitution', *Past and Present*, IX (April 1956), 42–64. Morrill's review of Manning's book in 'Provincial squires and "Middling Sorts" in the Great Rebellion', *The Historical Journal*, XX, 1 (1977), 229–36, is too sweeping in its dismissal of the contribution the first part of the book can make to our understanding of the dynamics of the early days of the Long Parliament.
35   See particularly Valerie Pearl, *London and the Outbreak of the Puritan Revolution* (1961); see also Robert Ashton, *The City and the Court* (Cambridge, 1979).

Structure and action in social analysis

Underlying the above discussion has been a distinction between forms of explanation focusing on action, and in particular on actors' motivations, and forms of explanation focusing on structural constraints and possibilities. The theoretical question of the relations between structural and motivational explanations is particularly complicated with reference to revisionist writings, since revisionists are on the whole somewhat ambiguous in their attitudes towards explanations both in terms of ideological motives and in terms of appeals to wider historical trends. Agreeing with Butterfield's critique of the Whig interpretation of history, revisionists wish to rescue men from being merely the agents of historical processes of which they were unaware, whether these processes be the rise of parliamentary constitutionalism or the rise of the capitalist mode of production and rule by the bourgeoisie.[36] Redescriptive phrases of these sorts, attempting retrospectively to encapsulate major historical changes, evoke in revisionists fears that their associated mystique implies an inevitability to the historical process. On the other hand, however, revisionists are against simple motive explanations of the English Revolution, preferring to downplay elements of ideological principle in the struggles. If the revolution was not caused by inexorable historical forces, nor was it caused by incompatible beliefs about the nature of right forms of government or the true nature of the Church. One substantive consequence of these positions, as Hexter has pointed out, is that revisionists have tended to raise naked struggles for power alone to a somewhat elevated causal status – there being little else left that the fight could have been about.[37] Revisionists have so far failed to come to terms in any explicit and satisfactory way with the truth embodied in Marx's dictum that 'Men make their own history, but they do not make it just as they please; they do not make it under circumstances chosen by themselves, but under circumstances directly encountered, given and transmitted from the past.'[38] Attempting to avoid both the Scylla of teleological determinism and the Charybdis of anachronistic revolutionary free-will, revisionists run the risk of shipwreck in a sea of theoretical confusion and largely negative assertions.

There can be little doubt that revisionists have performed a valuable service to social analysis in revealing the inadequacy of certain forms of motive explanation. 'Traditional' views, in so far as they involve concep-

---

36 See, for example, Ashton, *The English Civil War*, 17.
37 Hexter, 'Power struggle, parliament, and liberty in early Stuart England'.
38 Karl Marx, 'The Eighteenth Brumaire of Louis Bonaparte', in *Marx and Engels: Selected Works* (1970), 96.

tions of historically privileged classes, parties or institutions which are seeking to appropriate more power to themselves and acting accordingly, are shown by the revisionist critique to be substantively inadequate. Similarly, historical writing which substitutes appeals to reified evolutionary trends for genuine explanation of specific developments can be agreed to be unsatisfactory (if, at least in its more sophisticated versions, an evocative way of expressing the writer's own cultural concerns). But revisionists have drawn inappropriate conclusions from their critique. Rejecting certain forms of teleology, they have overreacted in celebrating the more conservative elements of the seventeenth-century heritage; and rejecting motive explanations in terms of conflicts of class interest, constitutional principle or ideological belief, they have highlighted instead struggles of faction and power. Men become in the revisionist world-view even more the prisoners of history: trapped in the perpetuation of conservatism and hierarchy, puppets of patrons in aristocratic struggles for power for power's sake. A new anti-orthodoxy is beginning to develop in mirror-image opposition to the old orthodoxies.

Nevertheless, it is possible in principle to combine a non-deterministic, non-teleological form of explanation which gives credence to the importance of actors' perceptions and ideas with a form of long-term explanation dealing with structural relationships and historical trends beyond the comprehension of the participants in the process. The contribution that certain Marxist and sociological approaches can make to our interpretation of available historical evidence is to suggest those long-term structural factors which render certain developments more likely or less likely, more or less plausible on the historical agenda. The arguments within Marxist and non-Marxist theoretical traditions are by no means resolved: determinist and voluntarist orientations confront each other within and across the intellectual boundaries.[39] But the less

39 Structuralist Marxists as against the Frankfurt school tradition, for example; or structural-functionalist as against phenomenological and action-theoretical traditions among non-Marxist approaches. Attempts are periodically and recurrently made to combine structural analysis (which incipiently tends towards determinism) with more voluntaristic theories of action, frequently resulting in ambiguities in the interpretation of a scholar's approach: Marx and Parsons are renowned cases in point. Recently German theorists have attempted to combine neo-evolutionary frameworks with an action-theoretical approach. This is obviously not an appropriate place to discuss such attempts; I wish merely to indicate that there is more to 'Marxist' and 'sociological' approaches than appears to have met the revisionists' eyes. See generally Alan Dawe, 'Theories of social action' in T. Bottomore and R. Nisbet (eds), *A History of Sociological Analysis* (1979); and, on historical conceptualization in terms of process and structuring as a way of transcending the structure/agency problematic, see Philip Abrams, 'History, sociology, historical sociology', *Past and Present*, LXXXVII (May 1980), 3–16.

determinist varieties of each – the approaches less concerned to conceptualize social wholes as functioning systems with logics of their own – which yet do not lose sight of the asymmetries of power and resources rooted in social relations and material conditions can provide fruitful starting points for the systematic analysis of the causes of the course and consequences of social action. In seeking to reject whole theoretical and historiographical traditions in the course of revising specific substantive hypotheses, revisionists are doing themselves and intellectual disservice.

Revisionism Revised: The Way Forward

How then, in the aftermath of the revisionist attack, is it best for those concerned to understand seventeenth-century England to proceed? Revisionists have made some useful negative points; let us take it that the straw men they have beaten so thoroughly are now beyond any hope of resuscitation. Let us take it also that serious scholars now would wish to consider all possible eventuations at any point of time, not foreclosing analysis simply through foreknowledge of what was actually to occur. Revisionists have certainly considerably redressed the teleological balance in highlighting so persistently the elements of stability, conservatism and consensus. The negative critique accomplished, it is time to develop more positive approaches to explaining, with a wider vision, what did, after all, actually occur.

The empirical inductivism of revisionists, and their somewhat strident anti-orthodoxy, have failed to provide adequate positive theses to fill the vacuum left by their negative critiques. The over-emphasis on the politics of patronage, apart from being inadequately established historically, suffers from theoretical and metatheoretical shortcomings.[40] Theoretically, it can really only tell us something about the *medium* of politics; it is an empirically open question whether or not there is any ideological content to the formation and struggles of different political factions. Metatheoretically, such exaggerated stress on patron–client relationships is at least as philosophically degrading as any other form of downplaying the autonomy of human action – such as seeing men merely as agents of historical forces – and should therefore be rejected by revisionists on their own arguments.

More positively, the work of Conrad Russell points in directions which are potentially promising. Russell's immensely detailed and thoroughly

---

40   On the empirical inadequacies, see the references cited at the end of fn. 1 above.

researched history of parliaments in the 1620s assures us that parliaments could only reflect processes taking place elsewhere.[41] They were the symptom of the Stuarts' difficulties, not the disease itself. Russell's suggestive remarks about the structural problems of the English state in terms of financial and administrative prerequisites for waging war, and about the coincidence of class discontents, have been referred to above, But Russell, with his repetitive concern to deny the 'inevitability' of the English Civil Wars, as well as to reduce the level of conflicts of principle allowed into explanation, has not as yet integrated these scattered comments into any sort of coherent explanatory framework. Indeed, on the evidence of Russell's unwillingness to see connections between Charles's political and religious policies, or between different class discontents, he appears to be leaning over backwards to avoid any such explicit framework.

Nevertheless, the debate has clarified the sorts of direction in which attempts at explanation should now be developed. First, any serious attempt must deal explicitly with long-term structural relationships having to do both with the form of the state and with socio-economic developments affecting the strengths, relations and potential alliances of different social classes. These features of state and society, while sustained by and reproduced through the actions of participants in the historical process, may not necessarily have been adequately comprehended by them. Retrospective explanation, while avoiding teleology, does not have to do away with all the advantages of the overview afforded by hindsight, and does not have to remain bound by the partial comprehension of contemporaries. Moreover, long-term structural arrangements and processes of change may bear no direct relation to the conscious intentions of historical actors: historians should not forget the problem of unintended consequences. Analysis which remains at the level of intentions, ignoring the brute facts of circumstances which render some aims more easily attainable than others, or which produce outcomes (such as Civil War) intended by nobody, is doomed to irrelevance.

In this sense, then, we need a structural analysis. But this does not imply a structural determinism. For, even if history is not a simple, rational matter in which individuals are the masters of their own destiny and intentions explain outcomes, nevertheless human-beings are not conversely mere puppets carried by currents beyond their control. Combined with analysis of structural constraints and possibilities must be interpretation of the mental world of participants. Revisionist historians have reminded us that in the 1640s there may,

41 Russell, *Parliaments and English Politics*, 417.

for many participants, have been less passion and principle than pragmatic desire to survive and maintain one's property intact (itself, of
course, reflective of an ideology). But for many others, there *was*
passion: there *were* conflicting conceptions about society, church and
state. These conflicts of principle may not be simply located in well-
organized, clearly-defined social or political groups, and they may have
cross-cut many other issues. They may in many cases have been more
a result of being forced into a practical decision about which side to
defend, than a cause of the revolutionary situation. But they were real
all the same. And conflicts of principle, over matters such as religion,
cannot simply be reduced to other factors: they must be interpreted on
their own terms.

More substantively, the most fruitful way forward now, it seems to me,
is to focus attention on that aspect of seventeenth-century history
which has been relatively neglected while the spotlight has been on the
concept of a 'bourgeois revolution' (or otherwise): namely, the problem
of absolutism. For if we can now agree that it was the ruler who was
the more innovative; and if we can now fairly well understand the bases
of the strength of resistance to absolutist rule, as rooted in the peculiarities of the English state and social structure; we nevertheless do not
yet have a comparable understanding of the drive towards absolutism
itself. Comparative European studies are revealing many of the elements
entering into the success or failure of estates to preserve the political
forms of the late mediaeval *Ständestaat*; but there are fewer acceptable
conclusions at present about causes of the rise of absolutist nation-
states.[42] For the English case, revisionists would doubtless argue that the
policies of Charles I had much to do with Charles's personality and
political decisions and mistakes; but there can be little doubt that in his
policies, decisions and mistakes Charles shared the aspirations and
strategies of numerous colleagues across the English Channel. To
explain the drive towards absolutism in functional terms of class necessity in an era of transition is not entirely satisfactory; to explain it purely
in terms of military exigencies is also insufficient; to reduce it to personal predilections of individuals is simply myopic. There exists a fertile
field of exploration in the area of explaining absolutism, and it is to this
that we must turn our attention if we are to attain a better understanding of the course of events of mid-seventeeth-century England,

42   See, for example, Koenigsberger, 'Revolutionary conclusions' and 'Dominium
regale . . .'; F. L. Carsten, 'Die Ursachen des Niedergangs der deutschen Landstände',
Historische Zeitschrift, CLXXXXII, 2 (1961), 273–81. For problems with Perry
Anderson's account of absolutism, see Mary Fulbrook and Theda Skocpol. 'Destined
pathways: the historical sociology of Perry Anderson' in Theda Skocpol (ed.), *Vision
and Method in Historical Sociology* (Cambridge University Press, 1984).

which were to be so important for the subsequent lineaments of English politics in contrast to continental lines of development.

The picture is by no means clear. Nevertheless, the fight in England was about fundamental issues. To reject, with revisionists, the limited hypotheses of 'traditional' approaches does not entail rejection of the wider concerns of these older historiographical traditions. The revisionist revolt has overstated its case: the long-term social, economic, political and constitutional causes of the English Revolution, as well as the specific short-term combinations of circumstances rendering Civil War an actuality rather than merely a possibility, remain valid fields of systematic historical investigation.

3

The British Problem and the English Civil War

Conrad Russell

Originally appeared as Conrad Russell, 'The British Problem and the English Civil War' in *History* 72. Copyright © 1987 Blackwell Publishers, Oxford.

The study of the English Civil War has so far created more problems than it has solved. The tendency of much recent research has been to show England before the Bishops' Wars as a society not sufficiently divided or polarized to make the war easily explicable. Professor Elton, indeed, has been moved to say that 'some of us wonder whether there really was a civil war since its famous causes have all disappeared'.[1]

It is perhaps a consolation, if not a help, to find that this sense of bewilderment at the Civil War was shared by some of those who lived through it. Sir Thomas Knyvett, in 1644, wondered whether 'the best excuse that can be made for us, must be a fit of lunacy'. In June 1642, Lord Wharton, an active enough Parliamentarian to be in a position to know, wrote to the Chief Justice Bankes, who was with the King at York, to ask what they were quarrelling about. He said those he knew at Westminster were not disloyal, and those who were with the King at York 'wish and drive at an accommodation'. 'How is itt then, hath all this kingdome noe person prudent enough according to theyr affections to prevent the ruine coming upon us; or is itt want of industry, or is itt the

This is a revised and expanded version of an inaugural lecture delivered at University College, London, on 7 March 1985. I would like to thank Peter Donald for numerous discussions of Scottish matters, and also my Yale pupils, notably Martin Flaherty, David Venderbush and Jim Wilson, who helped to stimulate my interest in matters British. The research for this article was done with assistance from the Small Grants Fund of the British Academy.

1   G. R. Elton, 'English National Selfconsciousness and the Parliament in the Sixteenth Century' in *Nationalismus in Vorindustrieller Zeit*, Herausgegeben von Otto Dann (München, 1986), p. 79.

wantonness of some few interested or unprovided people to pull downe more in one day, then the rest can build upp in yeares? Or is itt a judgement upon us immediately from the hand of God, for which no naturall or politique reason can be given?'[2]

Since the last of Wharton's explanations is not open to us, or at least not in our professional capacity, we are bound to supply a logical answer to his question. It does not help that both the types of explanation favoured over the past 40 years, based on long-term constitutional conflict and on long-term social change respectively, appear to have suffered irretrievable breakdown: we have to begin all over again.[3] There seem to be four possible ways of attempting the task.

One would be to say that we have not found long-term causes of the Civil War because there were none to find: that the war was the result of a short-term failure to solve a political crisis, together with the need to supply retrospective justification for actions taken in the heat of the moment. I am supposed in some quarters to have adopted this position already, and have been credited in one recent publication with having 'abolished the long-term cause of the Civil War'.[4] This report, like that of Mark Twain's death, is grossly exaggerated. Unlike some colleagues, I see no *a priori* impossibility in this type of explanation, but it remains highly improbable. It should be adopted, if at all, only on the application of Sherlock Holmes's law: 'when you have eliminated everything else, what remains, however improbable, must be the truth'. Since we are very far from having eliminated everything else, this approach remains premature.

A second approach, which I would associate with Peter Lake, Richard Cust and Ken Fincham,[5] would argue that the appearance of an undivided society is deceptive, and rests on the fact that a high proportion of our surviving sources were either addressed to the Privy Council, or written in fear of an accident to the posts. This approach contains much truth: it appears that in this period the private letter is often a less freespoken medium than the Parliamentary speech, but it will take some time for us to be sure how much truth it contains. It is clear that there

2 B. Schofield (ed.), *The Knyvett Letters* (Norfolk Record Society, 1949), xx, 133. I would like to thank Miss Ann Brophy for this reference. G. Bankes, *Corfe Castle* (1853), pp. 132–33.
3 This was written before the publication of J. P. Sommerville, *Politics and Ideology in England 1603–40* (1986). The book has not caused me to change this judgment, but it has convinced me that it needs more defence than can be offered here.
4 Christopher Haigh, *The Reign of Elizabeth I* (1985), p. 19.
5 Peter Lake, 'The Collection of Ship Money in Cheshire', *Northern History*, 1981, xvii, 71. Kenneth Fincham, 'The Judges' Decision on Ship Money in 1637: the Reaction of Kent', *Bulletin of the Institute of Historical Research*, 1984, lvii, 230–36. Richard Cust, *The Forced Loan and English Politics, 1626–8* (Oxford, 1987).

were significant divisions of opinion in England before the Bishops' Wars, and it seems clear that the effect of the Bishops' Wars was to exacerbate divisions which did exist, rather than to create others which did not. Yet it remains permissible to wonder how long these divisions, like fault-lines in rocks, might have remained latent if not subjected to the hammer-blows of outside intervention.

The third approach, which this article is designed to investigate, would argue that we have not found the causes of the English Civil War because the question involves trying to discover the whole of the explanation by examining a part of the problem. The English Civil War is regularly discussed as if it were a unique event, but it was not: between 1639 and 1642, Charles I faced armed resistance in all three of his kingdoms. In England and Ireland, civil war and resistance were simultaneous, but in Scotland five years elapsed between resistance in 1639 and civil war in 1644. This seems to be, not because Scotland was a less divided society than England or Ireland, but because the King of Scots, while resident in London, had so little power and patronage that he found the gathering of a party more uphill work in Scotland than in either of his other kingdoms. Charles appears to have regarded the absence of civil war in Scotland in 1639 as a political failure of his own, and his judgment deserves to be taken seriously.[6]

The tendency of dissidents in each kingdom to try to make common cause with sympathisers in the others ensured that the English, Scottish and Irish troubles could not remain three isolated problems: they triggered off a period of repeated intervention by the three kingdoms in each other's affairs, including Scottish intervention in Ireland in 1642, Scottish intervention in England in 1640, 1643, 1648 and 1651, and on a smaller scale, Irish intervention in England in 1643. This list is accompanied by a list of might-have-beens of which Strafford's supposed threat to use the Irish army is the most famous. Though the might-have-beens are not facts, the political hopes and fears they engendered are facts, and often influenced people's conduct. This period of acute British instability came to an end only with the English conquest of Scotland and Ireland in 1649–51.

When three kingdoms under one ruler all take to armed resistance within three years, it seems sensible to investigate the possibility that their actions may have had some common causes. We will not find them in constitutional development, for their constitutional structures were profoundly different. We will not find them in their social systems, for

6 *Calendar of State Papers Domestic 1639*, Vol. ccccxvii, nos. 3, 26, 65; Vol. ccccxviii, no. 50.

they were even more different: a social history of Britain in the early seventeenth century would be a stark impossibility. However, there are two obvious types of cause which are common to all three kingdoms. One is that they were all ruled by Charles I. It is perhaps fair to paraphrase Lady Bracknell, and so say that 'to lose one kingdom might happen to any king, but to lose three savours of carelessness'.

The other thing all three kingdoms have in common is that they are all parts of a multiple monarchy of three kingdoms. We now know, thanks to a large body of work, that the relations between multiple kingdoms were among the main causes of instability in continental Europe, and Professors Elliott and Koenigsberger have been asking for some time whether the rule which applies across the Channel also applies in Britain.[7] This article is intended to suggest that the answer to their question is 'yes'.

Thanks to them and many others, we now know a good deal about the normal flashpoints in multiple monarchies. They include resentment at the King's absence and about the disposing of offices, the sharing of costs of war and the choice of foreign policy, problems of trade and colonies, and the problems of foreign intervention. All these causes of difficulty were present in Britain. It is particularly interesting that Secretary Coke, probably in 1627–28, drew up a plan for a British version of Olivares' union of arms, and that the Scots in 1641 were demanding the right to trade with English colonies,[8] Yet these issues are surprisingly peripheral: it is possible to find them if we look for them, but only in Anglo-Irish relations between 1625 and 1629 does one of them (in this case the cost of war) become a central theme.[9] The absence of wars for much of the period between 1603 and 1640, and the overwhelming preponderance of the English revenue over those of Scotland and Ireland both contribute to this comparative silence.

This leaves only one of the normal causes of trouble within multiple kingdoms, that caused by religion. This one issue alone accounted for almost all the difficulties between the kingdoms of Britain between 1637 and 1642, and it caused enough trouble to leave very little room for any others. Some of the trouble seems to have arisen from the fact that religion for Charles, like arms for Olivares, was the issue on which he chose to press for greater uniformity. In Britain, as in the Spanish

---

7   J. H. Elliott, 'The King and the Catalans', *Cambridge Historical Journal*, 1953, H. G. Koenigsberger, *Dominium Regale and Dominium Politicum et Regale: Monarchies and Parliaments in Early Modern Europe* (London, 1975).
8   SP 16/527/44: BL Stowe Ms 187, ff. 51a, 57b.
9   Aidan Clarke, *The Old English in Ireland* (1966), pp. 28–60. Also W. Knowler [hereafter Knowler], *Strafford Letters* (1739), I, 238.

monarchy, it is the issue on which the centre demanded uniformity on which the liberties and privileges of the outlying kingdoms are most loudly asserted.

The rare cases in Europe of multiple kingdoms with different religions do not suggest that the British reaction is disproportionate. One case is that of France and Béarn, where Louis XIII, discovering, to his dismay, that he was King of the Protestant kingdom of Béarn (part of Henri IV's old kingdom of Navarre), decided to invade it and suppress it, even at the risk of war with Spain.[10] The most famous case of multiple kingdoms with different religions is that of Spain and the Netherlands, and that produced disturbances on the same scale as the British. Britain, moreover, offered the peculiar and illogical combination of difference of religions with a theory of authority in two kingdoms (or, as Charles believed, in three) vesting authority in the king as supreme head of the church. A British king who presided over different religions thus offered a built-in challenge to his own authority, something which Charles I was never likely to accept with equanimity. Though there are other cases in Europe in which one king presided over two religions, I am aware of none in which a single king presided over three. Moreover, Britain appears to be a unique case of multiple kingdoms all of which were internally divided in religion, and in all of which there existed a powerful group which preferred the religion of one of the others to their own. Perhaps the problem we ought to be trying to solve is not why this situation produced an explosion under Charles, but how James succeeded in presiding over it for 23 years without one.

The capacity of religion to cause political trouble in the seventeenth century did not just arise from the actions of zealots, though there were plenty of those. It was more serious than respectable conventional or governmental opinion accepted that it was its duty to enforce truth, and to repress error. The case for religious unity was such a conventional cliché that, as the Scottish Commissioners in London put it, it was accepted by 'sound . . . politicians'. It was the sound politicians' intellectual assent to many of the zealots' propositions which led them into actions which caused trouble. In the Scots Commissioners' words 'we doe all know and professe that religion is not only the mean to serve God and to save our owne soules, but it is also the base and foundation of kingdomes and estates, and the strongest band to tye the subjects to their prince in true loyalty'.[11] Conversely, as they said, 'the greater zeal in different religions, the greater division'. They even

10   J. Russell Major, *Representative Government in Early Modern France* (New Haven, 1980), pp. 449, 474.
11   National Library of Scotland [hereafter NLS] Advocates' Ms 33.4.6, ff. 142a–146b.

invoked Bede's account of the Synod of Whitby to support the proposition that it was unwise to allow the existence of different religions within the same island. In this, if in little else, the Covenanters agreed with Charles I.

Charles, at some date not later than 1633, and possibly as early as 1626,[12] decided to drop a match into this powder-keg by setting out to achieve one uniform order of religion within the three kingdoms. The task was the more necessary for the fact that Charles's interpretation of the English religious settlement, and especially of the 39 Articles, made the gap between the three churches appear considerably wider than it had done under James. Under James, it had been as true in a British as in an English context that Calvinist doctrine served for a 'common and ameliorating bond'[13] between those who disagreed about many other things. When Charles broke this 'common and ameliorating bond' between the churches, he not only widened the gap between them, but also offered a handle to his critics. It became possible for them to challenge Charles, as Pym did, through praise for the Irish Articles of 1615, or, as Peter Smart of Durham did, by publishing material highly critical of English authorities in Edinburgh.[14] It was, perhaps, essential to the survival of Charles's and Laud's Arminian innovations in England that Scotland and Ireland should cease to provide anti-Arminian Englishmen with a much more attractive alternative model. It was perhaps for this reason that Charles seems to have employed Laud as a sort of Secretary for ecclesiastical affairs for all three kingdoms. As early as 1634, Laud complained to Wentworth that 'I was fain to write nine letters yesterday into Scotland: I think you have a plot to see whether I will be *universalis episcopus*, that you and your brethren may take occasion to call me Antichrist'.[15] This attempt to make the three kingdoms uniform in order to protect Charles's changes in England was bound, to heighten theological resistance, to provoke fears that they were being dragged at English chariot wheels,

12 F. Larkin, *Stuart Royal Proclamations* (Oxford, 1983), II, 90–3. I would like to thank Dr N. R. N. Tyacke for this reference. Knowler, I, 187. I would like to thank Martin Flaherty for this reference.
13 C. Russell (ed.), *The Origins of the English Civil War* (1973), p. 121.
14 *Proceedings in Parliament 1628* edited by Robert C. Johnson, Mary Frear Keeler, Maija J. Cole and William B. Bidwell (New Haven, 1977), iv, 261, iii, 515; S. R. Gardiner (ed.), *Debates in the House of Commons in 1625* (Camden Society New Series VI, 1873), p. 181. Peter Smart, *The Vanities and Downfall of the Present Churches* (Edinburgh, 1628). I am grateful to Dr Tyacke for drawing my attention to the significance in this context of the citations of the Irish Articles against Charles's Arminian tendencies.
15 Knowler, I, 271. Laud was making fun of the 'Jonnisms' he associated with Wentworth's supposedly 'Puritan' upbringing in Cambridge.

being made, as Baillie put it, 'ane pendicle of the dioces of York',[16] and to encourage those Englishmen who resisted Charles's changes to rely on Scotland and Ireland for assistance in doing likewise.

Laud and Wentworth were both committed to this policy of uniformity between the kingdoms, which Wentworth even carried to the length of recommending that Scotland be governed by the English Privy Council as a dependency of England. Yet they both feared that, in his zeal to implement this policy, Charles did not see how difficult it was. In 1634, Wentworth wrote to Laud that 'the reducing of this kingdom (Ireland) to a conformity in religion with the church of England is no doubt deeply set in his Majesty's pious and prudent heart, as well in perfect zeal to the service of the Almighty as out of other weighty reasons of state and government' but, he added, in a typical Wentworth phrase, to do so without adequate preparation 'were as a man going to warfare without munition or arms'.[17] It is a warning to which Charles should have paid attention.

In trying to impose a uniform religion on Britain, Charles had to work through three very different legal and constitutional systems. Scotland was not in any way legally dependent on England, and it was of some importance to many Scots that in 1603 the King of Scots had inherited England, and not vice versa. The English Privy Council had no *locus standi* on Scottish matters, and even in 1639, between the Bishops' Wars, the Earl of Northumberland, who was a member of the Council Committee for Scottish affairs, was reduced to complaining that he knew no more of Scottish affairs than if he were at Constantinople.[18] The Committee for Scottish Affairs could advise on how, or whether, to use English military force to enforce the King's Scottish policy, but if any of them believed the policy itself to be mistaken, they had no authority to say so. Scotland had its own Privy Council, its own Parliament, and its own law. The Scottish Privy Council could govern so long as it was allowed an effective form of devolution, but whenever the King of Scots chose to form policy from London, his Scottish Council found it was not easy to advise him from Edinburgh. Scotland also had its own form of church government. It had bishops, but what authority they might have, and how that authority might be related to that of a General

16 Robert Baillie [hereafter Baillie], *Letters and Journals*, edited by D. Laing (Bannatyne Club, Edinburgh, 1841), I, 2 (further references are to Vol. I unless otherwise stated). Also Nicholas Tyacke, *Anti-Calvinists* (Oxford, 1987), pp. 230–34.
17 David Stevenson, *The Scottish Revolution* (Newton Abbot, 1973), p. 100 (Knowler, II, 190–92); Knowler, I, 187. I would like to thank Martin Flaherty for this reference.
18 *Historical Manuscripts Commission: De L'Isle and Dudley*, VI, 366, Kent Archive Office [hereafter KAO], U 1475 C.85/2.

Assembly, were to an extent matters of opinion. There was a widespread Scottish sentiment which held that the only ultimate source of lawful authority was the General Assembly, what Alexander Henderson called the 'representative kirk of this kingdom'. For such men as Laud, who protested during the Glasgow Assembly that 'for a national assembly, never did the church of Christ see the like', such theories were more than offensive: they were incomprehensible.[19] A pure Ullmanite ascending theory of power was equally beyond the comprehension of Charles, who believed, with little obvious justification, that he was supreme head of the Church of Scotland.[20] At the Pacification of Berwick, the Covenanters were faced with the task of explaining to Charles that he did not have a negative voice in a General Assembly as he did in an English Parliament, and he simply did not understand what they were talking about.[21] Moreover, Charles was offended by Scottish liturgical practice, as well as by Scottish doctrine and discipline. In 1633 when he went to Edinburgh to be crowned (eight years late) he insisted on using the English liturgy wherever he worshipped. In the *Large Declaration* of 1639, after he had officially abandoned the new Service Book, he complained of the 'diversitie, nay deformitie, which was used in Scotland, where no set or publike form of prayer was used, but preachers and readers and ignorant schoolmasters prayed in the church, sometimes so ignorantly as it was a shame to all religion to have the Majestie of God so barbarously spoken unto, sometimes so seditiously that their prayers were plaine libels, girding at sovereigntie and authoritie; or lyes stuffed with all the false reports in the kingdome'.[22] It perhaps highlights the difficulty in communication which difference of religion might cause that the way

19 John Leslie, Earl of Rothes [hereafter Rothes], *A Relation of Proceedings Concerning the Affairs of The Kirk of Scotland from August 1637 to July 1638*, edited by James Nairne (Bannatyne Club, Edinburgh, 1830), pp. 45–6, 5. Scottish Record Office GD 406/1 Hamilton MSS no. 547 [hereafter Hamilton MSS].
20 For the claim to the royal supremacy in Scotland, see the Scottish canons, Laud, *Works*, V, 586. For Laud's belief that such authority was inherent in all sovereign princes, as it had been in the Kings of Judah, see Baillie, II, Appendix p. 434. For a rare attempt to justify Charles's chaim in Scottish law and practice, see John Rylands Library, Crawford MSS 14/3/35, probably dating from the Pacification of Berwick. I am grateful to the Earl of Crawford and Balcarres for permission to use these MSS, and to Dr J. S. A. Adamson for bringing them to my attention. For the case Charles appears to have been discussing, see B. Galloway, *The Union of England and Scotland 1603–1608* (Edinburgh, 1896), p. 87. See also *Stuart Royal Proclamations*, II, 91.
21 Hamilton MSS M. 1/80. For the case for believing the supremacy was *jure divino*, and not founded on the municipal laws of any kingdom, see SP 16/288/88.
22 Gordon Donaldson, *The Making of the Scottish Prayer Book of 1637* (Edinburgh, 1954), pp. 42–3. *A Large Declaration* (1640), pp. 20, 16.

the Scots would have expressed the same point was that they did not have a reading ministry.

Ireland, by contrast, was not an independent kingdom, but, like Massachusetts or Virginia, a semi-autonomous dependency of the English Crown. Under the King, the Dublin administration was headed by a Lord Lieutenant, Lord Deputy or Lord Justices (the title varying according to the status of the holder). He and his Irish Privy Council were answerable to the English Privy Council, which could, and sometimes did, discuss Irish affairs. There was also an Irish Parliament though the operation of Poynings' Law firmly subordinated it to the English Privy Council. The English Parliament, before 1640, was not normally regarded as having any standing in Ireland: in British terms, the English Parliament was as much a local assembly as the Cortes of Castile.[23] In religion, there was an established Protestant Church of Ireland, run by Archbishop Ussher along lines acceptable to St John or Brereton, and to many of the increasing numbers of Scots settled in Ulster. Outside the Church of Ireland, the Catholic majority, handicapped by a formidable series of legal disabilities, enjoyed an intermittently Nelsonian blind eye.

Irish affairs also suffered from a threefold division of race. The New English, Protestants who usually controlled the government in Dublin, were English settlers who had arrived since the Reformation. For them, the key problem was always how to stop Ireland being Irish, an aim which became more and more closely identified with Protestantism and with a policy of plantation. The 'mere' or native Irish were excluded from the political nation, though with an apparently increasing number of exceptions. The pigs in the middle of Irish politics were the Old English, descendants of pre-Reformation English settlers, and often either Catholics or church-papists. The key to the Old English creed seems to have been the belief that it was possible to be a gentleman first, and a Catholic second. As owners of a third of the profitable land in Ireland, they felt increasingly threatened by the policy of plantation. The Earl of Ormond, threatened by one such scheme, commented that he was the first Englishman to be treated as if he were Irish.[24] He was not

---

23   This was the conventional view, but in *Calvin's Case* it had been argued that the Parliament of England could bind Ireland by express words: Coke, *Seventh Report*, 17. For the conventional view, stated by the Earl of Leicester, probably when about to take up appointment as Lord Deputy, see K. A. O. De L'Isle and Dudley MSS. Z 47. I am grateful to Blair Worden for drawing my attention to this uncalendared portion of the collection and to Viscount De L'Isle and Dudley for permission to quote from his family papers.

24   *New Irish History*, edited by T. W. Moody, F. X. Martin and F. T. Byrne (Oxford, 1976), III, 242.

the last: in 1641, one of the rebels marked the great watershed in Irish history by describing them as the 'new Irish'.[25]

It is no wonder that the complexity of these arrangements enmeshed Charles in many things for which the simplicity of his original plans had left no room. It is also important that though there was a Privy Council for each kingdom, there was no institutional equivalent of the Spanish Council of State, which could advise on issues affecting all three. Laud and Wentworth, or on occasion Hamilton and Lennox, might give British counsel, but only when the King asked for it. On most British issues, Charles, like the classic medieval tyrant, was without counsellors.

Charles's attempt at British uniformity was begun in Ireland, where some sharp political infighting between Lord Deputy Wentworth and Archbishop Ussher appears to have ended in a draw.[26] He was nearly 'surprised' by an attempt by Ussher's friends to secure confirmation of the Calvinist Irish Articles of 1615, but managed to secure Irish confirmation for the English 39 Articles. The attempt to set up an Irish High Commission was successful, and the attempt to impose new Irish canons produced a long battle between Ussher and Bishop Bramhall, Laud's chief Irish ally. Taken together with Laud's remark that there was no need to introduce the English liturgy because the Irish had it already, the programme sounds remarkably like the one which was tried out in Scotland from 1635 onwards.

It may have been the need to compromise with Irish resistance which moved Charles and Laud to act with so little consultation in Scotland. They consulted some of the Scottish bishops, who belonged to that faction in Scotland which welcomed moves towards uniformity with England. The use of proclamation, however, bypassed all the normal machinery of consultation. The Scottish canons appeared almost without warning, and though the new Prayer Book was expected, when ministers were commanded to buy it and use it, there were no copies available and none of them had yet seen it. The attempt to produce the Scottish Prayer Book as a *fait accompli*, however, cannot be regarded as a success.

It is fortunately unnecessary to recount the narrative of Scottish resistance to the Prayer Book: for the moment, it is the British implications which concern us. Two stories will perhaps help to illustrate them. Both tell of Covenanter conversations with the King's commissioner the Marquess of Hamilton. In one, the Covenanters explained that the

---

25   Aidan Clarke, 'Ireland and the "General Crisis"', *Past and Present* 1970, p. 81.
26   Knowler, I, 212, 298, 329. I would like to thank Martin Flaherty for these references.

Reformation of England was 'verrie farr inferior to the Reformatione of Scotland'.[27] This was an idea Charles could not allow to get loose in England. It also helps to explain why the Scots, who had had to admit to junior partner status in so much, clung so obstinately to the belief in the superiority of their Reformation, and so helps to explain their policy in England in 1640–41, when the boot was on the other foot. The other story describes how Hamilton told the Covenanters that his instructions allowed him to remove the Scottish canons and Prayer Book, but not to condemn anything in them 'which might reflect against any public order or any thing practiced, or allowed by my Lord of Canterburie and his followers in England or elsewhere'.[28] This story illustrates, both one of Charles's reasons for sticking to his guns, and the likely consequence for England of a Covenanter victory. The Covenanters' response, according to Baillie, was to insist that the doctrines be condemned because so many in their own church held them. Superb organisation and the King's absence enabled the Covenanters to claim to be much more representative of Scottish opinion than in private they ever believed themselves to be. We can see here the possibility of the anti-Covenanter opening which became crucial to Charles's Scottish policy in 1641 and beyond.

Charles first planned to invade Scotland with an Irish force under the Earl of Antrim, head of that clan who were Macdonnells in Ireland and Macdonalds in Scotland.[29] In doing so, Charles turned Argyll and his clan into devout Covenanters, since Antrim's chief motive had been to secure possession of lands in dispute between him and the Covenanters. As Baillie reflected, the ways of Providence were indeed strange.[30]

Charles finally decided to play his trump card of English intervention, and, to cut a long story short, lost at the battle of Newburn, on 28 August 1640. This was the day on which the apple was eaten: for some 14 years from Newburn onwards, the kingdoms were involved in each other's affairs with a daily urgency which had not been seen since the days of Edward I and Robert and Edward Bruce. When Hamilton told the Covenanters, shortly before war began, that if Charles turned to English intervention, he doubted if he would ever see peace in this kingdom again,[31] he spoke little more than the truth: he was executed in 1648 for leading a Scottish intervention in England on behalf of Charles I.

27   Rothes, p. 144.
28   Baillie, p. 120.
29   The suggestion of using Antrim appears to have originated with Hamilton. Hamilton MSS, 10,488, Hamilton to Charles, 15 June 1638.
30   Baillie, pp. 192–94.
31   Rothes, p. 137.

There is no sense, in an article of this type, in attempting a blow by blow narrative of the period from Newburn to the Civil War. It seems more sensible to examine the ways in which the affairs of one kingdom impinged on those of others.

The first way was by direct control, exemplified by the Scots in the 12 months after Newburn. They had an occupying army in Northumberland and Durham, while their commissioners negotiated a peace treaty in London. It was the Scots who dictated that Charles should call an English Parliament, since they refused to negotiate with any commissioners who were not appointed by King the Parliament, or to accept any treaty not confirmed by an English Parliament.[32] As Secretary Vane said in reporting this demand to Secretary Windebank, 'by this you may judge of the rest'. It was thus Scottish intervention which created an English Parliament, and which made a crucial contribution, by involving it in the treaty negotiations, towards giving it a share in executive power. It was also the Scots, by deliberately prolonging the treaty for the sake of their English friends, who made the first contribution to turning it into a Long Parliament.

The second way in which the kingdoms influenced each other was by direct copying. The Queries of the Irish Parliament appear to be a copying of the Petition of Right,[33] while their attempt in 1641, to impeach their Lord Chancellor, the Lord Chief Justice, Bishop Bramhall and the Laudian Provost of Trinity College, Dublin, was surely an imitation of what the English parliament was busy doing to Strafford. The committee they sent to negotiate with Charles in 1641 was empowered to act as a recess committee if there were a dissolution.[34] This was a Scottish idea, copied by the Irish and only subsequently by the English. The oath of Association of the Irish rebels in 1641, beginning 'I A. B. doe in the presence of Almightie God', is a copy of the English Protestation of May 1641, with a few intriguing alterations. The oath is taken in the presence of all the angels and saints, as well as Almighty God, the qualification 'lawful' is omitted from the things they engage to do in defence of religion, and the word 'Protestant' is at all points replaced by 'Catholic'.[35] Perhaps the Irish Rebellion was the greatest copying of them all. One of its leaders, arrested at the beginning of the rebellion, was asked what he was trying to do, and replied: 'to imitate Scotland, who got a privilege by that course'.[36] In England, the Triennial Act followed, at the Scots' suggestion, a

32   SP 16/466/36, 467/5; BL Harl Ms 457, ff. 3b, 4a, 6b, 8a.
33   SP 63/260/7.1; *C.J. Ireland*, I, 174ff.
34   *C.J. Ireland*, I, 165.
35   Bodleian Ms Carte 2, f. 137b.
36   *LJ*, iv, 415.

Scottish Act to the same effect,[37] and the proposals of 1641–42 that the Parliament should choose the great officers, were consciously borrowed from the Scottish settlement of September 1641.[38]

It is also possible to regard the Scots' drive to impose Scottish uniformity on England as a copying of what the King had been doing to them. Baillie said that they had 'good hopes to get bishops' ceremonies and all away and that conformitie which the King has been vexing himself and us to obtaine betwixt his dominions, to obtaine it now, and by it a most hearty nation of the kingdomes'.[39] It was also the Scots, first and foremost, who insisted on the death of Strafford, whom they regarded as the one Englishman unwilling to accept the verdict of Newburn as final. As the Scots painstakingly explained, using arguments almost comically like those used by Charles in 1639, they could not guarantee their own domestic security except by imposing profound changes on the domestic politics and religion of England.[40] They found, as Charles had done before them, that such attempts created considerable resentment.[41] It was these efforts by the Scots, and notably their paper of 24 February, which prevented Pym and his allies from reaching a peaceful settlement with the King, since a settlement which did not remove the Scottish army would be no settlement, and not worth reaching.

The existence of three kingdoms also created opportunities to fish in troubled waters, and these opportunities were much used. Any group who lost a round in their own kingdom could always make common cause with their sympathisers in another, and call in another kingdom to redress the balance of their own. The Scottish Arminians, who were very heavily dependent on English backing, were the first to learn this lesson, and only time prevented them from holding all the best bishoprics and deaneries in Scotland. The English Parliament learned it second, and the Irish Parliament, relying on the English Parliament for its remonstrance against Strafford, learned it third, but it was perhaps Charles who learned it most thoroughly. In May 1641, after the failure of the Army Plot, Secretary Vane expected Charles to settle with his

37   BL Stow Ms 187, ff. 9b, 41a. SP 16/471/22 shows the Scots pressing for such an Act in England, in order that any future disputes between the kingdoms should be considered in Parliament.
38   H. B. Wheatley (ed.), Diary of John Evelyn (1906), IV, 95, 97, 98.
39   Baillie, 278.
40   NLS Advocates' MSS 3.4.6, ff. 145–6; David Stevenson, The Scottish Revolution (Newton Abbot, 1973), pp. 218–21. The Scots' paper of 24 February is in BL Stow Ms 187, ff. 38–9, and Thomason Tracts 669 f. 3(4). It is worth remark that the Ms version is in Scottish spelling, and the printed version in English spelling.
41   LJ, iv, 216; BL Harl Ms 6424, f. 55a. NLS Advocates' MSS 33.4.6, ff. 130, 133. Edinburgh University Library Ms Dc 4.16, ff. 93a–94a.

English Parliament, 'there being in truth no other [course] left'.[42] In saying this, Vane merely revealed his ignorance of Charles's Scottish policies. Since 3 March 1641, Charles had been committed to a growing intrigue with Montrose which was designed to create a Scottish party to counterbalance the one at the disposal of his opponents, or (as in the event happened) to induce the Covenanters to withdraw from England before he could succeed in this attempt.[43]

Charles's opportunity came from growing hostility to the Covenanters inside Scotland. One of the major surprises of this work has been finding how strong this sentiment was. In the spring of 1641, it had reached the point at which the liturgy against which the Scots were fighting was being used inside the Scottish army.[44] Other things, such as Montrose's increasing jealousy of the power of Argyll, are the sort of thing which is part of the price of power. So are Scottish resentment at such things as the prohibition of salmon fishing on the Sabbath, or the occasion on which Baillie denounced his patron from the pulpit because at a wedding there was among the lords 'more drink than needed'.[45] The stages of Charles's intrigues with anti-Covenanter Scots are obscure, stretching through the plot of Napier, Keir and Blackhall,[46] the Incident in October 1641, and an abortive plan of May 1642 to secure Scottish intervention against the English Parliament.[47] The consistent theme underlying the details is Charles's desire to build a party of anti-Covenanter Scots, and to use that party to redress the balance of English politics. The schemes he began in 1641 were the ones he pursued until he pulled them off in 1648, and lost his head for it. The point which is immediately relevant to the origins of the English Civil War is that it was Charles's hope of breaking the Anglo-Scottish alliance which encouraged him to believe that Vane was wrong in insisting that he must settle with his English subjects. It is worth remembering that in September 1641, Charles did succeed in breaking the Anglo-Scottish alliance, and it was only the outbreak of the Irish Rebellion which kept the English Parliament in being from then on.

42   SP 16/480/20.
43   NLS Wodrow Ms fol. 65, ff. 65a, 72a–b. For the hardening line towards the Scottish Commissioners in London which accompanied this switch, see *LJ*, iv, 175.
44   NLS Advocates' MSS 33.4.6, ff. 119a, 121b.
45   Baillie, II, 6–7, 34–5.
46   S. R. Gardiner, *History of England* (1893), IX, 395–98, NLS Wodrow Ms fol. 65, nos. 12, 17.
47   This abortive plan was perhaps more important in Charles's strategy in 1642 than has been appreciated. See Gardiner, X, 203, and Stevenson, pp. 248–49. See also *RPCS*, VIII, 255–63, 264–65, *Letters of Henrietta Maria*, edited by M. A. E. Green (1853), pp. 53, 60, Hamilton MSS 1653, 1723, 1753, 1760, HMC *Buccleuch*, I, 298, and East Riding RO Hotham MSS DD/HO/1/4.

The existence of three kingdoms also provided dissidents with an alternative model, and thereby contributed to polarising the politics of all three. The English godly, who for so long had had to be content with half a loaf, found that having a Scottish army to press their demands had an intoxicating effect. When Burges, at the opening of the Long Parliament, preached on the delivery of Israel from Babylon by an army coming from the north, it was impossible to mistake his meaning.[48] As Baillie put it, 'God is making here a new world', and the reaction of many of the English godly was 'gramercies, good Scot'.[49] The opportunity encouraged D' Ewes to hold forth on the proposition that the English and the Scots were one nation, except for the Hebrideans, who were Irish, and to propose the setting up of a committee for the abolishing of superstition.[50] When the Root and Branch Bill passed in the Commons, Nehemiah Wallington commented 'Babylon is fallen, is fallen'.[51]

The polarizing effect of such utterances was because these men's hopes were other men's fears, and the fears tended to be expressed in the form of appeals to anti-Scottish sentiment. The Scots gave a particularly good opportunity for this when they asked for a euphemistically named 'Brotherly Assistance' of £300,000. Hyde's friend Thomas Triplett, who was pouring a stream of anti-Scottish sentiment into Hyde's ear from Newburn onwards, reported a rumour that the money for the Brotherly Assistance was to be raised by fining Alderman Abell the wine monopolist, 'and so lett Abel pay Cain'.[52] Gervase Holles, in the House of Commons, said the Scots might be our younger brothers, but, like Jacob, they were stealing our birthright – an image liable to boomerang on him.[53] The Earl of Bristol, the chief English negotiator, was surely not choosing his words at random when he described the Brotherly Assistance as a 'viaticum' for the Scots.[54] This anti-Scottish feeling grew steadily through the summer of 1641, and the emotions which led to Civil War were very near the surface when Sir Robert Harley reported

48   C. Burges, *The First Sermon* (1641), p. 6.
49   Baillie, p. 283. The poem to which Baillie refers is in *Diary of John Rous*, edited by M. A. E. Green, Camden Society, (1886), cxvi, 110–11, and NLS Advocates' MSS 33.1.1, XIII, no. 69.
50   W. Notestein (ed.), *Journal of Sir Symonds D'Ewes* (New Haven, 1923), p. 320, BL Harl Ms 163, f. 10a.
51   Nehemiah Wallington, *Historical Notices*, edited by Rosamond Ann Webb, I, 171. His text, *Rev* 18.2, describes the downfall of the Beast. See also Paul S. Seaver, *Wallington's World* (Stanford, 1985), p. 164.
52   Bodleian Ms Clarendon 10, no. 1514.
53   Yale University Beinecke Library, Osborn Shelves b 197, f. 40b.
54   Maija Jansson (ed.), *Two Diaries of the Long Parliament* (Gloucester, 1984), p. 18.

that Sir William Widdrington had been overheard saying that he looked forward to the day when any member calling the Scots 'brethren' would be called to the bar.[55]

The Scots' paper of 24 February 1641 demanding the Presbyterian-ising of England and the death of Strafford, gave this body of feeling its opportunity for organised expression. The debate on this paper on 27 February according to D'Ewes, 'raised one of the greatest distempers in the House that ever I saw in it'.[56] This debate marks the appearance of two-party politics in the Commons. The study of this and other debates bearing on the Scots shows that who spoke for and who against the Scots provides a better predictor of allegiance in the Civil War than any other issue, even Root and Branch or the Militia Ordinance. This fact is surely not purely coincidental. Charles was perhaps justified in accusing the Scottish negotiators in London of trying 'to stir up his people of England, and make a division between him and his subjects'.[57] Whether or not they tried, they certainly succeeded.

In the relationship between the three kingdoms, any rapproche-ment between two of them had a billiard-ball effect on the third, and for most of the first half of 1641, it was Ireland which came out third. The Scottish-Parliamentary alliance aimed, in the ominous phrase of the petition of the 12 peers, at 'the uniting of *both* your realms against the common enemies of the reformed religion'.[58] Ireland was a likely victim of any such unity. We are fortunate to have an early Irish reaction on this anti-popish drive. John Barry, an Irish Officer in the King's English army, reported that the Parliament had taken orders to cashier all popish officers, 'and among the rest myself. They call out bitterly against us, and begin to banish us out of town, and remove us from court; what will become of us, I know not, but we are in an ill taking at present.' Barry resented the imputation of disloyalty: 'Sir, I was never factious in religion, nor shall ever seeke the ruine of any because he is not of my opinion'.[59] For

---

55   BL Harl Ms 163, f. 696b.
56   *D'Ewes* edited by Notestein, p. 418; *Two Diaries of the Long Parliament*, pp. 12–13.
57   NLS Advocates' MSS 33.4.6, f. 129a. See also NLS Wodrow Ms Quarto 25, f. 117b, describing how the Scottish preachers in London were ordinarily invited to preach publicly to great auditories, and Surrey RO (Guildford) Bray MSS 52/2/19(8), Nicholas to Charles, 8 August 1641, reminding Charles 'what inconvenience pmitting the Scots comrs. to be in towne and treate hath beene to yet mats. affaires, and what a disturbance their daily presence did give to ye government'. I am grateful to Dr J. S. A. Adamson for drawing my attention to this important group of Nicholas Papers.
58   SP 16/465/16 [my italics].
59   HMC *Egmont*, I, 122.

him and many like him, the imputation was to become a self-fulfilling prophecy.

Barry was one of those who saw the increasing co-operation between the English Parliament and the Scots an opportunity for increasing co-operation between the Old English and the king. In the spring of 1641, Charles was negotiating with an Irish Parliamentary Committee at the same time as he was negotiating with the Scots, and their demands were to an extent alternatives. The main thing the Irish committee wanted was confirmation of the Graces, a set of royal concessions of the 1620s of which the key one was itself copied from England. It would have applied to Ireland the English Concealment Act of 1624, making 60 years' possession of an estate a valid title to it. In England, this merely stopped an unscrupulous way of raising money. In Ireland, it would have had the much more far-reaching effect of putting a stop to the policy of plantation. For this reason, it caused great alarm to the government in Dublin. When Charles confirmed the Graces, on 3 April 1641, he forged an alliance with the old English, but he also forged another, between the Lords Justices in Dublin and the English Parliament.

During 1641, many Irishmen came to realise that the greatest threat to their liberties came, not from the English king, but from the English Parliament. When the Parliament had set out to impeach Strafford for his conduct as Lord Deputy of Ireland without having any jurisdiction in Ireland they set out on a slippery slope. At first, they were very cautious, dealing with Irish petitioners by recommending, requesting and referring, but such caution could not last.[60] They were finally pushed over the edge by a series of cases of which the most important was that of Henry Stewart, the Don Pacifico of the British Civil Wars. Henry Stewart was an Ulster Scot, imprisoned by Wentworth for refusing to take an oath renouncing the Scottish Covenant, and the Scottish negotiators were demanding that those who imprisoned him should be punished. As a result, the English House of Lords summoned the whole of the Irish Privy Council to appear before them as delinquents. This was too much, and the Irish Privy Council and Parliament immediately protested.[61]

In denying that Ireland was subject to the English Parliament, the Irish were up against the Scots, who repeatedly assumed that it was. They also had to eat a number of their own words, dating from the anti-

---

60   *D'Ewes* edited by Notestein, pp. 3, 100–2, 224; SP 63/258/51. 53, 68.
61   House of Lords Main Papers, 9, 17, 30 July 1641. For an attempt by the Irish bishops to involve the English Parliament in Irish affairs, see SP 63/274/44.

Strafford phase in which the Irish Parliament had been busy claiming the liberties of Englishmen, and trying to make common cause with the English Parliament. Like many later Whigs, they hoped that the English Parliament gave more weight to its rhetoric about law and liberty than to its rhetoric about anti-popery, and they realised their mistake too late. If they faced subjection to an English Parliament in which they were not represented, they would be reduced to the unambiguous status of a colony, and with a Parliament as anti-popish as the English, the prospect was not inviting. In December 1641, when the Old English decided to throw in their lot with the Irish rebels, they accused the Lords Justices of having conspired 'to make this realm totally subordinate to the jurisdiction of the Parliament of England'. They said it was their aim 'to preserve the freedom of this kingdom without dependency of the Parliament or State of England'.[62] Thus, the Irish Rebellion was a reaction to changes in the power structure in England, brought about by Scottish intervention, which in turn had been provoked by attempts to impose English religion on the Scots, lest the Scots might set an evil example to English dissidents. There can be no better illustration of the fact that this subject does indeed have an Athanasian complexity.

This article has been intended to test two different, but not incompatible hypotheses. One is the hypothesis that when there are rebellions in three highly disparate kingdoms, one possible cause is the King who provides the most conspicuous common factor between them. This case appears to contain much truth. It is not given to historians to make controlled experiments, but the study of Charles I in a Scottish, an English and an Irish context is perhaps less remote from a controlled experiment than most things we are able to do. Variables, of course, are not eliminated, and it is particularly important that the Charles who handled the English crisis had already handled and suffered from the Scottish. Yet the man who appears in all three stories is perhaps more totally the same than, in such different situations, he should have been. The same convictions, the same imaginative blind spots, and the same defects in political methods, show up in all three situations. One constant characteristic is Charles's refusal to accept that he was bound by the limits of political possibility. His determination, during 1638, to force the Scots to give up the Covenant appears to have been immune to any advice that this was something he simply could not do. As Traquair reported to Hamilton in July 1638:

62 J. T. Gilbert, *History of the Irish Confederation* (Dublin, 1882), I, 251, 289.

I find nothinge sticke with his majestie so much as the covenant, he have drunk in [sic] this opinion, that monarchie and it can not stand together; and knowing the impossibilitie of haveinge it renderit upp, you may easily conjecture what will ensue if the king continue but a few days more of that mynd . . . If I was wearied in Scotland, my heart is broke heir, since I can see no possibilitie to satisfie our masters honor, so deeply doth he conseave himself interested, as the country from ruine.

When Hamilton, in September 1638, advised Charles how to gain a party for the Glasgow Assembly, 'his answer was, that the remedy was worse than the disease'.[63] This is surely the same man who believed, in January 1641, that he could enjoy the services of Pym as Chancellor of the Exchequer together with those of Juxon as Archbishop of York.[64] The King emerges, not only as a man who had difficulty in recognising the limits of the possible, but also as one who, when he did recognise them, was liable to conclude that peace could have too high a price. This is the same King who told Hamilton, in December 1642, that, win or lose, he would make no more concessions in the English Civil War, and would rather live a glorious king, or die a patient martyr.[65] He is perhaps an example of E. M. Forster's Law, that the tragedy of life is that one gets what one wants.

He also emerges in the Scottish and English stories as a man with a real allergy to Puritanism in all its forms. In many places, this prevented him from facing facts. His repeated promises to the Scots that there would be no 'innovation' in religion seem to have been made in all sincerity, and in blissful ignorance that they appeared to many of his honest subjects to contradict the policies he was then pursuing.[66] This is the same king who emerges from the tangled story of the English Arminians and the 39 Articles. This allergy also seems to be the main explanation for his obstinate, and apparently sincere, insistence that the Scottish troubles were not about religion at all, since he was unable to absorb that many Scots sincerely believed him guilty of innovation.[67] This blindness to the force of Puritanical conviction does not seem to have made it easy for him to handle a force whose very existence he was incapable of admitting.

Charles also emerges as a King subject to the political failing of saying 'never', and then retreating, thereby encouraging his subjects to believe

---

63   Hamilton MSS 718, 719.
64   HMC *De L'Isle and Dudley*, VI, 366; KAO U 1475 C 114/7.
65   Hamilton MSS 167.
66   *Cal SP Dom 1639*, Vol ccccxviii, no. 50; *RPCS*, VIII, 3–4; *Rothes; pp. 98–9; Baillie, pp. 25, 43.
67   *A Large Declaration* (1640), pp. 1–16.

that they could always press him harder, and he would retreat further. From the Petition of Right to the execution of Strafford, this habit handicapped Charles of England, and it is equally apparent in his handling of the Scottish service book. It was the Earl of Nithsdale, not the most conciliatory of his Scottish advisers, who reproved him for this habit: 'it would have been better to refuse them at the first, and better to grant what they ask with a seasoning to resent, then still to give ground'. As Hamilton explained after the Pacification of Berwick, this habit made life very difficult for Charles's servants. 'Those particulars which I have so often sworne and said your matie would never condiscend to, will now be granted, therefore they will give no credit to what I shall say ther after, but will still hope and believe, that all ther desires will be given way to.'[68]

It was a political style which tended to advertise the fact that concessions were made unwillingly and under duress. In instructing Traquair for the 1639 Scottish Parliament, he commented on the Act for abolishing episcapcy: 'we consent to this act only for the peace of the land, and in our own judgment hold it neither convenient nor fitting'. He then told Traquair to publish this opinion. At the same time, he reassured the Archbishop of St Andrews that 'you may rest secure, that tho perhaps we doe [erased] may [inserted] give way for the present, to that which will be prejudiciall both to the church and our government, yett we shall not leave thinking in time how to remedy both'. In September 1640, Loudoun commented that the King's actions 'beget a suspition that his matie doth not yet intend a reall peace'.[69] It is not surprising that Pym and Saye should have come to share this suspicion, and should have formed a desire to institutionalise Charles's concessions so thoroughly that he would be unable to reverse them. There is no reason to suppose Pym and Saye paid as much attention to the history of the Irish Graces as they did to that of the Scottish bishops, but had they done so, the story could only have strengthened a belief that Charles's concessions had to be bound in chains.[70] We are dealing with a king who invited resistance in all of his three kingdoms, and got what he was asking for.

Yet this stress on blame for Charles will not serve to eliminate the other major theme of this article, that the relationship between the three kingdoms itself, and not merely its mishandling, was a major cause of instability in all three of them. That Charles's English regime was in the event brought down through military defeat at the hands of the Scots

68 Hamilton MSS 883, 948.
69 Hamilton MSS 1031, 1030, 1218.
70 See my article, 'The British Background to the Irish Rebellion', *Historical Research*, 61 (1988).

is a point too obvious to need labouring. What perhaps needs saying is that this is not the intervention of a random factor like a stroke of lightning, but the results of a long-term difficulty in securing religious unity between Charles's three kingdoms. Charles's decision to impose the Scottish liturgy was not taken out of the blue, and 'folly' is not a sufficient explanation for it. It was the result of a long-standing conviction, known to Wentworth and Laud by 1634, that there must be a closer union in religion between Charles's dominions. The underlying thinking emerges in Laud's insistence, in 1633, that English *and Scottish* soldiers and merchants in the Netherlands should be compelled to use the English liturgy, or in his otherwise Utopian objective of sending a bishop to New England.[71]

It is clear that Charles was well aware that his Scottish policy had English implications. To take one example among many, in 1639, he would agree to Traquair, as commissioner, assenting to an Act of the Scottish Parliament declaring episcopacy contrary to the constitutions of the kirk of Scotland, but not to one calling it 'unlawful':

> If I doe acknowledge or consent that episcopacie is unlafull in the kirk of Scotland, though as you may have sett it downe in your consenting to the act, the word unlafull may seem to have only a relation to the constitt. of that kirke, yet the construction there of doth runn so doubtfull, as that it may too probably be inferred, that the same callin is acknowledged by us to be unlafull in any churches of our dominions.[72]

The political realism of a concern for unity in religion between the three kingdoms is perhaps best illustrated by the fact that Charles shared it with the Scottish Covenanters, with Pym and with James. The political danger of the objective is also illustrated by the fact that Charles shared it with all these people, and by the fact that no two of them were pursuing unity in the same religious position. The inherent difficulty of the situation has perhaps been masked by James's success in pursuing union in religion between the kingdoms so slowly, and so much by stealth, that Dr Galloway has even been moved to question whether he had the objective at all.[73] James's pursuit of episcopacy in Scotland was conducted by so many small stages, over such a long period of time, that there was no one moment at which it was obvious that its opponents should stand and fight. The process of reconciling moderate Presbyterian ministers to episcopacy stage by stage looks remarkably

71   Laud, *Works*, VI, i, 23; H. R. Trevor-Roper, *Archbishop Laud* (1940), pp. 157–62. See also S. R. Gardiner, *History of England*, viii, 167.
72   Hamilton MSS 1031.
73   B. Galloway, *op. cit*, pp. 86–9.

YALE COLLEGE LEARNING RESOURCE CENTRE

like the policy of separating moderates and extremists described for England by Dr Fincham and Dr Lake.[74]

Taken by itself, or even together with the Five Articles of Perth, James's commitment to Scottish episcopacy need not show that he was working towards unity between the three kingdoms. It looks much more likely that James had the objective when his commitment to Scottish episcopacy is taken beside his commitment to Calvinist doctrine for England and Ireland. From 1603 onwards, many Scots recognised an adherence to Calvinist doctrine as an essential ground for unity between the churches,[75] and James's policy seems to have been to build up a church with Scottish doctrine and English government. The choice of George Abbot to consecrate his Scottish bishops puts his policy in a nutshell.[76]

The difference between James and Charles, then, was not in the objective of unity between the three kingdoms, but in the theological position from which they pursued that objective. Charles pursued it from a position which markedly increased the number of influential Englishmen who preferred the Scottish model to their own. Also, Charles did not pursue unity, as James had done, by shifting each kingdom a little bit towards the others, but by shifting Scotland and Ireland towards that interpretation of the English settlement which, of all others, made it most remote from the Scottish and Irish churches. Charles's Arminian stance may have been barely sustainable as an English one, but it was certainly beyond the bounds of the possible as a British one.

It was by involving the Scots in English politics that Charles created that vital ingredient of a major political crisis, a serious rival power centre to himself. Over and over again, the Scots, by changing the bounds of the possible in England, drew Charles's critics to attempt what they would not otherwise have risked. The petition of the 12 peers, for example, had been discussed between Englishmen and Covenanters for a year before it surfaced.[77] It is not a coincidence that it ultimately did surface when the Scots crossed the Tweed, and was immediately reported to Edinburgh.[78] Indeed, Hamilton had warned Charles, as early

74   Kenneth Fincham and Peter Lake, 'The Ecclesiastical Policy of King James I', *Journal of British Studies*, 1985, xxiv, 169–207. W. R. Foster, *The Church Before the Covenants* (Edinburgh and London, 1975), pp. 12, 16, 18, 20, 22, 26, 29.
75   Galloway, pp. 6, 43; Foster, p. 2.
76   Foster, p. 29.
77   Hamilton MSS 985. The story emerged from a rash Covenanter boast to Traquair, and was relayed by Traquair to London.
78   NLS Advocates' MSS 33.1.1, no 28. I am grateful to Dr T. I. Rae for drawing my attention to this Ms. The Petition of the 12 Peers was reported together with the City petition, which was prepared jointly with it. For a text of the City Petition, see Yale University Beinecke Library, Osborn Shelves b. 197, f. 9v.

as June 1638, of the opportunity a Scottish war would give his English critics:

> the conquering totally of this kingdome will be a difficult worke, though ye were sertain of what assistans ingland can give you, but it faires me that they will not be so forwardt in this as they ought, nay that there are some malitious spereites amongst them thatt no souner will your bake be turned, bot they will be redie to dou as we have doun heir, which I will never call by a nother name than rebellioun.[79]

For such 'malitious spirits', for whom Burges and Marshall may serve as fair examples, and for those to whom they preached, Scottish intervention in England could serve 'in working up their hearts to that indispensable pitch of heavenly resolution, sincerely to strike through a religious and invoiable covenant with their God'.[80] It was Scottish intervention which turned the programme of 'further reformation' for which the Long Parliament Fast preachers were spokesmen, into practical politics.

Yet, by the very act of turning 'godly reformation' into practical politics, the Scots also presented Charles with an opportunity to recruit an English party. It is no coincidence that Falkland and Sir Frederick Cornwallis long before they were royalist MPs had been anti-Scottish volunteers in the First Bishops' War,[81] for it was anti-Scottish feeling, and fear of the 'further reformation' the Scots brought with them, which provided the cement between Charles and his new royalist allies of 1641. Falkland probably spoke for them all when he commented on the Scots' Brotherly Assistance that it was an English proverb not to look a given horse in the mouth, and he wished it were a Scottish one too.[82]

In this situation, Charles reacted with more than usual shrewdness. He appreciated that it was the Scots who conferred power on his English opponents, and from the beginning of the Long Parliament onwards, his strategy was designed to divide Pym and his group from their Scottish allies. For the first few months of 1641, Charles's terms for settlement, the preservation of episcopacy and the life of Strafford, were precisely those which would have the effect of separating the English Parliamentarians from their Scottish allies. From March 1641 onwards, he pursued the same objective by another method, and aimed, by Scottish concessions, to remove the Scots from English politics. In the autumn of

79 Hamilton MSS 327.1.
80 C. Burges, *The First Sermon*, Ep. Ded.
81 *Cal SP Dom 1639*, Vol ccccxvii, nos. 85, 92.
82 Bodleian Ms Rawlinson D. 1099, f. 22b.

1641, when he exacted promises of non-intervention in English affairs from Argyll and Loudoun as part of his Scottish settlement, he appeared to have succeeded.[83]

It was at this point that the Irish Rebellion drove Charles back onto the mercy of his English Parliament. The Irish Rebellion, like the Bishops' Wars, is regularly discussed as if it were a random intervention of an outside factor, like a stroke of lightning. In fact, it was not. It was the very measures taken to draw England and Scotland together which had forced England and Ireland apart.[84] It was demonstrated that one of the most Athanasian characteristics of the British problem was the way in which avoidance of one error led straight to the perpetration of another. For the second time, it was failure to handle the British problem successfully which led Charles to failure in England. Perhaps the point on which we should really be pondering is that it took five years of continuous British crisis to drive the English body politic to the point of Civil War. This might perhaps suggest that, in spite of all the strains to which it had been subjected, the English social fabric of 1637 was still very tough indeed.[85]

It is part of the Athansian quality of this subject that Charles's kingdoms provided three independent stories, as well as one combined one, and it is worth asking what were the peculiarities of each kingdom as they emerge from comparison. The order in which the kingdoms resisted Charles was Scotland, Ireland, England, and it seems that this may represent more than a chronological progression. Though the Irish troubles proved after 1649 to be more long-lasting, there are more senses than one in which the Scottish troubles may be regarded as the *primum mobile* of the British. The Scots, from the beginning showed none of that extreme hesitancy at the idea of resistance which characterised the English. Through Knox and Buchanan, they could draw freely on a tradition of resistance theory, which was subject to none of the taboos which inhibited it in England. With their ascending theory of power in a kirk which was 'ane perfect republic'[86] they were better equipped than the English with a rival ideology to that of Charles I. Over and over again the key measures and ideas of the

---

83   Hamilton MSS 1585, 1586.
84   See my article, 'The British Background to the Irish Rebellion', *Historical Research* 61 (1988).
85   For a very different route to a similar conclusion, see John Morrill and J. D. Walter, 'Order and Disorder in the English Revolution' in *Order and Disorder in Early Modern England* edited by A. Fletcher and J. Stevenson (Cambridge, 1985), pp. 137–65.
86   The phrase is from *Reasons for a Generall Assemblie* (Edinburgh?, 1638), STC 22,054 Sig B.1.

English Parliament, the Triennial Act, the notion of treason against the realm, or the election of the great officers in Parliament, turn out to have been anticipated in Scotland.

By contrast, the peculiarity of England is that, of Charles's three kingdoms, it was the one in which the King gathered the largest party. Since it was the kingdom in which Charles lived and the source of nine-tenths of his revenues, it is not surprising that he found it the easiest kingdom in which to gather support. Moreover, it was for his vision of the Church of England that Charles offended the Scots, and it is not surprising that the Church of England, like the Tory party after it, found more support in England than in the rest of Britain. The gravity of the English Civil War, when it came, was that it resulted from an even division of opinion: in no other kingdom did Charles muster the support of nearly half the kingdom. England experienced trouble, not because it was the most revolutionary of Charles's kingdoms, but because it was the least. Baillie was quite entitled to his observation that 'a gloom of the King's brow would disperse this feeble people, for any thing yet we see, if the terror of God and us afrayed not their enemies, if help from God and us did not continue their courage'.[87]

---

87   Baillie, 283.

4

Opposition to the Personal Rule of Charles I: the Diary of Robert Woodford, 1637–1641

John Fielding

Originally appeared as John Fielding, 'Opposition to the Personal Rule of Charles I: the Diary of Robert Woodford, 1637–1641' in *Historical Journal* 31. Copyright © 1988 Cambridge University Press, Cambridge.

Robert Woodford was an obscure man, the steward of Northampton from 1636 until his death in 1654, whose diary, which covers the period 1637 until 1641, tells us much about how provincial men viewed the growing political crisis which was to culminate in civil war. There are very few sources available from which to assemble a biography of the diarist. He warrants no article in the *Dictionary of national biography*, he is not recorded as having attended either university, nor to have registered at any of the inns of court. In a brief biography, his eldest son Samuel stated that his father was born in 1606, the son of a gentleman, Robert Woodford of Old in Northamptonshire, that 'he had but Ordinary Education', and that his 'meane Fortune' meant that 'he could never provide for us in Lands or Money'. He married Hannah, daughter of Robert Hancs, citizen of London, in 1635 at the church of Allhallows-in-the-Wall. The minute book of the Northampton Town Assembly furnishes us with a few brief details of his career as a provincial legal practitioner. In 1636, he was elected steward of the town of Northampton by the good offices of his patron John Reading, the outgoing steward, who relinquished the office in his favour. The climax of his career would seem to have been his appointment as under-sheriff of the county in 1653 until his death in 1654: he remained a provincial lawyer.[1]

1 The diary of Robert Woodford is New College Oxford MS 9502. It comprises 586 pages, but is unpaginated. The pagination used throughout, therefore, is my own. I hope at some stage to be able to produce an edition of the diary. The

From very scant external sources then we learn nothing exceptional about Woodford's life, career or opinions. The diary, however, permits us a rare insight into the private mental world of a provincial townsman, and private it certainly is. The first folio of the document bears the instruction that 'who ever finds this book (if lost) I pray be sparing in looking into it and send it to Robte Woodford at Northampton'. Furthermore there is internal evidence that the diary formed part of a series, although no other volumes have been found. The entries begin without any preamble or introduction in August 1637, and simply end without explanation in August 1641. Sections towards the end of the document, in which entries are repeated with alternative dates, suggest that, on some occasions at least, he wrote up incidents in his diary retrospectively, perhaps from rough notes. In this case it is possible that the diary was a fair copy of entries made over that four-year period.[2]

The diary belongs to the now familiar genre of puritan spiritual autobiography, the impulse towards which lay in a strict interpretation of Calvinist predestinarian theology. This stated the obligation of the committed christian to confirm to himself his calling or election by means of the practical syllogism, a process which Dr Kendall has called experimental predestinarianism.[3] This caused an intense introspection as the christian compared his own actions and feelings with the imagined ideal of one to whom god had granted true (saving) faith. Simply to acknowledge the initial calling was insufficient, since though many were called it was only the elect who would persevere by means of god's assisting grace. Growth in grace was the sign of true faith, the unregenerate would fall at last. Thus the search for the assurance which only the godly could find necessitated a study of the workings of grace over time.

brief biography of Woodford is to be found in Dr Samuel Woodford's *Paraphrase upon the Psalm of David* (London, 1678 edn), pp. 22–6. The will of Robert Woodford senior bears out his grandson's pessimistic estimation of his fortune. His inventory amounted to £36 12s. 6d. Moreover, he is not described as a gentleman, but alternately as a yeoman, and in the inventory itself, as a husbandman. Northamptonshire Record Office, Archdeaconry of Northampton Wills, First series, Book EV 575; Second Series, C168. For the diarist's career details see the minute book of the Northampton Town Assembly 1628–1744, Northampton Borough Records 3/2; and Northamptonshire Record Office, Tryon (Bulwick) MSS, 259: 2, 6.

2   Robert Woodford's diary, New College Oxford, MS 9502, p. 2. Henceforth abbreviated to Diary. Diary, pp. 554–72.

3   For the doctrine of assurance, especially in connexion with William Perkins, see I. Breward, 'The life and theology of William Perkins. 1558–1602' (unpublished Ph.D. thesis, University of Manchester, 1963), pp. 194–234. See also R. T. Kendall, *Calvin and English Calvinism to 1649* (Oxford, 1979), pp. 51–78. For a guide to puritan spiritual autobiography see Alan Macfarlane, *The family life of Ralph Josselin a seventeenth century clergyman* (Cambridge, 1970), pp. 6–8.

Works of this type exist in manuscript from the 1580s, although it was in the 1590s that such ideas found their way into print classically, of course, in William Perkins' *Golden Chain*. There is a continuity of underlying assumptions linking Woodford to these, and to future authors such as Nehemiah Wallington in the 1640s and beyond, culminating on the one hand in the separatist congregations demanding a spiritual autobiography as an entrance requirement for their churches, and on the other in the collection by Samuel Clarke of the biographies of saints showing how grace had transformed their lives.[4]

Woodford's diary does not include any narrative of the author's conversion which once more suggests that it formed part of a series. His initial calling predated the document, he was concerned in the diary to 'labour for grace'. His notes on the sermon of a local minister precisely describe the sort of process that he was going through in the pages of his journal. The sermon described the four stages in the soul's development once the first signs of grace had been perceived: 'poverty of sp[iri]t and sight of wants . . . sense of them with sorow and greife . . . hungringe and thirsting after grace and constancy in the holy dutyes . . . a combat between the flesh and the spirit . . .'.[5] The crucial concept was that the regenerate saw life in terms of a conflict between the opposing principles of flesh and spirit, Christ and Antichrist: it was the urgent need of the diarist, of course, to establish that he belonged to the world of the spirit, but Satan had many snares and traps for the godly.

Woodford encountered these most frequently in the day-to-day concerns of his family's subsistence. A regenerate man would take joy in spiritual things and would be indifferent to worldly misfortunes or to the accomplishment of worldly goals: Woodford felt sorely tempted by the cares of the world which threatened to batter down the castle of his faith. On one occasion he prayed:

> oh my g[od] save me for the waters are come up to my soule . . . I sit in the dust, in mercye rayse me up, my feet sink fast in the dunghill let thy goodnesse . . . lift me out. The fiery iniections and darts of Satan come thick uppon me the Archer hath shot sure at me with envenomed arrowes, but Ile take the sheild of fayth and in the name of g[od] Ile

---

4   For an early example of the genre in the 1580s, see Peter Lake, *Moderate puritans and the Elizabethan church* (Cambridge, 1982), pp. 116–68. Examples from the nineties can be found in M. M. Knappen (ed.), *Two Elizabethan puritan diaries* (London, 1933). See also Paul S. Seaver, *Wallington's world, a puritan in seventeenth century London* (London, 1985). For Samuel Clarke and the significance of saints' biographies see Patrick Collinson, *Godly people, essays on English protestantism and puritanism* (London, 1983), pp. 499–526.
5   Diary, p. 80.

quench and repell them . . . give me of the wine of thy consolacon, then shall I forget my poverty . . . let me never goe to Beelzebub the god of Ekron. . . .[6]

Prayer was seen as the most potent weapon against such onslaughts. Although he prayed fervently for the money needed to maintain himself and his family in health, his prayers were mainly his chance to show god that however much the corrupt part of his personality was necessarily sorely tried, he could distance himself from this in fervently desiring things spiritual. Thus he awoke early one morning to find himself subject to:

melancholly and the thorny cares of the world, but I remember a Christian is called to reiocyinge, and a good conscience is a continuale feast, and a christian in the lowest and worst estate and condition is farre better case, then a man out of Christ in his greatest wealth and Jollity, and hath more true cause of cheerfulnesse. I have prayed unto the Lord to help me against my infidelity and melancholly, to give me the use of my graces, for I am not able to stirre them up my selfe. Lord endue me with strength from on high, what a covetous[man] am I to be so long in learning this lesson to live by fayth in regard of outward things, and to be contented in the want of them: truly Lord I have a proud and carnall hart. Lord pardon and heale, inable me to dep[ar]te from every sinne . . . and in thy due time I beseech thee supply me, payinge my debts for me. . . .[7]

It must not be inferred, however, that Woodford regarded wealth as a sign of god's favour. He visited Lady Crane (widow of the recently deceased Sir Francis) and reflected upon the latter's great fortune: 'outward thinges cannot secure from the evills of this life and much lesse helpe after death'.[8]

God intervened actively in the lives of the saints, and only the regenerate could make a 'sanctified use' of every piece of good or bad fortune, interpreting it as a personal reward, punishment or warning. When a local lawyer, Edward Bagshawe, fell off his horse, Woodford praised God for his mercy in preserving him. Similarly when he was short of money to buy food with his servant Hatton one day, he found that 'g[od] had provided that there was left in hatton's hand 10 s for [a client] which he refused to receave so it was to remayne with me. Blessed be thy name oh Lord for this p[ro]vidence'.[9] He charted the course of his career (or

6   Ibid. pp. 298–9.
7   Ibid. p. 65.
8   Ibid. p. 23.
9   Ibid. p. 38.

'particular calling'), and listed his debts so that he could acknowledge providence in that area too.[10] Affliction was viewed as punishment for some personal inadequacy: thus the illness of his son John was seen as punishment of the parents for loving the child too much simply because he belonged to them: Woodford prayed that his children be made 'blessed comforts unto us and instruments of thy glory in due time and keepe our affection from exhorbitancy that we may love them in thee and for thee . . .'.[11] His wife Hannah was so badly afflicted with a swelled breast after the birth of one of their children that it was in danger of bursting. This was also seen as a punishment: he wrote: 'oh Lord thou art able to p[re]vent the breakinge of it, Lord pr[e]vent it if it be thy gracious will and sanctifye the feare of it to us p[ar]don our deadnes in seeking to thee'.[12]

The godly made a strict dichotomy between themselves and the unregenerate, whose sins and company were to be avoided. In Woodford's parlance pursuing worldly cares would lead one to indulge worldly comforts. Over-indulgence in drink was especially to be avoided since it placed one on a slippery slope to even more heinous sin: in recording that an old acquaintance had committed adultery Woodford observed that 'this is the fruit of his drunkennesse'.[13]

The puritan view was that only the elect were predestined to derive full benefit from the means of salvation: thus Woodford's attitude to these was connected to his search for assurance. Prayer was his greatest weapon against Satan: one night he prayed, and was rewarded with 'Lavishinge Comforts . . . the Lord even broke in uppon me he made even his glory to passe before me and [I] proclaymed the Lord gracious . . . to enjoye thy p[re]sence and to behold thee in thine excellence and glory by an eye of fayth is even heaven here uppon the earth'.[14] Though constantly assailed by the darts of Satan, he was certainly never wracked by the same doubts about his personal worthiness which brought the London apprentice Nehemiah Wallington to the brink of suicide.[15] Prayer, especially when performed on his own in secret, was for the diarist the most important ordinance, since it was the medium through which the penitent expressed his will to repent, though the Word ran it

10   For instance, on 8 December 1638 he noted that his debts amounted to £195 19s. 6d. His creditors were: Mr Watts, William Turland, Mr Chapman, Mr Spencer, Mr Bott, Mr Flood, Mr Greg, Mr Enyon, Mr Ragdale, Mr Sue, Mr Goodere, Mr Dillingham, Andrew Broughton (attorney), Mr Greene, Ned Coop, Mr Hopkins, Woodford's mother, Richard Rise. Diary, pp. 291–2.
11   Ibid. p. 17.
12   Ibid. pp. 36–7.
13   Ibid. p. 275.
14   Ibid. pp. 148–9.
15   Seaver, *Wallington*, pp. 21–2.

a close second. The sabbath could also be used to banish thoughts of the creature, as when 'worldly cares were ready to possesse my soule in the morning soone as I waked, but I brought the word of the Lord against them and they did not much p[re]vayle . . . I banished them by remembring the Sabath'.[16] Since the godly alone could fully reap the benefit of the Lord's Supper it was before communion that he agonized most intensely about his assurance. His criteria for a worthy receiving of this sacrament were an absence from the mind of carnal thoughts and worldly cares: 'Lord 'p[ar]don our unfittinge of our selves, our passion, our Idlenes, our deadnesse and dullnesse, oh the 7 abominacons that are in my soule! oh the denne of dragons that harbor in me, oh the multitude of locusts that swarm in my hart . . .'.[17] Only if these criteria were fulfilled, and the communicant received in an attitude of 'fayth and sincerity of hart', could the christian derive benefit, and be 'alive and quickened and may feel a sensible increase of grace and decay of sinne'.[18] The hope was that the outward sign would be indicative of an inward grace, and this was his wish on the night before one of his children was baptized.[19]

However, puritans in the pre-separation era before 1640, though at pains to prove themselves not of this world, still had to live in it, and consequently the godly/ungodly division was drawn less rigidly. Rather than avoiding the ungodly altogether Woodford was able to keep a clear conscience by confessing his wrong-doing to his diary retrospectively. After a night spent drinking he wrote that: 'my hart smote me for being in Company . . . with Mr. Burgnis . . . Sam Martin was with me tonight and blames himselfe for keepinge company some time with those that feare not god in drinkinge wine and takinge tobacco'.[20] It was above all the sins of the ungodly which were to be avoided. Thus he objected in company to the swearing of oaths in which god's name was mentioned, and noted one night at an inn that the company told 'many tales and Jestes which I dare not allow my selfe'.[21] Yet he was by no means totally abstemious and suffered pangs of guilt when, celebrating with friends after a particularly lucrative court day, 'instead of comfortinge my selfe with god's creatures I through want of moderacon was sicke'.[22] Puritans were perhaps less conspicuous in the social milieu than has often been imagined.

16 Diary, p. 111.
17 Ibid. p. 377.
18 Ibid. pp. 79, 208.
19 Ibid. p. 3.
20 Ibid. p. 271.
21 Ibid. p. 161.
22 Ibid. p. 335.

The conscientious diarist had to live in the world of the unregenerate: thus he contacted Mr Winstanley, keeper of the king's lodgings at Whitehall, to obtain a job in the royal gift even though he clearly found his company unwholesome: 'what doe I doe in such Company thou hast called me to holinesse and moderacon let not the cares of the world and melancholly cause me to put forth my hand unto evill . . . let me find cheerfullness in attendinge uppon thee without such squeezing of the Creature for that which it cannot yield'.[23] This even extended to papists, whom Woodford did not shirk from mixing with on a social level: on one occasion he went to a Catholic's house to take evidence in a court case 'where I conceive I supped with a demure priest . . . we had much discourse of gen[er]all papists in divinity my hart was affected'.[24] On another he travelled with one and 'used what arguments I could to convince him of his error and prayed unto the Lord in his behalfe'.[25]

The puritans believed that a true calling would make itself known externally through an impulse by the individual to form part of a wider godly community branching out from the family. Thus we see Woodford as *paterfamilias* repeating sermons to his wife, and reading Genesis with his children and servants, exhibiting as much concern about their spiritual welfare as any member of the better documented greater gentry. In March 1638 for instance Woodford registered 'great Comfort and Satissfaccon in speakinge with hatton [his servant] tonight I trust the Lord hath begunne the good work of grace in his Soule'.[26] Woodford and others took care to procure the godly minister Andrew Perne to baptize their children, and themselves stood witness to each other's offspring, as Thomas Pentlow's wife did for the diarist's son.[27] There was a close religious tie between the vicar and curate of the parish and this group, and Prayer Book services were sometimes fulfilled at home. In 1639 curate Newton churched Hannah Woodford at home and dined there the same night with Mrs Rushworth.[28]

The two principal public foci for godly activity in Northampton were the Thursday lecture and the Sunday service. It was traditional to have two sermons on Sunday at All Saints, and whenever in town Woodford never neglected to hear these, which were usually preached by Thomas

---

23   Ibid. pp. 255–6.
24   Ibid. p. 356.
25   Ibid. p. 172.
26   Ibid. p. 153. For the impulse of individual believers to form a godly community see Peter Lake, 'William Bradshaw, antichrist and the community of the godly', *Journal of Ecclesiastical History*, 36, 4, 570–89.
27   Diary, p. 406.
28   Ibid. p. 416. Hannah Woodford was also churched in Sept. 1640: ibid. p. 499.

Ball, vicar of All Saints, or his curate Charles Newton. These occasions allowed Woodford and his friends in town, who were mostly aldermen, substantial townsmen, clerics, schoolmasters and godly lawyers, to meet their gentlemen and clerical friends from the lecture's catchment area with whom they frequently dined and supped. Those who lived in town, such as alderman Francis Rushworth, or Peter Farren or Woodford himself, provided hospitality for the godly from out of town. In December 1637 he was joined by Nathaniel Watts, townsman, Andrew Perne and Thomas Pentlow, the latter two being his especial friends.[29] Perne was a popular godly preacher whom the local gentleman Thomas Pentlow had presented to his vicarage of Wilby. When the plague raged at Northampton these two provided a refuge for Woodford at Wilby, an equally lively preaching centre where Perne himself preached twice every sabbath. At the height of the Laudian regime, in this area of Northamptonshire at least, preaching was readily available, and such local puritans as Daniel Cawdrey, James Cranford and William Castle preached frequently at Northampton.[30]

Official religious activity was however merely the tip of the iceberg as far as the godly were concerned. They had their own distinctive communal forms referred to severally by Woodford as 'conventicles' or 'seekings' or being 'in dutye with god's people'. The vicar Thomas Ball was the most prominent member of the group, and at one such meeting at his house in 1640 Woodford, his wife, and others joined the vicar in 'seeking the Lord'.[31] Informal religious meetings of this sort were supplemented with even more private forms as when the diarist repaired to his friend Thomas Martin's house after a particularly edifying sermon to repeat his notes.[32] The godly provided each other with more tangible comfort as well – Woodford listed Perne, Martin, Watts and Turland amongst his many creditors – but it was ultimately the ties of spiritual aid and comfort which bound them together. A sense of common purpose to grow in grace together encouraged them to discuss their subjective experiences. When Thomas Pentlow was ill Woodford persuaded him of the need to 'labour for grace', and he was also sent for to comfort Mrs Rushworth who was 'in mighty horror roringe sometimes most hideously and cryeinge out she was damned she was damned'.[33] When shortly afterwards she died, he noted that the schoolmaster Daniel

29   Ibid. p. 87.
30   For Cawdrey see ibid. pp. 297, 444. For Cranford: ibid. p. 344. For Castle: ibid. p. 359.
31   Ibid. p. 502.
32   Ibid. p. 301.
33   Ibid. pp. 69, 219, 291–2, 546.

Rogers, a close friend of his and son of the great Essex puritan, was procured to preach at the funeral of his 'deare sister'.[34] Woodford himself was the recipient of spiritual aid from his friend John Bullivant, vicar of a neighbouring parish, to whom he confessed in private 'the temptacon which began uppon me this day three years'.[35]

The final earthly service the godly could perform for one another was to stand witness on the deathbed to perseverance in grace, as when Woodford and his friends travelled to a nearby town to see the death throes of one of their number called Thomas Freeman. According to the diarist they found him:

Cheerfull . . . but complayned that his body was become a very unfit organ for his soule to worke in . . . he prayed god he had got on the cloak of Xt, and that now he had but a step to heaven, and desired us to helpe lift him up by our prayers, and a little before he dyed he prayed god be with us all, and prayed when we could not well understand his words, and about 10 of the clock in the morninge he sweetly slept in the Lord without making any noyse onely ceased to breath . . . my mother closed his eyes at his depture. . . .[36]

In his educational background and career progress Woodford conforms to Christopher Brooks' characterization of the seventeenth-century provincial attorney as a non-graduate who was not a member of an inn of court, but who relied largely upon his master, a local practitioner, for training, and to gain employment.[37] Woodford's patron was John Reading of the Inner Temple, who was also part of the Northampton godly group. The steward, who was employed by the corporation, kept the town's manorial court by proxy for the mayor, the bailiff's court and the daily court of the record.[38] He supplemented his income by acting as clerk on the assize circuit, keeping the manorial courts of local gentry, and by executing the occasional special commission such as playing a minor role in representing the county's gentry at the earl of Holland's Forest Court, an employment secured for him by John

34   Ibid. p. 552. For an example of a more elevated (though similar) godly network of gentry, clerics, schoolmasters, etc. headed by Lord Brooke, see Ann Hughes 'Thomas Dugard and his circle in the 1630s – a Parliamentary–Puritan connection?' *Historical Journal*, 29, 4 (1986), 771–93.

35   Diary, p. 42.

36   Ibid. pp. 6–8.

37   C. W. Brooks, *Pettyfoggers and vipers of the commonwealth, the 'lower branch' of the legal profession in early modern England* (Cambridge, 1986), pp. 45–6.

38   J. C. Cox and C. A. Markham (eds.), *Records of the borough of Northampton* (2 vols., Northampton, 1898), II, 115–17.

Reading.[39] Clive Holmes has described these provincial lawyers as brokers who 'articulated provincial society into the national system of administration and law' by their advocation of litigation at the central courts in London.[40] For much of this sort of business Woodford relied upon his godly contacts in the county approaching him: thus Thomas Pentlow and Thomas Martin both asked him to draw up their wills.[41] In addition he helped to prepare Thomas Pentlow's case in the court of wards and the court of chancery as well as keeping his manorial court. Thomas Bacon, brother of John to whose house Woodford frequently repaired to pray, contacted him to help handle his ship money dispute which was to terminate only in the star chamber.[42] That the diarist could rely on his godly contacts for business is clear and it may indeed be the case that he was known as a lawyer to whom the godly could resort for help. On a more general level his professional position enabled him to socialize with a higher stratum of gentry society within the county; he and Pentlow dined several times at Sir Christopher Yelverton's house and Woodford handled some unspecified business for him. In December 1637 he also dined at Sir Christopher Hatton's with Thomas Martin, and the godly ministers Daniel Cawdrey and Thomas Ball.[43]

Thus business necessitated frequent trips to London, and indeed in the period November 1637 to December 1639 he spent just under one third of his time there. This allowed him to gain a wider professional experience. The inns of court offered him the opportunity of becoming part of a national legal culture, of establishing useful legal contacts, and of penetrating a more elevated job market; he visited Lincoln's Inn and mixed with other hopefuls there though he is not recorded as ever having become a member.[44] He also stayed at an inn of chancery, Clement's Inn, whose membership was made up of 'lower branch' attorneys such as himself, but the absence of sources prevents us from knowing whether he joined. In 1638 he sought employment as an auditor by looking through the Clerk of the Patent's book.[45] More reveal-

39   Diary, p. 21. For details of the duties of the clerk of the peace, see: T. G. Barnes, 'The clerk of the peace in caroline Somerset'. *University of Leicester department of English local history occasional papers*, 14, 1961.
40   Clive Holmes, *Seventeenth century Lincolnshire* (History of Lincolnshire, VII, History of Lincolnshire Committee, Lincoln, 1980), p. 51.
41   Diary, p. 246. See also Martin's will: he bequeathed to 'my loving friend Robert Woodford the writer of this last will twenty shillings to buy him a ring with this poosye (from a true frend)'. Archdeaconry of Northampton Wills, Northamptonshire Record Office, third series, A178.
42   Diary, p. 155 (March 1637/8).
43   Ibid. pp. 21, 99, 223, 95.
44   Ibid. p. 263.
45   Brooks, *Pettyfoggers*, pp. 158, 163. Diary, pp. 432–3, 257.

ingly the capital seems to have functioned as a job market for county-based employments too: he lobbied an attorney in Westminster Hall to elicit from him a deputation to hold an hundredal court in North-amptonshire.[46] Another potential avenue of promotion was through his father-in-law Robert Hancs who attempted to use his influence as Master of Weaver's Hall to obtain for Woodford a clerkship there, but once more the absence of records prevents us from discovering whether he succeeded.[47]

His sojourns in London also enabled him to experience a more sophisticated national culture, and to broaden his circle of acquaintance. He made friends with John Dillingham, a Northamptonshire man and newsletter writer who in 1643 was to become editor of the 'Parliament Scout' newsheet, and Sir John Wolstenholme, the city merchant.[48] He made fruitful contacts with the flourishing London godly in the persons of the famous ministers John Stoughton and William Gouge to whose arbitration he submitted a quarrel between himself and John Reading's son Daniel.[49] He visited his father-in-law's parish at Allhallows-in-the-Wall and took advantage of the far greater availability of sermons to hear nationally famous godly figures such as Stoughton himself, John Goodwin, Edmund Calamy, Simeon Ashe, and Stephen Marshall as well as the (in his eyes) infamous Thomas Turner and Willian Beale.[50] The provincial visitor acted as a channel for news, sometimes being a courier for letters from the capital, but more generally informing his local friends of news from the centre. For it was not only sermons which interested him; he was in London to witness the judgement in Hampden's Case, and frequently took time off for sight-seeing, on one occasion being given a conducted tour of the king's private apartments in Whitehall, on another watching with interest the installation of a new lord mayor.[51]

Peter Lake and Kenneth Fincham have recently drawn attention to the difficulty in establishing contemporary attitudes to the personal rule caused by historians' mistakenly seeking ideological opposition to the regime in official sources covering the administration of policy in the localities where it was not appropriate for such opposition to be

---

46   Ibid. p. 122.
47   Ibid. pp. 5, 202, 206.
48   A. N. B. Cotton, 'John Dillingham journalist of the middle group', *English Historical Review*, CCCLXIX (Oct, 1978), 817–34. See also D[ictionary] of N[ational] B[iography] under 'John Wolstenholme'.
49   Diary, p. 360.
50   Ibid. pp. 123–4, 371, 386, 513, 263.
51   Ibid. pp. 164–5, 254, 52–3.

expressed.[52] Woodford's diary is precisely the sort of private source that they recommend for the study of the nature of opposition in the 1630s, a decade which on the surface seems tranquil after the upheavals of the 1620s.

Woodford utilized three basic sources of information in compiling his political comments. Perhaps the most fruitful of these was the information he amassed on his many trips to London and elsewhere, either through witnessing events personally or through numerous conversations on the road and with his friends in the capital: this was supplemented by county gossip and rumour. On the road he can be seen discussing such matters as the altar policy or (when he met a Lancashire man called John Taylor) the imprisonment of Henry Burton.[53] In addition he received several letters from London, which contained items of news. In 1639 one such letter informed him that the City of London had refused to send the king 3,000 soldiers to fight the Scots.[54] His correspondents are unknown, but likely candidates include his father-in-law Robert Hancs and John Dillingham who in the same year showed Woodford a copy of the proceedings of the Scottish Assembly and seems to have acted as a source of information for his countrymen, notably Lord Edward Montagu of Boughton.[55] Lastly the diarist balanced these unofficial sources by referring to official government output, especially the three royal proclamations which were issued in connexion with the Bishops' Wars of 1639. As Richard Cust has shown, all these sources of information stressed conflict, though often from very different points of view, which reinforced the diarist's own theologically based tendency to perceive society in terms of polarities in conflict with one another.[56]

Woodford's political comments can be seen as an extension of his interpretation of providence to the collective level of the godly in the world with the twofold aim of on the one hand recording his own adherence to the forces of Christ, and on the other plotting the progress of the godly against Satan. Politics for Woodford (as for Thomas Scott, the author of *Vox Populi*) was a conflict between two opposing ideals of the commonwealth, which corresponded to the familiar dichotomy

---

52   Peter Lake, 'The collection of ship money in Cheshire during the 1630s', *Northern History*, XVII (1981), 71. Kenneth Fincham, 'The judges' decision on ship money in February 1637: the reaction of Kent', *Bulletin of the Institute of Historical Research*, LVII (1984), 230–7.
53   Diary, pp. 115, 128–9.
54   Ibid. p. 342.
55   Ibid. p. 307: Cotton, 'John Dillingham', p. 818.
56   For example: ibid. pp. 322, 336, 341. R. P. Cust, 'News and politics in early seventeenth-century England', *Past and Present*, 112 (Aug. 1986), 60–90.

between Christ and Antichrist. Though Woodford did not label these ideological poles 'court' and 'country' in the consistent way that Scott did, it is clear that he had a similar polarity in mind.[57] The opposite of the godly ideal was the corruption with which the commonwealth was afflicted from top to bottom. He came to believe that there was an Antichristian plot led by a party of papist malignants around the king, supported by the bishops and a whole host of clergy in the diocesan ecclesiastical courts and at parish level, to subvert both true religion and the laws of England. Thus he fulminated against the twofold threat posed by the 'antichristian power that is amongst us . . . vayne ceremonyes and some weak rudiments [oh Lord] purge thy floore blowe away the chaffe that is amongst our doctrine and in our discipline let pop[er]y and Arminianisme hide themselves . . .'.[58]

Doctrinal Arminianism threatened the diarist's fundamental predestinarian beliefs, as was demonstrated during a visit to Coventry when he argued with one Mr Naylor 'an armin[i]an [with whom] I had much dispute about pr[e]destinacon the Lord much moved my hart to defend his truth . . .'.[59] Furthermore the church's sacramental purity was jeopardized by Laudian ceremonialism, which substituted bodily (and therefore necessarily corrupt) worship for spiritual. For this the bishops were held mainly to blame. In August 1637 Bishop Francis Dee of Peterborough strictly enforced the altar policy in his diocese, through his commissioners Samuel Clarke and Robert Sibthorpe, insisting on the railing in of the communion table at the east end of the chancel, and on communicants coming up to the rails to receive the sacrament kneeling. Woodford saw such ceremonialism as popish, and idolatrous:

> why [he asked] should p[ro]phanesse be established or contenued by a law
> . . . why should the precepts of men be taught for doctrines, why should
> carnall ordinances and an earthly sanctuary still remayne, and the
> worship in spirit and in truth be yet refused, why should the whore of
> Rome, the mother of fornicacon and all the abominacons that are in the
> earth, remayne under these heavens and breath thy ayre, why should
> not Babilon fall and be cast rather into the botome of the sea like a
> millstone???[60]

57 Peter Lake, 'Constitutional consensus and puritan opposition in the 1620s: Thomas Scott and the Spanish match', *Historical Journal*, 25, 4 (1982), 805–25.
58 Diary, p. 385.
59 Ibid. p. 267.
60 Ibid. pp. 17, 337. Palace Green Library, Durham University, Visitation Articles for the primary visitation of Bishop Francis Dee (1634), S. R. 4. C. 11. (xvii. G. 22), article 3. And see especially the following for the execution of the altar policy in Northamptonshire: Peterborough Diocesan Records, church survey for 1637, Northamptonshire Record Office, X2159.

Archbishop Laud himself as the leader of the bishops was regarded by Woodford as one of the prime movers in the conspiracy: he was shocked one day to hear 'that the Archbp hath renounced the havinge a hand in the bringinge men up to the rayles to receive the sacramt . . . oh Lord thou art able to bring shame and confusion of face upon all favourers and p[ro]moters of supstition and Idolatry . . .'.[61] Bishop Matthew Wren of Norwich was similarly singled out. On hearing that Wren had preached before the king, he prayed god to 'bringe those that are faythfull to preach before his Ma[jes]tye . . . and remove the wicked from his throne'. Court preachers such as William Beale, who preached before the king condemning supralapsarians, and Thomas Turner, who preached in favour of bowing at the naming of Jesus, were also identified as promoters of false religion. His remarks concerning episcopacy are ambiguous at this stage: whilst he did note that he 'prayed agt wicked B[isho]ps and their h[i]erarchy . . .' it is not clear whether episcopacy itself was here being condemned, although it must be pointed out that his remarks concerning bishops were consistently slighting, and there is no mention of good bishops nor of any model of a good bishop.[62]

His model of political polarization was, however, present from the very beginning of the diary, and certainly predated the altar policy. Not surprisingly his portrayal of conflict at the local level is the most vivid. Here godly ministers, whom the diarist clearly expected to be leaders against Antichrist, were shown defending the truth against the enemy. In particular Andrew Perne was praised by his friend: 'Lord blesse his ministery still keep open his mouth notwithstandinge all the power of the adversary hold him as a starre in thy hand . . . Rayse up more Champions for thee even great Apolloes that may be mighty in the Scriptures.'[63] Yet the high profile of the ministerial calling left them vulnerable to attack by the enemy. As Perne was preaching one day, Dr Roane, an official in the church courts in the neighbouring county of Huntingdon, came to 'heare and (I doubt) to entrap Mr. Perne but he pre[eached] faythfully the Lord make it effectuall uppon us all that heard and uppon that supstitious doctor . . . I besought the Lord for his convercon'.[64]

Prominent among those whom Woodford perceived as collaborators in the episcopal plot was Samuel Clarke, surrogate to the archdeacon of Northampton, who in March 1638 appears to have challenged the tradition at All Saints of having an afternoon sermon on Sunday. On

61   Diary, pp. 369–70.
62   Ibid. pp. 263, 123, 49.
63   Ibid. pp. 10–11.
64   Ibid. p. 209.

Sunday 3 March he noted with disapproval that Clarke's order banning afternoon sermons was being obeyed; his response was characteristically violent: 'oh Lord though the adversary this wicked Haman and those of the Confederacye seeke to extinguish the light of thy glorious gospell . . . let thy truth breake forth . . .'.[65] Other local ministers were condemned, such as Richard Powell, that 'persecuting priest', who died whilst on his way to the church courts to present forty people, or Mr Forsyth, who spent a whole sermon condemning puritans.[66] The extent to which Woodford envisaged an elevated role for the godly minister in the war against Antichrist is further illustrated in the case of Richard Trueman's sermon. Trueman preached condemning idolatry only days before the execution of the altar policy at Northampton. He was promptly called before Clarke and later described the meeting to his friend Woodford:

> I understand by him that they threaten him that he is like to loose his life for the sermon the good and p[ro]fitable sermon which he preached here ag[ains]t Idolatry the last Sab[bath] day oh Lord defend him and susteyne him . . . I heare from London today that the bishop of Lincolne is like to loose his head the next tearme.[67]

Bishop Williams of Lincoln seems an unlikely hero for the godly, and his inclusion highlights the conceptual difficulties Woodford was experiencing in attempting to force the reality of politics to conform to his own simplistic pattern. He was on safer ground with his praise of those 'holy living martirs' Burton, Bastwick and Prynne whose release in 1640 he was to herald as 'the returne of the captivity from Babilon'.[68]

Woodford sought to associate such secular affairs as the ship money levy and the forest laws with the cause of religion. He regarded the former as illegal, and envisaged an elevated role for the magistrate (parallel to that of the minister) in speaking out for truth as is shown in his reaction to Judge Hutton's verdict in Hampden's Case, which he witnessed personally: 'Justice Hutton delivered his opinion freely and playnely against the businesse shewinge it to be contrary to the lawes of the Realme and answered the argument brought on the other side with much applause of the people. Blessed be God for also making him a man of courage.'[69] The inseparability in his mind of the attempts to subvert religion and the law is shown in his prayer

65   Ibid. p. 140
66   Ibid. pp. 215, 296.
67   Ibid. p. 19.
68   Ibid. p. 518.
69   Ibid. pp. 164–5.

to god to 'ease us of this great and heavy taxe if it be thy will and grant that the whole kingdome may live in p[er]fect peace and . . . in thy feare seeking the p[ro]motion of thy glorious gospell'.[70] The implication was that those who feared god would not impose such a monstrous tax, which breached the subject's liberty. Similarly when offered an employment by his master John Reading to represent the county's gentry at the forest court in 1637, he was reluctant to become involved in what he knew would be an unpopular issue. Most of all he and his countrymen resented the hectoring style of Judge Finch who 'hath much anticipated us in our evidence by declaring what hath bene already adiudged in this matter in other places wch he hath warned the Counsell to take notice of'.[71]

For Woodford the climax of his conspiracy came with the Bishops' Wars of 1639 to 1640. At no stage did he mention the initial cause of the crisis, the government's imposition of a new Prayer Book on Scotland, but he saw two conflicting ideologies at work. In the regime's handling of the problem he saw an extension of the popish plot. He notes having read the royal declaration of 27 February 1639, which stated that 'these disorders and tumults have been thus raised in Scotland and fomented by factious spirits and those Traiterously affected, begun upon pretences of Religion . . . the common cloak for all disobedience but now it clearly appears the aim of these men is not Religion . . . but it is to shake off all Monarchicall government . . .'.[72]

It is clear that Woodford regarded the Declaration as a subversive document, a product of those evil men around the king, since he immediately launched an attack on the enemies of true religion:

> let thy gospell break forth like the glorious sunne from under a cloud, that the eyes of the adversaryes may be inlightened, or they may be so ashamed that they may hide them selves in obscurity . . . the oposers of g[od] and true religion have said, we will devoure at once, they are in our hands, now shall we p[re]vale against those that they esteeme be off scowring of the world, and stayne with opprob[r]y[um] callinge them puritans sectaryes, etc.[73]

The regime's point of view also found supporters such as Woodford's neighbour Robert Sibthorpe, who wrote to his brother-in-law Sir John Lambe in June 1639 referring to the war: 'Bellum Episcopale as they

---

70   Ibid. p. 113.
71   Ibid. p. 32.
72   Ibid. p. 336. J. F. Larkin and P. L. Hughes (eds.), *Stuart royal proclamations* (2 vols., Oxford, 1973–83), II, 662–3.
73   Diary, pp. 336–8.

say some stile it [or] Rebellio Puritanica for soe I know it may be truely stiled . . .'.[74]

There is some evidence that Woodford identified with the secular so-called 'oppositionist' politicians on this issue, noting with distress that the 'godly and gracious' Lords Saye and Sele and Brooke were jailed at York for refusing to fight the Scots.[75] Thus, once more, in his mind the cause of religion was inextricably linked with that of the liberties of the subject, represented by the Scots, whilst the opposite view stressed obedience to the king's prerogative and daubed the Scots puritans and traitors. One victim of the crisis was John Dillingham, who during a visit to the capital by the diarist in 1639 had showed him a copy of the proceedings of the Scottish Assembly, and who was later arrested for harbouring a Scottish knight supposedly sent to contact English malcontents.[76]

If Woodford's radicalism lay in his detailed application of anti-papal rhetoric to the English political situation, it was also exhibited in his estimation of the degree of complicity of Charles I in the conspiracy. As we have seen, his support of the Scots was essentially treasonable. Woodford did not portray the king as a tyrant, whose policies could be legitimately resisted, but he went further than to merely suggest that Charles had been misled by evil counsellors. He regarded Charles as beset by evil men who had blinded him; as early as September 1637 he prayed 'for the Kings Ma[jes]tye for his Conveccon to inlighten his eyes to stirre him up to drive away ye wicked from ye throne and to make choyce of such as will be faythfull'.[77] Thus though the burden of blame must be placed on the counsellors they had undoubtedly convinced the king of their case. It is worth recalling the contexts of Woodford's previous use of the term 'unconverted'. We have seen him use it to express that state of unregeneration or carnality in which papists and drunkards wallowed. If the king had been blinded by others, then they were counsellors he himself had chosen; his blindness was a blindness to true religion; thus he prayed that god would make Charles into a worthy, and godly ruler: 'put it into the hart of his royall maiesty to love the good and hate the evill, to discerne betweene those that differ, that those that feare the Lord may be precious in his eyes . . . that he may improve the talent betrusted to him to the good of so great a people'.[78]

---

74   Huntingdon Library, California, Stowe MSS, unfoliated, Sibthorpe to Lambe, 3 June 1639.
75   Diary, p. 360.
76   Cotton, 'John Dillingham', pp. 817–34: P[ublic] R[ecord] O[ffice], S. P. 16/397/26.
77   Diary, pp. 27–8.
78   Ibid. p. 476.

It is symptomatic of the influence on Woodford's mind of the puritan imperialist tradition that he strove to think well of Charles I: on a sight-seeing tour of the king's apartments in Whitehall he visited the monarch's chamber and noted with pleasure the presence of the '4 Gospells the Acts of the Apostles and the Apocalypse in bookes all sett forth with pictures . . . Bless the King's Majesty and make him a nursing father to the Kingdoms committed to him'.[79] This episode is however exceptional; Woodford was already trying to allay his innermost doubts about the king's godliness and trustworthiness. After the king's army had flown from the Scots the diarist hoped that the subsequent peace treaty would imply the king's love for his Scottish subjects. That there was considerable doubt about this in his mind is demonstrated by his fervent wish that 'the good be accepted of him'.[80]

In juxtaposition to Woodford's formidable ideological opposition to the regime was his continued faith in traditional constitutional means to remedy the situation. He believed that a parliament would promote unity and consensus between monarch and subjects by removing the sources of grievance. It was the popish faction which had prevented Charles from taking the necessary steps to heal the breach with his people. Thus in 1637 rumour of the king's illness awoke hopes of his 'conversion' in Woodford's mind; the king, it was said, 'hath resolved uppon a Parliamt oh Lord prserve him in this life and keep him from all conspiracyes . . . move his hart to call a p[ar]liament which (being directed by thee) may conclude uppon wholesome lawes for the King-dome and may redress exhorbitancyes . . .'.[81] If he was beginning to doubt Charles I's ability to head a godly commonwealth his view of par-liament was highly idealized; it was the only institution he had complete faith would redress the subjects' grievances. For him as for Thomas Scott it was assumed to be an homogeneous body, the repository of that ideal vision of the country as a godly commonwealth which attained its representative credentials through the process of election and went on to purge the corruption out of the provinces.[82]

Woodford's diary demonstrates that the theory of a popish plot to subvert England's religion and laws, which had been espoused by John Pym and others in the 1620s, had by 1637 percolated down to the provinces and found support there. This leaves us, however, with the problem of explaining the diarist's apparently passive and obedient progress through these years; he is not recorded as having run foul of either the secular or the ecclesiastical courts, and even recorded paying

79   Ibid. p. 254.
80   Ibid. p. 355.
81   Ibid. pp. 75–6.
82   Lake, 'Constitutional consensus', pp. 815–17.

his levy to his local churchwardens for the execution of the changes demanded by the church courts.[83] His comparative silence suggests that, without a meeting of parliament, it was difficult for people with ideas such as his to express an ideological opposition to the government; this difficulty can be explored by uncovering what he regarded as legitimate ways to express his views.

Parallel to his concept of an individual christian's duty to condemn sin on the personal level was his concept of active citizenship: it was the calling of every christian to oppose sin (in this case the sin of popery) on a political level built on the premise that the fear of god was the cement that held every aspect of society together from the family to the godly commonwealth. The spur to action was god's providential anger as in the case of the altar policy. Woodford and his friends interpreted an outbreak of plague shortly after the episcopal visitation as divine punishment of the people of Northampton for permitting such antichristian innovation: 'the Rayle in the Chancell is now almost up and its confidently reported that the sickness is in the Towne'.[84] This approach lay behind his belief in the cause of the Scots. In April 1639 he met his friend, rector John Bullivant of Abington, and had 'much discourse about the Scottis[h] business [and how] we consider pr[o]cedinge and how justly the Lord may bringe uppon us the Judgm[en]t of the sword'.[85]

Woodford tended to keep a low profile, but there was more to his discretion than mere timidity; he was perhaps typical of puritans before 1640. As we have seen in his attitude to the godly's withdrawal from evil on the social level it was possible to conform to certain external observances whilst maintaining a clear conscience. This was achieved, in part at least, by agonizing about his duty retrospectively in the pages of his diary. Thus also he was able to attend a dinner party at Sir Christopher Hatton's at Kirby, though he must have known that their views were at odds. The evening passed without event until after the meal when Woodford and James Longman, Sir Christopher's chaplain, fell into conversation:

> about the times and altars and boweinge to them, he favors and maynteynes those innovations, I resolved to carry my selfe that he might not p[er]ceave my opinion but the fire brake out, and I spoke in the behalfe of gods true and sp[irit]uall worship, though with as much discrecon as I could and thought fitt.[86]

83   Diary, pp. 154, 347.
84   Ibid. p. 148.
85   Ibid. pp. 348–9.
86   Ibid. pp. 136–7.

Clearly the dinner table of his social superior was not an appropriate place for his views to emerge, and he goes on to describe the reason for his indiscretion. One could pardonably avoid stating one's opinions unless questioned individually on a matter fundamental to true religion, but then reticence was a sin:

> oh Lord keepe me from danger and questioninge if it be thy will, but if in thy p[ro]vidence thou hast ordeyned that I shall be called forth to wit- nesse to thy truth, I beseech thee, give me knowledge and wisdome and fayth and courage and . . . patience let me not feare the face of mortall men.[87]

The political temperature was plainly rising in a situation where even the relatively discreet Woodford was being forced into the open by the radical nature of the regime.

He did not see reticence such as his own as an acceptable response from the godly clergy. As more public figures it was their duty in his eyes to resist evil openly. After the 1637 visitation, he bemoaned the fate of the church in evil times by noting with disappointment the collabora- tion of certain godly ministers with the demands of the ecclesiastical courts: the prayers of curate Newton were derided (in a nice turn- around of the usual convention) as 'somewhat canonicall'.[88] In the same way he applauded the godly Burton, Bastwick and Prynne, and Judge Hutton who all spoke out against evil and commented that 'it is an evill time and the prudent hold their peace who so dep[arte]th from evill maketh himselfe a prey'.[89]

Woodford did not however believe in resisting royal authority. He was a vulnerable individual lacking a strong patron to protect him: outright resistance could prove disastrous to his career and livelihood. What options then did Woodford see as being open to the godly? One arena of action was professional; he acted as clerk for his friend Thomas Bacon of Burton Latimer who refused to pay what he stated was an unfair ship money assessment and was accused of persuading his tenants to mount a tax strike. The case was conducted throughout as an assessment dispute, but the personalities of the main protagonists reveal the ideological concerns that lay hidden beneath the surface. Woodford's attitude to the tax has already been discussed. His opponent, and the promoter of the case against Bacon, was Robert Sibthorpe, preacher of the infamous forced loan sermon in 1627 stating the subject's bounden duty to pay any tax imposed by the divine right monarch. The manifest

87   Ibid. p. 137.
88   Ibid. p. 139.
89   Ibid. p. 17.

impossibility of raising broad issues of principle in disputes which involved characters like Sibthorpe, who in another local case had dismissed as puritans those refusing to pay ship money, was shown in Woodford's response to him: 'I [went] to the Counsell table with Mr. Bacon and I am apt to think that Dr. Sibthorpe will therefore set himselfe against me and ruine me . . . [oh Lord] thou must deliver me from the mouth of the lyon and from the fingers of the wicked'.[90]

The godly community could also rally around their churchwardens. Woodford praised the actions of his friends Peter Farren and Francis Rushworth in taking on Dr Samuel Clarke by first refusing to move the communion table, then returning it to the body of the chancel at the administration of communion. This eventually resulted in their excommunication necessitating a trip to London to seek absolution at the court of arches, which was denied them. Their appeal to the court of delegates was, however, successful and Clarke's original verdict was declared invalid. In the capital they called on Woodford to afford them some (unspecified) legal aid.[91] Since redress at the ecclesiastical courts was impossible, the godly were driven to resort to the common law. Humphrey Ramsden, an informant of Sir John Lambe's at All Saints, was indicted for drunkeness whilst John Ponder of Rothwell prosecuted his curate at the assizes for administering the communion exclusively to kneelers.[92] Petitioning was another legitimate avenue of protest, and in September 1640 Woodford added his own signature to a list of Northamptonshire grievances to be carried to the king.[93]

The best chance of effective political participation for Woodford came with the Short Parliament elections of March 1640 when many of the issues and antagonisms which lay beneath the surface were made public. John Crew, ship money refuser and friend of John Pym, was elected unopposed to the first county place. Initially it seems Sir Christopher Hatton wanted to stand for the second place, but Woodford for one rejected the preliminary advances of his agent, and the election eventually became a contest between Deputy Lieutenant Thomas Elmes, the establishment candidate, and Sir Gilbert Pickering of Titchmarsh, who

90   Ibid. p. 367. S. P. 16/313/111, 317/46, 417/47: this was part of a wider dispute between Sibthorpe and Bacon, an excellent account of which is given in Victor L. Stater, 'The lord lieutenancy on the eve of the Civil Wars: the impressment of George Plowright', *Historical Journal*, 29, 2 (1986), 279–96. For the problems involved in trying to broach broad matters of principle in administrative disputes see: E. S. Cope, 'Politics without parliament: the dispute about muster master's fees in Shropshire in the 1630s', *Huntington Library Quarterly*, XLV (1982), 271–84.
91   H[ouse] of L[ords] R[ecord] O[ffice], Main Papers, 6 February 1641. Diary, p. 127.
92   Diary, pp. 22, 453.
93   Ibid. p. 501. I have not been able to find this.

was the godly candidate. Elmes seems to have been supported by the earls of Westmoreland, Peterborough, and Northampton along with such local figures as Dr Samuel Clarke and others in the ecclesiastical courts who can be seen canvassing on his behalf.[94] Pickering drew his support from the Northampton godly; Thomas Ball and some of Woodford's closest godly friends such as Thomas Pentlow and Thomas Martin seem to have acted as his campaign organizers. Ball persuaded a local godly colleague to preach in favour of Pickering's election and was later accused, with some of the aldermen, of browbeating the mayor of the town to do the same. Pentlow was charged with stating that no deputy lieutenant was eligible to stand since they were questionable in parliament for their part in raising conduct money for the Bishops' Wars.[95] This was a very serious charge. Recorded statements such as this connecting disapproval of conduct money with opposition to the war are necessarily very rare, since the Scots had, of course, been declared traitors. The defendants were also charged collectively with shouting 'A Pickering a Pickering, no Elmes, no deputy lieutenants' in the castle yard on the day of the election. Woodford maintained a characteristically low profile, but he certainly joined Pickering at Northampton, was polled for him, and described his eventual triumph as being 'to the joy of the harts of god's people'.[96] Thus even the timid diarist was able to take some political action albeit as a member of an anonymous crowd. Subsequently, there is clear evidence that these elections made issues public that had previously lain beneath the surface, and revealed deep rifts in county opinion. Woodford records visiting the house of Sir John Isham after the election where he had formerly found good hospitality. Isham was himself a moderate but Woodford found that 'his carriage was altered towards me in respect that I was for Sir Guilbt Pickeringe at the eleccon'.[97]

The policies of the 1630s appear to have revealed an ideological division between those such as the future royalist divine Robert Sibthorpe who perceived a threat to monarchy by seditious puritan popularity, and those godly such as Woodford, who by 1637 accepted not only the

94 Diary, pp. 456–8. Bodleian Library, Bankes MSS, 65/62. In this letter, which is written from Kingsthorpe (Dr Clarke's benefice), 'our doctor' is said to be canvassing for Elmes.
95 Bankes MSS, 44/13: Bedfordshire Record Office, St John (Bletso) MSS, 1369. Thirteen, including those mentioned, were called before the council. The matter was referred to Attorney General Bankes, and on his advice the king and council discharged them: Bankes MSS 42/55, 13/23: P. R. O., P. C. 2/52/427, 2/52/429. 2/52/471, S. P. 16/452/16, 452/56, 452/110, 473/24. I am very grateful to Nigel Jackson for references to the Bankes MSS.
96 Diary, pp. 456–7.
97 Ibid. p. 467.

assumptions but also the specifics of the arguments of a popish plot adduced by John Pym and others in the 1620s and again in the Grand Remonstrance. Unfortunately, little is known of Woodford's subsequent ideas and actions. He resisted the impulse to separation as yet, but his grave misgivings concerning Charles I laid the ground for his approval of limitations on the prerogative. Once the Long Parliament met, he was indeed afforded opportunities which were absent in the 1630s to pursue his enemies. His diary-keeping lapsed since its author was too busy helping to prosecute Sibthorpe and Clarke at the Committee for Religion, seeking redress of Thomas Bacon's grievances, and drawing up an anti-episcopal petition for his home county, to make time to write.[98] By April 1641 with Laud, Strafford and Wren out of the way, he was ready to see not only an end to episcopacy but a wholesale purge of the clergy of the sort undertaken by parliament after the Civil Wars; he called on god to:

> bring in the remaynder of the gentiles in America and otherwhere, and let the spirit of reformacon passe through this Iland and Ireland, and the adiacent kingdomes, pull downe that cursed Antichrist of Rome that Babilon the great . . . thou seest how the wicked B[isho]ps limbs of him here in this Kingdome have even darkened the sunne in the heavens thereof, and brought up a fog over the whole nacon, Lord cast them off roote and branch, in one day forever extirpate their hierarchy and set the Lord Christ upon his throne amongst us – breake the yoke of the oppressor as in the day of Midian. Strengthen the Parliam[en]t to that end.[99]

Robert Woodford's diary clearly has much to tell us about the way English politics were conducted before the Civil War. The diary reveals a high level of political consciousness amongst provincial townsmen, and demonstrates that it was not only clerics, Londoners and men with influential patrons who could have an informed view of the political crisis of the later 1630s. In some senses Woodford cannot be seen as being purely provincial: he had family, and business contacts in the capital. Of course, Woodford's level of religious commitment was out of the ordinary, but he can nevertheless be seen as a typical representative of that burgeoning local professional class made up of clerics, schoolmasters, and minor attorneys, which had developed in every English provincial town.[100] Yet if a high level of political consciousness was evident in the diarist's social circle, it is equally clear that severe restrictions existed upon the discussion of issues and upon the public expression of views

98 Ibid. pp. 518, 522, 534, 537. I cannot find any reference to this petition.
99 Diary, pp. 542–3.
100 Brooks, *Pettyfoggers*, passim.

like Woodford's which were opposed to those of the regime.[101] Another crucial hindrance was Woodford's lack of a powerful patron to protect him, with the result that he was forced to sublimate his views to preserve his career. It is disappointing that so little is known of his subsequent activities. His name does not appear in the papers of the Northampton County Committee during the Interregnum, but he certainly continued as steward throughout the rule of the Rump until his death in 1654. He was one of that tide of lesser men who came to prominence in those years through their acceptance of the legitimacy of the new regime. Indeed his close friend Thomas Pentlow was the most vigorous Northamptonshire J. P. in the years after the execution of the king in 1649, and it is significant that the climax of his own career, his undershrievalty, came in 1653/4, the first year of the Protectorate of Oliver Cromwell.[102]

101   For a discussion of the limits imposed upon political discussion, see Cust, 'News and politics', pp. 88–9.
102   P. R. Brindle, Politics and society in Northamptonshire 1649–1714 (unpublished Ph.D. thesis, University of Leicester, 1983), p. 138.

5

Why did Charles I Call the Long Parliament?

Conrad Russell

Originally appeared as Conrad Russell, 'Why did Charles I Call the Long Parliament?' in *History* 69. Copyright © 1984 Blackwell Publishers, Oxford.

At first sight, it might appear a superfluous exercise to explain why Charles I called the Long Parliament. Like so many other decisions of his, it may perfectly well be explained on grounds of necessity. After the battle of Newburn, on 28 August 1640, Charles faced the combination of a victorious invading army of Scots in front of him, and an empty treasury and public disaffection behind him. The Privy Council in London were advising him that they lacked the power to force any further supplies of men or money.[1] Moreover, since the line of the Tees is not defensible, Charles's forces had no secure line of defence behind which they could re-group. If Charles could not fight without a Parliament, he could not negotiate without a Parliament either, since the invading Scots were insisting that they would not consider any peace treaty unless it were confirmed by an English Parliament.[2] Since Charles had so little choice in the matter, it is perhaps necessary to say why his decision to call a Parliament needs explanation.

The decision to call a Parliament was not a substitute for a policy, but a choice of forum in which to pursue one. To explain events in any Parliament, it is necessary to understand the purposes the Crown called it to serve. Did Charles call the Long Parliament in order to retreat from the Scottish war on the most face-saving terms possible, or in order to

---

1 *Clarendon State Papers* ii 97–8. (Public Record Office) S(tate) P(apers) 16/466/1 and 5 appear to be rough notes for parts of this document. I would like to thank Professor Caroline Hibbard for reading and commenting on an earlier draft of this article.
2 S.P. 16/466/36, 467/5, 469/62.

gain English support for a renewed attempt to enforce the Scottish Prayer Book? Did he intend the calling of the Parliament as a cosmetic gesture to enable him to continue his English policies, or did he accept the advice of his Privy Council that the top priority was 'the uniting of your Majesty and your subjects together, the want whereof the Lords conceive is the source of all the present troubles'? This memorandum of the Privy Council appears to have begun the scheme for Charles to broaden the basis of his regime by taking some of his critics into his Council.[3] It is important to know whether, when the Parliament met, Charles appreciated that any such scheme would involve significant changes in his policies. Did Charles intend to make a virtue of necessity, and announce an about-turn in policy, or did he mean to hold what the French Ambassador, before the Short Parliament, called a 'Parlement à sa mode', an assembly which would virtuously rubber-stamp what he intended to do anyway?[4]

In the country at large, the decision to call the Long Parliament was one of the most popular decisions Charles ever took. This was in part because of attachment to Parliaments *per se*, a sentiment which had always been strong, and which Ship Money and the Bishops' Wars appeared to have strengthened.[5] Yet the enthusiasm for a Parliament was not merely about the chance to have a meeting: it was also because conventional wisdom associated the calling of Parliaments with specific policies which were more likely to find support in Parliaments than outside them. The petition of the twelve peers is a good example of this association. Among these policies, Dr Hibbard has mentioned alliance with France, hostility to Spain and criticism of the Laudian church as policies pro-Parliamentary Councillors were likely to associate with the calling of a Parliament.[6] By 1640, this list should include abandonment of the Scottish Prayer Book and the end of the Scottish Wars. Before the Short Parliament, George Wyllys, writing to his father in Connecticut, found the prospect of a Parliament 'gives many hopes of better times and a thorough settlement of a peace with the Scotts'.[7] Before the Long Parliament, Rossingham

3 *Clarendon State Papers, ubisupra.*
4 P.R.O. 31/3/71, p. 154.
5 Anthony Fletcher, *The Outbreak of the English Civil War* (New York and London, 1981), pp. 1–2; Esther Cope, *The Life of a Public Man: Edward, First Baron Montagu of Boughton* (Philadelphia, 1981), pp. 160–167, and Kenneth Fincham. 'The Judges' Decision on Ship Money in February 1637: The Reaction in Kent', *Bulletin of the Institute of Historical Research* 57 (1984).
6 Caroline Hibbard, *Charles I and the Popish Plot* (Chapel Hill, 1983), p. 21.
7 George Wyllys the younger to George Wyllys the elder, 8 April 1640, *Wyllys Papers*, Connecticut Historical Society, vol. 21, p. 9. The younger Wyllys had returned from Connecticut in order to sell the family land in England.

reported to Conway that 'we are all mad with joy here, that his Matie does call his Parliament, and that he puts the Scotch business into the hands of his peers, who, the hope is here, will make peace upon any condicions'.[8] The Parliament was so widely welcomed partly because it was thought to symbolize a decision for peace with Scotland. It is then important, in judging Charles's relations with the Long Parliament, to know whether he understood or shared the symbolism associated with its calling.

The story begins with the English defeat at Newburn, on 28 August 1640. This rapidly led to a decision to summon a Great Council of Peers, which met at York on 24 September 1640. Charles announced his decision to call a Parliament in his opening speech to the Council of Peers. The Parliament was called for 3 November, leaving the statutory minimum of forty days between the issue of the writs and the meeting of the Parliament.

After the defeat at Newburn, the King seems to have remained determined to continue fighting,[9] while a group of Privy Councillors, among whom Secretary Vane is the best documented, became more and more articulate in their determination to get out of the war on the best terms possible. By 20 September, the peace faction on the Council appeared to have prevailed, and Vane reported to Roe that 'for ventringe all of a day, I conceive there is no danger of that'.[10]

During the period before the meeting of the Council of Peers, the Privy Council twice discussed the possible calling of a Parliament. The first time, in the week of Newburn, it discussed whether to call a Parliament or a Council of Peers. The rival arguments were those of Dorset and Cottington. Dorset's view was that since a Parliament would happen anyway, the Council rather than the peers should get the credit for advising the King to call it. Cottington's advice, which prevailed, was to let the peers take the responsibility for advising Charles to call a Parliament.[11] The second time, on 16 September, the Privy Council explicitly advised a Parliament, apparently on the motion of Arundel and Laud. This advice had reached Charles by 18 September, but Vane still reported that 'I doe not finde in his Matie yett any certaine resolution for the same'.[12]

Six days later, the King had not merely taken his decision, but announced it. Vane, whether by inside information or by a lucky guess,

---

8 S.P. 16/468/86. See also P.R.O. 31/3/72, p. 269 for the French ambassador's belief that the calling of the Parliament implied peace with Scotland.
9 S.P. 16/466/28, 467/28, 467/101.
10 S.P. 16/467/120.
11 S.P. 16/466/11 and 12.
12 S.P. 16/467/75 and 101.

foresaw the decision before it was announced.[13] There is no reason to suppose the decision was known to anyone else before it was made public. Indeed, there is some evidence that it was *not* known to some key people before it was made public. In deciding to call a Parliament in exactly forty days from his announcement, Charles put the Lord Keeper and the Clerk of the Crown under considerable pressure to issue the writs promptly. In his speech to the Council of Peers, Charles, using the past tense, claimed that he had 'already given order to my Lo. Keeper to issue the writs instantly'.[14] Charles's use of the past tense appears to be incorrect. The Lord Keeper's instruction to the Clerk of the Crown to send out the writs instantly, and to remember to date them that day, is written on the bottom of a list of commissioners chosen to negotiate with the Scots. These commissioners were not chosen till the afternoon after the King's speech. With this letter, Vane sent a message from the King asking for the Queen to be told of the decision for a Parliament, so it would appear that she too had no advance knowledge of the decisions.[15]

Charles, as he said, took the decision to call the Long Parliament 'of my selfe'. In this, it was like many of Charles's major decisions: he had taken advice, but the final decision was a solitary one, and the thoughts which led to it were not shared with anyone. It is, then, necessary to explain Charles's decision, not in terms of the advice he received, but in terms of his own words and actions. The speech in which he announced the decision shows that, at this date, he had not seen any connection between calling a Parliament and making peace. It is a thoroughly belligerent speech. He told the peers they had been called because of sudden invasion, and 'this being our condicion at this tyme, and an army of rebells lodged within this kingdome, I thought it most fitt to conforme myselfe to the practise of my predecessors in like cases, that with your advice and assistance wee might iointly proceede to the chastisement of these insolencies, and securing of my good subjects'. At the time Charles announced the decision to call a Parliament, he saw it in conjunction with a desire to continue the Scottish war.

That afternoon's debate in the Council of Peers might have done something to show Charles that he was following two incompatible policies. It was begun by a motion by Bristol to enter into treaty with the rebels. According to Vane, 'most lords' believed they had it in their power to make peace, and this should probably be interpreted as meaning that

13 S.P. 16/467/135.
14 For this and subsequent quotations from the King's speech at York, see S.P. 16/468/1.
15 S.P. 16/468/16 and 22.

they wished to do so. The peers' choice of commissioners to negotiate with the Scots strengthened the impression that they were opposed to the war. About half the commissioners chosen were signatories of the petition of the twelve peers, and none of them was a known supporter of the war. Vane, emboldened by the pacific sentiment around him, plucked up courage to tell Windebank that 'I told you so', and said that the Councillors going south at the end of the Council would tell Windebank 'many good passages' in which 'the Earl of Bristol hath spoken much and freely'.[16]

This impression of 'a free and frank exchange of views' is strengthened by the official communiqué of the Council of Peers. This document, signed by 57 peers for the benefit of potential lenders in the City of London, is drawn up in careful antiphonal phrases which seem designed to give full weight to both sides in a debate. The antiphonal phrases perhaps represent a debate inside the committee responsible for drafting the letter, which consisted of Strafford, Finch, Manchester, Bristol, Hertford, Bedford, North, Goring, Littleton, Bankes and Vane. The peers said they were treating for:

> such an accommodation as may tend to the honner of his matie and ye perfect union of both kingdomes; wherein as wee rest most assure that his Matie will bee no way wanting in his grace and goodnesse to listen to the just and reasonable demands of his subjects of Scotland; so, if they shall insist upon terms dishonnerable for his Matie and ye English nation to condiscend unto, wee should all hold our selves obliged in honner and duty to preserve and defend this kingdome from all invasions and spoyles by any kind of enemy whatsoever.[17]

These exchanges with the peers might have marked the point at which Charles was persuaded to abandon the Scottish war, and the antiphonal phrases might have been intended to save the royal face.

16   S.P. 16/468/23, 39, 83. The Venetian Ambassador claimed that *all* of these 16 commissioners had declared themselves in favour of the Scots, and were 'equally zealous' for the calling of a Parliament. The assertion is not now verifiable, but it is probably only a slight exaggeration. *CSPV 1640–2* p. 86, 2/12 October 1640.

17   West Devon Record Office, Drake of Colyton MSS 1700/M CP 17: Alnwick MSS vol. 15, British Library Microfilm no. 286, f. 98 r–v. I am grateful to His Grace the Duke of Northumberland for permission to use these MSS. The word 'communiqué' may sound anachronistic, but I can think of no other accurate description of the type of document involved. Hardwicke State Papers, London 1778, ii 213. All the other documents in this section of the Hardwicke collection are from genuine originals in State Papers. It appears probable that this is a perhaps imperfect transcript of Sir John Borough's original notes, and that the original has disappeared from State Papers between 1778 and the making of the *Calendar*.

Yet, though the communiqué alone might have borne such an interpretation, it will not bear it when seen in the context in which Charles placed it. For Charles, it seems that 'terms dishonnerable' meant anything which conceded more than the Pacification of Berwick, in which Charles had refused to abandon either the Scottish Prayer Book or Scottish episcopacy.[18] If these were Charles's objectives, then, whether Charles knew it or not, they were ones which could not be achieved without war.

The impression that Charles gave this communiqé a hard line interpretation is strengthened by the words in which Windebank, who had not been at York, but was in close contact with the King, reported it to Hopton in Madrid. Windebank's version was this:

> if they [the Scots] will accept of such conditions for theire return into
> Scotland as shalbe thought fitt, they will have an offer of such made unto
> them: but if they shall refuse such reasonable and fayre conditions, they
> are to be pursued by force as traitors. . . . If either this money be leavied,
> or the nobility will continue firme to his Maty for the repulsion of the
> Scotts, there is no doubt but this black storme wilbe dispersed[19]

The most interesting word in this report is the verb 'continue'. The record of what happened at York has never looked to anyone else as if the peers were 'firme to his Maty for the repulsion of the Scotts'. If Charles had got this impression, he must have treated attempts to preserve the minimum appearance of courtesy as expressions of support for a possible resumption of the war. If so, he was desperately deluded. It is also hard to remember, reading Windebank's confident phrases, that he was making plans for a *defeated* army.

It appears, then, that Charles came south to meet his Parliament still believing that he could impose on the Scots terms resembling those which had originally provoked the war, and that he would enjoy public support for resuming the war if the Scots did not meekly agree to such terms and make themselves scarce. Maybe, as Clarendon suggests, he had become convinced that a Parliament would be more sensible of his

18   S. R. Gardiner, *History of England* (1893), ix 209: David Stevenson, *The Scottish Revolution* (Newton Abbot, 1973), p. 211. *Hardwicke* S.P. ii 220–223.
19   Bodleian Library, MSS Clarendon, vol. 19, no. 1437, 1 October 1640. In citing Clarendon MSS, I have used the piece numbers from the Ogle and Bliss Catalogue, rather than folio numbers. The money to which Windebank refers was to be borrowed by the peers from the City of London to keep the King's army together until negotiations were completed. It was not intended to finance a resumption of war. A week earlier, on 24 September, Windebank had told Hopton that the rebels must be chased out, and the only way to do *this* was judged to be the speedy calling of a Parliament. *Ibid* no. 1430.

honour than the commissioners who were negotiating at Ripon. As Charles put it in the Council of Peers on 6 October, he hoped it would be 'a shock of Parliament to give invaders or rebels money'. At moments during this day's debate, Charles seems to have been trying to get the Council of Peers to support resuming the war rather than accept the Scots' financial demands in the Treaty of Ripon. He asked 'whether better to give rebels money or to stop them?' and 'whether to give them any thing, or remove them by force'.[20] As Clarendon also suggested, Strafford was still prepared to think of resuming the war.[21] Strafford contained his anti-Scottish feelings until the Scots' financial demands were made known, and then began to argue, with the accuracy of a self-fulfilling prophecy, that 'to grant them any dishonourable terms, he will first die'. On 17 October he quarrelled sharply with Lord Keeper Finch, who had called it a 'hopeful treaty'. Under extreme pressure from Bristol, he reluctantly conceded what the King would not concede, that he 'would not answer for the success' of a battle. He did, however, offer to bring over the Irish army at two days' notice, if he were given shipping. It is in these last debates at the Council of Peers that Strafford, as he in part foresaw, ensured that he would be cast as a scapegoat for the Scottish war. For whatever reason, Charles seems to have been quite unable to imagine that a Parliament, faced with a rebellious and invading army, could have any reaction but a desire to get it out again. It is possible to understand Charles's bewilderment, since English willingness to back a Scottish invading army against their own king is a somewhat startling phenomenon. Yet, bewildered, and even outraged, though Charles may have been entitled to be, after the debates at York, his belief that he could gain Parliamentary support for resuming the war cannot be classified in terms less harsh than a flight from reality.

When the Parliament met, on 3 November, Charles began by telling them that if what he had said about the Scots to the Short Parliament had been believed, none of this trouble would have happened, 'but it is no wonder that men are soe slow to believe that soe great sedition should be raysed upon so little ground'. The belief that the Scots had rebelled on a 'little ground' is a somewhat startling one. For agenda, Charles said he would not mention the 'support' he was justly entitled to expect, since there were at that time 'twoe points merely considerable. First

20   *Hardwicke S.P.* ii 241–6.
21   Edward, Earl of Clarendon, *History of the Rebellion* (Oxford, 1732), I 159. Hardwicke S.P. ii 246–7 (6 October), 264, 266 (12 October), 279, 280 (17 October), 284, 287, 288 (18 October). For the King answering Bristol's questions by maintaining that the army was strong enough to fight, see *ibid.* 230 (28 September).

the chasing out of the rebells, and the other is the satisfying your just grievances'.[22]

This speech seems to have caused some surprise, since two days later, Charles came back to 'explain myselfe'.[23] He repeated that the Scots were rebels, but said that since he was in treaty with them, they were his good subjects too. He said he hoped the treaty would have been concluded by this time, but, after his attempts to give a soothing impression, concluded with the words: 'I doubt not but by your assistance I shall make them know their dutyes or by your assistance make them returne whether they will or noe'. Between the two speeches, Charles had made a tactical retreat. In the first speech, he proposed war. In the second, he offered the Scots the chance to avoid war by withdrawing and conceding most of the points in dispute, with the threat of war to follow if they did not do so. It is a retreat which probably seemed less significant to others than it did to Charles.

It seems clear, then, that Charles called the Long Parliament in the hope of getting Parliamentary support to resume the war against the Scots. In this, he had made a grievous misjudgement of the public mood. In taking his decision, he was following his own counsel. He had, in the main, concealed his intention from his Councillors, and seems to have regarded his lonely decision to call a Parliament as an appeal, over his Councillors' heads, to a wider public from which he had expected a greater concern for his honour. Moreover, he expected, in a way reminiscent of 1628, that the Parliament would tackle the Scots *first*, before dealing with the domestic situation. What Charles meant by *just* grievances there is no source to tell us, but his use of the phrase in 1626 and 1628 suggests that he placed considerable limiting force on the adjective. The Privy Council, on hearing of the decision to call a Parliament, had assumed it was to be followed by an announcement of the abolition of Ship Money,[24] but when the Parliament met, no such plan was in evidence. There was counsel available to Charles to tell him that he could not expect a Parliament to take action against the Scots before they had dealt with their own frustrations. On 22 October Northumberland wrote to his brother-in-law Leicester:

22   Neither of Charles's opening speeches is noted in the *Journals*: see no. 33 below. The speech of 3 November survives in House of Lords Main Papers, 3 November 1640, S.P. 16/471/13 and Bodleian Library MS Clarendon vol. 19, no. 1446. There are verbal variations of no great apparent significance between these texts. I have used the House of Lords text on grounds of provenance.
23   House of Lords Main Papers, 5 November 1640.
24   S.P. 16/468/17, undated Privy Council notes in the hand of Edward Nicholas. These must be dated between 24 September and 3 November 1640, and the editors of the *Calendar* are probably right in assigning them to the earlier part of this range.

untill we have setled those points that were in agitation the last
Parlament, wch was matters of religion, proprietie of goods, and
libertie of person, and peradventure some others, we shall hardly
bring the Parlament to any resolution that may free us from this army
of rebells.[25]

This, as the event showed, was a more accurate assessment of the situation than Charles's own, but it represented a line of policy which, every time he had the choice, he rejected.[26]

The House of Commons almost totally ignored the agenda Charles had proposed for them. There was just one moment when they paid attention to the type of arguments Charles wanted them to discuss. This was on the morning of 10 November when Sir William Widdrington, knight of the shire for Northumberland, delivered a petition about the distress of the occupied county of Northumberland. This, if anything, should have been the cue for the sort of patriotic anti-Scottish reaction Charles expected. In the course of his speech, Widdrington, like Charles, called the Scots 'invading rebels'. Immediately, Holles and Glyn moved that he should either explain himself or be punished. Widdrington, somewhat ambiguously, said he 'called them no more rebells seing his Majestie called them otherwise', and the matter was allowed to drop with a note that his words were 'ordered to be entred in the Journal as language disliked by the House'.[27]

The Widdrington case raises the question of the exceptional silence of the anti-Scots in the second half of 1640. Charles was right that there was still a considerable body of anti-Scottish sentiment in England, and it can still be found in private letters. Young Richard Dyott, for example, regarded the twelve peers as, in effect, in collusion with the enemy.[28] Hyde's correspondents Archdeacon Marler and Thomas Triplett (admittedly both clergy) continued to express anti-Scottish sentiments.[29] Why did these not surface in public until very much later in the Long Parliament? It is possible that the fact of Widdrington deterred others who might have wished to speak to the same effect. Free speech in the Long

25   Kent Archive Office, U 1475/C.44. I am grateful to Viscount De L'Isle and Dudley, VC., KG., for permission to quote from these papers.
26   Caroline Hibbard, *op. cit.* p. 227.
27   *The Journal of Sir Symonds D'Ewes*, vol. I, ed. W. Notestein (New Haven, 1923), pp. 20, 531. *Commons' Journals* II 25. See also Sir John Holland's speech of 9 November which appears to follow the York communiqué, D'Ewes, *op. cit.* p. 16.
28   Staffs. R. O. Dyott MSS, D 661/11/1/5. (7 September 1640).
29   Bodleian Library MSS Clarendon, vol. 20, nos. 1506, 1514, 1528. See Triplett's suggestion (no. 1514) that Alderman Abell's fine should go towards paying the Scots, 'and so lett Abell pay Caine'. (The Scots were requesting a 'Brotherly Assistance'.)

Parliament, as Gervase Holles, Digby, Palmer and Dering were all to discover, was somewhat selective.

However, it is more important that from the battle of Newburn onwards, there were two different lines of criticism of the Scottish war. These lines started from ideologically different positions, but led to practically similar conclusions. For Denzil Holles and Glyn, criticism of the war was based on the fundamentalist assumption that the Scots were right. There is no reason to suppose that the whole country had suddenly been converted to this very Calvinist view. Its strength can only be assessed on later evidence, but on that, it looks as if it appealed to about half the House of Commons. The other line of criticism, with which Vane, Arundel, Northumberland and Bristol should be associated, involved no objection of principle to the Scottish war. To these critics, the war was wrong because it had failed.[30] It had proved, as the Privy Council pointed out on 3 September, unduly divisive in English politics. Moreover, because it had ended in defeat, it had left the King in a very dangerous situation from which he could only extricate himself by cutting his losses and unambiguously making peace. The key spokesman for this case was Bristol. As he put it in the Council of Peers on 26 September 'if his Majesty were in case, it were best to bring them on their knees. But now, considering their strength, Newcastle and the two provinces taken, we must now speak of the business, as to men that have gotten these advantages'. On 12 January 1641, Bristol outlined the case for the treaty to the Lords. He said many might think it a dishonour to relieve an invading army, but it was not so 'as the case now standeth'. He said the nation 'could hardlie be brought to this condicon, were it not for want of unitie and discord amongst ourselves'. He regarded the restoration of unity as an essential preliminary to the recovery of the nation's honour.[31] People of this stamp were never pro-Scottish, but the time when they rallied to an anti-Scottish line was in the spring of 1641, when it became apparent that the Scots were endeavouring to interfere in an *English* settlement.[32] It was this line of criticism, that the policy needed to be abandoned *because* it had failed, which moved most of those on whom Charles might otherwise have relied for ideological support. Charles had no excuse

30 For Northumberland's views see K.A.O. U 1475 C 85/3 (7 November 1639) and C 44 (22 October 1640) on the Scots, and *ibid.* C 2/42 (7 May 1640) and C 85/17 (18 June 1640) on the impracticality of the war.
31 *Hardwicke S.P.* ii 225: Bodleian Library MS Dep. C.165 (Nalson Ms 13), 12 January 1640/1. See also *H.M.C. 10th Rep.* VI, p. 137.
32 For an early attempt to rally anti-Scottish sentiment, led by Hyde, Capel, Strangeways and Hopton, see the debate of 27 February 1641. D'Ewes, *op. cit.* pp. 417–8.

for being unaware of this line, since it was widely held within his own Privy Council.

It was Charles's failure to understand that most of his potential friends had been convinced by this case that left him so startlingly isolated in November 1640. This isolation had profound political consequences in his relations with the Parliament. When the Long Parliament met, they, and many of the Privy Council too, were looking for symbols of Charles's willingness to abandon the policies with which Laud and Ship Money were associated, since the conventional wisdom of November 1640 was that, right or wrong, these policies had ceased to be viable. The longer such a change of policy was put off, the bigger the symbols needed to convince members that it was being undertaken would grow. The later Charles's concessions came, the bigger they would need to be.

It is a crucial misfortune for all concerned that it was not until early December that Charles was convinced it was necessary for him to make peace with his Scottish subjects and make concessions to his English ones. In the first month of the Parliament, when such a policy would have been easiest to follow, there was a deafening silence from the King. This silence did much to establish the Parliament as a sort of alternative government, paying the armies and negotiating with the Scots while they waited for the King to wake up to the true situation. This royal inability to perceive the true situation did much to begin the Privy Council's and the Long Parliament's habit of carrying on government as if the King were incapacitated. When someone wanted to look at his speech of 5 November, threatening war against the Scots, it is no surprise to find that Secretary Vane, as a good servant, claimed to have 'lost' it.[33] In the growth of the tendency to push the King into a back seat, and in the ultimate failure to reach a settlement between him and the Long Parliament, this month's delay before Charles could believe the evidence of his own ears may have a greater importance than it has ever been given.

33　H.M.C. De L'Isle and Dudley, VI 370–1. Vane had lost the clerk's original, and it was claimed that 'no other copie can be had'.

6

Why did Charles I Fight the Civil War?

Conrad Russell

Originally appeared as Conrad Russell, 'Why did Charles I Fight the Civil War?' in *History Today* 34. Copyright © 1984 History Today Ltd, London.

Civil wars are like other quarrels: it takes two to make them. It is, then, something of a curiosity that we possess no full analysis of why Charles I chose to fight a Civil War in 1642. Yet the early seventeenth century was in many ways a good period for gentry, and a bad period for kings. If we were to search the period for long-term reasons why the King might have wanted to fight a Civil War, we would find the task far easier than it has ever been to find long-term causes why the gentry might have wanted to fight a Civil War.

Why, then, has the task never been attempted? The trouble, I think, comes from our reliance on the concept of 'revolution.' Revolutions are thought of as things done *to* the head of state and not *by* him. The result is that Charles has been treated as if he were largely passive in the drift to Civil War, as a man who reacted to what others did, rather than doing much to set the pace himself. This picture is definitely incorrect. Whether the notion of an 'English Revolution' is also incorrect is a question I will not discuss here. Anyone who is determined to find an 'English Revolution' should not be looking here, but later on, in the years 1647–1653, and those years are outside the scope of this article. This article is concerned with the outbreak of Civil War, an event in which the King was a very active participant.

If we look carefully at the slow process of escalation by which the political crisis of 1640 was transformed into the Civil War of 1642, it was usually Charles who raised the stakes by introducing threats of force. It was Charles, in August 1642, who raised his standard and legally began a state of war. This fact repeated a pattern which was already visible. In January 1642, it was Charles who left London, and thereby first separated the combatants into two armed camps. The physical division of the political community caused by the rival summonses to rally to York and to Westminister made an enormous contribution to the creation of an atmosphere in which Civil War became a real possibility. Moreover, the week before Charles left London, it was he who brought armed guards to arrest the Five Members, not the Five Members who brought armed guards to Whitehall Palace.

If we trace the cycle of failed deterrents backwards, and ask who first introduced the threat of armed force, the answer is again Charles. The first threat to use armed force to resolve the deadlock at Westminster was the Army Plot of April and May 1641, and this was clearly Charles's plot. The first Parliamentary strivings towards control of the militia begin the week after the Army Plot, and this is a case where chronology is the best guide to causation. If we go farther back still, and ask who first introduced armed force in the British Isles, the answer is Charles, in the misguided attempt to conquer Scotland, the first round of the conflict which was later localised as the English Civil War.

In the light of these facts, it seems hard to deny that Charles made some contribution to the drift to war. It is, then, important to ask, both how big this contribution was, and what motives, short and long term, might have led Charles to make it.

To understand Charles's contribution, it is necessary to understand the aims of his opponents. They were not aiming at Civil War, though from Charles's point of view, their actions were at least as provocative as if they had been. His opponents were following a strategy with precedents going back at least to Simon de Montfort, in which the object was to impersonalise royal authority by putting it into the hands of a Council and great officers, to be nominated in Parliament and answerable to Parliament. As a Parliamentary declaration put it in May 1642, Charles was to be treated as if he were a minor, a captive or insane. Charles's opponents, many of whom were experienced Privy Councillors, believed government was too important to be left to Kings.

This strategy depended for its success, not on skilled party leadership but on keeping the community united. If it succeeded, there would be no civil war. If it failed, the idea was to be able to blame the King, as Simon de Montfort and Thomas of Lancaster had done, in effect for waging war against his own government. It was thus a secondary objective to be able to blame the King if the strategy failed and fighting did result. This impersonalisation of public authority, under the doctrine of the King's Two Bodies, actually went so deep that Parliamentary declarations complained that gathering of forces round the King might lead to a breach of the King's peace, and that the King's forces might start a 'rebellion'.

Every time this strategy had been used in the past (1215, 1258, 1311, 1386), it had produced the same result. Each time, after a delay of two years or more, it had produced a civil war in which the King had been the apparent aggressor. Each time, the delay in the outbreak of fighting had depended on the length of time the King's critics were in power before they built up their own body of enemies, and thereby presented the King with a party. Each time, this baronial strategy had forced the King to play a waiting game, until he could divide his critics enough to raise a force and fight back. The situation was one which forced the King to divide the nation, as it forced his opponents to try to unite it. Thus, some part of the appearance that the King began the war is illusory: it is the result of Parliamentarian tactics which put the pressure to fight, and therefore the blame for doing so, squarely onto the King's shoulders.

Yet, though this appearance is in part illusory, it is also in part genuine. True, Charles was under pressure to fight, but it was a pressure he showed no great determination to resist. Indeed, he nearly threw away his chance by trying to fight too soon. Twice, over the Army Plot and over the attempt on the Five Members, Charles moved before the reaction in his favour had gone far enough, and thereby did his critics the priceless service of reuniting them. Richelieu, before the Army Plot, had wisely advised him to wait until the wheel of fortune turned, but Charles was too impatient to take his advice.

Charles, then, had become eager to fight. In creating this eagerness, he was influenced by short-term indignities he suffered during the Long Parliament, but he was also influenced by long-term frustruations, and the study of those frustrations tells us something important about seventeenth-century government.

Among these frustrations, the issue of money is somewhere near the centre of the stage. All through his reign, he had tried to do, and indeed was expected to do, things for which the money was simply not available. On a number of occasions, notably 1626, his Parliaments had made helpful noises about the shortage of money, but no action had ever followed. By August 1642, Charles was quoting Rudyerd's 1626 offer to make him 'safe at home and feared abroad' as simply a piece of mockery. In 1628, after agreeing to the Petition of Right, Charles had expected a grant to allow him to collect Tonnage and Poundage legally, to be faced instead with a remonstrance for collecting it illegally. In 1629, he had called another session of Parliament largely in the hope of getting a legal grant of Tonnage and Poundage, only to find that the Commons wanted instead to punish those who had obeyed his orders to collect it. In 1640, he had listened to Parliamentary offers to give him a legal grant of Tonnage and Poundage and a new book of rates to assess it by. Instead, by the end of 1641, he had been given a series of grants for a few weeks at a time, no new book of rates and an Act of Parliament saying he could not collect it without Parliamentary assent. Since over 50 per cent of his ordinary revenue was covered by Tonnage and Poundage, it is no wonder that Charles's hope of ever getting a permanent grant had grown slim, and his irritation had grown large in proportion.

It was clear by 1642 that royal revenue had failed to keep up with the previous century's inflation. Some major new source of revenue was needed, and Charles was entitled to his scepticism about whether the House of Commons was ever likely to provide it. The Bill of Tonnage and Poundage has been rightly described as 'the bill the Commons never seemed to have time to pass', and other proposals for revenue reform had made even less progress than Tonnage and Poundage. By contrast, Charles's attempts in the 1630s to increase his revenue without Parliamentary assent had been comparatively successful. If, as appears probable, Charles decided sometime around December 1641 that he would never be solvent until he ceased to rely on Parliaments concerned to ease burdens on their constituents, it is not possible to dismiss his conclusion as against the weight of the evidence.

More specifically, Charles appeared to be facing a situation in which he could not fight when relying on Parliaments. Over the century before the Civil War, the costs of war had inflated more than most other costs, and the growth of firearms, together with the need for standardisation they implied, had increased the proportion of military costs which had to fall on public funds. In 1624–5, Charles believed with some plausibility that he had entered into a war with Spain which a Parliament really wanted him to undertake, only to find, when the war came, that the next Parliament would only vote a paltry supply, and the next none at all unless they could impeach his chief minister. Yet in 1626, even the sums the Commons had offered to vote if they could impeach Buckingham were less than half what the King needed. What was the point of making his peace with Parliaments, at great political cost, if they did not then give him enough to avoid arbitrary taxes likely to lead to another crisis? No king during the Thirty Years' War could accept a situation in which he could never fight. If Charles, as appeared likely, could never fight with parliaments, he might have to make himself able to fight without them.

It was also Charles's misfortune to rule at about the time when the Augsburg principle of *cuius regio, eius religio* became out of date. With each generation since the Reformation, confessional loyalties became more established, and therefore harder to change with a change of monarch. When Charles looked back at the history of the Church of England, he could see that Henry VIII, Edward VI, Mary, Elizabeth, and to an extent James had all been able to make it in their own image. In trying to introduce Laud's brand of ceremonial Arminianism, Charles was only trying to do what they had done. Moreover, this commitment seems to have been, for Charles, something which was not negotiable. Even in January 1641, when he went farther in exploring possible concessions than at any time before or after, he still hoped the Arminian William Juxon could succeed Laud as Archbishop. If he hoped, as he appears to have done, that he could have Juxon as Archbishop at the same time as he had Bedford as Lord Treasurer and Pym as Chancellor of the Exchequer, he was living in cloud cuckoo land. He simply did not see that what had been perfectly possible for Edward VI and Mary was not possible for him. If he believed, as he appears to have done, that a situation in which he could not enforce his own religion was one in which he would have lost a substantial part of his authority, we must allow that he was probably right. Since both Charles and his critics took it for granted that religious unity must be enforced, if Charles could not enforce his religion on the country, he would have to let the country enforce theirs on him. One may understand why he found such a notion a threat to his authority.

The belief that it was the duty of a ruler to enforce uniformity in the true religion was one which caused difficulties for other authorities, as well as Charles I. A century after the Reformation, religious choice was too established a fact to be very easily denied, and rulers who believed that it was their duty to enforce one form of religion were increasingly obviously setting themselves an impossible task. Philip II in the Netherlands failed in this task for reasons not altogether different from those of Charles I. Both felt themselves obliged to fight rather than give up the struggle.

Other rulers in Europe also found it difficult to achieve harmony between multiple kingdoms, but Charles was the only one who faced the problem of religious unity blended with the problems of multiple kingdoms. For him, then, the problem of religious unity was one of unity between kingdoms, even more than of unity within one kingdom. On this point, Charles's Scottish opponents agreed with him. They too thought that unless there was unity of religion and church government between England and Scotland, there would be permanent instability. Just as Charles was prepared to fight to enforce English religion on Scotland, so the Scots were prepared to fight (and remained so through the Civil War), to enforce Scottish religion on England. Charles, moreover, did not only have a King of England's resistance to Scottish notions of Presbyterianising England: he also had to view such a proposal through the eyes of the King of Ireland. A religious settlement in which it would have been a key point that no papists were to be tolerated would hardly have led to stability in Ireland, and any responsible King of Ireland had to resist such a proposal, by force if need be. Of all the participants in the crisis of 1640–42, Charles was the only one whose position forced him to a genuinely British perspective, which did a lot to restrict his freedom of manoeuvre. It was also his British perspective which led him, back in 1639, to start the war against the Scots from which all the later troubles followed. In thinking of his supposed duty to achieve religious unity between all the parts of the British Isles, Charles could well have repeated Laud's words on his appointment to Canterbury: 'there is more expected of me than the craziness of these times will give me leave to do'.

Indeed, if one were to write a job description of the British monarchy in the early seventeenth century, it would not be an attractive one. The King was expected to cut a major European figure on an income which bore no comparison with those of his European colleagues, and to do so without raising illegal taxes. He was expected, in religion, to enforce both unity and truth, while anyone who did not believe that what he was enforcing was the truth could exclaim: 'we ought to obey God rather than man'. He was expected to solve the problem of multiple kingdoms, in a context in which religious differences merged with the various nationalisms of his kingdoms. The tasks conventional contemporary opinion assigned to Charles I were ones no ordinary political skills could have discharged, and if he finally tried to cut the Gordian knot, we should, perhaps, not be too surprised. It is certainly easier to understand why sheer frustration might have driven Charles to fight than it has ever been to understand why the English gentry might have wanted to make a revolution against him.

For further reading

S. R. Gardiner, *History of England* vols ix and x. (Longman, 1893); Valerie Pearl, *London and the Puritan Revolution*, (Oxford University Press 1961); G. E. Aylmer, *The King's Servants* (Routledge and Kegan Paul, 1961); Caroline Hibbard, *Charles I and the Popish Plot* (University of North Carolina Press, 1983); Anthony Fletcher, *The Outbreak of the English Civil War* (Edward Arnold, 1981); David Stevenson, *The Scottish Revolution* (David and Charles, 1973); *A New History if Ireland*, vol. III, ed. T. W. Moody, F. X. Martin and F. J. Byrne (Oxford University Press, 1976).

Part III The Course of the Civil War

Introduction to Part III

Historical research into the course of the English civil war which formally began on 22 August 1642, when Charles I raised his standard, and which ended in summer 1646 with a complete military victory for parliament, has generated far fewer disputes and divergent theories than has research on the causes of the war. We are, after all, now considering just four years rather than interpreting four decades or more. The different approaches adopted by historians working on causation are also found in studies of the course of the war. Thus some civil war historians adopt a top-down viewpoint, focusing on the political and/or military leadership, while others take a bottom-up approach, exploring the world of the common people, soldiers and civilians; some adopt an urban, county or regional perspective; yet others explore the war as a national (that is, English and Welsh) or a 'British' conflict. As before, historians examine or emphasize different aspects or elements of the story – political, military, administrative, religious, social, economic, elite, popular and so forth. However, with relatively few exceptions, work on the course of the war has not given rise to major and durable historical debates, to fundamental divisions comparable with, say, the controversies over class-based interpretations of the causes of the war which dominated the historiography of the middle decades of the twentieth century.

The broad military outline of the civil war has long been well-established. Most historians accept and retell a similar account of the national war, stressing the campaigns and battles of the major or combined armies – the indecisive campaigning during the opening months, with the drawn battle of Edgehill, the royalist victories and territorial advances of 1643, and the parliamentarian fight-back thereafter, including victory in the north in 1644, associated especially with the battle of Marston Moor, and in the midlands in spring and summer 1645, associated especially with the battle of Naseby, and the 'mopping up' of the latter half of 1645 and the first half of 1646, especially in Wales, the south and the south-west, culminating in complete military victory.[1] In the course of war both sides sought to overhaul their military machines, with a growing degree of 'professionalization', and historians now stress that by the end of the war

1   Sound, mainly military accounts of the war include M. Ashley, *The English Civil War* (Stroud, 1990); M. Bennett, *The Civil Wars in Britain and Ireland, 1638–51* (London, 1997); J. P. Kenyon and J. Ohlmeyer (eds), *The Civil Wars. A Military History of England, Scotland and Ireland, 1638–60* (Oxford, 1998); S. Reid, *All the King's Armies. A Military History of the English Civil War, 1642–51* (London, 1998).

many of the officers in both the parliamentary and the royalist armies were successful and experienced soldiers drawn from outside the traditional elite.[2] Most military historians go on to stress that beneath this national picture lies a much less tidy and more complex story of the conflict at a regional or county level, the dour territorial war fought between rival garrisons and smaller county forces, a war of raiding and counter-raiding, of fortifying or refortifying castles, manor houses, churches and urban centres, of sieges and relief operations, of skirmishes and minor field engagements.

There are some distinct variations within this military account. Thus some historians search for a 'turning-point' in the military struggle, the reverse from which the royalists were set on a course of defeat, and identify this variously as the king's failure to smash his way into London in November 1642, his failure to take Gloucester and to crush parliament's relieving army in summer 1643, Prince Rupert's decision to give battle at Marston Moor in summer 1644 and his disastrous defeat there or the defeat at Naseby in summer 1645. Depending upon how far they are convinced by the recent 'British' approach to the mid-seventeenth century as a whole, historians lay differing emphases upon the degree to which the English (and Welsh) civil war was transformed into a British civil war during the winter of 1643–4 in the wake of parliament's alliance with the Scots, allowing the entry into England of a Scottish army, and the king's truce with the Irish Catholic rebels, allowing him to bring over troops from Ireland to fight on the mainland.[3] Mark Kishlansky, Ian Gentles and Austin Woolrych have reached different conclusions about the novelty of, and the level of radicalism within, the New Model Army created by parliament in spring 1645.[4] And historians rank in different order the list of factors which eventually brought parliament victory and the king defeat – the variable quality of the overall high command, the senior military commanders and their armies, the variable quality of the political leadership and of the central and local administrative machines, differing levels of (religious and secular) motivation, parliament's possession of the navy

---

2   P. R. Newman, *The Old Service: Royalist Regimental Colonels and the Civil War, 1642–6* (Manchester, 1993); I. Gentles, 'The New Model Officer Corps in 1647: A Collective Portrait', *Social History* 22 (1997).
3   Compare the British outlook of Bennett, *The Civil Wars in Britain and Ireland* and of Kenyon and Ohlmeyer (eds), *The Civil Wars. A Military History* with the Anglocentric approach of Reid, *All the King's Armies*.
4   M. Kishlansky, *The Rise of the New Model Army* (Cambridge, 1979); I. Gentles, *The New Model Army in England, Ireland and Scotland, 1645–53* (Oxford, 1991); A. H. Woolrych, *Soldiers and Statesmen. The General Council of the Army and its Debates, 1647–8* (Oxford, 1987).

and of the more populous and affluent parts of the country, especially London, and differing levels of demographic, economic and material depletion in royalist and parliamentarian territories as the war continued. However, none of these issues have caused broad historiographical chasms to open. Indeed, some of the most complex and bitter disputes over military interpretations of the civil war focus on points of detail, such as the precise ground upon which armies deployed for particular battles, the role and location of specific regiments during a large engagement and the colour and style of garb worn by particular ranks, regiments or armies in a campaign. Thankfully, preoccupation with technical details of this sort is more the preserve of war-gamers and re-enactors than of academic historians.

While the military history of the civil war has been the subject of serious academic as well as of popular study since the nineteenth century, only more recently have the political and administrative machines established by both sides during the war years received detailed attention. Despite the work of Ronald Hutton, Peter Newman and others,[5] it is also true that the parliamentarian political and administrative structures have been studied more closely than those of the royalists. In part, this is a consequence of the imbalance of extant primary source material, for far more records survive relating to the victorious parliamentary cause than to the defeated royalists. Never the less, it is clear that in the course of the war both sides established similar administrative machines, built principally upon the county unit, with county committees imposing a similar range of fiscal and other levies to keep the royalist and parliamentarian war efforts supplied with money, men, horses, food and other materials. At the centre, royalist political and executive leadership rested with the king himself, elements of the old Privy Council and a new Council of War and with a rather weak Oxford Parliament comprising existing MPs and peers loyal to Charles. Parliamentary political and executive leadership rested with the now rather depleted Long Parliament and with a range of councils and committees established by it. Research has revealed that the royalist and parliamentarian machines alike suffered from overlapping and ambiguous authorities, from personal power struggles and factional in-fighting and from tensions and divisions created by the differing levels of commitment to the war as well as the differing political, constitutional and religious outlooks of the men who ran them.

5   R. Hutton, *The Royalist War Effort, 1642–6* (2nd edn, London, 1999); P. R. Newman, *The Old Service*; Newman, 'The Royalist Officer Corps, 1642–60', *The Historical Journal* 26 (1983); Newman, 'The Royalist Party in Arms', in C. Jones, M. Newitt and S. Roberts (eds), *Politics and People in Revolutionary England* (Oxford, 1986).

These problems and divisions are apparent both within and between the local and the central machines. The main strands of this story have now been well-established, on the parliamentarian side at least, and are widely accepted.[6]

There have, however, been significant disagreements over the interpretation of specific points. Thus in the middle decades of the twentieth century there was a sharp if narrow dispute over how to classify the factions or groupings which emerged amongst the politicians who continued to sit in the Long Parliament. The existing interpretation based upon two parties, dominated by differing religious outlooks, was discredited, though for a time there was disagreement over what framework might be erected in its place.[7] That dispute has now died down with widespread acceptance of an interpretation based upon 'war', 'middle' and 'peace' groupings, but stressing the loose and fluid nature of outlooks, accepting that many MPs cannot clearly or consistently be assigned to any of the three groupings, and seeing religion as only one (and perhaps not the most important) of many determining factors. More recently, in the early 1990s, a briefer dispute flared up in the wake of John Adamson's argument that the Lords and the titled aristocracy played a powerful and dominant role during the war years, part of his promotion of a 'baronial context' for the civil war. Mark Kishlansky sharply criticized Adamson for misusing primary source material and more broadly many historians were sceptical and felt that the case had been exaggerated.[8]

6 See, for example, C. Holmes, 'Colonel King and Lincolnshire Politics, 1642–6', *The Historical Journal* 16 (1973); Holmes, *The Eastern Association in the English Civil War* (Cambridge, 1974); L. Beats, 'The East Midland Association, 1642–4', *Midland History* 4 (1978); A. Hughes, 'The King, the Parliament and the Localities during the English Civil War', *Journal of British Studies* 24 (1985); J. Morrill, *Revolt in the Provinces. The People of England and the Tragedies of War, 1630–48* (2nd edn, Harlow, 1999).

7 See particularly J. H. Hexter, 'The Problem of the Presbyterian-Independent', *American Historical Review* 44 (1938), and the on-going debate at its height during the 1960s conducted by D. Underdown in the *Journal of British Studies* 4 (1964) and 8 (1968), L. Glow in the *Bulletin of the Institute of Historical Research* 38 (1965), V. Pearl in *Transactions of the Royal Historical Society*, 5th series, 18 (1968), S. Forster in *Past & Present* 44 (1969) and the various contributors to *Past & Present* 47 (1970).

8 J. Adamson, 'The English Nobility and the Projected Settlement of 1647', *The Historical Journal* 30 (1987); Adamson, 'Parliamentary Management, Men-of-Business and the House of Lords, 1640–9', in C. Jones (ed.), *A Pillar of the Constitution: The House of Lords in British Politics, 1640–1784* (London, 1989); Adamson, 'The Baronial Context of the English Civil War', *Transactions of the Royal Historical Society*, 5th series, 40 (1990). Adamson was savaged by M. Kishlansky, 'Saye What?', *The Historical Journal* 33 (1990), to which Adamson replied, 'Politics and the Nobility in Civil War England', *The Historical Journal* 34 (1991). Kishlansky returned with the equally critical 'Saye No More', *Journal of British Studies* 30 (1991), which apparently concluded the debate.

And historians continue to disagree over which side developed the more efficient and effective administrative machine, which maintained better relations with the civilian population, and which in seeking to resource a long and expensive war acted more ruthlessly and in practice felt less restrained by traditional procedures and existing laws.[9] The patchy nature of the surviving source material on both sides, but especially for royalist administration and territories, means that it is unlikely that these questions can ever be completely answered and comprehensively resolved.

Martyn Bennett has recently been at the forefront of exploring the military, fiscal and administrative structures of the war, both nationally and via detailed studies of the north midlands. In an article first published in 1992 (Chapter 7), one of several linking the military and administrative histories of the war years,[10] he analyses the war-time administrations established during 1642–3 in the midlands counties of Derbyshire, Leicestershire, Nottinghamshire, Rutland and Staffordshire. This was a divided region, and different though overlapping parts of it were controlled by crown and parliament or passed from one to the other in the course of the war. Accordingly, rival administrations were set up at the outbreak of war. Bennett traces their origins in the rival structures which king and parliament put in place during the summer in an attempt to secure those counties, to tap their existing military resources and to recruit there. The article brings out how both sides undertook similar administrative and financial reorganizations in 1642–3, once it became clear that the war would continue for some time, though Bennett detects differences between the royalist and parliamentarian administrators, in terms of background and status, participation and commitment. Both sides, he argues, had sought to construct war-time administrations 'based on peace-time methods of

---

9   See, for example, the line taken by A. Hughes in 'Militancy and Localism: Warwickshire Politics and Westminster Politics, 1643–7', *Transactions of the Royal Historical Society*, 5th series, 31 (1981); Hughes, 'The King, the Parliament and the Localities during the English Civil War', *Journal of British Studies* 24 (1985); Hughes, 'Parliamentary Tyranny? Indemnity Proceedings and the Impact of the Civil War: A Case Study from Warwickshire', *Midland History* 11 (1986). Hughes has criticized the work of Hutton, *The Royalist War Effort*, and Morrill, *Revolt of the Provinces* (first published in 1976); Morrill has replied in the revised and slightly retitled edition of this work, *Revolt in the Provinces*, pp. 194–7.

10   See also M. Bennett, 'Contribution and Assessment: Financial Exactions in the English Civil War, 1642–6', *War & Society* 5 (1986); Bennett, 'Leicestershire's Royalist Officers and their War-Effort in the County, 1642–6', *Transactions of the Leicestershire Archaeological and Historical Society* 59 (1984–5); Bennett, 'Damnified Villagers: Taxation in Wales during the First Civil War', *Welsh History Review* 19 (1998).

government', an example of the way in which many people caught up in the civil war 'tried to cling on to the wreckage of their society'.

Much of the recent research and writing on the civil war of 1642–6 has focused on a small number of key issues. The first, and by some way the most complex, is the attempt to identify and to explain the divided allegiances seen in England and Wales, especially during the opening months of the war. Surviving evidence makes it easier to chart the allegiances of the elite than those of the common people. The actions taken by members of the two Houses of Parliament – to continue sitting in London, to join the king, to absent themselves from both London and Oxford or a combination of them – can be traced, the records of sequestration and compounding identify and throw light upon the actions of hundreds of landowners who allegedly did not support parliament (though this is, of course, a biased source), the identities of many of the officers who served in the royalist and parliamentarian armies can be discovered and the positions adopted by many other members of the literate elite are revealed through their correspondence, memoirs, commonplace books and such like. It has to be admitted, however, that almost every study of elite allegiances within a county or region has failed to uncover the positions adopted by a significant proportion of that area's gentry families; they cannot safely be classed as 'neutral' and must remain 'unknown'. As John Morrill and others have argued, even those who, sooner or later, voluntarily or under a degree of duress, made a clear stand and so can be labelled 'active' royalists or parliamentarians, did so for a wide variety of reasons and often with widely differing degrees of enthusiasm and levels of commitment; many on both sides wavered, supported peace movements during the war and hoped for a compromise settlement. It is, therefore, misleading to interpret motivation as if the royalists or the parliamentarians were monolithic blocs.[11] Moreover, it is one thing to show that a member of the elite who was active on one side or the other possessed strongly-held religious views, had spoken out on a particular issue during the opening years of the Long Parliament, had supported or been hurt by royal policies during the pre-war period and so on, but quite another to demonstrate that those beliefs and experiences had motivated him to support one side in the war, to prove tangibly or at least beyond all reasonable doubt which conviction, fear or aspiration drove him on and determined his allegiance.

Very occasionally, surviving personal papers do contain fairly clear and explicit explanations of why the writer chose to support one side or

---

11 See especially Morrill, *The Nature of the English Revolution*, chs 8–9; Morrill, *Revolt in the Provinces*, pp. 64–74, 185–90.

the other. For example, a letter which Sir Thomas Salusbury wrote to his sister in June 1642 laid out the grounds which led him actively to support one side, in his case the royalists; he cites biblical injunctions to serve and obey a king, and relates his strong belief that the crown offered the best defence against looming chaos, dislocation and schism in both secular and religious affairs.[12] In contrast, Jonathan Langley of Shropshire explained in a letter of February 1643 his inability to support either side and his determination to remain neutral; he wrote that he could not choose between the two sides, for he owed loyalty to both king and parliament and felt that they both, in their ways, supported the Protestant church, though he was clearly disgusted that the former was accepting the support of Catholics and the latter of 'sismatikes'.[13] But such clear explanations of motivation are unusual. More often, historians have to reconstruct the factors which may have motivated members of the literate elite to support one side or the other, or to attempt to remain neutral, from a range of evidence including their surviving personal papers, works which they published, records of public or parliamentary speeches and so forth. The process leaves plenty of room for doubt and disagreement.

It is clear that the elite were deeply divided, with significant numbers supporting each of the two sides in the war, though many more apparently did not commit themselves to either. Crude or more sophisticated headcounts have revealed regional variations in the proportions supporting each side and in many cases more sided with the king than with parliament. However, there evidently were deep divisions within the ranks of the landed elite and historians have sought to explain them. It is also fairly clear that a range of different factors could and did determine why members of the elite supported crown or parliament. Some might be seen as positive, such as ideological support amongst royalists for (constitutional) monarchy[14] and for the existing church and constitution, and amongst parliamentarians for reform of religion and the constitution. Others might be seen as negative, a reaction against accurate or distorted images of the goals of the other side. For some, who rallied to the king, this might be a belief that the policies of the parliamentarians would lead to the destruction of church and state, religious schism, rampant heresy, lawlessness, popular violence and an overturning of the established social order; for others, who rallied to parliament, this might be fears that the king was unbalanced or untrust-

12 Reproduced most accessibly in W. J. Smith (ed.), *Calendar of the Salusbury Correspondence* (Cardiff, 1954), no. 251.
13 Reproduced most accessibly in Morrill, *Revolt of the Provinces*, document 10.
14 See D. L. Smith, *Constitutional Royalism and the Search for Settlement* (Cambridge, 1994).

worthy and at the first opportunity would overturn the reforms of 1640–1 and resume a tyrannical path, together with a deep-seated belief in a 'popish plot' around the king to overthrow the reformed church.

Attempts to find broad socio-economic dividing lines amongst the landed elite, perhaps with hereditary peers on one side and gentry on the other, economically flourishing members of the elite supporting one side and declining members the other, or members of the elite with office at court supporting one side and those out of office the other, have proved as unsuccessful in the context war-time allegiances as they are in the context of the causes of the civil war. On the other hand, geographical location probably did play a part in some instances. Thus with parliamentarian London and large numbers of parliamentary troops on their doorstep, many of the Kentish elite who probably sympathized with the king found it wiser to remain neutral or to display a minimal loyalty to the parliamentary cause.[15] In several counties, such as Leicestershire, Wiltshire, Somerset and Cheshire, pre-war factionalism amongst some members of the elite, springing from family rivalries or squabbles for precedence, spilled over into the period 1642–6 and helped to determine the war-time allegiances of groups of families.[16] In some areas it is perfectly plausible to suggest that deference played a role, that the stance taken by one of the great territorial magnates helped to persuade lesser members of the elite thereabouts to support the same side. However, most historians go on to suggest that in most cases deeper factors were involved, that ideologies played a significant part in dividing the elite and determining allegiances.

John Morrill has argued strongly that religion was the principal factor which drove some members of the elite onwards to continue to oppose the crown and to become active parliamentarians (whether as soldiers, politicians or administrators) during the war. He has repeatedly emphasized the centrality of radical puritanism and associated anti-popery in driving forward the parliamentary cause as well as in motivating many of the leading figures within the parliamentary camp.[17] One of those leading figures was Sir William Brereton, who was prominent in opposing some of the crown's policies during the opening years of the Long Parliament and who became the dominant figure in the parliamentary war effort in Cheshire and the surrounding area throughout the war, in many ways the pre-eminent 'county boss' of the era, only to fade from

15   A point made by P. Young in a lecture, as recalled and recounted by Morrill, *Revolt in the Provinces*, pp. 189–90.

16   Ibid., pp. 64–8.

17   Morrill, *Nature of the English Revolution*, part 1.

the scene very rapidly after 1646. In an article first published in 1985 (Chapter 8), Morrill looks at the record of Brereton's life and works during the 1630s and 1640s and seeks to explain his motivation. For Morrill, Brereton was 'a firebrand on religious issues', an 'austere Calvinist' in doctrine, an anti-Catholic and 'a model Puritan magistrate'. Like Woodford and many others, he kept his head down during the 1630s and outwardly conformed to Charles's government, but his opposition to royal policies quickly surfaced in the Commons in 1640–1, where he was very prominent in pressing for religious reform; in contrast, Morrill argues, he was far less prominent in the battles for political and constitutional reform. He was one of the religious militants who mobilized for parliament at the outbreak of war and although his role as leader of the Cheshire war effort forced him to devote much of his time to military and administrative matters, he continued to emphasize the importance of religious reform and renewal. Morrill suggests that his rapidly waning enthusiasm after 1646 was caused by disillusionment at the failure of the victorious parliament to press ahead with religious reform.

Historians generally accept the importance or centrality of religion in motivating many, perhaps most, of the relatively small number of the elite who distinguished themselves as leaders of the parliamentary cause, who stood out during the summer and autumn of 1642 as unhesitating and enthusiastic, willing not only to take up arms themselves but also to raise troops and to work to secure their home region for parliament. There are, as Morrill concedes, exceptions. Few were more radical and outspoken than the ungodly Henry Marten, whose motivation clearly did not spring from a deep and zealous puritan faith. But religion may also have been less central in driving forward many of the less prominent members of the parliamentarian elite, the less enthusiastic but more typical MPs and gentlemen who supported the cause rather than led and shaped it. A desire to reform religion and to carry forward the incomplete process of reformation begun in the sixteenth century and a fear of a popish plot hatched by the king or those around him certainly helped to motivate many such people, but so too might support for continuing political and constitutional reform and a suspicion that until further reform had been completed the king could not be trusted and the good work of 1640–1 might be reversed. There may have been 'no constitutional militants' as there were religious militants on the parliamentary side,[18] but political and constitutional factors could shape perfectly solid parliamentarianism.

18   Morrill, *Revolt in the Provinces*, pp. 188–9.

There was also a religious element to elite support for the king. Although most Roman Catholics kept their heads down during the 1640s, a significant number of Catholic gentlemen actively supported the royalist cause.[19] More broadly, the king drew support from many who supported the Church of England and Prayer Book of Elizabeth I and James I, who by 1642 felt that Charles's ringing declarations of support for the church he had inherited and his abandonment of Laudian innovation were sincere and who – like Salusbury – feared more the continuing reformation and overturning, the religious schisms and social disorder, which leading parliamentarians seemed about to unleash. But as Ronald Hutton, Peter Newman and others have pointed out, the elite royalists as a whole, and the prominent royalists in particular, generally do not display anything like the level of concern for religion, a passionately held faith visibly central to their motivation, apparent in figures such as Brereton and Cromwell on the other side.[20] Prominent royalists were more likely to stress issues of loyalty to the crown. Many had supported the parliamentary reform programme of 1640–1, but by 1642 they saw the king as the upholder of the established (pre-1625) constitution and the rule of law, against continuing attempts to undermine monarchy, unbalance the political order and, by accident or design, cause social turmoil and overturning, as well as to create religious instability. Charles was certainly portraying himself in that way by 1642.

Sir Edward Dering cannot be seen as a typical royalist any more than his fellow MP Brereton was a typical parliamentarian. Although he supported the king at the outbreak of war and raised a cavalry regiment for him, by 1643 Dering was ill at ease and increasingly disenchanted and by the time of his death in 1644 he was attempting to return to the parliamentary fold. He was, at best, a reluctant and unenthusiastic royalist. His surviving papers allow historians to explore the process which transformed Dering from a critic of royal government in the opening months of the Long Parliament to a somewhat uneasy supporter of the crown by the end of 1641. Derek Hirst's article (Chapter 9) charts that course, exploring the reasons behind Dering's 'defection' to the royalists. Unconvinced by the 'county community' thesis, at its height when he was writing in the early 1970s, Hirst instead stresses the informed

---

19 This has been confirmed by the work of P. R. Newman, referred to above at n. 5.

20 See, for example, Hutton, *Royalist War Effort*, pp. xxi–xxiii. Indeed, Morrill has conceded that 'while I would still argue for a spiritual imperative impelling most of those who made others make intolerable choices for Parliament in 1642, I would no longer claim that things were so straightforward on the royalist side', *The Nature of the English Revolution*, p. 43.

interplay between Dering and his Kentish constituents over national policies, especially religious policy. Dering comes across as yet another conformist during the 1630s – an image largely confirmed by subsequent work by S. P. Salt[21] – whose doubts about Caroline religious policies quickly surfaced in the Long Parliament. During the opening months of the parliament he played a prominent part in opposing Laudianism and pressing for ecclesiastical reform; in so doing, he was in tune with opinions expressed by many of his constituents and was keen to keep them informed of his actions. Yet during the spring and summer of 1641 Dering became concerned where some reforms, especially the complete abolition of the episcopal system, might lead, and at rising levels of violence and disorder which he saw around him and which the reformist tendencies of some of his more radical colleagues seemed to be encouraging. Here, too, many of his constituents shared Dering's fears and some of them were actively lobbying him during 1641. By the time of the Grand Remonstrance in the autumn he was critical of parts of the continuing reform programme and contemptuous of the opposition's alleged attempts to win popular support. In consequence, he openly if unenthusiastically supported the crown as war began. Although he raised troops and took up arms himself, Dering's royalism was clearly very different from that of enthusiasts such as fellow MPs George Goring or Sir Ralph Hopton, reinforcing the point that 'active' royalists and parliamentarians were of many different hues.

In recent years historians have stressed that it is not enough to explore the allegiances and motivations of members of the elite alone. During the first autumn of the war over 40,000 men took up arms in England and Wales and by summer 1643 that number had risen to over 100,000. Duress, blind obedience, unthinking deference and even the lure of regular pay and food cannot explain why so many had decided to fight and risk life and limb. Historians have recently sought to discern and to explain the patterns of non-elite or popular allegiance. Such studies often link divisions within society to the causation of the war and many have already been reviewed in the introduction to Part II. Thus we have seen that some historians, such as Brian Manning and Christopher Hill, have stressed the prominence of an urban or rural 'middling sort' (variously defined) in pushing for reform and supporting the parliamentary cause.[22] Many historians have remained uncon-

21   S. P. Salt, 'The Origins of Sir Edward Dering's Attack on the Ecclesiastical Hierarchy, c. 1625–40', *The Historical Journal* 30 (1987).
22   B. Manning, *The English People and the English Revolution* (2nd edn, London, 1991); for C. Hill see, amongst others, *Change and Continuity in Seventeenth Century England* (2nd edn, London, 1991), *Puritanism and Revolution: Studies in the Interpre-*

vinced and point out that such interpretations do not fully explain popular royalism. It has been suggested that in a number of provincial towns the divisions of the civil war years followed on from and were shaped by pre-war cleavages between religious traditionalists and an emerging godly faction, sometimes reinforced and mirrored by rivalry between an established mercantile oligarchy and a group of lesser merchants, retailers and artisans.[23] In Part II we also noted David Underdown's attempts to interpret the divided allegiances of society in three south-western counties in terms of an 'ecology' of allegiance, built upon differing religious, social and cultural outlooks, themselves springing from different settlement patterns, land use and occupations.[24] That pattern works in some areas but not others and has not won wide acceptance. For example, Mark Stoyle's detailed and important study of popular allegiances in the neighbouring county of Devon does not fully support the Underdown thesis, any more than it finds deference to the elite or pre-war political outlooks adepuate explanations of war-time allegiances. Although some patterns emerge, with Devon's tinners and those in the more remote rural areas inclined to support the king, and clothworkers, seamen and those living in large towns to support parliament, there were significant exceptions to this. Stoyle stresses religion as a key factor in determining popular allegiance in Devon, with those favouring further reform of the state church – found particularly in the ports, towns and cloth working districts – tending to support parliament, and those who were more conservative and less reformist in outlook – found particularly in the moorland and interior of the county – tending to support the king.[25] In contrast, Buchanan Sharp, Andrew Wood and others have argued that for some members of the non-elite, allegiance was determined by practical rather than ideological reasons. Thus some of the miners in the Forest of Dean supported parliament and those in parts of Derbyshire supported the king in the hope and expectation that those allegiances would help them in long-running

tation of the English Revolution of the Seventeenth Century (London, 1958), especially part 1, and Society and Puritanism in Pre-Revolutionary England (London, 1964), esp. ch. 4.

23   M. Stoyle, From Deliverance to Destruction: Rebellion and Civil War in an English City (Exeter, 1996); D. Underdown, Fire From Heaven. Life in an English Town in the Seventeenth Century (London, 1992); the mercantile/commercial division emerges from several urban studies in R. C. Richardson (ed.), Town and Countryside in the English Revolution (Manchester, 1992).

24   D. Underdown, Revel, Riot and Rebellion. Popular Politics and Culture in England, 1603–60 (Oxford, 1985).

25   M. Stoyle, Loyalty and Locality: Popular Allegiances in Devon during the English Civil War (Exeter, 1994).

disputes against local grandees, namely the royalist Sir John Winter in Dean and the parliamentarian Sir John Gell in Derbyshire.[26] Whilst 'functional' royalism and parliamentarianism of this type have been shown to be important in some specific areas, they are likely to be the exception rather than the norm.

There is no doubt that a large proportion of the adult male population sought to avoid clear commitment to one side or the other. In the opening months of the war, leadership was seized by a fairly small number of committed activists, who were willing to take up arms, and who struggled to overcome a conspicuously low level of enthusiasm displayed by many, at elite and non-elite levels. In several counties or wider regions, many of the gentry sought during the opening months of the war to reach formal or informal truces, non-aggression pacts or demilitarization agreements, in order to restore or maintain peace in those areas. Even though they were overwhelmed during 1643 by the war machines of both sides, there is ample evidence of a continuing disinclination to fight, of a deep-seated sense of revulsion at the violence and bloodshed which the war engendered and of considerable tension between civilian populations and the military and administrative burdens imposed upon them by king and parliament. However, as the theory that England and Wales were made up of self-contained, inward-looking county communities has faded in recent years, so the arguments that neutralism borne of localism was the dominant mood during the civil war have been questioned or stressed less heavily by some recent historians. Thus, for example, Mark Stoyle's work on popular allegiance in Devon[27] certainly accords a place to neutralism, but nothing like the prominence which it was given in several works of the 1970s, such as Ronald Hutton's *The Royalist War Effort* or John Morrill's *Revolt of the Provinces*.

The question of neutralism and of active antipathy to the war leads on to a second significant theme of recent work on the course of the civil war, namely the origins and nature of the clubmen movements of the latter half of the war. Although no full-length study of the clubmen has (to date) been published, during the closing quarter of the twentieth century the writings of a number of civil war historians, including David Underdown, John Morrill, Ronald Hutton, Martyn Bennett and

26   B. Sharp, 'Rural Discontents and the English Revolution', in Richardson (ed.), *Town and Countryside*; Sharp, *In Contempt of All Authority: Rural Artisans and Riot in the West of England, 1586–1660* (Berkeley, 1980); A. Wood, 'Beyond Post-Revisionism?: The Civil War Allegiances of the Miners of the Derbyshire "Peak Country"', *The Historical Journal* 40 (1997).
27   Stoyle, *Loyalty and Locality*, esp. ch. 6.

C. D. Gilbert, threw new light on the clubmen movements.[28] In the wake of smaller anti-war movements in 1643 and 1644, in December 1644 and on through 1645 there emerged in certain regions – parts of Somerset, Dorset, Wiltshire, Herefordshire, Worcestershire, Shropshire and South Wales, with lesser ripples in other western and southern counties – larger and better organized groups of local civilians which worked to control and reduce the impact upon the civilian population of royalist and parliamentary forces and to press for peace and a return to traditional, peace-time forms. Leadership usually rested with articulate and literate members of the middling sort, sometimes supported by local clergymen; on occasion some of the lesser gentry became involved. The bulk of the clubmen were often drawn from the middling ranks of rural society, from the yeomanry and the upper ranks of husbandmen. The clubmen movements were active in different and often quite specific geographical areas as well as at different times during the latter half of the war. Thus conclusions about the movement in one county may not necessarily hold good for clubmen movements elsewhere.

Depending upon the local circumstances which prevailed, there are examples of clubmen working with or against royalist and parliamentary forces, dealing with, curbing or physically opposing officers, garrisons and field armies of king and parliament. Leading on from this, historians have reached different conclusions about what lay at the heart of clubmen allegiances and outlooks. Some have seen them as genuine neutrals, engaged in a locally-based uprising against the depredations of war perpetrated by whichever side happened to be active in that locality at that time.[29] Essentially, they were neither royalist nor parliamentarian in outlook, though for tactical reasons they were perfectly willing to negotiate with either or both parties and even to cooperate with one side if that might ease the burdens imposed upon them by the other and bring peace closer. Thus in some areas they cooperated with the New Model Army in defeating and expelling royalist forces,

28 D. Underdown, 'The Chalk and the Cheese: Contrasts Among the English Clubmen', *Past & Present* 85 (1979), and reprinted in R. Cust and A. Hughes (eds), *The English Civil War* (London, 1997); Underdown, 'The Problem of Popular Allegiance in the English Civil War', *Transactions of the Royal Historical Society*, 5th series, 31 (1981); Underdown, *Revel, Riot and Rebellion*; Morrill, *Revolt of the Provinces*, chapter 3; Hutton, *The Royalist War Effort*, ch. 15; Hutton, 'The Worcestershire Clubmen in the English Civil War', *Midland History* 5 (1979–80); Bennett, *The Civil Wars in Britain and Ireland*, ch. 8; C. D. Gilbert, 'Clubmen in South West Shropshire, 1644–5', *Shropshire History and Archaeology*, 68 (1993); Gilbert, 'The Worcestershire Clubmen of 1645', *Transactions of the Worcestershire Archaeological Society*, 3rd series, 15 (1996); see also P. Gladwish, 'The Herefordshire Clubmen: A Reassessment', *Midland History* 10 (1985).
29 This is the line taken by Morrill in *Revolt of the Provinces*.

though they were motivated not by parliamentarian sympathies but by a desire to be rid of the military party which was then occupying their area and disrupting their lives. Other historians, however, have questioned the neutrality of the clubmen and have seen them springing, not from spontaneous and non-aligned anti-war protests, but from longer-standing divisions within society rooted in royalist or parliamentary sympathies.

In the 1980s David Underdown was the leading proponent of this interpretation, arguing that in Dorset, Wiltshire and Somerset there were different groups of clubmen, some of them actively royalist, others actively parliamentarian. Their allegiances were shaped, not by reactions to the local conditions which existed in 1645, but by the type of community in which they lived. In other words the allegiances of the clubmen, like those of other members of the community, were shaped by Underdown's arable versus wood–pasture division or, as he put it in his work on the clubmen, between the sheep-corn downland 'chalk' areas of royalist clubmen and the woodland and pasture 'cheese' areas of parliamentary clubmen. In fairness, he recognized that this pattern did not always work well, even in his three south-western counties. But the important point is that Underdown strongly argued that the clubmen movements generally sprang from divided and partisan regions and had clear and deep-seated royalist or parliamentary allegiances.[30] Although Underdown's interpretation of the south-western clubmen, like his broader ecology of allegiance thesis in which it was grounded, was criticized when it appeared and has been sceptically received, the recent work of Mark Stoyle on Devon seems – on the subject of the clubmen – to offer some support. Although not one of the major centres of club activity, during 1645 there were a number of clubmen outbursts, based in distinct parts of the county, criticizing and opposing the royalists who then controlled Devon. Stoyle argues that these districts of clubmen activity were overwhelmingly those in which popular parliamentarianism had been evident earlier in the war. Accordingly, Stoyle sees the stance of the Devon clubmen movements as determined by 'pre-existent allegiance patterns' (in this case, pro-parliamentarian), 'rather than an automatic response to military depredations', noting that the 1645 risings occurred in precisely the same districts as, and should be seen as a continuation of, anti-royalist risings earlier in the war.[31] Underdown's interpretation that the clubmen were partisans rather than neutrals is therefore supported by the Devon evidence.

30   Underdown's most concise statement of this thesis is found in 'The Chalk and the Cheese'.
31   Stoyle, *Loyalty and Locality*, ch. 6; the quotations are from pp. 131–2.

While arguments over the neutral or partisan nature of the clubmen have focused on the south-western counties, attempts to explain why risings occurred in some areas but not in others have tended to focus on the (west) midlands and the Welsh Marches. Historians have sought reasons why clubmen activity is seen in particular parts of Hereford-shire, Worcestershire and Shropshire and why it is not found elsewhere in those counties and in most neighbouring and nearby midland counties. Ronald Hutton, C. D. Gilbert and others have pointed to distinctive characteristics found in clubmen areas in the Welsh Marches – some were physically remote and economically conservative, some contained few resident gentry, some supported religious reform, encouraged by radical ministers in those areas, and displayed strong anti-Catholicism, and some had suffered particularly badly from the burdens of war and at the hands of locally active (mainly royalist) officers and soldiers. There is, however, a two-fold problem here. Firstly, these factors are not common to all the areas in the Welsh Marches which saw clubmen activity – they cannot all plausibly be described as remote, for example, and religious conservatism rather than radicalism seems to character-ize some clubmen movements in the region. Secondly, none of these factors alone or even combinations of them are unique or particular to areas which saw clubmen activity. There were plenty of other parts of Marcher counties and plenty of neighbouring regions which might be seen as rather remote, which had few gentry, which had certainly suf-fered heavily during the war and so forth, and yet there is no sign of clubmen activity in those areas.

Simon Osborne's 1994 article (Chapter 10) addresses this problem by exploring five midlands counties, one of which (Worcestershire) saw clubmen activity, while the remainder (Warwickshire, Northampton-shire, Leicestershire and Rutland) did not, and by searching for factors found in the former but absent from the latter which might explain this. He concludes that the answer does not lie in the differing burdens of war endured by these counties, for all suffered a range of military activity, from the attention of field armies, raiding, skirmishing and larger engagements, heavy taxation and plunder. He differs from Hutton, who had argued that until 1645 the western part of Worcestershire (one of the main clubmen zones) had largely escaped the depredations of war and that what triggered the clubmen rising there was the imposition in 1645 of a new association which would for the first time impose the full burdens of the war effort on the area.[32] Osborne, in contrast, contends that western Worcestershire had suffered its share of the war-time plun-

---

32 Hutton, *The Royalist War Effort*, ch. 15; Hutton, 'The Worcestershire Clubmen in the English Civil War'.

dering, destruction and exhaustion found throughout the region and had not hitherto escaped the burdens of war. Instead, he argues that what distinguishes the clubmen zones of Worcestershire from other parts of the county and from the other four counties is their unusual remoteness from permanent or strongly-established garrisons. He claims that, as well as imposing a burden of their own, garrisons also provided the surrounding civilian population with a degree of security and order, affording protection from raiding and plundering by enemy troops. In this way, the presence of 'strong, well-ordered' garrisons throughout most of the region was 'crucial to the maintenance of popular support', and this popular support in turn ensured a steady flow of volunteers and meant that neither royalists nor parliamentarians had to resort to large-scale impressment in much of the region. Western Worcestershire was exceptional in its remoteness from permanent or firmly-established garrisons (of either side). In spring 1645 the area suffered from the particularly disruptive activities of some royalist cavalry units and, with no garrison nearby from which they could seek help and which might, in turn, maintain order in the area, some of the local civilian population took up arms to defend themselves. Elsewhere in the region the regular and heavy presence of often well-ordered garrison troops both inhibited the rising of armed, self-defence civilian bodies and, by offering a degree of security and protection, made such action less pressing.

By no means all historians who have worked on the clubmen are convinced by this interpretation. Gilbert, for one, has criticized Osborne for focusing on Worcestershire alone and for paying little attention to clubmen activities in Herefordshire and Shropshire. He argues that elsewhere in the Marches long-standing garrisons did not prevent clubmen outbreaks in the area and, indeed, that the presence of garrison troops actually provoked the risings.[33] Martyn Bennett, too, is sceptical. His work on the north midlands also leads him to suggest that the regular garrisons there were effective in minimizing incursions and maintaining order, stability and a regular system of taxation for much of the war. However, by 1644–5, 'the most destabilised period' of the civil war in the north midlands, royalist control over parts of the region was crumbling. Yet the region did not see significant clubmen activity in 1644–5, even though 'so many of the prerequisites found in areas marked by club risings' could be found there. Bennett suggests that club activity sprang from other factors, not apparent in much of the midlands. The presence of Roman Catholic officers in the royalist armies might be an important trigger, for while many in the

33   Gilbert, appendix to his article 'The Worcestershire Clubmen of 1645'.

Welsh Marches were angered by the prominence of Catholics in the proposed new Marcher Association, they played little role in the royalist military and administrative organization in the north midlands. More importantly, perhaps, Bennett suggests that the civilian population, including community officials such as constables, could react against the war-time administrations and their military and civilian representatives if, under the growing strains of war, and a war which by 1645 the royalists appeared to be losing, the (royalist) administration either broke down or, through desperation and disorder, adopted arbitrary, damaging and unacceptable practices. In contrast, where reasonable order was maintained, even during the latter half of the war – as it was, Bennett argues, in the north midlands – there was little clubmen activity.[34]

The third significant theme of recent work on the course of the civil war, an emphasis upon the disruptive and destructive impact of the war and its exceptionally high costs in men, money, materials and property, has given rise to fewer disputes and has been widely accepted by historians. Portraits of the civil war as a conflict which largely passed by the bulk of the population and during which everyday life continued much as it had before 1642, and tales of puzzled and bemused farmers unsure what was happening when they chanced upon soldiers marching across or fighting on their land, unaware that a civil war was in progress, are now given little credence. More recently, the work of historians such as Stephen Porter, John Morrill, Charles Carlton, Philip Tennant and Martyn Bennett has stressed a very different and in many ways darker image of the civil war.[35] It is now argued that the civil war involved most of the country, either directly as combatants – Morrill has estimated that one in three or four of the adult male population of England and Wales

34 M. Bennett, ' "My Plundered Towns, My Houses Devastation": The Civil War and North Midlands Life, 1642–6', *Midlands History* 22 (1997); Bennett, *The Civil Wars Experienced. Britain and Ireland, 1638–61* (London, 2000), pp. 109–20, from which the brief quotations are drawn.
35 S. Porter, 'The Fire-Raid in the English Civil War', *War & Society* 2 (1984); Porter, 'Property Destruction in the English Civil Wars', *History Today* 36 (1986); Porter, *Destruction in the English Civil Wars* (Stroud, 1994); J. Morrill (ed.), *The Impact of the English Civil War* (London, 1991), including Morrill's own introduction; C. Carlton, 'The Impact of the Fighting', in Morrill (ed.), *The Impact of the English Civil War*; Carlton, *Going to the Wars. The Experience of the British Civil Wars, 1638–51* (London, 1992); P. Tennant, *Edgehill and Beyond. The People's War in the South Midlands, 1642–5* (Stroud, 1992); Bennett, *The Civil Wars in Britain and Ireland*; Bennett, *The Civil Wars Experienced*; see also B. Donagan, 'Codes and Conduct in the English Civil War', *Past & Present* 118 (1988); Donagan, 'Prisoners in the English Civil War', *History Today* 41 (1991); Donagan, 'Atrocity, War Crime and Treason in the English Civil War', *American Historical Review* 99 (1994); J. A. Dils, 'Epidemics, Mortality and the Civil War in Berkshire, 1642–6', *Southern History* 11 (1989); M. Stoyle, 'Whole

was mobilized for war at some stage and that one in nine was in arms at any one time during the campaigning seasons of 1643, 1644 and 1645[36] – and administrators, or indirectly as members of a civilian population which was hit by unprecedentedly heavy taxes, plundering and by the presence and (often free) quartering of soldiers. In addition to up to 85,000 direct military fatalities in England, perhaps an additional 100,000 perished through the increased prevalence of disease in war-time, producing an overall death-toll in the civil war, viewed as a proportion of the national population, slightly higher than that suffered in the First World War and much higher than that in the Second.[37] Agriculture and manufacturing, trade and commerce were badly disrupted and scores of castles, churches, manor houses, suburbs and towns were attacked, ruined or completely destroyed. Far from being a civilized, almost genteel affair, a 'war without an enemy'[38] contested by gentlemen according to gentlemanly rules, the civil war is now seen as bloody, brutal and, at times, truly barbaric.

Although they did not lead on to a full-length study, during the 1970s Ian Roy produced some important articles, exploring and stressing the disorder and destruction of the civil war. In one striking case study, he looked at the actions taken by the local population in summer 1643 when the king and his ill-disciplined army, having captured and sacked Bristol, plundered their way through Gloucestershire en route to besiege Gloucester. Some of the locals waged a guerrilla war against the king's army, with bodies of armed farmers roaming the countryside, picking off stragglers, scouts and messengers, and even ambushing whole cavalry units, eighty-strong. They also withheld the supplies and labour which the royalist siege army needed, only to replenish parliament's relieving army upon its arrival. If multiplied over a wider area, this popular action, 'a subterranean form of conflict' Roy called it, had the potential to alter the course of the war.[39] In a broader paper, read in 1977 and published the following year (Chapter 11), Roy compares the experience of the civil war in England (especially western England) with

Streets Converted to Ashes: Property Destruction in Exeter during the English Civil War', *Southern History* 16 (1994); R. Hutton, 'The Experience of the Civil War in the West', *Proceedings of the Somerset Archaeology and Natural History Society* 138 (1995).

36   Morrill, *Revolt in the Provinces*, p. 190.

37   Carlton, 'The Impact of the Fighting', in Morrill (ed.), *The Impact of the English Civil War*.

38   From Sir William Waller's letter to Sir Ralph Hopton, written shortly before the two clashed at the battle of Lansdown.

39   I. Roy, 'The English Civil War and English Society', in B. Bond and I. Roy (eds), *War and Society. A Yearbook of Military History, I* (London, 1975); the quotation is from p. 42.

that of Germany during the notoriously bloody and destructive Thirty Years War of 1618–48. He finds a number of links and similarities, such as the participation in the civil war of many who had gained experience in the continental war, and the employment in England of continental weaponry, fortifications and experts. Equally, the hard-line attitudes of both sides, careless of the rights and welfare of the civilian population, as they waged a bitter war to control the disputed Severn valley, 'was not distinctly different' from type of warfare waged to control important but disputed territory in Germany or the Low Countries in the Thirty Years War. Although Roy concedes that the civil war experience of the Severn valley may have been worse than that of other English regions, especially London and the south-east, he concludes that the plunder, extortion and deliberately destructive raiding, the deployment of fire and sword in towns and villages, and the disruption or prohibition of trade and commerce practised in western England, brought levels of misery and suffering to that region 'very comparable to those suffered by the war zones in Germany'. Oglander's image of a murderous, 'miserable [and] distracted' civil war is back in fashion.

7

Between Scylla and Charybdis: the Creation of Rival Administrations at the Beginning of the English Civil War

Martyn Bennett

Originally appeared as Martyn Bennett, 'Between Scylla and Charybdis: the Creation of Rival Administrations at the Beginning of the English Civil War' in *The Local Historian* 22. Copyright © 1992 British Association for Local History, Salisbury.

This article will examine the outbreak of the civil war in the five counties of Derbyshire, Leicestershire, Nottinghamshire, Rutland and Staffordshire. These counties became a Royalist association under the command of Henry Hastings, Lord Loughborough, who continued in this command throughout the first Civil War (1642–46) and they were also part of a parliamentarian association under Lord Grey. During this period both sides established administrative systems in order to co-ordinate the military, financial and general affairs of the counties. These bodies, the royalist Commissions of Array and the parliamentarian County Committees, met with false starts and many problems in their attempts to govern the regions. This study will explore the way many people tried to cling on to the wreckage of their society, by firstly looking at the creation of the rival organisations, as King and Parliament attempted to construct war-time administrations based on peace-time methods of government. The article will then turn to examine the membership of these bodies, and assess how successful the rival sides had been in using the traditional officers and organs of government.[1]

Both the King and Parliament spent the spring and early summer of 1642 attempting to gain the political support of prominent government and local figures. In addition to this, both were trying to create some kind of armed force to supplement the political pressure which they hoped to exert on their opponent. In the shires many people, who would later become supporters of one side or another, observed this with undisguised horror. On 18 June 1642 a group of men from Leicestershire drafted a petition to King Charles I requesting that he

> accord with your Parliament, and comply with them to restrain the violent malice of the bloud-thirsty Rebels in Ireland. To settle a Godly, Learned and Industrious Ministry. To disarme the Papists seeing they reioyce in this discord, and insolently speake words full of Arrogancy. To separate from you that subverting Councell who dare not stand to the goodnes of their Cause nor can indure the Test. To cashire those Cavaliers and other unnecessary undependants.[2]

It was a mixture of local and national concerns, expressing the fear that social anarchy, exemplified by the arrogance of the papists, might ensue from the division between the King and his Parliament. On a local level, the cavaliers that they referred to included Henry Hastings, second son of the earl of Huntingdon, who, they understood, was about to try to raise the county militia in the King's name by virtue of a Commission of Array. Further, they reminded the King that the last civil war – the Wars of the Roses – had seen fighting in their own county, at Market Bosworth. Seeing themselves bereft of 'castles or any other places of strength by Sea or Land' and feeling themselves to be in the 'Middest of your Kingdome of England, and in the Middest of our great feares', they moreover complained of the King's military intent.

A fortnight later, on 1 July, diverse knights and gentlemen of Nottinghamshire sent a letter to their knights of the shire, Sir Thomas Hutchinson and Robert Sutton, esquire, requesting that they adhere to

1   The title of the article is taken from Henry Oxinden who wrote in July 1642 that 'Meethinks my condition betwixt the commission of array and ordinance of Parliament is like his that is between Silla and Carybdis, and nothing, butt *Omnipotencie* can bring mee clearly and reputably off.' Cited in Morrill, J., (ed.), *The Revolt of the Provinces. Conservatives and Radicals in the English Civil War 1630–1650* (1976), p. 139.
2   Leicestershire Record Office (henceforth LRO) 66'34 To His Kings Most excellent Majestie. The Humble Petition of the Knights, Ministers, Gentry, Freeholders and many thousands of the inhabitants of the countie of Leicester, 18 June, 1643.

the King out of their duty to the laws of England, made by the King, Lords and Commons working together, and not to 'engage us in a civil war'.[3] Many of the signatories were later to become Royalists, five of them had been named as commissioners of array for the county, along with Hutchinson and Sutton, on the same day that the Leicestershire men drafted their petition. Despite the probability that the two documents come from opposite ends of the political spectrum, both include statements which could be gauged to appeal to the many people who occupied the middle ground. Both referred to the established laws, and the necessity of adhering to those laws created in full collaboration between the three estates, monarchy, aristocracy and commons. Both stressed the importance of a strong Protestant church, and referred to recent oaths or tests imposed to re-affirm loyalties. Moreover both placed emphasis on their authors' fears of civil war, brought home to them by the fact that there were now two camps arming, one to the north and one to the south of their own localities, which seems to have acted as the spur to both petitions.

It was out of the argument over who should control the Militia and the subsequent issue, by Parliament, of the ordinance giving it power to nominate the lords lieutenant, that the obvious need for the king to react to the emasculation of his military powers grew. The threat to which Charles was exposed, after Parliament passed the Militia Ordinance on 5 March 1642, was a very real and dangerous one.[4] Yet Parliament's attempt to seize the military initiative had not met with immediate success either and it was May before any concerted efforts to act on it began to be made. In effect the Militia Ordinance had replaced all the existing lieutenants with men of Parliament's choosing.[5] However, several of the sitting lieutenants had not wished to make the journey to Westminster to submit their commissions for cancellation, since no doubt the dubious legality of the ordinance caused concern. The King's delay in declaring the ordinance illegal must have salved consciences and eventually the changes were effected. In the Midlands the changes appeared to be quite dramatic. In Nottinghamshire, the Pierrepoint family in the shape of Henry Pierrepoint, Viscount Newark, was displaced from the lieutenancy by the Holles family led by the earl of Clare.

3 Deering, C., *Nottinghamia Vetus et Nova or An Historical Account of the Ancient and Present State of the town of Nottingham* (Nottingham, 1751), pp. 342–44.
4 This was true in a political sense too. It had dispensed with the need for the King's signature, because, although ordinances were issued in the absence of the monarch – and he was in York – they were passed strictly on the understanding that they would become an act upon the monarch's return.
5 Gardiner, S. R., (ed.), *The Constitutional Documents of the Puritan Revolution* (3rd. edn., reprinted 1979), pp. 245–48.

In Derbyshire the branch of the Cavendish family headed by the earl of Devonshire was displaced by the Manners family, led by the earl of Rutland. In Leicestershire, the Hastings family had held the lieutenancy since the 1580s. Henry, Earl of Huntingdon and his heir, Ferdinando, Lord Hastings, held a joint lieutenancy over the counties of Leicestershire and Rutland. The ordinance divested them of both. Rutland was handed to David Cecil, Earl of Exeter, and Leicestershire's lieutenancy was passed on to the Hastings family's chief rivals in the county, the Greys, led by the earl of Stamford.[6]

Not all of these appointments were successful ones from the point of view of Parliament. The earl of Essex was appointed lieutenant of several counties including Staffordshire, and eventually he was given command of Parliament's army. He was unable to devote much time to Staffordshire, and so he appointed Walter Wrottesley of Wrottesley, esquire, as his vice-lieutenant. Wrottesley was assiduously courted by the Royalists and eventually threw in his lot with them. In Rutland, the earl of Exeter seems to have undertaken no direct action in line with his duties as lord lieutenant which could have furthered the Parliamentary cause.[7] Nevertheless, in other areas the militia was being assembled by active Parliamentarians. In Leicestershire, for example, the earl of Stamford assembled the county forces on 8 June in Parliament's name.[8]

The King responded to this challenge by issuing the Commission of Array, which had been used to call together the leading gentry of the shires to command the county militia until the reign of Elizabeth, when its duties had been superseded by the lieutenancy's assumption of permanent status. There had been a brief attempt to use commissions during the war with Scotland in 1640, but generally the commissions had been in abeyance for about a century. The King issued the first Commission of Array in late May 1642 to the gentry of Lancashire, at the same time as he issued his counterblast to the use of the Militia Ordinance. Most of the commissions were issued during June and July. Some members of these original groups continued to meet throughout the war, operating in different regions with differing functions and varying

6   Northampton Record Office, Finch Hatton Mss 133 contains the lists of the new Lords Lieutenant and the Commissions of Array.
7   Staffordshire County Record Office (henceforth SRO) D948/4/6/2 6. Wrottesley, G., 'History of the Wrottesley Family', *Collections for a History of Staffordshire History*, New Series, vol. 6 part 2, pp. 312–19. Hutchinson, L., *Memoirs of the Life of Colonel John Hutchinson* (Oxford, 1973).
8   Rushworth, J., (ed.), *Historical Collections* (London, 1721–22), vol. 3, part 2, pp. 669, 676; Nichols, J., *The History and Antiquities of the County of Leicestershire* (London, 1804), vol. 3, part 2, appendix 4, pp. 19–22.

degrees of success. In their initial stages, they were generally regarded as a failure, and had the war been shorter, they might never have functioned successfully at all. The King put the commission for Leicestershire into the hands of Henry Hastings on 12 June. The Commissioners called together by this document and its subsequent issues, were specifically empowered to 'array and train our people, and to apportion and assess such persons who have estates and who are not able to bear arms to find arms for other men.' These arrayed men were to be organised into companies, under commanders 'as convenient'.[9] The cost factor was an important one and there was a concomitant attempt to allay fears about the commissions' aims. The commissions were very different from the Militia Ordinance, which did not require the new lords lieutenant to call out the trained bands immediately. In contrast the commissions were brought together specifically for the purpose of calling together the trained bands. The potentially adverse effect which this might have had on public opinion had to be eased as much as possible: the commissioners were instructed not to have the militia assembled permanently and they were not to augment their numbers.[10]

The response of those named as commissioners of array was not unanimous. In Leicestershire, Henry Hastings was not aided by either his father or by the earl of Devonshire, who were the premier commissioners. This undermined Charles' aim, which was to place the militia in the hands of the nobility and specifically, in the North Midlands, giving the responsibility to those who had been his lords lieutenant.[11] Further, it was hoped that members of the nobility would form the quorum of three necessary to hold the meetings. In the Midlands, it was not to be; the earls of Huntingdon and Devonshire, commissioners for both Derbyshire and Leicestershire, avoided taking action; Edward Noel, Viscount Camden, the leading nominee to the county's commission, seemed to undertake no action in Rutland; whilst in Staffordshire, Lord Paget alone of the nominated three lords undertook to raise troops. In Nottinghamshire, only former lord lieutenant Lord Newark mustered the trained bands in July. Generally speaking, wherever concerted efforts were made to raise the trained bands in the North Midlands, it was the gentry or younger members of noble families who were prominent: Henry Hastings, second son to the earl of Huntingdon, Sir Richard Roberts of Sutton Cheney, and Sir John Bale of Saddington and Carlton in Leicestershire; Sir John Fitzherbert, heir to Lord Norbury and Christo-

9   Gardiner, *op cit*, pp. 245–47.
10   British Library (henceforth BL), Add Mss 34217, f70; Instructions to the Northamptonshire Commissioners.
11   Fletcher, A., *The Outbreak of the English Civil War* (London, 1985), p. 323.

pher Fullwood of Middleton, esquire, in Derbyshire; Viscount Newark and John Digby of Mansfield Woodhouse, esquire, in Nottinghamshire, actively attempted to raise forces in their counties. These attempts were not successful. Hastings was prevented from mustering the Leicestershire forces on the Horsefair Leas at Leicester on 23 June. Fullwood found that the leading Parliamentarians, the earl of Rutland and Sir John Gell, had a greater sway in the county than he did until the King made tax concessions to the Derbyshire lead miners. In Nottinghamshire, Digby and Lord Newark found it impossible to gain control of the county munitions supply.[12] Even so, there was an attempt to co-ordinate the actions of the Commissions. In order to control communications within each county, the King had included the high sheriffs of the counties in the commissions. Where the sitting sheriff proved antagonistic, as did Leicestershire's sheriff, Archdale Palmer of Wanlip, esquire, the King replaced him. Accordingly, Hastings was appointed sheriff in Palmer's place and the other sheriffs in the region were ordered to cooperate with Hastings. John Digby, who was the sheriff of Nottinghamshire, assisted Hastings to transport arms and ammunition into Leicestershire on 1 July. The commissioners for Derbyshire had already been instructed to call together their militia to aid Hastings.[13] However, it was clear by August that the commissioners across the country had failed to raise significant numbers of the trained bands in the King's name. A mixture of Parliamentarian opposition and the part-time soldiers' desire to avoid embroilment had defeated them. On top of this was the lack of commitment amongst significant numbers of the commissioners who, like the soldiers, wished to escape involvement.

As Dr Ronald Hutton has demonstrated, it was only by issuing commissions to individuals that the King raised an army; and the same was true for Parliament, as neither side could overcome the general apathy expressed towards their respective causes by the members of the trained bands. Many of the regiments which formed the King's early forces were raised by commissioners of array, acting as individuals, by virtue of their commissions as officers in their own troops and regiments.[14] In Staffordshire, Lord Paget and Sir John Beaumont began to raise regiments for the King. In Leicestershire, Henry Hastings was commissioned Colonel of Horse in early August and other commissioners of array, like

12   Nichols, *op cit*, vol. 3, part 2; appendix 4, pp. 20–21, 22–24; Rushworth, *op cit*, vol. 3, part 1, pp. 618, 669, 670, LRO Br 18/22/155: Historical Manuscripts Commission, *Report on the Manuscripts of the Late Reginald Rawdon Hastings* (1930) (Henceforth HMC *Hastings,*), vol. 2, p. 84.
13   Journal of the House of Commons, vol. 2, p. 645. HMC *Hastings*, vol. 2, p. 85.
14   Hutton, R., *The Royalist War Effort* (1982), p. 22.

Sir John Pate of Sysonby, were to raise regiments later. In Derbyshire, commissioners Sir John Harpur of Swarkstone, Sir John Fitzherbert of Norbury and John Freschville of Staveley, esquire, raised regiments for the King. In Nottinghamshire, sheriff John Digby was one of the earliest to raise forces and he was to be joined by commissioner Isham Parkyns of Bunny, esquire. In Rutland, Viscount Campden and his eldest son, Baptiste Noel, had raised forces between them by the end of the year. These regiments and part-regiments marched to join the King as he progressed through the Midland region and other commissioners provided material support. In August 1642, the forces raised by Hastings in Leicestershire were sent south to assist Sir Nicholas Byron and the earl of Northampton in Warwickshire, where they attempted to halt the progress of Lord Brooke's successful recruitment campaign and to take Warwick castle, where Brooke had stored the county magazine. The King himself added his weight to this action in his attempt to seize Coventry on 20 August. The city refused to allow the King in when he was accompanied by soldiers, so instead he left his tiny army outside the town to effect a siege and returned northwards. On 23 August the two sieges in the county ended after larger numbers of Parliamentarian forces arrived there. Meanwhile, King Charles had returned to Nottingham. On 22 August the royal banner was raised outside the castle, signalling the official commencement of a war against Parliament. The omens were reckoned to be bad when the standard blew down in fierce winds.

The Royalist cavalry joined the King in late August, camping in south Nottinghamshire, at the Bunny home of commissioner Isham Parkyns.[15] On 26 August, under the leadership of the King's nephew Prince Rupert, the horse attacked the Bradgate home of the earl of Stamford in order to seize the Leicestershire county ammunition the earl had stored there. On 6 September Prince Rupert, using the presence of the horse as a threat, 'requested' that the people of Leicester show their loyalty by offering the King £2,000. The King repudiated the demand within days, but kept hold of the £500 which the town had sent him as an initial instalment.[16] The King was sending two clear, if contradictory, signals. Firstly, he did not want his military leaders to act arbitrarily and so alienate the local communities, but secondly he showed that his need for money sometimes outweighed these principles.

15 Firth, C., (ed.), 'The Journal of Prince Rupert's Marches', *English Historical Review*, vol. 13, 730.
16 Nichols, *op cit*, vol. 3, part 2, appendix 4, p. 31. Stocks, H., (ed.), *Records of the Borough of Leicester, 1603–1689* (Cambridge, 1923), pp. 317–19.

On 12 September 1642, Charles left Nottingham and marched westwards, through Derbyshire, where his forces camped on the Swarkstone estates of commissioner Sir John Harpur, into Staffordshire to the estates of commissioner Sir Harvey Bagot at Field.[17] With the King went the vast majority of committed royalists and forces gathered from the North Midland counties. Hastings and Freschville, amongst others, served at the battle of Powick Bridge on 23 September and at Edgehill on 23 October and went on to fight at Brentford on 12 November and at the stand-off at Turnham Green the following day. The King had intended to create a field or marching army, and to this end all available forces were brought together at Shrewsbury and then taken south. This left the North Midlands unguarded except for a force of dragoons heading southward through the region and a small garrison at Bretby in south Derbyshire.

Into this vacuum stepped Sir John Gell of Hopton in Derbyshire, the lead mine lessee who had earlier blocked commissioner Fullwood's attempts to raise forces for the King. Gell had gone to Hull whilst the King had been in the region, and taking soldiers from Hull and from forces stationed in Sheffield, he drove the royalist Sir Francis Whortley and his dragoons out of Derbyshire. A troop of horse was raised in Nottinghamshire and a garrison established under John Hutchinson of Owthorpe in Nottingham castle. The garrison at Bretby was driven out and Whortley repulsed once again from Derbyshire.[18] In Staffordshire, Whortley's abrupt appearance prompted the county gentry to hold a special sessions of the peace in November 1642 which included Royalist commissioners of array, like Sir Harvey Bagot. The J.P.s proposed a third force – an armed body to keep both the King's forces and those of Parliament out of the county. This was part of a larger attempt to maintain a neutral stance, evidence of which was also seen in Cheshire and Lincolnshire.[19]

Both the King and Parliament acted swiftly to deal with the problem. Charles ordered High Sheriff Comberford and Sir Francis Whortley to garrison Stafford. Thomas Leveson of Wolverhampton, esquire, was to garrison Wolverhampton and Dudley castle.[20] Hastings was sent back from the King's capital at Oxford with his regiment of horse, a commission to raise a regiment of dragoons and ammunition for a regiment of foot. He was to establish a base at Ashby-de-la-Zouch

17   Firth, *op cit*, p. 730.
18   Derbyshire County Record Office (henceforth DRO), D830 M29, Copybook of Sir George Gresley, np; Glover, S., *The History, Gazetteer of the County of Derby* (Derby, 1829), vol. 1, Appendix, p. 64.
19   Pickles, J. T., 'Studies in Royalism in the English Civil War, with special reference to Staffordshire', unpublished M.A. thesis, Manchester (1968), p. 61.
20   SRO, Quarter Sessions Order Book, 15 November 1642; Pickles, *op cit*, p. 63.

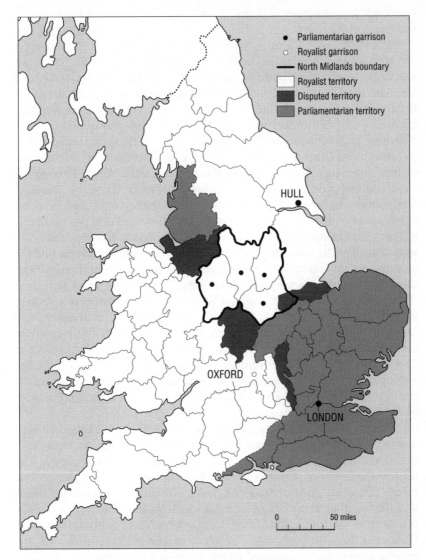

Map 7.1 The division of Britain at the end of 1643 (the North Midland counties are heavily outlined)

from which to take control of Leicestershire as a first step to gaining possession of the region for the King. John Digby was sent back to Nottinghamshire from Oxford to work with the earl of Newcastle's man, Sir John Henderson, in establishing a presence in Nottinghamshire. Other leading Royalists returned to the region; Ferdinando Stanhope

was sent home to join his father, the earl of Chesterfield, now en-
sconced in Lichfield.[21]

Parliament also began a systematic reorganisation of its resources
throughout the country. In the North Midlands this necessitated a con-
solidation of the work done by Gell and Hutchinson. Before the end of
the year, county committees had been established in Nottinghamshire,
Leicestershire, Rutland and Derbyshire. In Derbyshire and Nottinghamshire the committees were centred on the two prominent activists
Gell and Hutchinson. In Leicestershire, the Earl of Stamford's heir,
Thomas, Lord Grey of Groby, became the leading figure in the absence
of his father who was serving in the south west.[21] Within the month
these county committees were associated with those of Rutland,
Northamptonshire, Buckinghamshire, Huntingdonshire and Bedfordshire with the aim of creating a larger and more efficient logistical and
military organisation. In order to give the impression of aristocratic participation, Parliament appointed Lord Grey commander-in-chief of the
association: he was only twenty-three years old.[23] Within the next four
months, the committee system developed. By February 1643, all five of
the counties in the North Midland Region had committees meeting on
a regular basis, responsible for the raising and training of forces. For
three of the committees, the county towns of Derby, Nottingham and
Leicester were securely in Parliamentarian hands at the beginning of
1643, but the Rutland committee could not use Oakham until the following year, and the Staffordshire committee could not meet in the
county town until May 1643, when it was captured from the Royalists
by Sir William Brereton.

The reorganisation of administrative affairs by the Parliamentarians
also involved the progression from being dependent upon loans to a
taxation system more geared to a longer-term financial need. The
central part of this taxation system was the weekly tax – the Assessment. This was supplemented by a policy of sequestrating estates aimed
at utilising the resources of the Royalists within the region.[24] Sub-
committees of the main Militia Committees dealt with these taxes.
Further sub-committees were created as the responsibilities of the
county committees in general grew. A sub-committee for the 'punish-

21   HMC *Hastings*, vol. 2, p. 87; Roy, I. (ed.), *The Royalist Ordnance Papers* (Oxford,
1964), vol. 1, P. 70; Glover, *op cit*, appendix, p. 62.
22   DRO, D803 M29, np; Glover, *op cit*, appendix, p. 71; Nichols, *op cit*, vol. 3, part
2, appendix 4, p. 31.
23   Firth, C. H. and Rait, R. S. (eds.), *Acts and Ordinances of the Interregnum,
1642–1660* (London, 1911), vol. 1, pp. 49–51.
24   Ibid, pp. 85–100, 106–117; Northamptonshire Record office, Finch Hatton
Manuscript, passim.

ment of scandalous ministers' was created at the same time as the taxation sub-committees, giving the county Parliamentarians powers over religious affairs. The creation of these sub-committees from the same body of men may have been aimed at limiting the potential for disagreements and for preventing individuals from creating powerbases for themselves within the administration. If this was the aim, it was only a partial success. John Hutchinson in Nottinghamshire and Sir John Gell in Derbyshire both created and led factions on their respective committees. Basil Fielding, Earl of Denbigh, created a faction on the Staffordshire committee to try and secure its cooperation once he had taken effective command of the West Midlands Association in March 1644. Denbigh was never technically a member of the committee and his interference was divisive.[25]

In the meantime the Royalists had also reconstructed their administration in the region. The commissions of array had largely fallen into abeyance once the King had created his marching army and there is little evidence to suggest that the commissions met once the campaign began in September 1642. Some of the Staffordshire commissioners felt that their primary allegiance lay with their county, and so they had participated in the special sessions of November 1642, which had proposed a third force to fend off incursions from either side. Nevertheless, it was the commissions which formed the basis of the renewed Royalist organisation in the shires. Even the Staffordshire commission was certainly at work again by late November. In the following February all of the region's commissions of array were ordered to cooperate with each other and on 23 February, Henry Hastings was given command over the region, bringing the North Midlands Royalists together in an association similar to that over which Lord Grey held command for the Parliamentarians.[26] The various commissions established themselves at principal centres (although none were in the county towns except perhaps for the Staffordshire commission during the spring of 1643) throughout the region. Leicestershire's commission sat at Ashby for most of the war, except when it undertook circuits of the county, and in mid-1645 when it was temporarily driven out by plague. Nottinghamshire's commis-

25   For a full discussion of the role of factions on the committees see, Lloyd, P., 'Politics and the Personnel of Politics in Nottingham 1642–1688', unpublished M.Phil. thesis, Nottingham University, 1983, passim; Beats, L., 'Politics and Government in Derbyshire 1640–1660', unpublished Ph.D. thesis, Sheffield University, 1978, passim; and Pennington, D. H. and Roots, I. A. (eds.), *The Committee at Stafford* (Manchester, 1957), p. 356 and passim.

26   Bodleian Library, Dugdale Ms19, f6: Public Record Office, Chancery Lane, Black, W. H., 'Docquets of Letters Patent and other Instruments of Government', p. 9; HMC Hastings, vol. 2, pp. 94–95.

sioners were established at Newark and those for Staffordshire generally met at Lichfield, especially after May 1643. The Derbyshire commission sat at Tutbury, just over the border in Staffordshire, and also at various times in Chesterfield and Ashbourne. The Rutland commission seems to have met in the county at Burleigh House, but also at Belvoir in Leicestershire on some occasions.

By late 1642 the Royalists, like the Parliamentarians, had gradually changed their means of raising money, by moving away from the inadequate loans system to the collection of regular taxes. It is not a simple task to trace the activity of the North Midland Commissioners, as most of their papers were destroyed in the closing stages of the war to limit the evidence available to the Parliamentarian investigators. For Worcestershire and for Glamorgan, working papers produced by the commissions are in existence; but there is no equivalent for the Midland Royalists. Instead their work had to be reconstructed from materials culled from a wide range of sources, such as constables' accounts, rare garrison account books, private papers, and small collections of letters to and from prominent Royalists in the region. The commissions had roughly the same responsibilities as the county committees. They too administered a weekly tax, in this case called the Contribution, and from early 1643, they also ran the sequestration of Parliamentarian estates. From 1644 there was also a Royalist excise tax administered by a sub-commission, but there is little evidence of its collection in the North Midlands.

It is clear that in each county the membership of the commissions of array was smaller than the committee against which they were pitched.[27] Many of the people named by the King in the original commissions issued during the summer of 1642 do not appear to have taken any part in the work of the commissions at any time during the war. Out of the 128 men who were nominated commissioners for the five counties in 1642 and 1643, fifteen became active Parliamentarians, and a further seven died early in the war, or had been captured and prevented from participation by Parliament. There were thirty nominees who made no appearance for either side. These men may have been passive Royalists who sought some form of neutrality; no less than fourteen of them were fined by Parliament for royalism. Sixteen of the nominees who were active royalists, like the earl of Newcastle, a member of three of the commissions, served outside the region throughout the war. The total of sixty possible activists in

27   A full discussion of the figures given below is given in Bennett, M., 'The Royalist War Effort in the North Midlands, 1642–1646', unpublished Ph.D. thesis, Loughborough University, 1986, pp. 35–53, 88–105.

the region represents approximately 47 per cent of those chosen by the King.

Parliament saw a higher proportion of its nominees actually participate in its county administration. Approximately 70 per cent of the 174 men appointed to the committees in the region during the war took some part in the work. Some of the reasons for this discrepancy in participation are easy to appreciate. The King had generally made his appointments before the war had begun and before many people had been obliged to take sides. In some cases too, the appointment was offered to those who may have already expressed hostility to the Royalist cause, in the hope of attracting their support. This policy had at least one success, for it did gain the material support of Walter Wrottesley, the earl of Essex's vice-lieutenant in Staffordshire, who not only sat as a commissioner, but also supplied the Royalist cause with iron from his Wrottesley iron works throughout the war. Parliament seems to have attempted the same policy, for it tried to lure Sir Edward Littleton, of Pillaton Hall, on to its Staffordshire committee well into 1643 before admitting failure. Yet, although Parliament had the advantage of appointing its committeemen after the war had broken out and when loyalties were easier to detect, nine of its nominees, including Wrottesley and Littleton, became active Royalists. That there were fewer mistakes of this kind is perhaps a reflection of Parliament's choice of local activists like Hutchinson or Gell to serve on its committees rather than initially choosing those who were socially prominent, as had been the King's policy when appointing the nobility to lead his commissions of array. The result of this had been that many local nobles like Devonshire and Huntingdon had sought to avoid commitment.

The difference in levels of commitment was matched by other differences between the active committeemen and commissioners. The working commissioners of array tended to have a higher pre-war social status than the committeemen. Approximately 96 per cent of them came from the squirearchy and above, compared with just over 50 per cent of the committeemen. Nevertheless, for both groups, the largest number of active men were labelled as esquires in contemporary documents ranging from the College of Heralds' visitations, official letters and papers emanating from local and central government and personal correspondence.[28] In both instances, the proportion of esquires was approximately 40 per cent of the total number of activists. The differ-

28 In ascribing social rank, I have generally followed the practices and tests of status put forward by Dr Wanklyn and others. These are neatly explained and summarised by Dr Morrill, in Morrill, J., 'The Northern Gentry and the Great Rebellion', *Northern History*, vol. 15, 66–87.

ence was that for the Royalists, esquires represented the lowest social group whilst for the committees, possibly as many as 49 per cent of the members were below the rank, including mere gentlemen (24 per cent), and at least one yeoman was appointed later in the war. From the earliest days of the committees there was also a small group of committeemen drawn from urban hierarchies and involved in trade, like Edmund Craddock in Leicester or William Nixe of Nottingham (four men representing 4.3 per cent), and a large number whose rank is obscure or imprecise (20.5 per cent).

In the royalist commissions there was a greater tendency for the active commissioner to be the head of his family: almost 80 per cent were heads of families, like Sir Gervaise Clifton of Clifton, Nottinghamshire, and a further 11 per cent were eldest sons like Sir John Fitzherbert. For the Parliamentarians, only 45 per cent of those for whom familial status can be ascertained (this is reduced to 30 per cent if all committeemen are included) were heads of families, but a further 36 per cent were eldest sons. This more comparable proportion suggests that there was at least familial prominence to support the selection of the committeemen. This is important when turning to the administrative, political and educational backgrounds of the two groups. The King had selected his commissioners largely on the grounds of the standing in the community which they had achieved already. The absence of any pre-Militia Ordinance lords lieutenant from the commissions highlights the inactivity of the nobility. Most had avoided any connection with the commissions at the outset and Lord Newark, the former lord lieutenant of Nottinghamshire, was probably at Oxford throughout the war. Every other branch of county government was represented. There were among the commissioners fifteen men who had been M.P.s at one time or who had been elected to the Long Parliament; at least eleven deputy lieutenants; eighteen men who had been high sheriffs; and at least eighteen men who had once been J.P.s. Over half of the active commissioners had certainly attended university and 20 per cent had been at one of the inns of court. Despite its greater number of activists, on the five committees Parliament could muster only five M.P.s, two deputy lieutenants, nine high sheriffs, ten J.P.s and four men who had shared in urban government. Just over a third of the committeemen had been at one of the universities, but around a quarter of them had attended one of the inns of court. No doubt this poorer showing in most areas of public life is a reflection of the social status of the committeemen, and is a result of Parliament's attempt to include proven supporters. It also illustrates the perceived social dilution of county government during the war years, so mocked by Royalists during the war and noted afterwards by the Loughborough poet, John Cleveland: 'Upon Sir Thomas Martin, who subscribed a Warrant thus, We the Knights and Gentleman of the committee etc, When there was no Knight but himself.'[29] This poem, dealing with another county at a later date, would have been no less appropriate to Rutland's county committee during the first civil war when only Sir Edward Harrington of Ridlington, knight and baronet, bore any such title. Whilst Parliamentarian committees were run by people with less experience of public affairs and a corporate lack of social standing, their larger size and greater social variety allowed for a greater input and range of ideas to be brought to bear on the administrative process.

It cannot be denied that the greater experience and social cohesion of the commissions of array benefitted the Royalist war effort: the methods and means of taxation owed a lot to pre-war practice, for money was collected by virtue of warrants issued by the high sheriff or the clerk of the peace, via the usual channels of high and petty constables. Those members of the commissions with experience as tax gatherers, such as high sheriffs and the J.P.s, particularly those who had served as commissioners for the Forced Loan in the late-1620s, would no doubt be of considerable assistance to the work of the commission. As the Contribution seems to have used some of the principles established by the collection of ship money in the 1630s, it was significant that six of the region's ex-sheriffs who sat as commissioners had been involved with ship money. One, Sir Henry Skipworth of Cotes, had the reputation in Leicestershire of being a particularly ruthless collector. There was no one actively serving on the Rutland or Nottinghamshire commissions who had been involved with ship money. The J.P.s had always been responsible for solving grievances over taxation matters, either in private sessions, or especially during the previous few years, in full court, dealing with ship money defaulters.[30] This fitted them for their new war-time role as arbiters in cases of over-taxation. Those who believed that they were being assessed unfairly were instructed to pay the sums required to the constable as usual and make an appeal after two months to the J.P.s on the commission.

Parliament's county committees also had representatives of those responsible for many of the functions of local government serving on them. In Nottinghamshire the active J.P.s of 1642 had divided three ways upon the outbreak of war, three becoming Parliamentarian committeemen, three commissioners of array and three remaining aloof

29 Cleveland, J., *Poems By J.C., With Additions, never before printed* (1653), pp. 8–9.
30 Bennett, M., 'People and Government: Civil Disobedience in the North Midlands' unpublished paper presented to the Seventeenth Century Studies Conference, Durham University (1987), pp. 22–29.

from both sides. Four of the five committees in the region had J.P.s on them, with only Staffordshire appearing to be the exception. Gell, the leading figure on the Derbyshire committee, was himself a notorious ship money sheriff who whilst in office had actually insisted that the county could pay more money, and the Nottinghamshire and Rutland committees also contained ex-ship money sheriffs, Sir Francis Thornhaugh of Fenton and Sir Edward Harrington, respectively. The latter had also been a commissioner for the Loan in the 1620s.

This brief study of the commissions of array and the committees has shown something of the nature of their composition. For the most part, the Royalist commissioners were not leading members of the aristocracy or magnates with huge estates in a number of counties. There was a cross-section of local gentry society. Although most of them were esquires or titled gentry, between them they were able to muster no small degree of administrative experience, having held county offices such as high sheriff, J.P. and deputy lieutenant. Many could bring some degree of legal training to the commissions on which they served. All of these factors would be of value to the work which they were called upon to do. Moreover, as they were important local figures, immersed in the counties in which they lived and over which they held authority, they were able to contribute vital local knowledge; a sense of knowing how the community operated, what it could bear and what it could not, could be conveyed to the commissions upon which they sat. The Parliamentarian committees were drawn from a similar social group, although right from the outset the committees involved a greater proportion of people from the lower rungs of the gentry ladder, urban gentry and even yeomen. Nevertheless, these men were predominantly landowners who would have the same qualms as their Royalist counterparts about the effects of war upon the communities in which they lived. The Parliamentarian committeemen brought less experience to their task than did the Royalists; but even so ex-members of county government were present, even if in smaller numbers. Their collective knowledge would be utilised and their experience built upon. Such experience was to be very necessary to both the commissions of array and the county committees. For the duration of the war, under a variety of circumstances, the rival administrations were faced with the collection of taxes necessary to the war's prosecution. The problems of collecting the heavy and unremitting tax burden were complex enough without the constant necessity of fending off enemy incursions. But the end of 1643, Henry Hastings and the Royalists had ringed the area with eight major and sixteen minor garrisons. Each was involved in the collection of the taxation upon which they depended; each was responsible to the commissions of array which decided the levels of taxation required. The system was subject to internal struggles and the interference of central government in Oxford. These problems were compounded by constant skirmishes with local Parliamentarian forces and by the major defeats inflicted during and after the summer of 1644. The region's Parliamentarians hung on to their county town bases, but had major funding difficulties until that same summer, after which the committees were able to extend their own hold on the region. By the end of the war it was to be the committees which dominated the region, with the local Royalists reduced to pockets of territory from which they could collect taxation. For the women and men of the region, the financial burden was a constant one and one which may well have dominated their collective experience of the war. It is an experience which merits further examination, beyond the constrains of this paper.

8

Sir William Brereton and England's Wars of Religion

John Morrill

Originally appeared as John Morrill, 'Sir William Brereton and England's Wars of Religion' in *Journal of British Studies* 24 (July 85): 311–32. Copyright © 1985 by The North American Conference on British Studies. All rights reserved. Reproduced by permission of The University of Chicago Press.

Historians have begun to rediscover the Puritan Revolution. A number of recent studies concentrating on the Long Parliament, on particular counties, or on clusters of religious ideas have found religious divisions at the heart of the collapse of early Stuart government.[1] This article tries to consolidate this trend by looking at the behavior of one prominent individual. If it was indeed religious conviction that drove active minorities to take up arms, then it is essential to find men who have left enough evidence of a sufficiently intimate kind to permit us to pry into the feelings and longings that determined their particular responses to the developing crisis in church and state. While it is hoped that such a case study can help to clarify general issues, it is obviously not possible to claim that one case study demonstrates any particular theory of allegiance. This article presents an instance of a general theory and no more.

This is a revised version of a paper given to the North American Conference on British Studies in Toronto in October 1984. The author is grateful to Paul Christianson and Michael Finlayson for their constructive criticism of the conference paper and to Norman Dore and Jamie Hart for answering fiddly and time-consuming queries.

1   For example, A. Fletcher, *The Outbreak of the English Civil War* (London, 1982); W. Hunt, *The Puritan Moment* (Cambridge, Mass., 1983); M. Fulbrook, *Piety and Politics* (Cambridge, 1983); C. Hibbard, *Charles I and the Popish Plot* (Chapel Hill, N.C., 1982); and J. S. Morrill, 'The Religious Context of the English Civil War,' *Transactions of the Royal Historical Society*, 5th ser., 34 (1984): 155–78.

The subject of the first part of this article is Sir William Brereton (1604–61) of Handforth in Cheshire, who will be examined as a Puritan magistrate in the 1630s, as a Parliamentarian activist in the early 1640s, as a county boss in the war years, and as an increasingly disillusioned 'honest radical' from 1646 and especially from 1653. He is probably better documented in the public records than all but twenty or so M.P.s in the Long Parliament, and his fifteen hundred extant letters plus a collection of private papers and travel journals from the 1630s make him probably the best documented of all county bosses, at least down to 1646.[2]

Brereton was the head of a cadet branch of an ancient Cheshire family, but his branch was among the thirty or so wealthiest families in Cheshire, and its estates were concentrated in the northeast of the county not far from Stockport.[3] Although he acquired lands in Staffordshire by marriage and in New England by purchase, he was essentially a Cheshire man. His father and grandfather had both served on the commission of the peace, and his father had twice served as knight of the shire. Sir William himself was put on the commission of the peace as soon as he was released from wardship,[4] and he served in the parliament of 1628 and in both parliaments of 1640, thus becoming the first man ever to serve as knight for Cheshire in three successive parliaments and only the fourth since 1543 to represent the county three times.[5]

2   Five letter books are known to have survived; the chronological sequence is: Cheshire Record Office (RO), DDX/428 (never previously used by scholars); British Library (BL), Additional (Add.) MS 11331, Add. MS 11332, and Add. MS 11333; and Birmingham Reference Library (RL), MS 595611. Cheshire RO, DDX/428; and BL, Add. MS 11331, have now been calendared; see R. N. Dore, ed., *The Letter Books of Sir William Brereton*, Lancashire and Cheshire Record Society, vol. 123 (Gloucester, 1984). There is also a miscellany of Brereton's papers relating to 'public affairs' in the Chester City Archives Office (CAO), CR63/702. His travel journals were published; see E. Hawkins, ed., *Brereton's Travels*, Chetham Society, vol. 1 (Manchester, 1844).
3   His family background is well covered in G. Ormerod, *History of Cheshire*, rev. by G. Helsby, 3 vols. (Chester, 1882). For the Breretons' involvement with the Boleyn faction in the 1530s and its effects on local politics, see E. W. Ives, ed., *The Letters and Accounts of William Brereton of Malpas*, Lancashire and Cheshire Record Society, vol. 116 (Chester, 1976).
4   His father and mother both died in 1609, and he was brought up in the household of his mother's family, the (Puritan) Hollands of Denton. He married the daughter of Sir George Booth, *custos rotulorum* in Cheshire, which probably explains his precocious appointment to the bench and perhaps his early appointment as a deputy lieutenant. For his early years, see R. N. Dore, 'The Early Life of Sir William Brereton,' *Transactions of the Lancashire and Chester Antiquarian Society* 63 (1953): 1–8.
5   J. S. Morrill, 'Parliamentary Representation,' in *Victoria History of the County of Chester* (hereafter *VCH Cheshire*), vol. 2, ed. B. Harris (Oxford, 1979), pp. 101–3, 106–8.

Between 1629 and 1640, he attended over 80 percent of all quarter sessions (the *custos* or chairman attended 60 percent and no one else more than 40 percent). The files contain more than twice as many documents with his signature as with the signature of any other justice, suggesting that he was also the busiest justice out of sessions. He displayed especial zeal in suppressing alehouses and pursuing Catholic recusants. He was a model Puritan magistrate. There is no evidence that he approved of the policies of the government, but neither is there any evidence of flagging zeal in the face of royal policies. He was also an active deputy lieutenant; he cooperated over the Book of Orders and with the commissioners for distraint of knighthood; he paid his forced loan promptly; and he did not obstruct the payment of ship money.[6] His actions in 1640–41 suggest that he resented royal fiscal policies and doubted their legality. None of this imposed an intolerable strain on his conscience. Brereton, a militant in 1642, did not engage in any acts of passive disobedience in the 1630s. He was certainly not one of those who contemplated emigration as an alternative to subjection to tyranny. He combined active magistracy with a thrusting and prosperous pursuit of business interests, such as the construction of the first commercial duck decoy anywhere in the country.[7]

The most telling illustration of this relative constitutional complacency was his attitude toward ship money, especially as he has often been wrongly accused of obstructing its collection.[8] In the mid-1630s, the Corporation of Chester launched a series of legal actions against exempt jurisdictions within its bounds, hoping to secure a legal victory in respect of ship money that could then be extended to include a variety of other financial and administrative burdens. One of their targets was Brereton's former monastic property, which was known as the Nuns. As far as the city was concerned, the central issue was whether his tenants should perform watch and ward. The Privy Council found for Brereton in his dispute and specifically noted the fact that he had promptly paid his assessments.[9]

6   For his role in local government before 1640, see Dore, passim; J. S. Morrill, *Cheshire, 1630–1660* (Oxford, 1974), chaps. 1, 2; and G. Higgins, 'County Government and Society in Cheshire, c. 1590–1640' (M.A. thesis, University of Liverpool, 1973), chaps. 2, 3. For his intense interest in the local government in the Netherlands and Scotland, esp. the relief of the (deserving) poor, see Hawkins, ed., pp. 14, 21, 46, 50, 106–10.

7   Dore, pp. 5–8; Chester CAO, CR63/702, pp. 1–115 and passim.

8   As, e.g., by J. T. Cliffe in *The Puritan Gentry* (London, 1984), p. 195.

9   See A. M. Johnson, 'Some Aspects of the Political, Constitutional, Social and Economic History of the City of Chester, c. 1550–1662' (D.Phil. thesis, Oxford University, 1970), pp. 120–38; P. Lake, 'The Collection of Ship Money in Cheshire,' *Northern History* (1981): 44–71; Public Record Office (PRO), State Papers (SP)

Brereton is as easily labeled a Puritan in the 1630s as any gentleman can be.[10] He was a Protestant nationalist with marked anti-Catholic views.[11] He displayed a hostility to the imposition of 'popish ceremonial' in the 1630s; he disapproved of the Book of Sports; he rejoiced to hear of churches where sermons were preached twice on a Sunday and of towns where it was possible to hear up to six in a single day;[12] he admired Archbishop Ussher and Bishop Moreton and disapproved of Archbishop Spottiswoode.[13] In Holland he visited and admired the worship of separatist congregations such as those of Hugh Peter and Thomas Paget. He liked what he saw of the Lutherans and much of what he saw of the Scottish Kirk.[14] Although his travel journals from Holland, Ireland, and Scotland preserve a cool, neutral form (they were probably intended for circulation among his friends), the topics he chose to include and an occasional transparency of manner reveal a marked Erastianism together with some anxiety that freedom in religion could run to license. He was at his most eloquent on the work of lay elders in the Kirk.[15] He comes across as an ideal Collinsonian Protestant, with an openness and eclecticism in matters of practice, as an austere Calvinist in doctrine, and as a very sensitive antenna that picked up even the remotest trace of popery. All this would have made him react strongly against the pretensions of Laudianism.[16]

Brereton sat as knight of the shire in both the Short and the Long Parliaments. On both occasions his return followed boisterous canvassing and caballing among the greater gentry.[17] In the spring, the county establishment was united against an intrusive, overbearing court and against religious innovation. The contest, in Cheshire as elsewhere, was not between court and country but between local groups vying for

16/317, no. 100, SP 16/347, no. 20, SP 16/354, no. 7 and Privy Council Register (PC) 2/47, fols. 422–23; BL, Harleian (Harl.) MS 2093, passim, and Add. MS 36915, passim.

10   See the sources cited in n. 59 below.

11   Dore, pp. 15–18; Hawkins, ed., passim, but esp. pp. 6–7, 13, 45–46, 59–60, 63–64, 67–68, 79–83, 100–10, 121, 135–44.

12   Hawkins, ed., pp. 59–60.

13   Ibid., pp. 79–82, 99, 115, 134–43.

14   Ibid., pp. 6, 10, 11, 24, 57, 63, 67, 106–10.

15   Ibid., pp. 106–10.

16   For 'Laudianism' in Cheshire, see R. C. Richardson, *Puritanism in North-West England* (Manchester, 1972), passim; H. R. Trevor-Roper, *Archbishop Laud*, 2d ed. (London, 1965), pp. 173–74, 323; B. W. Quintrell, *The Troubling of Bishop Bridgeman*, Transactions of the Lancashire and Cheshire Historical Society, vol. 132 (Liverpool, 1982), pp. 67–102.

17   Morrill, *Cheshire* (n. 6 above), pp. 29–34; *VCH Cheshire* (n. 5 above), pp. 107–9.

primacy of honor, each claiming to be better able to secure redress of agreed grievances. Brereton ran in harness with Sir Thomas Aston (future champion of non-Laudian episcopacy and future Royalist activist but also an ex-sheriff who had become a knowledgeable critic of ship money).[18] They both appear to have run under the aegis of a wealthy group of families headed by Lord Cholmondeley of Cholmondeley.

In the autumn election, Brereton and Aston were on opposite sides, Aston being paired with Cholmondeley's son-in-law and Brereton apparently running as an independent. This turnaround may have been occasioned by no more than a reluctance to breach the hitherto unbroken tradition that the county seats be occupied by rota, which made Brereton's search for a third term unacceptable. But it is more likely that there were growing qualms about his religious views. While he appears to have sat mute in the Short Parliament,[19] his private conversations with Aston or with other local gentry about events in the spring and summer may have isolated him. Certainly a commentator on the election hitherto sympathetic to him indicates that he set out to secure the support of 'the religious' against the county establishment – highly successfully, as it turns out, for he was returned in first place.[20] There was no major rift, however. He was fully engaged, as were Aston and members of all gentry factions, in the preparation of a petition of grievances that he presented to the House of Commons in the early weeks of the new Parliament. Brereton's petition concentrated on secular grievances – principally, ship money and coat and conduct money.[21]

There is no reason to suppose that Brereton dissented from any of the remedial secular reforms passed by the Long Parliament in 1641. But he took little part in the debates and sat on only one relevant committee (the committee on the bill for annual parliaments, out of which came the Triennial Bill).[22] By contrast, he spoke frequently on the need for ecclesiastical reform and religious renewal and was seconded onto many important religious committees, such as those for the reform or aboli-

18   For Aston, see Lake, passim; and a forthcoming article by Judith Maltby.
19   The parliamentary diary of Sir Thomas Aston, which increases our knowledge of the number of speeches tenfold (and which appears to be remarkably comprehensive), has recently come to light and is being prepared for publication by Judith Maltby; it will be published by the Camden Society. The diary records no speech by Brereton.
20   BL, Harl. MS 2125, fol. 133.
21   *Calendar of State Papers, Domestic* (*CSPD*), *1640–41*, pp. 146–47; Cheshire RO, Quarter Sessions Order Book, 1640–50, fol. 13.
22   *Journals of the House of Commons* (*JC*), 2:60.

tion of High Commission, for the investigation of the activities of Bishop Wren and Bishop Piers, for the bill against scandalous ministers, for the security of the true religion, for the reformation of the universities, and for establishing grounds to dissuade Charles I from proceeding to the consecration of five new bishops in the autumn of 1641.[23] Meanwhile he was actively involved in the promotion of root-and-branch petitions from Cheshire and in securing a favorable hearing for such petitions from other counties on the floor of the House of Commons.[24] In regard to the Cheshire petitions, Brereton was to find himself isolated among the county elite. No other leading magistrate associated himself with the abolition of episcopacy, and he found himself working with and through a group of lesser gentry and substantial farmers (men with solid experience of county affairs through regular service on grand juries) together with some of the merchants of Chester who had gained notoriety for their entertainment of Prynne in 1637 as he passed through Chester to prison in Caernarvon after his brutal physical punishment in London for libeling the bishops. This petitioning campaign gained the support of few of the parish clergy and became clearly linked in the minds of most of the county establishment with outbreaks of iconoclasm, in which Brereton's second wife and other members of his family were implicated.[25] One erstwhile supporter spoke of having heard a friend of his say that he 'loved Sir William Brereton well, but yet, as I do, loved order, decency and good discipline better.'[26] Brereton may also have already been linked to the radical congregationalist Samuel Eaton, just returned from exile in New England, whose sermons not only challenged the basis of all existing church government, discipline, and liturgy but also took up radical social causes. From the outset, Eaton received the patronage of Brereton's most prominent ally among the gentry, Robert Duckenfield of Duckenfield.[27] Brereton's group was, then, a radical minority, and it was opposed by a group led by Cholmondeley and Aston committed to the defense of 'the pure religion of Queen Elizabeth and King James' (i.e., non-Laudian Anglicanism) and by the bulk of the county establishment, whose preference appears to have lain with a reduced episcopacy. There can be little doubt, given his support for Sir Henry Vane's proposals in June 1641, that Brereton had come to reject any church

23 Ibid., passim.
24 Morrill, *Cheshire*, chap. 2; Fletcher (n. 1 above), pp. 104–8.
25 BL, Add. MS 36914, fols. 210, 225.
26 Ibid., fol. 215.
27 Morrill, *Cheshire*, pp. 35–37; W. Urwick, *Historical Sketches of Nonconformity in Cheshire* (Manchester, 1864), pp. 288–90 and passim; Bodleian Library, Tanner MS 65, fol. 214.

settlement that was merely a modification of the existing one: he was for a fresh start.[28]

Two things remain uncertain. The first is whether the radicalism that is so evident in 1641 had been there all along but is hidden from us by his prudence and self-censorship or whether that radicalism represents a clarification, a demystification under the impress of events in the early months of the parliament. The second is whether he knew what should take the place of the old religion: commitment to the dismantling of the Elizabethan settlement did not necessarily mean commitment to a particular alternative. These are matters that can only be resolved in the wider perspectives that will be explored later.

By the summer of 1641, Brereton had made no impact on the Long Parliament's concern with secular misgovernment, but he was clearly marked out as a firebrand on religious issues. In the second session, after the summer recess, he again took little part in the main constitutional debates over the Grand Remonstrance, the Militia Ordinance, and the Nineteen Propositions, and he made no effort to mobilize support by petition or grand jury presentment on constitutional issues. But he continued to organize provincial lobbies for religious renewal, and he became increasingly caught up with the Irish crisis. As soon as news of the Catholic massacres of Protestants in Ulster reached London, he was dispatched to the northwest to organize recruits, equipment, and shipping for the relief forces and also to interrogate refugees in order to identify 'planted' papist agents. His letters reveal a credulity both in the probability of similar outrages on the mainland and in the possibility of the king's implication in the rebellion. He shared the conviction of many that the king was deranged, so deluded by papist advisers that he was abdicating his role as protector of the realm and protector of Protestantism. The king was not a papist but a man no longer able to discern the dangers of popish infiltration of church and state.[29]

---

28   The general context of this paragraph derives from *JC*, vol. 2, *passim*; the parliamentary diaries of d'Ewes and Moore, both published sections (namely, W. Notestein, ed., *The Journal of Sir Simonds d'Ewes from the Beginning of the Long Parliament to the Opening of the Trial of the Earl of Strafford* [New Haven, Conn., 1923]; W. H. Coates, ed., *The Journal of Sir Simonds d'Ewes from the First Recess of the Long Parliament to the Withdrawal of the King from London* [New Have, Conn., 1942]; and W. H. Coates, A. S. Young, and V. F. Snow, eds., *The Private Journals of the Long Parliament, 3 January to 5 March 1642* [New Haven, Conn., 1982]) and unpublished sections; W. A. Shaw, *A History of the English Church during the Civil Wars*, 2 vols. (London, 1900), vol. 1; and W. Abbott, 'The Issue of Episcopacy in the Long Parliament' (D.Phil. thesis, Oxford University, 1981).

29   This paragraph is culled from a mass of material in *JC*; the journal of Sir Simonds d'Ewes (BL, Harl. MS 162, and Harl. MS 164); uncalendared material in

In the summer and autumn of 1642 Brereton seized the initiative in Cheshire and created a Parliamentarian movement. Until his arrival, no attempt had been made to implement the Militia Ordinance, and without him it is hard to see who was in a position to seize the initiative for Parliament. Brereton's standing as a veteran deputy lieutenant and as a member of parliament, conjoined with his energy and drive, was enough to seize the initiative from the commissioners of array. A clear majority of the gentry dithered, unable to decide between allegiance to king or to Parliament and determined that a civil war was unnecessary. A powerful minority, consisting almost entirely of those who had organized themselves to defend the Elizabethan church settlement, declared for the king, but the men they raised and armed were mostly subsumed into the royal marching army and went off to Edgehill and beyond. Brereton, working with and through a group of middling gentry who had helped him to organize the antiepiscopal petitions of the previous eighteen months, gained control of most of the trained bands and fortified Nantwich, the second town of the county, though the prize of the city of Chester eluded them. By the time the county establishment split, no longer able to dream of keeping Cheshire out of the war, Brereton and his men were in control of the war machine.[30] There was to be continual friction over the next four years between Brereton's group and the county magnates over the conduct of the war, but the triumph of Brereton's 'russet-coated captains' was the product less of their zeal during the war than of their precocious actions in the summer of 1642. Those who chose to fight in 1642, as opposed to those drawn into the fighting in 1642, were primarily driven by their religious views.

There is no need to repeat here the account that has long been available of Brereton's qualities as a war leader.[31] His engrossment of power, his breadth of strategic vision, and his dynamism and pragmatism can be taken as read. It is only necessary to emphasize his characteristic belief in the end justifying the means, his indifference to the breaches of those legal nostrums that many believed the war was intended to preserve (his free use of arbitrary imprisonment, martial law, and distraint, his rigorous application of the sequestration rules against 'neuters' as well as against 'malignants,' etc.), and his distinctive commitment to religious

Chester CAO (Cowper MSS) and Cheshire RO, DCC/14 (Cowper MSS); and BL, Add. MS 11332 (a few letters at the back of the volume).

30   Morrill, *Cheshire*, pp. 56–69; which has been supplemented and improved on by Fletcher, pp. 338–417; and R. Hutton, *The Royalist War Effort* (London, 1982), chaps. 1, 2. His role is well elucidated by the sequence of letters in Historical Manuscript Commission , *Portland I*, pp. 44–46, 51, 94–96, 140–41.

31   See Morrill, *Cheshire*, chaps. 3, 4; R. N. Dore, *The Civil Wars in Cheshire* (Chester, 1966), passim; Dore ed. (n. 2 above), introduction.

renewal. He was precocious in his employment of officers as lay preach-ers;[32] his troops met as a gathered church for prayers before his major engagements;[33] he renewed his acquaintance with Hugh Peter and kept up a heady correspondence with him;[34] he personally supervised the expulsion of 'scandalous ministers,' including many moderates who had received the patronage of his senior colleagues on county committees;[35] and he protected and patronized Samuel Eaton, a radical congregation-alist who had spent the 1630s in New England.[36] His language was as redolent of the language of providence and divine immanence as that of any civil war commander; he said of the spire of Lichfield cathedral, which his cannonades destroyed: 'It was erected in ressemblance of the Pope's Triple Crowne and if soe this downfall may be ominous and prognostick of another downfall';[37] and to those who protested against another act of iconoclasm: 'You insist much upon defacing the ancien-teth monument of Christian piety in these parts and will see the hand of God's judgment upon the same for the ignorance and superstition that hath been nourished and practised in that place.'[38] His rhetoric remained fundamentally religious. His vision of the future he was fighting for was articulated solely in terms of man's response to God's invitation to follow his path. Throughout his fifteen hundred letters there is no trace of any commitment to political or constitutional *ends*.

In 1645 and the first half of 1646 he was one of the most powerful and influential men in England. But with the end of the fighting there was a rapid decline in his prominence. His attendance and activity in Parliament became increasingly fitful. He was very active in the summer of 1646 and the spring of 1647 and then absent for several months (for which he was heavily fined).[39] He was active on army committees during the second civil war, and he sat in the Rump from shortly after the exe-cution of the king.[40] But his attendance record was below average, even

---

32   For example, Jerome (or Hieronymus) Zanckey. Many of Zanckey's letters to Brereton are in BL, Add. MS 11332, and Add. MS 11333. See J. E. Auden, *Sir Jerome Zanckey of Balderstone*, Transactions of the Shropshire Antiquarian Society, vol. 50 (London, 1950). For the preaching officers, see Dore, ed., pp. 79ff.

33   Cambridge University Library, Syn.7.64.236[63] ('Cheshire's Success,' March 1643, no. 4).

34   For example, Dore, ed., p. 88; R. P. Stearns, *The Strenuous Puritan* (Urbana, Ill., 1954), pp. 293–94.

35   Morrill, *Cheshire*, pp. 139–79.

36   Birmingham RL, MS 595611, p. 166; Morrill, *Cheshire*, pp. 164, 167n., 264–70.

37   Birmingham RL, MS 595611, pp. 250–51.

38   Ibid., pp. 262–63.

39   *JC*, 5:337 and passim.

40   A. B. Worden, *The Rump Parliament* (Cambridge, 1974), pp. 65, 376n.

for that assembly. He squeezed onto the Council of State (in last place) in 1651.[41] His postwar committee work consisted almost entirely of military and religious matters.[42] He abandoned almost all his positions in local government and appears to have lived in semiretirement in the archiepiscopal palace at Croydon, which he had acquired in the late 1640s. He played no part in the public affairs of the Protectorate except to contest Cheshire in the 1656 elections as an opposition candidate,[43] but he resumed his seat in the restored Rump in 1659. Despite some damaging testimony against him given at the trial of Hugh Peter in 1660 in which it was alleged that he was one of those urging Cromwell in December 1648 to establish the High Court of Justice to try the king, he was left unmolested.[44] He died soon afterward, and we lose sight of him as his coffin was swept away in a flash flood as it was being taken across a ford on its way back to Cheshire.[45]

The explanation of this atrophy is not easy to discover. In part, no doubt, the unpopularity of his hard-line policies in the North Midlands led to an erosion of his power base, especially with the disbandment of provincial armies in late 1646 and 1647. Then at last the greater gentry who had been his reluctant allies on the county committees set out to reestablish their own primacy through the traditional organs of local government. On this account, Brereton's power base in Westminster, which rested on the ability to deliver the goods in the North Midlands rather than on his abilities as a speechmaker, would crumble in consequence. Being the only M.P. for Cheshire in the House between 1642 and 1646 gave him considerable importance as a linkman, but it also meant that he was not the leader of a phalanx of M.P.s and that he probably commanded no man's vote but his own. But this is not an adequate explanation. Although the restoration of great, quarter, and petty sessions eroded the domination Brereton had achieved through his packing of wartime committees, it did not destroy it. His closest ally, John Bradshaw, was appointed chief justice of Chester, close wartime colleagues controlled local garrisons and the militia, and his group retained a powerful presence on the commission of the peace and won as many tussles as they lost within the sequestration committee. Brereton was a battler, and his abandonment of his home, offices, and friends needs further explanation. He may have been dismayed and disillusioned at the smear campaign mounted by his Cheshire critics and amplified by the press and

---

41   *JC*, 6:553; for his modest attendance record, see *CSPD, 1651*, p. xxxv.
42   *JC*, vols. 5–7, passim; *CSPD, 1646–53*, passim.
43   Morrill, *Cheshire*, pp. 287–92.
44   *An Exact and Impartiall Accompt of the Indictment, Arraignment, Trial and Judgment . . . of 29 Regicides* (London, 1661), pp. 167, 248.
45   J. P. Earwaker, *East Cheshire*, 2 vols. (London, 1887), 1:259.

by enemies within the House of Commons. He was charged with corruption by his nephew, young George Booth, with seizing Eccleshall
Castle for himself and for his own profit rather than that of Parliament,
and with handing Dudley Castle back to its Royalist owners for considerations linking him to certain London goldsmiths. Such accusations
followed him into the 1650s, one pamphleteer speaking of his 'prodigious stomach to turn the archbishop's chapel at Croydon into a
kitchen.' In August 1646, he gained notoriety when a debate in the
Commons about his possible confirmation in possession of Eccleshall
Castle as a reward for military service led to a debate so heated that Sir
John Clotworthy moved that a ballot box be brought in so that the issue
could be settled by a secret vote. Yet even this seems insufficient as an
explanation. Almost all prominent M.P.s and county bosses were
accused of peculation. Brereton was no more pilloried by his critics than
were many others. A more compelling explanation of his lassitude after
1646 may lie in his particular disillusion at the failure to settle true religion.[46] Norman Dore, the greatest authority on Brereton, concluded
that 'his political ineffectiveness after the civil war was partly due to an
inability to decide between the orderliness of presbyterianism and the
mental freedom of Independency.'[47] That tension is very evident both in
the 1630s and in the early 1640s. It reminds us again that the precise
form of the new church was subordinate at that time to a generalized
yearning to fall in with the ways of God and the promotion of agreed
norms of godliness. Forms could be left to an assembly of divines. For
men like Brereton, the how was subordinate to the hither. The events of
1646–47 forced men like him to adopt a particular form of church government or to seek toleration outside it. His preference almost certainly
lay with an alternative form of national church. He did not want either
the scheme of the Westminster Assembly or the license of total freedom.
He may well have been shaken not only by the course of events at Westminster but also by the strength and pervasiveness of the discredited old
religion. Never having seen constitutional checks and balances, let
alone popular sovereignty, as the imperatives to civil war, he could take
no consolation from regicide and the establishment of the republic. Such
an interpretation is speculative, but it is wholly consistent with the
evidence that survives for the years after 1646.

46   Most of the material in this paragraph comes from a lecture on the Civil War
in the West Midlands given by R. N. Dore in Birmingham on November 25, 1984.
The reference to Brereton's prodigious stomach is from *The Mysteries of the Good Old
Cause*, 2d ed. (London, 1663), p. 3; and the debate on Eccleshall Castle is discussed
in M. Kishlansky, *The Rise of the New Model Army* (Cambridge, 1979), p. 137. See
also P. W. Thomas, *Sir John Berkenhead* (Oxford, 1969), pp. 104–5.
47   Dore, 'The Early Life of Sir William Brereton' (n. 4 above), p. 17.

Let us turn, as the preacher of a Fast sermon would have said, to the applications.[48] While Brereton was clearly not typical of all M.P.s or even of all those who became Parliamentarians, he appears to represent a crucial group or at least to represent an important way of thinking. However, first of all he is a reminder of the hazards of agglomeration, of drawing up – whether for the 1620s or for the 1640s – a catalog of grievances against the king and his ministers and a list of all who expressed concern about one or more items from the catalog and then assuming that everyone on the list suscribed to everything in the catalog. This is almost as serious a fault in historiography as is the tendency to isolate all the issues on which there was conflict of opinion without setting them into the context or perspective of those issues on which there was consensus. Historians should emulate engineers, one of whose functions it is to determine where the stress points are in, say, a bridge. There will always be stress points, and changes in the structure can shift the patterns of stress. But it is also the task of engineers to estimate how and in what circumstances the stress will become too great, resulting in fractures and, ultimately, in collapse. Some materials are capable of absorbing great stress. Historians of the 1630s and 1640s must imitate the engineers. They must study the patterns of stress and isolate the points of maximum stress, but they must also establish how and in what circumstances fractures will occur. It is inadequate merely to chronicle the pattern of stress, let alone to aggregate all the stresses. It is asserted here that, notwithstanding the claims of some recent works, Charles I's government of church and state occasioned widespread alarm, dismay, and anger and that much of the alarm and anger was the product of deeply felt conflict of belief and not just dissatisfaction with the distribution of office and patronage dressed up in rhetorical flourishes. But equally, there has never been a political community in which there were not conflicts of interest and ideology. What the historian has to discover is how far critics of royal policies in the 1620s and 1630s believed that remedies for grievance remained open within the political and constitutional framework and how far they were forced to reexamine the assumptions that defined the limits of political obligation. Few men were more militant in their support for the Parliamentary cause in and after 1642 than Sir William Brereton. Yet, as we have seen, there is no evidence that in the 1630s his perception of the scale

---

48   The following paragraphs are a digest of Morrill, 'The Religious Context of the English Civil War' (n. 1 above), and 'The Attack on the Church of England in the Long Parliament' in D. Beales and G. Best (eds), *History, Society and the Churches* (Cambridge, 1985).

of royal misgovernment led him seriously to contemplate rebellion. In this, Brereton seems to represent the view of most of the gentry and most of the nation. The magnitude of the crown's assault on liberties was insufficient and the impracticability of mounting effective resistance was too great.

England had the kind of civil war that it had because early Stuart government was so strong. Since their title was so secure and since there were no rival claimants, the easiest remedy of the aggrieved – to rally to the banner of a pretender – was unavailable. This certainly reduced the risks of civil war, but it also meant that if civil war did come it would be more radical and more violent (since it would involve the questioning of deeper and more fundamental values). Levels of political violence were declining decade by decade from the late sixteenth century onward (fewer treason and sedition trials, less and less resort to arms to settle disputes, less brigandage, more recognition of the ubiquity of royal justice, etc.). Fewer royal officers were killed or maimed, and there was more law-abidingness (and hence more litigiousness) than elsewhere in Europe. Until 1640 there is no evidence at all of a country sliding out of control, of a weak and increasingly unheeded monarch presiding over anarchy. That too would have produced a different kind of civil war, one more akin to the Frondes. It was not so. There were structural weaknesses in the Todor-Stuart state, but there was an immense momentum of obedience too. And while Charles I was a thoroughly incompetent, shifty, and unreliable monarch who buckled under pressure, there was more that he and his critics would have agreed on at a conference on the nature of kingly power than they would have disagreed on. Most of those whose opinions we can determine, among the gentry and beyond, held, by 1640, a limited but firm belief in a partial royal tyranny. The king, albeit as a consequence of wicked counsel, was misusing his powers. But let us be clear what that means. There was no criticism of monarchy per se; there was no criticism of the long-term development of the early modern state; there was no demand for a fundamental change in the nature of royal power. The complaints were very specifically about misgovernment under a particular king, Charles I, and they were about the abuse of power, not the attempt to usurp new powers. The king was not accused of trying to make law outside Parliament or of claiming new prerogatives or fresh arbitrary powers. He was accused of using approved powers in inappropriate circumstances, powers that he possessed *pro bono publico* (for the public good), *pro bono suo* (for his own benefit). This was a limited perception of tyranny. There is little evidence that most men believed that approved modes of protest – in and through Parliament, in petitions to the king in council, or in extremis by passive disobedience or emigration – were exhausted. The pressure on liberty, estates, and consciences was considerable but not extreme. Those who had preached passive obedience to the Catholics in the late sixteenth century could not, or at least did not, bring themselves to contemplate the right to resist. No single cause was dramatic enough as a focus of resistance, no person or institution existed as a rallying point in the way in which Parlement, provincial Estates, or the households of *Les Grands* acted as a magnet for malcontents in France. Until Parliament met in wholly unique circumstances in the autumn of 1640 (able to command its own destiny)[49] there was a helplessness at the prospects of organizing resistance. Members of the Short Parliament had recognized that the king could either make concessions to them in order to secure a grant to renew his war with the Scots or else make concessions to the Scots and be rid of them. They therefore set their sights low.[50] Members of the Long Parliament were conscious that the king had willfully blundered away his initiative and that with the Scots' occupation of Newcastle he was forced to wait on the willingness of the Houses to vote the supply to send them home. They therefore set their sights high. This had given them what would probably have been a once-for-all opportunity to put things right.[51]

The Long Parliament agonized over but was not polarized by the constitutional issue.[52] There was indeed quite a limited constitutional debate in the country in 1641. While the presses poured out sermons, tracts, and broadsides about the fate of episcopacy and the Book of Common Prayer, the conservatively conceived, restorative constitutional/institutional measures were reported but were not as extensively debated. Even when, in 1642, the Militia Ordinance and the Nineteen Propositions divided the Houses and the country, the intellectual debate was amazingly limited, tended to follow events rather than to lead them, and found both sides adopting a conservative, defensive posture.[53] Those who were primarily concerned with secular misgovernment, with legal and constitutional issues, were not primarily responsible for the taking up of arms. The perception of men like John Selden, Bulstrode

49   Despite Charles I's fantasies about retaining Parliament only if it would grant him supply (for which, see C. Russell, 'Why Did Charles I Call the Long Parliament?' *History* 69 [1984]: 375–83), he was not a free agent.
50   As will be shown by the publication of the parliamentary diary of Sir Thomas Aston (see n. 19 above).
51   For a rather different recent emphasis, see S. Lambert, 'The Opening of the Long Parliament,' *Historical Journal* 27 (1984): 265–88.
52   Morrill, 'The Religious Context of the English Civil War,' passim.
53   Ibid., p. 70; and M. Mendle, 'Politics and Political Thought, 1640–1642,' in *Origins of the English Civil War*, ed. C. Russell (London, 1973), pp. 226–32 (which is developed at greater length in his 'Mixed Government, the Estates and the Bishops' [Ph.D. thesis, Washington University, 1977], pp. 396–432).

Whitlocke, and Benjamin Rudyerd that the king could not be trusted to abide by the settlement of 1641 led them to vote for the Militia Ordinance and the Nineteen Propositions. But it did not lead them to vote for measures to impose those guarantees by force. They knew which side they had to be on if there was a war, but they did not will that war.[54] Similarly, men like Sir Edward Hyde on the Royalist side, those dominated by a constitutional propriety and constructionism that forbade innovation in accidentals in order to preserve the essence of the constitution, were necessarily at the king's side but in despair at the drift to war.[55] Those who took the initiative in 1641–42, either in London, with the peripatetic royal court, or in the provinces, were those who, whether they shared the perception of limited royal tyranny or were indifferent to it, were specifically driven to one of two polarized sets of religious imperatives.

In the early months of the Long Parliament more than six hundred cases were brought on appeal to the House of Lords from common law or conciliar courts. They reveal widespread abuses of the rule of law by officers of the crown since the accession of Charles I. Yet cases involving the henchmen of Archbishop Laud, or otherwise connected with religious policy, were far more numerous and damaging than were those involving secular officers of the crown. Ship money and coat and conduct money threw up only a handful of cases, the imposition of Laudian rulings at least forty.[56] This is just one aspect of a larger problem.[57] No ship money sheriffs and few M.P.s were disciplined for zealous implementation of unpopular royal policies; there was certainly no widespread purge or political witch-hunt. Once leading councillors had been harried from office, there was an end to persecution. The opposite happened in the church: there was an escalating pursuit of the bishops, individually or in groups; scores of ministers were investigated by committees and many of them were deprived of their livings; and those who had been persecuted for religious offences in the 1620s were rehabilitated and lionized (in contrast to the victims of political persecution such as the M.P.s imprisoned after the scenes at the end of

---

54   For the later months of 1642, see Fletcher (n. 1 above), chaps. 7–12; and the early parts of J. H. Hexter, *The Reign of King Pym* (New Haven, Conn., 1940). For Selden, see R. Tuck, 'The Ancient Law of Freedom: John Selden and the Civil War,' in *Reactions to the English Civil War*, ed. J. S. Morrill (London, 1982), pp. 137–62; for Whitlocke, see R. Spalding, *The Improbable Puritan* (London, 1979); for Rudyerd, I am indebted to David Smith for letting me see work in progress.
55   B. H. G. Wormald, *Clarendon* (Cambridge, 1950), pt. 1.
56   J. S. Hart, 'The House of Lords and the Reformation of Justice, 1640–1643' (Ph.D. thesis, Cambridge University, 1985), chap. 3.
57   Morrill, 'The Attack on the church of England in the Long Parliament,' passim.

the 1629 parliament, who got scant recompense). Intense lobbying of Parliament by petition, by the Scots, and by the city of London led to a split over religion that was not paralleled by any split over the constitution. When the Long Parliament opened, most M.P.s sought a return to non-Laudian Anglicanism. They bitterly resented the clericism, the imposition of particular patterns of worship, derivable from but not vibrant within the traditions and injunctions of the church over the previous seventy years. Many resented the new emphasis on the sacraments, at the expense of the pulpit, and the ban on that penumbra of religious observances that had grown up in many parishes and many households around the prayer book. (For Laud, a particular style associated with the prayer book was not only necessary: it was sufficient.) Yet for many, the great majority perhaps, their reflex was conservative, restorative; they sought to protect the Church of England from innovation and subversion by returning to the status quo *ante* Laud.[58] There was a continuity with the arguments of the later 1620s. For them the program of the Long Parliament in religious matters was precisely to parallel their program in constitutional matters. But from the outset there was a strong minority in both Houses whose diagnosis and prognosis of the religious situation went much deeper.[59] These men saw the malaise in the church as more fundamental, as a fatal flaw in its creation and constitution. What was needed was not reform but re-formation, not restoration but renewal. The Elizabethan settlement itself was to be dismantled and a new system of government instituted. Such men had made no such call in the 1610s and 1620s because the church of James I, for all its faults, was moving, if painfully slowly, in the right direction: toward an all-graduate preaching ministry and a church less vulnerable to lay predators and more adiaphorous in its requirements than it was under the old queen, who was stiff in her attitude toward externals. Magistrates who had been brought up to pray for hotter Protestantism yearned for more to do, not for less, and could carry through enough of their reformation of manners to make tarrying for Constantine worthwhile. It was this illusion (if it was an illusion – what

---

58 This follows the argument of M. Finlayson, *Historians, Puritanism and the English Revolution* (Toronto, 1983), pp. 79–119, for the 1620s but not entirely for 1640–42.

59 This account leans heavily on the work of P. Collinson, as in *The Religion of Protestants, 1558–1625* (Oxford, 1982), and *Godly People* (London, 1984). It is also much influenced by the articles of P. Lake, esp. 'Sir Richard Grosvenor and the Rhetoric of Magistracy,' *Bulletin of the Institute of Historical Research* 54 (1981): 40–53, and 'Thomas Scott and the Spanish Match,' *Historical Journal* 25 (1982): 805–25; by P. Christianson, *Reformers and Babylon* (Toronto, 1978); and by Hunt (n. 1 above).

if James had been succeeded by Henry IX?) that was shattered by Laud, who frog-marched them toward a papistical Zion of his own carnal imaginings. While the degree of secular tyranny was inadequate to drive men to radical solutions, the betrayal of Protestantism was adequate to rekindle religious radicalism.

The constant revelations of the months after November 1640 – in the petitions, in the investigations of parliamentary committees, and in the discovery of the penetration of papists into royal counsels, of the king's negotiations with English, Irish, and Scottish papists, even with Spain and Rome, and of his attempts to crush the Covenanters – persuaded an increasing number of M.P.s that the threat to the Protestant foundations of the church was so great, and the penetration so deep, that remedial action was insufficient: only the demolition of the existing edifice and the purification of the site could prepare the way for the Temple that would protect God's chosen people from Antichrist.[60] This is precisely the point hammered home by the preachers whose rhetoric we should take at face value.[61] Preacher after preacher spoke of the Word of God embodying tales of judgment and mercy contingent on the people turning to him and emphasizing human ability to exercise agency. More precisely, preachers like Cornelius Burges, Stephen Marshall, Edmund Calamy, and Thomas Goodwin took Old Testament stories of God's offers to Israel and the consequences of human acceptance or rejection of those offers, and they matched those stories precisely and literally to the present crisis: 'If a nation do evil in God's sight, God will repent of the good he intended. . . . when God begins to draw back his mercies from a Nation, that Nation is in a wofull plight. . . . But on the contrary, if we turn from our evil ways, God will perfect his building, and finish his plantation, he will make us a glorious Paradise.'[62] These were religious imperatives and not just ecclesiastical ones. They were also invitations

---

60 In general, I am persuaded by Hibbard (n. 1 above); esp. in the light of D. Stevenson, *Alasdair MacColla and the Highland Problem in the Seventeenth Century* (Edinburgh, 1981), and *Scottish Covenanters and Irish Confederates* (Belfast, 1981). I am, in fact, inclined to go further and to see a symbiotic link between a heightened fear of popery and the necessity of godly reformation. In explicating the political thought of 1642, this article owes most to W. M. Lamont, *Richard Baxter and the Millennium* (Brighton, 1979); and to conversations with Howard Moss, who is completing a thesis on the thought of Henry Parker.

61 This draws heavily on J. F. Wilson, *Pulpit in Parliament* (Princeton, N.J., 1969); and on a reading of the Fast sermons (for which, see R. Jeffs, ed., *Fast Sermons to Parliament, Nov 1640–Apr 1653*, 34 vols. [London, 1970–71]).

62 BL, Thomason Tract E 131 (29) (Edward Calamy, *England's Looking Glass* [1641], pp. 3, 58), although Thomason Tract E 133 (9) (Stephen Marshall, *Meroz Cursed* [1641]) is usually the first mentioned. See also BL, Thomason Tract E 147 (13) (Thomas Goodwin, *Zerubbebel's Encouragement to Finish the Temple* [1642]).

to action, not a blueprint of what would be found in the promised land. They were injunctions to 'reform the reformation,' to 'throw to the moals and the bats every rag that hath not God's stamp upon it.'[63] They were imperatives to a fresh start, but not to a particular fresh start. We must beware of confusing a lack of zeal for an articulated Presbyterianism with religious moderation. The language of the debates in the Long Parliament from January 25, 1641, demonstrates the folly of this. No particular pattern of ecclesiastical reform was introduced because there was no unity or even a simple majority behind any one scheme and because the House of Lords imposed a legislative stymie. Yet a majority did vote in June 1641 to supplant the existing church by interim bodies of lay and clerical administrators in every diocese, and many M.P.s did become convinced that if bishops survived at all they would do so only as part of an entirely new system rather than with a reduced role in the old system. It is simply not true that religious issues were left on the back burner while constitutional issues were resolved.[64] While a plethora of bills foundered, there was an administrative assault on the church that had transformed it by the summer of 1642. Thus bishops and church courts were suspended or superseded, while the Houses, together or singly, suspended or deprived dozens of ministers of their freeholds and livings, appointed lecturers, reversed orders degrading ministers from the ministry, permitted ceremonies banned by the bishops and the courts, licensed iconoclasm, and pardoned those involved in schismatical services. Every aspect of ecclesiastical government was subsumed into the administrative competence of the Houses. There was no need to rush to legislative remedy: the 'reformation intended' was already in hand.

Yet such activities and such rhetoric repelled as many as they attracted. While it was all too possible to see Charles I in 1641 as at best mendacious, at worst the helpless tool of a papist conspiracy, it was also possible to see him as a chastened and wiser king, as a man who had accepted major constitutional reforms, remodeled his council, abandoned the Laudians, and appointed moderate bishops. It was also possible to lay alongside the threat of popish risings the reality of popular disturbances in London and elsewhere that constituted a threat to social order that many prominent M.P.s at the very least condoned. A great many of those who denounced most bitterly the innovations of the Laudians did so out of concern for

---

63 Both are quoted in G. Yule, *The Puritans in Power* (Sutton Courtney, 1982), p. 108.
64 The next two paragraphs are based on Morrill, 'The Attack on the Church of England in the Long Parliament.'

and love of the evolving practice and piety of the Elizabethan and Jacobean church. They were not unmoved by the revelations of 1641, but they put them into a different context. Less obsessive in their anxieties about Catholicism, they looked harder and less indulgently at the fissures within radical Protestantism, at the spread of separatism, and at the doctrines of social leveling preached by some of the separatists.

Such men rallied first to the defense of episcopacy and the prayer book and later to the defense of the crown. Active Royalists were most usually those who identified the defense of the church with the defense of the social order. Those who were concerned less with religion than with the law, less with the apocalypse than with questions of constitutional propriety, were united in the search for peace but divided on whether the Nineteen Propositions or the king's reply to them offered the better basis for settlement. Constitutionalists sought to avoid war but had preferences that determined their reaction to a fait accompli. In 1642 those who believed that there was a stark choice between either obedience to God or else collapse into anarchy were active Parliamentarians.

And so we return to Sir William Brereton. He seems to exemplify these crucial distinctions. Like Robert Harley, Alexander Rigby, and many of the Essex gentry studied by William Hunt or the Lincolnshire gentry studied by Clive Holmes,[65] Brereton moves from active magistracy in the 1630s to Puritan militancy in 1642 in a way that determines the shape of the Revolution. None of them was driven to passive, let alone active, disobedience by the secular policies of the 1630s; none of them demonstrates any commitment to the constitutional issues of 1642 except as a means to an end, a religious end, to overthrow popery and to perfect the Reformation. Those who mobilized for Parliament in 1642, as against those who threw in their lot with Parliament, were the religious militants, and this is at least as true of the provinces as it is of Westminster. Thus we need to distinguish different types of reaction to the reign of Charles I. Elsewhere it has been argued that there are three separable perceptions of misgovernment or modes of opposition: the first, 'localism,' led naturally to neutralism in 1642; the second, 'legal constitutionalism,' determined the nature of the crisis in 1640 but not in 1642 and lacked the momentum to drive men to war; the third, the 'reli-

---

65 For Harley, see J. Levy, 'Perception and Belief: The Harleys of Brampton Bryan and the Origins and Outbreak of the Civil War' (Ph.D. thesis, University of London, 1983); Hunt, pp. 279–310; and C. Holmes, *Seventeenth-Century Lincolnshire* (Lincoln, 1980), chaps. 8–10. For Alexander Rigby, I have relied on parliamentary diaries, on *JC*, and on conversations with J. J. Bagley.

gious' mode, alone had the dynamism to drive minorities to take up arms. It alone proved a solvent to the deeply ingrained resistance to resistance theories. Brereton is an unimpeachable example of someone immune to the first perception and suffering from a mild dose of the second and a powerful dose of the third. It may have been the classic diagnosis of Parliamentarian militancy.[66]

Such an analysis can help to explain some of the central paradoxes and problems of the Revolution: why the Parliamentarians used a conservative, defensive rhetoric in their political thought and a radical, eschatological one in their religious thought; how England moved from the placidity of the 1630s to the violence of 1642–46; how the activists can be distinguished from those dragged into the fighting; and why the Parliamentarian movement fell apart in and after 1646.

For those Parliamentarians whose primary concern had been the rule of law, the Parliamentary victory constituted a disastrous defeat.[67] In order to win the war, the Houses had violated every clause of the Petition of Right. In order to prevent counterrevolution, the Houses had to sustain a large army, the burden of paying for which further alienated most of the political nation. In the eyes of many Parliamentarians, one form of tyranny had come to replace another. Many drifted into passivity and even into obstruction. Others edged toward the various de facto positions most clearly articulated in 1649 and 1650.[68] Successive regimes found that they could command acquiescence but not consent. For men like Brereton the problems were even more agonizing. The tension within him between the search for religious freedom and the search for good order and discipline had been sustainable in 1641–42. The intolerable and arrogant anti-Christian practices and claims of the Laudians made even the license of the iconoclasts and the separatists understandable if not excusable. But in 1646–47, as we have seen, the heady rhetoric of building the Temple had given way to tawdry parliamentary debates about a particular set of plans for the Temple. Many of those who had assumed that the post-Anglican church would suit them found that they had

66   Morrill, 'The Religious Context of the English Civil War' (n. 1 above), passim.
67   This is an amalgam of J. S. Morrill, *The Revolt of the Provinces* (London, 1976); and of R. Ashton, 'From Cavalier to Roundhead Tyranny,' and D. Pennington, 'The War and the People,' in Morrill, ed. (n. 54 above), pp. 185–208, 115–36. It also draws on D. E. Underdown, *Revel, Rebellion, and Riot* (Oxford, 1985).
68   See esp. the article by Q. Skinner, 'Conquest and Consent,' in *The Interregnum*, ed. G. E. Aylmer (1972), pp. 79–98, but also much else. For an important attempt to demonstrate the providentialist arguments at the center of the Engagement controversy, see the forthcoming article by Glenn Burgess.

to choose either to accept the 'lame erastian presbytery' that had emerged from the Westminster Assembly or to seek freedom outside that church. For those whose Calvinism dictated an alliance of minister and magistrate to bring all men to loving obedience of God by the Word and by the sword but whose preciseness made them uneasy with features of the new church, the issues were distressing and protracted ones. Those who could cut free from the theocracy of Calvinism (most easily by adopting – small *a* – arminianism) could rejoice in the freedom of the saints. But Brereton could not seem able to take that way out. Perhaps, too, his self-confidence in being able to discern the workings of Providence evaporated. The war had destroyed Protestant unity just as it substituted parliamentary for royal tyranny, and everywhere the church was beset and reformation strangled by the tares of Anglican survivalism.[69] In the end he was a fellow traveler of the radicals as they moved forward to regicide and beyond, but there was about his record in those years the very lassitude one sees in the conservatives who drifted to war in 1642 without the stomach for a fight. It was thus, as we know, a minority of a minority who willed the Revolution of December/January 1648/9. Those who willed his trial and execution were men who saw Charles's taking up of arms as a sacrilege, as an attempt to overturn the judgments of God;[70] they saw his death as a necessary atonement for the horrors visited on England.[71] Whatever the really rather feeble legal arguments put forward to rationalize the Revolution after the event, it was again religious perceptions that impelled Cromwell forward.

If Brereton's nerve broke in 1647, Cromwell's sustained him until (almost) the end of his life. Cromwell was not an especially intelligent man, and the streams of consciousness to which he treated his parliaments hardly constitute and orderly exegesis of his political thought.[72] But they do make clear how loyal a student of the Fast sermons he had been. It is true that he eschewed their favorite tales from the Babylonian Captivity for the events of the Exodus in constructing his typologies. Englishmen were God's latest chosen people, called forth out of bondage in Egypt and wandering in

---

69   J. S. Morrill, 'The Church in England,' in Morrill, ed., pp. 103–14.

70   See, e.g., the events and declarations surrounding the trials and executions that followed the sieges of Colchester and Pembroke in 1648 – unlike anything in the first civil war.

71   P. Crawford, 'Charles Stuart, That Man of Blood,' *Journal of British Studies* 16, no. 2 (1977): 41–61.

72   This derives vicariously from the vast literature on Cromwell. For a fuller statement of the main theme, see J. S. Morrill, 'King Oliver?' *Cromwelliana* (1981–82), pp. 20–26.

the desert. They could choose to follow the pillar of fire set up by God (i.e., the triumphs of the army) to guide them to Canaan or they could choose to dawdle in the desert. Cromwell's pervading sense of Providence is the most obvious thing about his thought. It proved a powerful solvent of much that the Parliamentarians held dear. It could free him from prescriptive rules and the bonds of customary law. He believed that the end justified the means so long as the end was conformity to the will of God (what Cromwell, echoing the schoolmen, called necessity). Doing that which conformed to the will of God and brought the nation closer to the promised land justified arbitrary imprisonment, arbitrary taxation, unconstitutional legislation, the creation of major generals, and the declining of the kingship. It helped also to free him from an awe of existing political and religious institutions – dross and dung in comparison with Christ. Being the creation of man, human institutions were as imperfect as man himself. Institutional evolution was a facet of man's evolution toward obedience to the divine will. Thus constitutional and institutional forms were disposable, to be retained or rejected as they proved capable of shaping that progress. Hence too the belief in religious toleration. In the world as it was, no church could claim a monopoly of truth. Fragments of God's truth were vouchsafed to men spread throughout the churches and the sects. Men with the 'root of the matter' in them lay scattered, and each must contribute his fragment to the building up of a mosaic of truth: at its loftiest and least practical, this led to Barebones; more generally, it underpinned and shaped the scope of toleration in his thinking.

In the end, what bound the militants of the 1630s, the 1640s, and the 1650s together was the impossible vision of perfecting man by perfecting human institutions. William Laud, William Brereton, and Oliver Cromwell were just three of the many who yearned to create a better world by this means. Each in his own time faced disillusion and defeat. Each experienced the exhilaration of divine blessing on his undertaking and then experienced divine betrayal or abandonment. This is, arguably, the central and crucial fact of the Revolution. After 1660, very few, in the Anglican church or beyond, sought to change man by creating a theocratic state. The attempt to eternalize religion, to infuse human institutions with divine imperatives, was abandoned. Religion was internalized; the churches set out to teach men that the world was a flawed and irredeemable place and that men should strive to build temples of grace within themselves. Government, economics, and the natural world operated within empirically determinable and amoral principles. God would speak through their hearts and minds and not by thundering through the events of history. Skepticism gave way to cynicism. Much became possible, even the Industrial Revolution. Religious argument continued. But England, like Europe, had seen the last of the wars of religion.

9

The Defection of Sir Edward Dering, 1640–1641

Derek Hirst

Originally appeared as Derek Hirst, 'The Defection of Sir Edward Dering 1640–1641' in *Historical Journal* 15. Copyright © 1972 Cambridge University Press, Cambridge.

Historiography of the years immediately preceding the English civil war has tended to conceive of two disparate entities in politics, Westminster and the localities. There are in practice two distinct kinds of history, reflecting this division, which connect only on rare occasions. The latest major work on the period can, despite its title, limit itself almost entirely to the confines of Westminster and the court,[1] while the student is faintly aware of volumes of local works which contain scarcely a hint of what passes outside the town wall or beyond the county boundary. Parliament was indeed an aggressively self-conscious and independent body, and the county or borough was frequently particularist and introverted, but this did not preclude all contact between the two. Dr Pearl has demonstrated how vulnerable parliament was to the influence of London, and vice versa, and there have recently been several local studies which illustrate the close relationship between the county and the centre.[2] But by and large, Clarendon's assessment of the importance of the Buckinghamshire petition against the attempt on the Five Members, and the obvious prominence accorded by Commons leaders of both sides to petitioning, has not been sufficiently appreciated. Par-

As will be immediately apparent to the reader, I am indebted to Dr W. M. Lamont for many aspects of this article, and for his kindness in suggesting the initial subject of enquiry to me.

1 P. Zagorin, *The Court and the Country* (London, 1969).
2 V. Pearl, *London and the Outbreak of the Puritan Revolution* (Oxford, 1961); and cf. R. Howell, *Newcastle upon Tyne and the Puritan Revolution* (Oxford, 1967); and C. A. Holmes, 'The Eastern Association' (unpublished Cambridge Ph.D. thesis, 1969).

liament was deeply concerned about what might be termed 'public opinion': events in the localities, and the reactions to parliament's policies.[3]

This interaction was more than a matter of mere political fact, but was raised to the level of constitutional debate in the propaganda warfare of 1641–2. As polarization increased, attempts to coerce persons of unsympathetic views became more frequent. Parliament's treatment of offending individuals is well known,[4] but the process could be reversed. Sir John Strangways and the bishops were not the only men to be assaulted, and irate Londoners were not the only assailants. The gentry of Nottinghamshire in 1642 remonstrated with their knights for exceeding their commission by involving them in the arbitrary orders of the Houses, suggesting that it was no part of the representatives' function to tell the country what to do, for they were rather the country's servants: '. . . we hope you will not be unwilling to follow our sence, so far as you conceive it to be the sence of your County whose you are, and for whom you serve'. The elder Sir John Hotham objected to the Yorkshire pacification of 1642 on the grounds that it was an attempt to call the resolutions of both Houses before 'the Bar of Yorkshire', and by implication to make the localities sovereign over their elected representatives. One of parliament's defenders attempted to counter this tendency towards separation of the people from their representatives by asserting that the commonalty were 'obliged in all duty and service to those Noble Gentlemen, and others of their own chusing', by virtue of the fact that they had chosen them, and consented to commit their rights and privileges to them, and must therefore not attempt to desert them. Such a defence as this was necessary in view of the increasing frequency of questions about the nature of the Houses' position and power. An opponent of Henry Parker asked, 'May not the People withdraw the power of representation, which they granted to the Parliament,' and even some alleged disaffected parliament men were to be found a few months

---

3   Clarendon, *History of the Rebellion*, ed. W. D. Macray (Oxford, 1888), I, 512; and it was commonly accepted that popular support was essential for the two Houses: cf. *Persecutio Undecima* (1648), p. 63; J. Nalson, *An Impartial Collection of the Great Affairs of State*, II (1682–3), 187; *The Moderator Expecting Sudden Peace or Certaine Ruine* (1643), p. 15.

4   For Parliament's reactions, see B. S. Manning, 'Neutrals and Neutralism in the English Civil War 1642–1646' (unpublished Oxford D.Phil. thesis, 1957), esp. 16–108; and cf. also Pym's and Ven's attempts to stir up feelings against the Kentish petition of 1642 and the impending one from Somerset [B.M. Additional MS 14827, fo. 77v.].

later urging the kingdom 'to Reassume the Power which hath been so abused' by the parliament.[5]

Despite frequent assertions of supremacy for the Houses by virtue of the fact that they represented England,[6] many parts of England clearly did not consider themselves irrevocably bound by the decisions of the Houses, and felt free to question those decisions. This could create problems for a member for a dissident constituency, as the younger Harbottle Grimston appears to have found at Colchester, where he was driven to appeal to his colleague, Sir Thomas Barrington, to restore his shattered credit.[7] A study of this interrelation between local community and centre can help to explain the final alignment of sides for the war, in that it illustrates the pressures forcing an individual member, or an area, in a given direction.

Thanks to the large body of material surviving, it is possible to examine the career of Sir Edward Dering in the context of his relationship with Kent, his constituency, and to appreciate the manner in which he was driven from his early committed reformist standpoint in response to promptings from his county on the subject of his duty to it. That it should be possible to study the interaction of Kent and one of its members is of particular value, for, as an unwitting result of the large body of recent work on the county, Kent has now become the paradigm of the county community, the locality striving to preserve itself isolated and intact from the upheavals at the centre.[8] An analysis of Dering's career suggests that the paradigm is perhaps misleading, that it is possible to depict the county community as too strong an entity: for such a study reveals that polarization was evident as early as 1640, and that therefore the pressures which Dering had to face were not entirely centrifugal, but much more positive.

The career of Dering is of further interest in that it can be taken as exemplifying some of the problems facing the so-called 'constitutional

---

5   *The Resolutions of Divers of the Gentry of Nottingham . . . sent to . . . Knights of the County of Nottingham* (1642), p. 5; Manning, op. cit. p. 38; *A Short Discourse Tending to the Pacification of all Unhappy Differences* (1642), p. 1; *Animadversions upon those Notes which the Late Observator hath Published . . .* (1642), p. 12; *A Present Answer to the Late Complaint unto the House of Commons by divers Members of the said House* (1642), p. 5.

6   Thus, *The Declaration of the Lords and Commons in Parliament Assembled, concerning His Majesties last Message about the Militia* (5 May 1642); H. Parker, *Observations upon some of His Majesties late Answers and Expresses* (1642), pp. 9–10.

7   Essex Record Office, Morant MSS, XLVII, 31, 67.

8   A. M. Everitt, *The Community of Kent and the Great Rebellion* (Leicester, 1966); P. Laslett, 'The Gentry of Kent, 1640', *Cambridge Historical Journal*, IX (1948), 148–64; F. W. Jessup, *Sir Roger Twysden 1597–1672* (London, 1965); C. W. Chalklin, *Seventeenth Century Kent; a Social and Economic History* (London, 1965).

opposition' of 1640–1, the opposition which subsequently divided as the political crisis worsened. Dering's course in these fateful months can be outlined briefly, the details being clearly set out in the *D.N.B.*: soon after the opening of the Long Parliament, he took a major part in the attack on Laud by presenting the petition of a persecuted minister, Thomas Wilson, for which he was rewarded with the chair of the sub-committee for examining the sufferings of the clergy; he followed this early venture with a consistent commitment to ecclesiastical reform, which culminated in support for the London Root and Branch petition, presentation of the Kent Root and Branch petition, and the moving of the Root and Branch bill against episcopacy in April 1641; in June he abandoned his earlier stance, and spoke in favour of a moderate form of episcopacy, and after this, moved further away from the reforming group, supporting the Kent neutralist petition in early 1642, for which he was expelled from the House as a malignant, and imprisoned. He eventually, and apparently reluctantly, joined the king.

The traditional view of him is very much conditioned by the vindication he published in 1642 to defend himself against charges of betrayal.[9] His initial support of Root and Branch he alleged had never been total, but rather conditional on its replacement of the episcopal system with some less obnoxious alternative: he had been misled in this respect by Vane, Haslerig and the radicals into introducing the Root and Branch bill, but when he found that they aimed only at destruction, he rapidly dissociated himself from them, and maintained a determined consistency in a policy of purging a corrupted institution. His own interpretation of his actions has been adopted by most modern historians until Dr Lamont: thus, Professor Everitt saw him and his friends in Kent as 'provincials and conservatives rather than radicals'.[10] But this is not only to accept Dering's characterization of himself as the archetypal enlightened moderate, but it is also to attribute too great a unity to society, split only between the hot-heads at Westminster and the more rooted and saner forces in the local community. To many contemporaries, there were few more committed members than Dering in the early months of the Long Parliament, an assessment for which his initial activity would seem to provide ample warrant: he was stigmatized later as the most culpable turn-coat after Lord Digby, suggesting that his early role had been a major one.[11] The transformation of this religious zealot into the victimized malignant of 1642 merits examination, for not only

9   Sir Edward Dering, *A Collection of Speeches* (1642).
10   W. M. Lamont, *Godly Rule 1603–1660* (London, 1969), pp. 83–93; Everitt, op. cit. p. 85 – this is a judgement which largely concurs with that in the *D.N.B.*
11   *The Coppie of a Letter written unto Sir Edward Deering* (1642); J. Vicars, *God in the Mount* (1642), p. 84.

does it suggest that the drift of part of the opposition of 1640 into the royalist ranks of 1642 was not necessarily a coherent one, but more importantly, it illustrates the folly of attempting political delineations at this period in purely parliamentary terms. The policies of parliament were capable of alteration by the views and actions of those in the country – the act of electing a member did not end the constituent's role – and more obviously, the localities were greatly affected by speeches and resolutions in parliament.

Dering's turn-coat character was easily accounted for by some. One Kentish contemporary attributed it to a scholar's instability when finding himself on the political stage[12]; Simonds D'Ewes even doubted that there was a problem:

> for mine owne part I doe not thinke him to bee guilty of Apostacy for I never thought him a convert which made mee when I first heard him speak . . . earnestlie in the matter of Religion to stand up and say that I was very glad to heare that gentleman speake as hee did for it was the first time that ever I heard him speake in the maintenance of a good cause.[13]

To a large extent, either of these notions is plausible, for the volatility of Dering's career seems to betoken a great instability of character. However, a study of that career demonstrates that the great change of front of the summer of 1641 was caused by more than mere personality defects. Dr Lamont has rightly suggested that Dering's apparent adoption of the Root and Branch cause in the opening months of the Long Parliament was genuine, despite Dering's later protestations to the contrary, and has outlined some of the considerations which caused him to abandon his earlier commitments.[14] But it is necessary to look further back than the beginning of the session in order to comprehend the confusion of Dering's later actions, for this confusion is to be found some time before April 1641. Furthermore, an examination which begins in November 1640 fails to take into account the society which elected Dering, and makes it possible to minimize the extra-parliamentary factors.

12   Henry Oxinden (of Barham) observed in Feb. 1642, 'itt did ever runne in my head, that Sir Edward Deereing has so used to turne round in his Studie that hee would doe the like in the Parliament House. Pray God his much turning hath not made his head dazie, and that hee doth not turne out of his right witts.' *The Oxinden Letters 1607–1642*, ed. D. Gardiner (London, 1933), p. 296; see also Laslett, op. cit. pp. 156–7.
13   B.M. Harleian MS 162, fo. 366. I am grateful to Dr C. A. Holmes for this reference.
14   Lamont, loc. cit.; cf. Dering, op. cit. p. 2.

The surviving evidence must question the belief that Dering was elected by a conservative, in-grown community: Kent in 1640 was politically split, and was concerned about national issues not only in so far as they affected the independence of the community, but at a more general level. Gentry seeking election had perforce to take note of the diversity of opinions, and shape their actions accordingly. In the unprecedented political crisis of 1639–40, the election of an M.P. was clearly seen by many to be a political act, which could be anticipated to have political repercussions. It was not merely something to be done unthinkingly. Electors were patently concerned about the views and character of their representative, and in some cases seem to have voted accordingly, and to have expected, and striven to ensure, that he would conform to their expectations. Similarly, it is clear that candidates were conscious of the desires of their constituents, and appealed for votes on the basis of these desires. Understandably, problems were created if performance failed to cohere with promises. That is, a continuing relationship was created between constituency and M.P. by the election, because a clearly defined course of action was, probably for the first time, expected of him.

In his years as Lieutenant of Dover Castle in the 1630s, Dering seems to have been an active servant of the government, both in its religious and its secular policies, striving to advance the commissions for knighthoods and ship money, and being one of the main persecutors of separatists in the area. Indeed, this was apparently one of the prime causes for his defeat in the Short Parliament election for the county. Dering's own assessment of the reasons for his defeat lends support to this contention, for he wrote, 'Plain it is that the puritan faction made Twysden' [his opponent], for 'the obscure and peevish sort that are separatists and lovers of separation did make itt theire cause to have a childe of theires in the house'. His list of the accusations that were circulating in rumour form against himself shows clearly that his role as a courtier, an ex-client of Buckingham, and a furtherer of the ship and knighting monies, militated against his success at the election.[15]

But even at this early date, the ambiguity of Dering's position is striking. In 1639, he had protested his dutifulness over ship money (in order to excuse his non-attendance on the king in the north), and he had earlier been commended by the earl of Suffolk for his endeavours in that service,[16] yet in his private notebook, he seems to have been to some

15   B.M. Stowe MS 743, fos. 85, 106; Kent County Archives U350 c/2/26, c/2/54; Bodley MS Top. Kent c6, quoted by J. H. Plumb, 'The Growth of the Electorate in England from 1600 to 1715', *Past and Present*, XLV (1969), 106; and also Stowe 743, fo. 140.
16   Ibid. fos. 106, 132.

extent setting himself against the tax.[17] Although his account of the March 1640 election sees his defeat as partly attributable to his association with the Court, at the same time he noted that it was objected against his candidature that he was opposed to the Lord Chamberlain, to Sir Henry Vane the elder, Treasurer of the Household and Secretary, and to the deputy lieutenants. Furthermore, he averred that he had at the start of the campaign 'absolutely resolved that in times so desperate [he] would contribute no helpe to any privy counsellor or deputy lieutenant'; this attitude could well have been an accurate response to public opinion on his part, for his opponent, Sir Roger Twysden, noted in the middle of March, 'Trwly the common people had been so bytten with shippe money they were very averse from a courtyer.'[18] Religious alignments, however confused, also appear to have played a part in the contest. Dering had indeed incurred the hostility of the 'puritan faction' within the county for his persecuting activities, but Twysden informed him that he lost the election because he was 'none of our church', it being imputed against him that he 'never would goe up to the rayles to receive the communion', an explanation which Dering's own account bears out, suggesting as it does that he was seen as one of the preciser sort by some voters.[19] Although the line-up of forces was very unclear, and Dering, unfortunately for his chances of success, appeared to stand for all things to all men, it is evident that political and religious considerations were important in the decisions of some electors to vote as they did.

By the time of the Long Parliament elections, Dering's views were no more definable. Professor Everitt has maintained that these, whatever they were, played little part in either of the essentially local and personal elections of 1640.[20] The case he has made out is convincing, yet the very confusion of the political and religious issues may have led to their being under-estimated. The fear that puritan machinations were working against Dering was still present. Richard Browne, his opponent, had been 'sett up by the precise party', in the words of Dering's partner Sir John Colepepper, and had been greatly strengthened by 'his bangleeared

---

17   Add. 47787, fo. 32v.

18   Bodley MS, loc. cit., *Proceedings in Kent in 1640*, ed. L. Larking (Camden Soc., 1862), p. 6.

19   Stowe 184, fo. 10. Yet even in this, he seems to have been trying to hedge his bets. In the attempt to apprehend the separatist leader John Fenner in 1636, Dering appears to have been reluctant to proceed. He wrote that he knew Fenner was at home, but protested somewhat implausibly, 'Night or day I would willingly bestowe my labour with successe but I should be very sorry to make Fenner more wary by affrighting him.' He was also allegedly in doubt as to the authority by which he could break down a door to seize the local sectary. K.C.A. U1551.

20   Everitt, op. cit. ch. 111.

props out of the durt', as Dering's active supporter Sir John Sedley had it.[21] In support of this implication that a lowly 'precise' interest worked against Dering just as much in this election as in the previous one, there is at least one piece of evidence that suggests that some voters supported Dering on account of his moderate religious position, despite the apocalyptic tones in which the letter is couched.[22] In the secular sphere similarly, Dering's correspondent, the minister Robert Abbot, testified that 'some whispered against yow the knighting business'.[23] While not according with the view that this second election was a mere local personality clash, this evidence would tend to support Professor Everitt's hypothesis that Dering was a provincial conservative.

A letter written to Dering shortly before the Long Parliament met, however, runs counter to this notion. A correspondent in Ashford (one of the main bases of Dering's support in the election, as the poll list shows), after attacking the institution of episcopacy, prayed that God's aid would be vouchsafed to Dering, 'that so your friends that have ingaged their creditt for your faithfulnes may have just cause to blesse God for you, and that those that are not as yet perswaded of your sincerety may be of another mind'. That is, Dering was expected to oppose episcopacy, and had received support in the election on this understanding. And in order to further his projected campaign against Antichrist, Dering's constituents lost no time in lobbying him. The conclusion that emerges from this conflicting evidence is that many participants, both candidates and voters, in these elections were unclear as to what issues were involved, and even more, who was involved with what issues. In the absence of political traditions or effective communications, the political divisions were predictably confused and contradictory, but they were clearly present, and were seen to be so by some contemporaries.[24]

21   Stowe 743, fo. 149; Stowe 184, fo. 15. His correspondent Robert Abbot wrote in March 1641 that at this election the 'Brownists' (i.e. separatists, rather than supporters of Richard Browne) had been preparing to petition against Dering for his rigorous practices towards them. Ibid. fo. 27.
22   Sir John Skeffington to Dering, at the height of the latter's activist period in Dec. 1640: 'You have abus'd my sorrowes: I had engag'd as many for you as my dry braine could affoard. By the waters we sate downe and wept to consider what an advantage you had given Babylon.' Skeffington went on to protest against the way in which Dering, now 'in power and State', was calling 'pale Soules' before his 'tribunall'. Stowe 744, fo. 17.
23   Stowe, 184, fo. 27.
24   Lamont, op. cit. p. 86. Compare the opening of Abbot's letter in Mar. 1641: 'We are happy in our choise. All my arguments could not perswade this, till your worships and your partner in this noble service, had made yourselves knowne by your speaches.' Stowe 184, fo. 27.

The question of which way the pendulum of Dering's religious beliefs would swing was soon settled, possibly as he came under the influence of stronger minds than his own in the House. By mid-December, the Canterbury Cathedral chapter were talking of him as 'dangerously sicke in mind (in plaine tearms madd)'. Dr Lamont has demonstrated that Dering's immediate support for the Root and Branch minister Thomas Wilson meant more than Dering would have liked people to think when he came to write his vindication.[25] One of his correspondents hinted at the end of November 1640 that Dering was somewhat closer to the centre of power in the House than the characterization of him as a provincial conservative would warrant,[26] and some observers appear to have been well aware of this. The anonymous author of *Persecutio Undecima* still remembered Dering as having been a dangerously potent radical some years after the events: the justifications, the affair of the Kentish petition of 1642, and the flight to the king, had not altered the impression:

> Let the sword reach from the North to the South, quoth Sir Edward Deering, rather then his phantasticall new Church Government should be hindred, reviling the established forme of Gods service . . . and this railing against the Clergy was the only way to be made a Chaireman of a Committee, or to be designed for some great preferment, and to be the worshipfull Golden Calves of the people, the only ambition of those popular Speech-makers . . .[27]

Dering was clearly seen as having achieved prominence in the House, not because of his moderation, but because of his commitment to change. In justifying his support of the Kent Root and Branch petition, he claimed that he forwarded it only after having 'taught it a new and more modest language'[28] but this is not borne out by the evidence. Although the phrase 'Root and Branch' of the original was omitted, the final version which Dering espoused concluded with the significantly vague prayer 'that this Hierarchicall power may be totally abrogated'. Taken in conjunction with Dering's cheerful approbation of the London Root and Branch petition in his introduction of the Kent one, it left D'Ewes at least, as Dr Lamont observes, in no doubt that he was hearing a plea for the

---

25 *Proceedings in Kent*, p. 23; Lamont, op. cit. pp. 85–7.
26 Sir Richard Skeffington, from whom Dering had difffered in late 1638 because the former was 'so much for the Puritans' [K.C.A. U350 c/2/59], referred to their mutual 'deare freinde Mr. Pyme'. Stowe 184, fo. 19.
27 *Persecutio Undecima*, p. 17; also Nalson, op. cit. II, 248.
28 Dering, op. cit. p. 17.

abolition of the bishops.[29] Furthermore, in the debate on the London petition, when Hyde, Colepepper, Waller, Selden, Hopton, Digby, Falkland and all his future colleagues of the Grand Remonstrance debates were advocating that it should not be committed, Dering was strongly in favour of it, and was ultimately a teller for the 'ayes'.[30]

This parliamentary activity took place in the context of Dering's relations with his constituency. The alacrity with which one of his supporters established contacts with him, even before the session opened, has been pointed to, and Abbot similarly observed that Dering had been lobbied by Brownists soon after the opening.[31] The Kent Root and Branch petition was accompanied by a number of letters urging him to forward it, and expecting him to do so, which suggests that they were informed of his past actions in the House.[32] They saw him as their political instrument, and he was quite willing to be seen in this light: he was 'their servant', he did 'appear for them' in the matter.[33] But it is noteworthy that such a concept of delegation could only prevail when there was harmony between the member and his constituents. By the time of the Grand Remonstrance, which attempted to strengthen and define that relationship, Dering was totally out of favour with the concept, scorning to 'remonstrate downward, tell stories to the people'. He assured the House that the people 'do not expect to hear any other stories of what you have done, much less promises of what you will do' – activity which he himself had clearly indulged in earlier.[34] Dering's attitude to the people changed as he parted company from the more active of them. When furthering the Root and Branch cause, he had been prepared to use popular felings in debate, and even to manipulate those feelings: he is alleged to have maintained close contacts with Kent religious activists, providing them with arguments, and advising them how to proceed against unsympathetic ministers.[35] For this service, the Brownists' petition against him, with which he had been threatened for

29   When talking of the London petition, he assured the House that 'my heart goes cheerfully along therewith' [ibid. p. 18]; for D'Ewes's reaction, Lamont, op. cit. p. 88. Similarly, Sir Thomas Peyton saw it as no different from any of the other Root and Branch petitions then being presented. Bodley MS Film 39, p. 66.
30   *The Journal of Sir Simonds D'Ewes*, ed. W. Notestein (New Haven, 1923), pp. 337, 343.
31   See above, p. 214; and Stowe 184, fo. 27.
32   K.C.A. U350 c/2/86–88, the first of which praises Dering's 'zeale for Gods matters', and the last claims that Dering's activity in God's cause alone emboldened him to write; also, *Proceedings in Kent*, pp. 25–6, where the petitioners maintain that they 'have cause to praise God' for Dering's service.
33   Dering, op. cit. p. 19.
34   J. Rushworth, *Historical Collections*, IV (1682), 425.
35   Stowe 184, fos. 27, 33.

his actions in the eleven years, was withdrawn. Abbot complained at this time that Dering's speeches and letters were stimulating his parishioners in the depths of Kent to agitate against him.[36] The effectiveness of such communication suggests that the purpose of the publication of separates of speeches was not just to keep the public at large or in London informed, but also to inform constituents of their members' doings. In this case, they were certainly informed – Henry Oxinden's letters provide further evidence of Dering's speeches coming into Kent, and of their popularity.[37] Supporting the contention that Dering was concerned for the popular reception of his speeches, the Register of the Stationers' Company shows that Dering approved the printing of his speeches (and he was not the only member so to do), despite his repeated denials in his vindication that he had done so.[38] *Persecutio Undecima's* charge against him, that he had indulged in 'publishing those Speeches in print on purpose to infect the people, and fire their mindes', would seem to have been accurate.[39] There was little wonder then that the radical clerical pressure groups in the Commons' lobbies, of whom Dering later complained, should have been surprised at his ensuing change of front. As late as the end of May 1641, he still retained the favour of the London mob, and seems to have been highly gratified by this.[40] But when his concerns became different from those of his more vociferous lobbyists, his attitude to the people's will, as exemplified in his Grand Remonstrance speech, and even more in the preface to the vindication, changed to one of contempt.[41] Public opinion was only a factor to be consulted when it accorded with the M.P.'s own predilections.

In the spring of 1641, then, Dering took a sympathetic view of popular agitation against episcopacy, and even encouraged it in order to provide further support for the efforts of himself and his parliamentary collaborators. But unfortunately for the solidarity of the opposition cause within the House, the fruits of the activities of such men as Dering were becoming evident at this juncture. The sea-change this could induce can be observed in the relationship between Dering and his most voluble correspondent, the minister at Cranbrook, Kent, Robert Abbot.

36   Ibid. fos. 27–9. For a further instance of local hostility to activists' contacts with the centre, see Lamont, op. cit. p. 89.
37   *The Oxinden Letters 1607–1642*, pp. 270, 298.
38   *A Transcript of the Registers of the Worshipful Company of Stationers; from 1640–1708 A.D.*, ed. G. E. B. Eyre (London, 1913), I, 20, 24; Dering, op. cit. pp. 49, 65, 96, 155. I am grateful to Mr M. J. Mendle for this information.
39   *Persecutio Undecima*, p. 17.
40   Dering, op. cit. p. 2; *Proceedings in Kent*, p. 47.
41   Rushworth, op. cit. IV, 425, 428; Dering, op. cit. Dedicatory Epistle.

Possibly because Abbot's religious views were not totally opposed to those of Dering,[42] he eventually succeeded in detaching the latter from his Root and Branch colleagues, by stressing the disorders that the actions of the Commons were causing in the countryside. He was not alone in this realization. *Persecutio Undecima*, when talking of Dering and the other 'popular Speech-makers', pointed out that although they were 'little dreaming of the Puritans plots', they 'themselves opened the Gappe, kindled the fire which others of meaner condition (but of different intentions) blew up to such flames, as since have burned the kindlers owne neasts'. Such an awareness had a massive political effect: Thomas May observed that 'many Gentlemen who forsook the Parliament, were very bitter against it for the proceedings in Religion, in countenancing, or not suppressing, the rudenesse of people in Churches'.[43] The resolutions of the House of Commons were near to creating greater social dangers than the rule of 'Thorough' had done. Abbot protested to Dering that the latter's speches and contacts with 'some of mine' had made his position in his parish untenable: his parishioners had become obstreperous, at Dering's (perhaps unwitting, allowed Abbot) instigation, and if petitioning were as easy and as assured of success as Dering had encouraged them to think, then 'I knowe not what minister in the Church of England could hold his station'. The gist of his letter was not a theological or an historical defence of the existing order; it was purely a plea for order. Dering's utterances, and especially his attack on the validity of the Laudian Canons, on the grounds that nothing could be universally binding unless consented to by all men, had been seized on by the common people, and used as a justification for demanding that their opinions be consulted. But, warned Abbot, unlike Dering, they did not attack bishops alone, but the whole established Church structure: they would oppose all preachers 'who issue not in a popular way'. However well-intentioned Dering might be, the repercussions of his actions in London were threatening to destroy the whole local social fabric.[44]

42　Thus, Abbot asserted in Mar. 1641 that he would be glad if the Prayer Book were reformed and ceremonies 'layed aside', and he bracketed the papal Church and the school of Arminius together. Stowe 184, fos. 28–28v.

43　*Persecutio Undecima*, p. 17; Thomas May, *The History of the Parliament of England*, I (1647), 115. The King himself made exactly the same point in a speech to both Houses at the end of Jan. 1641 attacking the Root and Branch agitation: 'distractions' were 'occasioned through the cause of Parliament though not by the Parliament . . . and petitions in an illegall way given are neither dismitted, nor denyed'. Harl. 4931, fo. 106.

44　Stowe 184, fos. 27–9.

Despite such warnings, Dering pressed forward on his original course, presenting the Root and Branch bill in May, apparently sincerely enough: even in his vindication, Dering admitted that he had accepted the bill's provisions.[45] The stories that he was tricked into presenting it by Vane and the radicals seem as much special pleading as does his attempt to minimize the extent of his sympathy for Thomas Wilson. He appears to have remained in the forefront of the Commons' activity for the whole of May, being added to the very important Committee of Seven for the security of Dover, Portsmouth and the Isle of Wight (called by D'Ewes 'the secrett Committee'), and he was on the committee of 20 May for the disbanding of the armies, as well as the strongly puritan committee for making St Paul's Covent Garden, into a parish.[46] But he lapsed into a period of silence in the first half of June, failing to be re-appointed to the committee of 10 June on the armies, and by the 19th his doubts were made manifest by his action in presenting a subsidy bill without leave of the House, which 'the House did not like'.[47] Finally, on 21 June, he made the speech advocating a moderated form of episcopacy in committee on the Root and Branch bill which cost him 'the prayers of thousands in the City', as he was told the next day.[48]

It can be suggested that what caused him to abandon his earlier commitment was just that fact which Abbot was so concerned to stress, the increasing level of disorder in the country, and in particular the tumults consequent on the Commons' Protestation of 3 May – tumults with which Dering came into early contact as a member of the House's committee of May to enquire into the disorders in the city and elsewhere, and the assault on the Queen Mother's household.[49] For it is significant that Dering's objectionable speech was delivered on the day after a remarkable sermon by Henry Burton to the House which must have wholly confirmed Dering's worst fears. The fact that Burton should preach on Church government immediately before a scheduled Root and Branch debate presumably gave rise to apprehensions that he was voicing the policy of a dominant group within the House, and that therefore his views must be allotted due consideration.[50] The emphasis of Burton's diatribe against Church government might have been

45   Dering, op. cit. pp. 63–4.
46   *Commons Journals*, II, 146, 152, 156; Harl. 163, fo. 191.
47   *C.J.*, II, 172, Harl. 478, fo. 93v.
48   Dering, op. cit. p. 77.
49   *C.J.*, II, 143.
50   H. Burton, *Englands Bondage and Hope of Deliverance* (1641); *C.J.*, II, 181. On the subject of parliamentary sermons in general, see H. R. Trevor-Roper, 'The Fast Sermons of the Long Parliament', in *Religion, the Reformation and Social*

thought to reflect the views of the extreme Root and Branchers around Vane, who had argued on 11 June for the total destruction of the episcopal organization, as a corrupt institution, although he had allowed that 'Church-government, in the generall, is good, and that which is necessary, and which we all desire'. In April and May there had been three similar attacks on the government of the Church in unofficial sermons before members of the House, suggesting a planned campaign by ministers and members in support of the bill.[51] But Burton's demands were more far-reaching. After having asserted that the present hierarchy was nothing but a limb of Antichrist, he proceeded to give cold comfort to those whose concerns were social rather than millenarian. In answer to the cry, 'What! shall wee have no Government', Burton replied that Christ had left the Church tied to no form of order: indeed, Burton regarded discipline as 'a Babilonish garment', and held that its institution was 'the service of the divell', and had done more than anything else to destroy true religion. Again asking himself whether there should be any order or discipline at all, he provided no answer, other than urging destruction. Such a programme could not seem other than a counsel of despair to those who were becoming anxious at the increase of popular activity. Burton was plainly aware of the problem of disorder, as his references to those who demanded some form of order show, but he held that such considerations were unimportant beside the need to extend Christian liberty to the godly.[52]

In this context, when reckless destruction seemed likely to be the avowed policy of certain Commons leaders, Dering's speech the next day becomes thoroughly comprehensible. Its concern was with order and not with the nature of episcopacy. He could no longer give his assent to Root and Branch unless 'we may have . . . a future government, in roome of this that goes out', and given the inevitable intransigence of the Lords over the establishment of a non-episcopal substitute, some other form of order had to be sought. For this very political reason, he went on to outline his 'right forme of primitive Episcopacy'. His theme was exactly that stressed by Abbot at the end of March: merely to abolish the existing form of Church government as Burton demanded would be fatal, for

Change (London, 1967), pp. 294–344; that at least one contemporary was aware of the connexion outlined by Prof. Trevor-Roper can be seen from Add. 11045, fo. 144v.

51   *Sir Henry Vane his Speech in the House of Commons, at a Committee for the Bill against Episcopall-Government* (1641), p. 3; John F. Wilson, *Pulpit in Parliament* (Princeton, 1969), pp. 47–8.

52   Burton, op. cit. pp. 23–30.

nobody was agreed on an alternative, and some evidently wanted none at all.[53]

But he had not yet found a solution to the problems of Church order. He complained early in 1642, in his vindication, that his religious proposals of the summer of 1641 had been three times printed before in an 'imperfect Copie', and they contain what was apparently the scheme which Dering cited a few months later. There were, however, some significant variations. The proposals for the financial endowment of the 'bishops and presbyters' in the early versions would have made them markedly poorer than would the proposals in the final scheme. And more important, while the contemporary accounts of Dering in the summer of 1641 provide that the clergy shall have *no* secular employment, the Dering of 1642 ordains that 'No Bishop or other Clergy man [is] to have the constant manage of any Temporall office', and that the bishops shall have an advisory capacity in the House of Lords.[54] If Dering's protest about the 'imperfect' nature of the earlier printing is taken to be as self-serving as all his other similar claims in the volume undoubtedly were, and that the early versions record what Dering was in fact advocating in the summer of 1641, then it can be seen that Dering's period of indecision was not limited to the month of June, and that his reconciliation with the establishment was by no means complete at that date – and moreover, that his claims to consistency in aim, if not in detail, are thoroughly questionable. The contention that he was still undecided in the summer receives support from his statement in another Root and Branch debate in July that he did not object to the idea of abolition itself, but to the alternatives to episcopacy proposed by others, to the fact that what faced the House was a 'growinge bill'.[55] The situation confronting the erstwhile opposition was clearly a complex one.

Fears on the subject of social order were realized as the summer wore on, and the stimulation provided by the Commons' destructiveness took effect. Abbot prayed early in July that at least something be done, 'and special order taken against this disorder'. He feared lest 'from private

53 Dering, op. cit. pp. 66–77.
54 Ibid. pp. 155–8; the other versions of the proposals are to be found in *Master Grimstons Argument Concerning Bishops. With Mr. Seldens Answer. Also severall Orders, concerning Church Government* (London, 1641), pp. 2–5; *The Order and Forme for Church Government By Bishops and the Clergie of this Kingdome* (London, 1641); *Sixteene Propositions in Parliament. Touching the manner and forme for Church Government, by Bishops and the Clergie of this Kingdome* (London, 1642). I am indebted to Mr Mendle for these identifications, and for pointing out that John Moore transcribed the scheme into the volume of his diary which covers the summer of 1641 [Harl. 479, fos. 175–173v (reverse foliation)].
55 Ibid. fo. 71v.

motion and popular authority' in his parish, he should be compelled to break the laws for the ordering of religion, 'before the wisedome of the House hath layed them downe or made better'. He inveighed bitterly against the way in which both the Protestation and Burton's *Protestation Protested* were being used by the populace as a justification for iconoclasm and for attacks on the Prayer Book, as Burton had urged.[56] That Burton's tract, or at least the arguments it contained, should have penetrated to the meaner sort of the Kentish countryside is remarkable, and demonstrates the extent of the contacts between politics at the centre and different social groups in the localities. Abbot's unease at the growing social crisis remarkably parallels the content of Dering's first anti-Root and Branch pronouncement: the concern of both is essentially eirenic rather than doctrinal, and in this there is a marked contrast with Dering's earlier speeches, which had focused on doctrinal technicalities – which might suggest that those following were made under the influence of something other than his personal interests alone. For Abbot continued to press his complaints to Dering about the harm being done by the religious policy, or lack of one, being pursued by a section of the commons. In October he protested that his parishioners, following the religious orders of the House of the previous September which allowed parishioners to take the initiative, were preparing to institute a lecturer in his parish, who, he feared, would 'crosse shinns with mee to the fomenting of popular spirits against lawes'; and none would please the people but one that condemned the Prayer Book. He professed that he would gladly leave his cure in consequence.[57] The impact which Abbot's anxieties about impending anarchy had on Dering can be appreciated from the fact that Dering, in a speech of 23 October on disorders in the Church, cited him and

---

56   Stowe 184, fo. 43v. Similar reports, that the Protestation, binding individuals to further the godly cause, was being used to foment disorder in churches, were coming to London from places as far afield as Tewkesbury and Yorkshire, and from men as sympathetic to the general aim of religious reform as John Geree and Thomas Stockdale, Fairfax's agent and later recruiter M.P. John Geree, *Vindiciae Voti* (London, 1641), sig. C; *The Fairfax Correspondence*, ed. G. W. Johnson (London, 1848), I, 381–2.

57   Stowe 184, fos. 47–47v. On this score, Burton seems to have been speaking directly to Abbot: if such a problem arises, and the minister's position is endangered, he should reform himself, and then he would not lose his flock [H. Burton, *The Protestation Protested* (1641), sig. C2v.–C3] – advice which was hardly calculated to ease social tensions. It should be noted that such concern for the fate of the Prayer Book, and alarm at the extent of the religious disorders, swayed a majority of the House by the end of August, and was strong enough to move men as zealous as William Strode, Serjeant Wilde and John Crew. Northants. Record Office MSS, FH 2881; B.M.Add. 11045, fos. 142, 143v.

another minister as examples of the unfortunate clergy whose 'now infected sheepe, after long pastorall vigilancy, and faithful ministery . . . runne and staggle from them more in these last ten moneths then in twenty yeares before'.[58] The dating of ten months past would take the dawn of the troubles back to the first agitation over Root and Branch. As Dr Lamont has pointed out, contemporaries saw Abbot as one of the main factors in Dering's desertion of the anti-episcopal cause,[59] and it is plain that by the autumn of 1641 Abbot's thesis had been completely accepted.

This became the major concern of Dering's important speech in defence of the liturgy in the debate leading up to the Grand Remonstrance. He maintained that, by virtue of the House's destructiveness, no settled doctrine remained with which to combat recusancy. Although 'this mischiefe growes not by our consent', there was now 'such a leud licentiousnesse . . . as never was in any age, in any Nation, untill this Parliament was met together', and cited in particular the prevalence of artisan preaching.[60] He well warranted the rebuke for inconsistency which D'Ewes administered to him in these debates,[61] but Dering could have replied that he had changed his opinions because he was not too blinded by them to realize the adverse effect that they were having on the country at large. To him, ideological commitment was evidently a commodity which could be ill afforded in this turbulent period, but this his erstwhile collaborators failed to acknowledge.

The vulnerability of Dering to such considerations as the state of opinion in the locality is well illustrated by an episode during the summer recess. Throughout the session, the House had been assuming an executive capacity, a process which was to culminate in the passing of the wartime ordinances with the Lords. A major development in this trend was the orders on religion of September 1641, permitting parishioners to establish lectureships on their own initiative, and to remove idolatrous ornaments from Churches. This increase in the House's power seems to have been strongly opposed in Kent: Sir Roger Twysden made frequent condemnations in his journal of the validity of the executive orders of the Commons, on the grounds that the members were there to do what was enjoined by the country, and not to issue commands. He maintained that he was supported in this opinion by

58   Dering, op. cit. p. 93.
59   Lamont, op. cit. p. 91.
60   Dering, op. cit. pp. 96–105. And perhaps the chief fear he manifested in his famous speech in the Grand Remonstrance debate two days later was of what effect it would have on the 'common people'. Rushworth, op. cit. IV, 425–8.
61   *The Journal of Sir Simonds D'Ewes*, ed. W. H. Coates (New Have, 1942), pp. 151–2.

many other J.P.s in the county, and Abbot likewise made a similar point in his letter to Dering at the beginning of October, commenting on the authority of the Committee of Recess, that the 'committee hath not a legislative power alone'.[62] But Dering initially did not concur. There is no record of his having opposed the earlier orders of the House, and when taxed by other Kent justices during the recess as to the legality of the September orders, he would make no positive answer, only affirming meekly 'that the howse of Commons meant all good to the Protestant religion', which was hardly in dispute.[63] Yet immediately after the recess, on almost the first available opportunity, he used exactly the arguments which his neighbours had used earlier, and in terms suggesting that they were adopted as a consequence of local pressure upon him. He informed the House that

> There want not some abroad, men of birth, quality, and Fortunes; such as know the strength of our Votes here as well as some of us . . . men of the best worth, and of good affyance in us, and no way obnoxious to us: They know they sent us hither as their Trustees, to make and unmake Lawes; They know they did not send us hither to rule and govern them by arbitrary, revocable and disputable Orders; especially in Religion.[64]

For all its inconsistencies, then, the meaning of Dering's progress in 1640–1 seems clear. A study of his actions demonstrates that the members of the House of Commons were not laws unto themselves, as an exclusive concentration on the activities of King Pym and his colleagues might suggest. He was subject to pressures from the 'blacke walkers of Westminster Hall' and the city mob, as is well known. But equally, he was exposed to the often conflicting fears and beliefs of men in varying stations in his county.[65] To assume otherwise would be to impose a distorted perspective on these years, and to render Dering's unstable behaviour singular in the extreme. The justification advanced

---

62 *Archaeologia Cantiana*, I (1858), 187–9; ibid. II (1859), 179–80, 188, 214; Stowe 184, fo. 47v. The grievance is also to be found in clause XII of the Kentish petition of 1642. *Arch. Cant.*, I, 208.

63 Ibid. I, 190–1.

64 Dering, op. cit. p. 79.

65 Dering was clearly influenced by strident cries from the local governors that disorder was endemic; now, whether these cries were genuine, that is, whether they accurately reflected contemporary social conditions, is another matter entirely, and not wholly relevant to the argument that Dering reacted in response to certain pressures. Dering's correspondents are supported by Henry Oxinden's prognostication in Nov. 1641 that the sectarian tumults in Kent indicated 'the latter day to bee very neare att hand' [*Oxinden Letters 1607–1642*, 257]. Unfortunately, no sessions papers survive, but it is interesting that the calendar of prisoners in gaol awaiting

by his correspondents for lobbying him was that he had been elected for a specific political purpose, and that a mutual relationship between elector and elected had been created to this end. Abbot informed him that he dared to attempt to guide him 'because I, and all my friends are engaged in our votes for your worship, I could not but intimate my heart unto yow'.[66] Just as the connexion of the locality with the M.P. was a continuing one, which handicapped the attempts to create clear political delineations at Westminster, so vice versa. The local community was almost as riven, although more confused, in 1640 as it was to be in 1642, and in such circumstances the Protestation, for example, could not remain a mere attempt to put parliamentary pressure on the Crown to eliminate Strafford. There were close contacts between Westminster and the locality, and the volatility of both entities meant that each was eminently susceptible to influence from the other.

---

trial shows no significant increase in the number of detainees in 1641 when compared with the two previous years, and a slight decrease from the 1636–8 level (which could, of course, reflect a decline in efficiency of law enforcement) [K.C.A. Q/SMc I, no foliation]. It would be tempting to read from this that Abbot and others were playing a devious political game, comparable to that of Sir Thomas Aston's 1641 petitioning campaign from Cheshire, another attempt to get local pressure to work on Parliament. But in the absence of further information, the question must remain unanswered.

66   Stowe 184, fo. 29; see also Stowe 744, fo. 17; *Proceedings in Kent*, p. 22.

10

The War, the People and the Absence of the Clubmen in the Midlands, 1642–1646

Simon Osborne

Originally appeared as Simon Osborne, 'The War, the People and the Absence of the Clubmen in the Midlands 1642–1646' in Midland History 19. Copyright © 1994. Reprinted with permission of The University of Birmingham.

The central aim of this essay is to examine the impact of the civil war upon communities in the midlands, with a view to advancing an explanation for the scarcity of concerted popular neutralist movements in the region.[1] In particular, it seeks to explain why it was that out of five midland counties (namely Leicestershire, Rutland, Northamptonshire, Warwickshire and Worcestershire), all apparently heavily affected by the war, a Clubman movement arose in just one, and even there was restricted to a particular part of it. It will be suggested that the answer does not lie in a geographically variable popular experience of the war. Although there was such a phenomenon, the variation was more localised than some authorities have suggested, and Clubmen were absent from even the worst affected areas. Instead, it will be suggested that the answer lies in variations in the capacity of the military to affect the *response* to this experience: that is that ultimately the outbreak of Clubman risings in the midlands was dependent upon the strength (or weakness) of the military.

The impact of the civil war and the various Clubman movements have received considerable attention from recent historians.[2] Despite

---

1   Much of this essay is based on S. Osborne, 'Popular Religion, Culture and Politics in the Midlands, c. 1638–1646' (University of Warwick Ph.D. thesis, 1993), chs. 4–6.

2   See especially I. Roy, 'The English Civil War and English Society', in B. Bond and I. Roy (eds.), *War and Society: A Year Book of Military History* (London, 1976); D.

Everitt's characterisation of the war as one which did not badly disrupt everyday civilian life or the economic and social fabric,[3] most recent authorities have emphasised how, especially in a factious region like the midlands, the war did indeed affect most communities to a significant degree. Although these recent studies all have different perspectives and emphases, an orthodoxy may be said to have emerged. Broadly speaking, this is that until recently the destructive impact of the civil war has been underestimated, and that the war must be regarded as a disruptive and traumatic experience not only for those who fought it, but for the communities that were caught up in it. A related orthodoxy pertains regarding the Clubmen. This is that they were a reaction to the demands and brutalities of the war, a burst of popular neutralism born out of war weariness and the collapse of military-civilian relations (such as they were) by the latter stages of the conflict.[4] A recent study of the Clubman movement in Herefordshire refers also to the importance of impressment and anti-Catholicism; but the only work to exclude the role of military depredation entirely is Hutton's study of the Worcestershire Clubmen.[5] A logical inference from the prevailing orthodoxy would be that where we find communities long exposed to the vagaries of the war, we might also expect to find Clubmen.

A problem with this is that as pointed out by Hutton, the Worcestershire Clubmen were from an area of the county apparently *least* affected by the war, and certainly removed from the main garrisons, supposedly one of the main agents of the burdens and abuses that gave rise to Clubman movements elsewhere.[6] It has been pointed out more recently that this problem does not apply to the Clubmen in neighbouring Herefordshire.[7] Indeed, it will be shown below that the Worcestershire Clubmen areas *were* heavily affected by the war,

Pennington, 'The War and the People', in J. Morrill (ed.), *Reactions to the English Civil War* (London, 1982); C. Carlton, *Going to the Wars: The Experience of the British Civil Wars, 1638–1651* (London, 1992). On the impact of the war in the midlands, see especially A. Hughes, *Politics, Society and Civil War in Warwickshire 1620–1660* (Cambridge, 1987) and P. Tennant, *Edgehill and Beyond: The Peoples' War in the South Midlands 1642–1645* (Stroud, 1992).

3   A. M. Everitt, *The Local Community and the Great Rebellion* (Historical Association, 1969).

4   J. Morrill, *The Revolt of the Provinces: Conservatives and Radicals in the English Civil War 1630–1650*, (London, 1976), 98–111; D. Underdown, 'The Chalk and the Cheese: Contrasts among the English Clubmen', *Past and Pres.*, 85 (1979), 25–48; P. Gladwish, 'The Herefordshire Clubmen: A Reassessment', *Midl. Hist.*, X, (1985), 62–72.

5   Gladwish, 'Herefordshire Clubmen', 63; R. Hutton, 'The Worcestershire Clubmen in the English Civil War', *Midl. Hist.*, V, (1979), 40–50.

6   *Ibid.*, 40–2.

7   Gladwish, 'Herefordshire Clubmen'.

if not as heavily as some other parts of the region. But if there is a direct relationship between the burdens of supporting garrisons and armies and the outbreak of Clubman risings, we also need to explain the absence of the Clubmen from Warwickshire, Northamptonshire, Leicestershire and Rutland. These counties were in the thick of the war. They were host to a network of major and petty garrisons, and saw many skirmishes throughout the conflict, frequently playing host to soldiers from both sides. Field armies crisscrossed them, and clashed at Edgehill and Naseby. On the face of it, they should have been breeding grounds for the sort of popular neutralism that arose in west Worcestershire. But despite being a major arena of the civil war, these parts of the midlands never saw a concerted popular neutralist movement.

One possible explanation for this is that the experience of Worcestershire was qualitatively different from that of the other counties under consideration here: i.e. the impact of war was more severe in the far west. This could accommodate Everitt's conservative characterisation of the war, which was based on a discussion of Leicestershire and Northamptonshire. More recently, it has been argued that, largely through the efforts of local commanders to mitigate the conflict, the impact of the war in Leicestershire was less than it was elsewhere.[8] This might help in explaining the absence of Clubmen in the eastern part of the region. No such claim has been made for Warwickshire, and indeed a recent study has provided ample evidence of the pervasive impact of the war there, particularly in the south and in neighbouring parts of Oxfordshire and Northamptonshire.[9]

In fact, a similar picture may be painted for the whole of the present region, including the east. Certainly, there was little variation in the distribution of garrisons, although there was a slightly heavier concentration to the west.[10] There were major garrisons at Worcester, Coventry, Northampton and Leicester. In the east, the royalists soon established important garrisons in north-west and north-east Leicestershire, at Ashby-de-la-Zouch and Belvoir Castle respectively. Sympathetic royalist gentry set up smaller and shorter-lived garrisons in the south of the county and at Grafton House in Northamp-

---

8   Everitt, *Local Community*; M. Bennett, 'Leicestershire's Royalist Officers and the War Effort in the County, 1642–1646', *Trans. Leics. Arch. & Hist. Soc.*, LIX (1984–5), 44–52, 47ff.

9   Tennant, *Edgehill and Beyond, passim*.

10   For the garrisons in the region, see Osborne, 'Popular Religion, Culture and Politics in the Midlands', ch. 4, and also the good military narratives available in J. W. Willis Bund, *The Civil War in Worcestershire 1642–1646* (Birmingham and London, 1905); R. Hutton, *The Royalist War Effort* (London, 1982); P. R. Newman, *Atlas of the English Civil War* (London, 1985) and Hughes, *Warwickshire*.

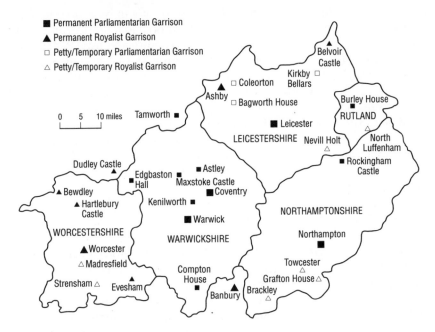

Map 10.1   Garrisons in the Midlands, 1642–1646

tonshire.[11] In late 1643 small royalist garrisons were created at Brackley and Towcester in south Northamptonshire, but soon ran in to problems of supply and had to be abandoned.[12] At approximately the same time, Colonel Thomas Waite was more successful in establishing a parliamentarian garrison at Burley House in Rutland,[13] whilst the Rutland Committee had in the meantime sat at the garrison at Rockingham Castle in north-east Northamptonshire.[14] By May 1645 the parliamen-

11   For the capture of the Rutland petty garrisons, see *Certain Informations*, (16–23 January 1643), British Library (hereafter B.L.), E85(45), 2; *Certain Informations*, (20 February–6 March 1643), B.L., E92(3), 51; Historical Manuscripts Commission (hereafter H.M.C.), *Thirteenth Report, App. I, Portland I (1892)*, 82, 99. For Grafton House, see *Calendar of State Papers Domestic* (hereafter *C.S.P.D.*) *1641–3*, 508–9. Press accounts of its capture are in (for example) *Mercurius Civicus*, (21–28 December 1643), B.L., E79(18), 344–5; *A True Relation of the Taking of Grafton House*, (1643), B.L., E79(24).
12   Bodleian Library (hereafter Bodl.), MS Eng. Hist. C53, fos. 93v–96v, 107–107v, 112; B.L., Add. MS 18980, fos. 144, 168; Bodl., Firth MS C6, fo. 193; *Mercurius Civicus*, (18–25 January 1644), B.L., E30(7), 379.
13   Waite first mustered his company of foot and troop of harquebusiers at Burley on 6 December 1643: Public Record Office (hereafter P.R.O.), SP 28/121A/373, Musters of Colonel Thomas Waite.
14   Bodl., MS Tanner 62, fo. 438; *Mercurius Aulicus*, (7–13 May 1643), B.L., E103(10), 237.

tarians had small garrisons in north Leicestershire at Bagworth house, Coleorton and Kirkby Bellars.[15] Parliament also had a number of small garrisons in north Warwickshire, at Astley, Kenilworth Castle, Maxstoke Castle, Tamworth and Edgbaston Hall. In June 1644, parliamentarian forces captured the royalist garrison at Compton House in the south of the county.[16] In Worcestershire, the garrisons were all royalist. The main ones were concentrated in the north and east: at Worcester, Evesham, Dudley Castle, Bewdley and Hartlebury Castle. There were minor, late-established garrisons at Strensham and Madresfield, the latter possibly not established until the autumn of 1645. Massey's capture of Evesham on 26 May 1645 gave the parliamentarians a secure base within the county for the first time.[17]

The juxtaposition of so many garrisons in the region resulted in a process of raid and counter-raid that lasted for much of the war. Outside the areas close to the main garrisons, much of the countryside was an effective no-man's land, with the unfortunate towns and villages subject to the demands and plundering of both sides. Thus Worcestershire was heavily affected by the proximity of the parliamentarian garrison at Gloucester, with the east particularly affected by the nearness of Edgbaston and Warwick.[18] South Warwickshire and Northamptonshire were the sites of repeated clashes between forces from royalist garrisons at Worcester, Oxford and Banbury and from parliamentarian garrisons at Coventry, Warwick and Northampton.[19] Disputed territory extended in an arc upwards into Rutland and parts of Leicestershire, where both sides had garrisons, and forces from Newark and the Eastern Association were also active.[20] In such areas, the suffering of civilian communities was particularly severe; whereas those in the shadow of a major garrison at least only had to endure the burdens imposed by one side. Thus we

15   C. E. Long, (ed.), 'The Diary of the Marches of the Royal Army During the Great Civil War Kept By Richard Symonds', *Camden Society* (Old. Ser. LXXIV, 1859), 178.
16   Hughes, *Warwickshire*, 195, 208; *The Parliament Scout*, (6–13 June 1644), B.L., E50(35), 410–11.
17   Willis Bund, *Civil War in Worcestershire*, 16–17, 112, 146–7, 178; Hutton, *War Effort*, 100–4, 178.
18   For the military situation in the midlands by April 1643, see Edward, Earl of Clarendon, *The History of the Rebellion and Civil Wars in England*, ed. W. Dunn Macray (Oxford, 1888), II, 472–3. For Worcestershire, see Willis Bund, *Civil War in Worcestershire*, 3–13.
19   For the heavy military activity in the south midlands, see Tennant, *Edgehill and Beyond*, Introduction, and the many descriptions of skirmishes between garrison forces, as recorded in the contemporary press.
20   Everitt, *Local Community*, 11; C. Holmes, *The Eastern Association in the English Civil War* (Cambridge, 1974), 72, 86, 91. There are many press accounts of clashes in the east and north midlands between parliamentarian forces and forces from Ashby-de-la-Zouch.

can speak of geographical variations in the suffering of midlands people. But it will be shown that these variations were *within* counties, and do not support arguments based upon distinctions between the west and east of the region, or between particular counties. Moreover, Clubman movements failed to develop even in the hardest hit areas.

Some of the thousands of soldiers present in the garrisons occasionally left the region for service in field armies, but as these armies themselves traversed the midlands, there was little if any overall easing of the burden.[21] Both Worcestershire and Warwickshire frequently hosted field armies. The earl of Essex's army marched across both these counties in the opening campaign of 1642, and Warwickshire was crossed by both Brooke and Rupert in the campaigns based around Lichfield in early 1643. Waller's army was present in Worcestershire in the spring of that year. In August 1644 Basil Fielding, Brooke's successor as commander of the West Midland Association, was in Warwickshire, and Charles moved his army down through south-east Worcestershire in order to avoid him. In 1645, Charles again passed through eastern Worcestershire in the campaign that culminated at Naseby,[22] whilst both Warwickshire and Worcestershire hosted the New Model in 1646. The inhabitants of these two counties also hosted the Scots in 1645 and 1646.[23] But the east was by no means totally spared. Rupert passed through Leicestershire on his way to relieve Newark in early 1644, and a year later Sir Marmaduke Langdale had a stormy passage through Northamptonshire and Leicestershire on his way from Banbury to the relief of the siege of Pontefract.[24] The Naseby and post-Naseby campaigns saw both main field armies in Northamptonshire and Leicestershire. In September 1645, Sydenham Poyntz marched forces from the east midlands and the north through Uppingham and Wellingborough on his way to Banbury and then Tewkesbury.[25] No part of the region escaped the burden of supporting field armies at some stage or other.

The financial demands made to support war efforts were heavy in themselves. The levies were many and included weekly or monthly assessments; levies on designated parishes for the maintenance of garrisons and individual troops and companies; and an excise tax on essential goods. Field armies made levies on the communities through which

---

21   Much in this section is drawn from Newman, *Atlas*, and J. Kenyon, *The Civil Wars of England* (London, 1988).

22   Bodl., Firth MS C8, fo. 27.

23   *C.S.P.D. 1645–7*, 56; H.M.C., *Portland I*, 233.

24   H.M.C., *The Letter Books, 1644–5, of Sir Samuel Luke*, ed. H. G. Tibbutt (1963), 204, 217.

25   *C.S.P.D. 1645–7*, 102–4, 109, 122.

they passed. Parliament levied taxes for the army in Ireland, the Scots army and the New Model Army. The weekly/monthly assessments began in the winter of 1642–43. In Worcestershire, the royalist £3,000 monthly assessment soon proved unpopular, and dragoons had to be used to collect arrears as early as March 1643. Later in the war, loss of territory and increasing influence of parliamentarian forces added to the problems.[26] But in Rutland too financial demands – this time parliamentarian – quickly proved onerous. By December 1643 the Committee (still at Rockingham Castle) were complaining at having not only to levy a weekly assessment of £62 10s., but to raise money for Waite to raise a regiment of horse, 'which in itself would be an unsupportable burden'. They had also recently been obliged to raise a fortnight's pay for Lord Grey's regiment at Leicester, and £500 for the Scots. The Committee pointed out that the county had until very recently been subject to much 'oppression' by royalist forces, but even parliamentarian forces had proved burdensome in their seizing of horses and provisions.[27] In Northamptonshire, incursions from Banbury and Oxford were making parliamentarian collection of taxes difficult by June 1644, and money due from the county to the Scots was in arrears by February 1645.[28] Clearly, the problems of having to collect money under the noses of the enemy bedevilled parliamentarians (and therefore civilians) in the east, as well as royalists in the west.

Garrisons also made heavy financial demands. Northamptonshire villages were commonly required to pay a weekly sum to those at Northampton and Rockingham, as well as contributions to others outside the county, usually Lynn, Cambridge, Huntingdon, Stamford, Newport Pagnell and Bedford.[29] Garrison and troop commanders were able to range far and wide in their quest for money. In south Worcestershire in 1644–45, John Gyles, captain of a troop of parliamentarian horse probably based in Tewkesbury, was able to levy as far west as Bransford, near the Malverns, and as far east as Cleeve Prior, near Evesham. His colleague Captain William Gouge, based at Evesham, was assigned thirteen villages in the Vale of Evesham in July 1645. Major George Purefoy, parliamentarian governor of Compton House, was authorised to collect weekly contributions from thirteen parishes in

26 Bodl., Rawlinson MS D924, fo. 152. See also Hutton, *War Effort*, 76–81 and *passim*.
27 Bodl., MS Tanner 62, fo. 438.
28 *C.S.P.D. 1644*, 208; *Commons Journals*, IV, 41.
29 See for example P.R.O., SP 28/173, Sutton Bassett Accounts, Stoke Doyle Accounts; SP 28/172, Harringworth Accounts, Harrington Accounts; H.M.C., *Salisbury (Cecil)* (1971), XXII, 380 (payments made by Nicholas Jackson, Bailiff of Brigstock).

south Warwickshire and twelve in Oxfordshire.[30] Many of these communities would also have had to help support the royalist garrison at Banbury, and probably the garrison at Northampton too. The latter garrison was certainly able to levy as far south as the countryside near Banbury itself; while the royalist Colonel Gerrard Croker was authorised to levy for his regiment of horse in several towns in south Warwickshire, north Oxfordshire and Gloucestershire.[31] Similarly, the constables of both Waltham-on-the-Wolds and Branston in north Leicestershire recorded regular taxes to both sides.[32]

Thus communities in disputed territory were especially vulnerable to the burdens of double taxation. But even in relatively secure areas such as north Warwickshire, protected by Coventry and the smaller garrisons to the north, the burden was heavy and occasionally unsupportable. Taxes for the Maxstoke Castle garrison were over £35 in arrears after eighteen months; the total weekly tax for the Tamworth garrison in December 1645 was just over £24, but a note on the garrison accounts records that it was not wholly collectable, 'by reason that it is taxed upon so poor men, and upon such lands where there is not distress to be had'.[33] However, these problems were as nothing compared to those where military weakness allowed the enemy to disrupt matters. Thus in May 1644, Lord Newcastle's horse, sent out of the north to join Goring at Newark, were out collecting money in supposedly parliamentarian areas of Staffordshire and Leicestershire. As late as November 1645, the absence of the Northamptonshire horse with Poyntz was allowing the royalists to plunder 'to the very walls' of Northampton. Following the recapture of Leicester, Fairfax ordered that a garrison of 1,500 be maintained there. But the town and countryside were so exhausted, and the royalists at Newark still so strong, that it was feared it could not be done.[34] The Towcester garrison quickly exhausted the south Northamptonshire countryside, already torn between Banbury and Northampton. By November 1643 the royalists were short of quarter for both men

---

30 P.R.O., SP 28/138, Accounts of Captain John Gyles, 1644–5; SP 28/138, Accounts of William Gouge, governor of Hawkesley Hall; SP 28/136/37, Accounts of Major George Purefoy at Compton House garrison, June 1644–February 1645.
31 *The Parliament Scout*, (26 April–3 May 1644), B.L., E44(23), 374; *Mercurius Civicus*, (25 April–2 May 1644), B.L., E45(1), 485–6; B.L. Harleian MS 6852, fo. 81.
32 Transcribed in T. G. Daniels, *Waltham-on-the-Wolds Constables' Accounts 1608–1706* (1984, no other publication details: copy consulted in Leicestershire Record Office), 188; Leicestershire Record Office (hereafter L.R.O.), DE 720/30, fos. 53–4v, 63.
33 P.R.O., SP 28/182, Accounts of Henry Kendall, Governor of Maxstoke Castle; SP 28/122, Tamworth garrison musters.
34 *C.S.P.D. 1644*, 171; *C.S.P.D. 1645–7*, 219; H.M.C., *Portland I*, 253.

and horses, and some of the horses in Towcester itself stood 'backside about the fetlocks in dirt'.[35] In December the governor, John Cochrane, complained that hundreds orginally assigned to him had been given to the Banbury garrison, and those he did have were exhausted by the presence of horse regiments. By the end of the month, with parliamentarian forces all around, he was unable to collect a farthing.[36] But the mere presence of royalist forces so close to Northampton also created problems for the parliamentarians. That same December, the Northamptonshire Committee wrote to the Speaker that the recent proximity of the enemy had hindered the gathering of taxes for the garrison, whose charges (by their own admission) were 'very great'.[37] Both sides accused the other of resorting to plunder.[38] The problems of the Worcestershire royalists in maintaining a war effort on a shrinking power base have been well described.[39] But we should note that in such a hotly disputed region as the midlands few communities found it easy to pay their bills.

Of course, fiscal demands were not the only burden placed upon civilian communities. Armies and garrisons needed food, horses, raw materials and manual labour. They also required accommodation and sustenance for troops on the move, often taken as 'free quarter'. As the war dragged on, taxes became ever more difficult to collect, and soldiers' pay became more infrequent. This resulted in a blurring of the distinction between sanctioned free quarter and mere foraging and plunder. This was in addition to the ravages of the war itself, in which plunder was frequently a tactical device, especially as punishment for communities perceived as disaffected.[40]

Even civilians in relatively secure areas suffered badly. In Coventry, thirty-eight inhabitants of the Spon Street ward alone drew up accounts of losses to parliamentarian forces, claiming from £1 16s. 4d. to £128 7s. 0d. The case of one of these people illustrates the range of losses that could be involved. Henry Smith, a baker, paid a variety of taxes, sent in cheeses, gave pewter to make into ordinance, and provided free quarter. This did not save him from having his horses taken away or having a barn burned down by order of the Committee.[41] So many

35   Bodl., MS Eng. Hist. C53, fo. 93v.
36   B.L., Add. MS 18980, fo. 159.
37   Bodl., MS Tanner 62, fo. 430.
38   See for example *Mercurius Aulicus* (10–16 September 1643), B.L., E68(4), 504; *The Parliament Scout*, (17–24 November 1643), B.L., E76(27), 191.
39   See Hutton, *War Effort*, ch. 9, esp. 95–9.
40   I. Roy, 'England Turned Germany? The Aftermath of the Civil War in its European Context', *Trans. Royal Hist. Soc.*, 5th ser., XXVIII (1978), 127–45, esp. 135–7; Osborne, 'Popular Religion, Culture and Politics in the Midlands', 208–11.
41   P.R.O., SP 28/182, Accounts of the inhabitants of Spon Street Ward, Coventry.

houses were pulled down in the city suburbs (in order to deny royalists cover) that people had to gather in the churchyards for shelter.[42] In nearby Stoneleigh, forty inhabitants drew up accounts of their losses, of which a number included sections for 'losses by the Scot'. The Scots' shopping list suggests more than mere foraging for essentials: they also took linen, pewter and petticoats. In Brinklow (north Warwickshire), a troop of Sir William Brereton's men took a similar variety of goods, including horses, sheep, beer, tobacco and a hawk.[43]

But communities in contested areas undoubtedly had the worst of it. In such areas civilians were frequently subject to the demands and plunder of both royalist and parliamentarian forces. In the present region, Worcestershire is the most familiar but by no means the sole example. Charles was concerned as early as December 1642 that lack of pay would result in 'some violence upon the country' in Worcestershire. In February 1644, Rupert made strenuous efforts to stabilize the situation, temporarily increasing the monthly assessments and outlawing free quarter. But there were more complaints about soldiers' conduct at the Michaelmas quarter sessions.[44] By 1646 the royalist soldiery was out of control. Colonel Samuel Sandys, Governor of Hartlebury Castle at this time, was alleged by Henry Townshend to have 'so sharked the country thereabouts, that for beef, malt, hay and bacon he lived in free cost'.[45] During the siege of Worcester, soldiers pulled down citizens' property and sold the materials for drink. It has been estimated that overall perhaps a fifth of Worcester's buildings were burnt or destroyed.[46] By the latter part of the war, parliamentarian forces were adding to the misery of the county's inhabitants, especially in the north and east. Inhabitants in communities such as Kidderminster, Flyford Flavell, Fladbury and Chaddesley Corbett were plundered by parliamentarian soldiers from garrisons in Warwickshire, as well as those in field armies under Essex, Waller, Poyntz and the Scots.[47]

A broadly similar story may be told of the east. The lack of accounts of parishioners' losses in Leicestershire and the absence of royalist

42 B.L., Add. MS 11364 (Annals of the City of Coventry), fo. 17v; *Certain Informations*, (7–14 August 1643), B.L., E65(8), 231. On the theme of property destruction generally, see S. Porter, 'Property Destruction in the English Civil Wars', *Hist. Today*, 36 (1986).
43 P.R.O., SP 28/182, Stoneleigh Accounts; SP 28/182, Brinklow Accounts.
44 J. W. Willis Bund (ed.), *The Diary of Henry Townshend of Elmley Lovett 1640–1660* (Worcs. Hist. Soc., 1915–20), II, 90, 160, 174–5.
45 *Ibid.*, I, 106.
46 *Ibid.*, I, 128; Porter, 'Property Destruction', 37.
47 P.R.O., SP 28/187, Kidderminster Accounts; SP 28/188, Flyford Flavell Accounts; SP 28/187, Fladbury Accounts; SP 28/187, Accounts of Chaddesley Corbett.

Committee papers or a 'diarist' such as Townshend makes an assessment difficult. But other evidence suggests that communities suffered just as much in this area as they did further west. It is true that early on there was some attempt to mitigate the impact of war in these parts. In January 1643 Hastings offered to prevent plunder of parliamentarian sympathisers, if Grey would reciprocate. In Ashby-de-la-Zouch, Hastings had a proclamation posted on the market cross forbidding plunder and robbery by soldiers, on pain of death.[48]

But Hastings's offer came to nothing, and anyway he was not the only commander operating in Leicestershire and Rutland. Plunder soon became common. The payment of taxes to both sides in parishes like Waltham-on-the-Wolds and Branston indicates not tacit co-operation, but military impasse. Indeed, there is at least one case of an attack on the enemy in one of these very parishes. In December 1643, Thomas Waite attacked a party of royalists quartered in Waltham, and the royalist response threatened severe escalation. Waite wrote that a party of Belvoir horse rode into Rutland, 'swearing that unless I would be gone from Burleigh they would not leave one town in Rutland worth a penny'.[49] Early the following summer, with the Eastern Association horse bogged down by mud and rain, the earl of Newcastle's horse plundered villages near Leicester, before moving north. A little later, a party of royalist horse under Colonel William Nevill plundered several towns and villages between Belvoir and Leicester.[50] Both the Leicestershire gentry and Hastings complained about the conduct of Lucas, imposing oppressive taxes in the north of the county, and threatening plunder. Waite added to the misery of the inhabitants by taking oxen and 200 sheep from near Belvoir in March 1644.[51] Hastings himself resorted to force in order to collect taxes. The source for this is 'Mensalia, or monthly passages', an unpublished royalist journal of propagandist tone, dealing with military affairs in the east and north midlands. 'Mensalia' noted that when in June 1643 a troop of Hastings's men came to Bagworth and other villages in west Leicestershire to collect the levy for Ashby, they found it not ready. In response, the troopers seized the constables, 'other men of sufficiency', and some horses, and took them back to Ashby.[52] In March 1644, a successful skirmish with some of Hastings's men at Hinckley resulted in the release of about thirty countrymen taken prisoner from the south-western villages of Cosby

48   H.M.C., *Hastings*, II (1930), 87–8; Bodl., MS Add, C132, fo. 39v.
49   Bodl., MS Tanner 89, fo. 27. See also H.M.C., *Portland I*, 165.
50   *C.S.P.D. 1644*, 190–1, 304.
51   B.L., Add. MS 18982, fos. 42–3; Bodl., Firth MS C8, fo. 374; *The Scottish Dove*, (8–15 March 1644), B.L., E37(24), 172.
52   Bodl., MS Add. C132, fo. 50v.

and Leire.[53] It is clear that the war in these parts was as bitter as it was further west. As early as 1643, 'Mensalia' commented that plunder, pillage and the seizing of horses were so common, 'that we take them for no instances of wonder or speciality of recording'.[54]

The strain on communities and individuals was immense. Between October 1643 and October 1644, the constables in Waltham-on-the-Wolds recorded one hundred and fifty individual disbursements of money. Twenty-seven (18 per cent) of these recorded supplies for soldiers quartered in the town. The supplies included oats, peas, ale, cheese, tobacco, mutton, bread and even a pack of cards. Soldiers were quartered in the town on seventeen separate occasions in that period, including 320 men on 19 October 1643. This was in addition to the village sending supplies to Belvoir, providing horses, and paying contribution money.[55] Unsurprisingly, the Waltham constables were obliged to emulate their counterparts in Branston in paying soldiers money not to take horses.[56] From Rutland, the gentleman Abel Barker wrote that he dared not keep money about him, as every day he expected to be arrested and his house plundered. Because of the disruption caused by the war, he did not expect to receive one half of the rents due to him.[57] Hastings testified to the exhaustion of Leicestershire when explaining his surrender of Leicester in 1645. He had been desparately short of supply and horse, and 'the country people being all prisoners or pillaged there came in not a days pay while I was in the town'. The Leicestershire Committee echoed this in a letter to Fairfax of March 1646: 'This country is so extraordinarily plundered and impoverished that they cannot continue the ordinary taxes'.[58]

Similar problems affected other heavily contested parts of the region. Lacking a secure base in south Northamptonshire, royalist forces were dependent of plunder for provision. The town of Brackley and the surrounding area is a good example. Byron told Rupert that he used four hundred and fifty horse and dragoons to 'drive the country of such horses and cattle as can be found near the town' whilst he was quartered in Brackley in July 1643.[59] In December 1644, the town hosted about five hundred of Prince Maurice's men, and just four days later four hundred men under Sir John Digby.[60] The following February, the New

53 *A Letter to the Lord Grey of Groby*, (6 March 1644), B.L., E37(9).
54 Bodl., MS Add. C132, fo. 46.
55 Daniels, *Waltham-on-the Wolds Constables' Accounts*, 118–23.
56 *Ibid.*, 118; L.R.O., DE 720/30, fos. 53, 54.
57 H.M.C., *Fifth Report* (1876), App., Field MSS, 388.
58 Bodl., Firth MS C8, fos. 5–6; Bodl., MS Tanner 60, fo. 516.
59 B.L., Add. MS 18980, fo. 80.
60 *Letter Books of Sir Samuel Luke*, 679–80.

Model made its presence felt when Captain Abercromby arrived and raided the market, taking away horses, meat and corn. In March, a party of horse from Warwick seized 'prisoners and oxen' from the countryside between Brackley and Aynho.[61] In east Northamptonshire, Brigstock in Rockingham Forest was afflicted not only by heavy taxation but by plunder of cattle and illegal ploughing up of the park. Some tenants deserted their land.[62] Parliamentarian soldiers committed 'great spoil' in Salcey Forest, whilst Cromwell allegedly plundered 'all the chief gentry' in Northamptonshire in late April 1643.[63] In south Warwickshire, the people of Brailes, despite being 'well affected' to the royalist cause, were heavily taxed and threatened with plunder by Gerrard Croker, whilst from Compton House the people of nearby Tysoe were threatened by the parliamentarian George Purefoy.[64] Foot soldiers at Warwick Castle kept horses stabled in the town so that they might go out on their own plundering missions; the inhabitants of Cubbington petitioned that no more troops be quartered on them, as their provisions were all used up.[65] But the south Warwickshire people were also affected by the ability of forces from Banbury occasionally to plunder as far as Warwick itself.[66] In similar tones to the Leicestershire Committee, the Warwickshire Committee warned in 1648 of the devastation caused by the war to the local people and economy: 'the present dearth of provision and deadness of trading this county is so impoverised that we fear we shall not be able to answer the parliament's expectations . . . .'.[67]

It seems then that there was no axiomatic relationship between oppressive taxation, depredations by the soldiery, etc., and the growth of Clubman movements. This may appear to lend support to Hutton's argument that the Worcestershire Clubmen were not a response to such phenomena at all, occurring as they did in the hilly districts of the west which had been least affected by the war. Hutton argues that the Worcestershire Clubmen were responding to the threat by the newly formed Western Association fully to involve them in the war effort for the very *first* time.[68] The possibility arises that factors other than mili-

---

61   *Ibid.*, 150, 182.

62   H.M.C., *Salisbury*, XXII, 380; P.A.J. Pettit, *The Royal Forests of Northamptonshire 1518–1714* (Northants. Rec. Soc., XXIII, 1968), 176–7.

63   *Letter Books of Sir Samuel Luke*, 380; *Mercurius Aulicus*, (7–13 May 1643), B.L., 103(10), 237.

64   B.L. Add. MS 18980, fo. 58; Hughes, *Warwickshire*, 202–3.

65   P.R.O., SP 16/511/57; H.M.C., *Fourth Report* (1874), App., Earl of Denbigh MSS, 272.

66   See for example, *Letter Books of Sir Samuel Luke*, 87.

67   Bodl., MS Tanner 58, fo. 719.

68   Hutton, 'Worcestershire Clubmen', and *War Effort*, 161ff.

tary depredation may explain the restriction of the Clubmen to the far west of the region. Certainly, the prominence of the Catholic earl of Shrewsbury in the Western Association, and the impressment by the Association of hundreds of men in the west, created special antagonisms there. At one stroke, the impressment warrants aroused a combined popular hatred of Catholics and conscription.[69] In addition, there is no evidence of similar large scale, systematic impressment in any of the other counties under consideration here.[70] There was then an apparent relationship between impressment and Clubmen movements. However, this does not apply to east Worcestershire, which despite also being subject to the demands of the Western Association did not produce Clubmen. Clearly the relationship was not a simple one, and in distinguishing west Worcestershire some other fact or set of factors was at work.

We cannot identify this factor as the absence of military lawlessness in the far west. Both the Worcestershire and the Herefordshire Clubman movements were at least in part provoked by the misdemeanours of the royalist soldiery. Although it is true that western Worcestershire was not as heavily affected by the war as the east of the county, the Clubman communities *were* reacting to military depredation. The Worcestershire Clubmen produced their first declaration, drawn up on Woodbury Hill, on 5 March 1645. The centre of activity was Woodbury, bounded, Hutton suggests, by the county border and the rivers Severn and Teme.[71] It is this very area which Townshend describes as exhausted by the demands of the royalist soldiery in 1645: 'All the country between Severn and Teme and on the banks of the Severn (which are his Majesty's only secure quarters) . . . are by free quarter of the horse eaten up, undone, and destroyed'. The horse regiments had extorted money, and threatened to fire houses, murder and pillage.[72] Moreover, Townshend's description bears a striking resemblance to the language used in their declaration by the Woodbury Clubmen themselves: 'We having long groaned under many illegal taxations and unjust pressures . . . we, our wives and children, have been exposed to utter ruin by the outrages and violence of the soldier; threatening to fire our houses; endeavouring to ravish our wives and daughters, and menacing our persons'.[73] A second, undated declaration was produced by Clubmen in the south-west, at Malvern

---

69   Hutton, 'Worcestershire Clubmen'; Gladwish, 'Herefordshire Clubmen', 63.
70   Osborne, 'Popular Religion, Politics and Culture in the Midlands', 261–4.
71   *Townshend Diary*, III, 222–3; *The Kingdom's Weekly Intelligencer*, (11–18 March 1645), B.L., E247(2), 727–9; Hutton, *War Effort*, 160.
72   *Townshend Diary*, III, 239–40.
73   *Ibid.*, 222–3.

Link.[74] These people may well have suffered at the hands of soldiers from both sides. Essex's army passed that way in 1642, and as we have seen John Gyles's troop of horses were levying contributions right across the south by late 1644. From Gloucestershire, Edward Massey had constantly raided this part of Worcestershire. Indeed, the origin of the Western Association itself lay in desire to stop the 'daily incursions, plunders, rapines and murders' committed by parliamentarian soldiers.[75] Certainly, the Herefordshire Clubman made it clear they were defending themselves from 'all insolencies and violences whatsoever offered us or our estates at home'.[76] Sir William Brereton thought the Herefordshire and Worcestershire Clubmen were alike in reacting against royalist plundering.[77]

What, then, distinguished west Worcestershire? In explaining the distribution of popular neutralist movements, the remoteness of the Worcestershire Clubman areas from the permanent royalist garrisons remains important. Equally important is the profusion of garrisons and soldiers in other parts of the region. This is because the garrisons were not simply parasitic on the local community: there was also a more positive aspect to the relationship. In heavily disputed territory, strong garrisons provided shelter from enemy forces engaged on their own plundering missions. Protection from enemy plunder was, as we shall see below, what was expected of garrison forces by civilians in such territory, in return for their continued support. No garrison could honour this in full; but in the present region there were enough garrisons of sufficient strength – especially on the parliamentarian side – to negate wholesale disillusion. Many communities too far from the major garrisons to benefit from protection were nevertheless close enough to minor ones to make possible the policing of the inhabitants' activities. Both the protective and the policing functions required strong, effective garrisons; but the net result of the juxtaposition of garrisons in the present region was a high degree of military authority in many areas.

It may be, therefore, that the main reason for the absence of Clubmen from such large parts of the midlands is because there were so *many* garrisons within a heavily disputed area. That is, the proliferation of garrisons in the region held out the hope – however poorly realised – of defence against the enemy, or failing that, the promise of swift action

74 *The Kingdom's Weekly Intelligencer*, (18–25 March 1645), B.L., E274(24), 735–7.
75 *Townshend Diary*, II, 181–2.
76 R. N. Dore (ed.), *The Letter Books of Sir William Brereton*, 2 vols. (Rec. Soc. of Lancs. & Cheshire, 1984 & 1990), I, 62–3; Gladwish, 'Herefordshire Clubmen', 63–4.
77 *Letter Books of Sir William Brereton*, I, 110.

against disaffected civilians. Removed as they were from the worst of the fighting and the permanent garrisons, and plagued by the long stay of the horse regiments, the people of west Worcestershire still had the embittering experience of free quarter and plunder, without either the compensation of protection by garrison forces, or a permanent sense of military authority. Their counterparts to the east, however, were able at least occasionally to benefit from the shelter provided by a nearby garrison, and had less inclination and opportunity to organize themselves into a third force.

With garrisons and field armies to sustain, both royalists and parliamentarians needed the support of civilians. Raw materials and foodstuffs were constantly required, and the high rates of wastage in the local forces meant that there was an on-going demand for fresh recruits.[78] Extortion, pillage and impressment were ways of meeting these demands; but voluntary support was more effective and where obtainable was generally preferred.[79]

In turn, sustained voluntary support was dependent on the ability of the military to protect the local populace. Both sides recognised this. Thus when it was the fear of being 'deserted' – i.e. left to the mercy of the enemy – that lay behind the 'discontent and murmur' that arose one day in Ashby in January 1643, Hastings made a show of his presence the next day, and feasted the townspeople in the evening.[80] The earl of Denbigh was informed as early as August 1644 that recent parliamentarian gains in Worcestershire had shown the country people 'how unable, or at least how slow, their Worcester friends are in protecting them', and that many people were now switching their allegiance to the parliamentarian forces.[81] Popular parliamentarianism was equally conditional. This applied in even partisan Northamptonshire. In February 1643 a letter from the county, subsequently printed, warned of the growing disaffection of ordinary people, due to the seeming inability to protect the county from the royalists. A recent spate of raids in the Daventry area had not been resisted, and 'country fellows' in the parliamentarian forces were on the verge of mutiny, as they saw 'nothing done to ease them, or relieve them'.[82] Shortly before the royalist storm of

---

78   For wastage in midland forces, see Osborne, 'Popular Religion, Culture and Politics in the Midlands', 233–4, 243–4. For wastage in parliamentarian regiments in Warwickshire, see also Hughes, *Warwickshire*, 199–200.
79   See for example H.M.C., *Fourth Report*, App., Earl of Denbigh MSS, 264; B.L., Add. MS 18980, fo. 58; Harleian MS 6804, fo. 139.
80   Bodl., MS Add. C132, fo. 38v.
81   H.M.C., *Fourth Report*, App., Earl of Denbigh MSS, 270.
82   *The Latest Intelligence of Prince Rupert's Proceedings in Northamptonshire*, (2 February 1643), B.L., E18(3), 2–3.

Leicester in 1645, Grey was advised that the Committee there had fortified only the Newark area of the city (in which they were living), and that discontent was spreading rapidly among the townspeople, who believed they had been abandoned to the whims of the enemy.[83] In their protracted dispute over the command of the Warwickshire forces, both the Warwickshire Committee and Denbigh referred to the deleterious effect the dispute was having on popular support, because of the feelings of insecurity it generated.[84] Coventry citizens petitioned parliament in October 1643, complaining of the suffering of the county at the hands of the cavaliers. *Mercurius Aulicus* quoted what it claimed was the text of the petition: 'the want of due protection . . . to the great disadvantage and disheartening of many, and daily falling off of others, who have contributed to the parliament for their future safety'.[85] Even if fictitious, the use of this passage as propaganda reveals much about what was expected of the military by civilians. Another petition, printed in the parliamentarian press in August 1644, made the situation clear. Claiming to represent the 'inhabitants' of Warwickshire, it complained not only of taxes and free quarter, but of 'frequent plundering, almost throughout the whole county'. The result was 'a general discontent' which was discouraging people from supporting the parliament.[86] Popular allegiance had a price, and protection from plunder was one of the major requirements.

The presence of strong, well-ordered garrisons was therefore crucial to the maintenance of popular support. Much of the preceding discussion has shown that in very few parts of the region were civilians entirely free from plunder by at least one side. Indeed, there were times when the major garrisons were little more than islands in a sea of plunder. In the summer of 1644 it was said that no part of Leicestershire was free of royalist plundering; even Northamptonshire was at one time 'much infested' by royalist forces, and the Committee were 'not able to defend their own county'. The Warwickshire Committee summed up the problem: 'when there are garrisons on all sides it is impossible to protect every village'.[87]

83   John Nichols, *The History and Antiquities of the County of Leicester*, 4 vols. (London, 1795–1815), III, Pt. II, App. IV, 41–2.
84   *Lords Journals*, VI, 321, 325.
85   *The True Informer*, (28 October–4 November 1643), B.L., E74(21), 55; *Mercurius Aulicus*, (22–28 October 1643), B.L., E75(13), 602–3.
86   *The Humble petition . . . of the County of Warwick and the City of Coventry*, (1644), B.L., E7(20), 3–4.
87   *Lords Journals*, VI, 627–8; *C.S.P.D. 1644*, 208; *C.S.P.D. 1645–7*, 219; H.M.C., *Sixth Report* (1877–8), App., House of Lords MSS, 27–8.

But the garrisons, particularly the larger, permanent ones, did not fail entirely. Many people came from towns and villages further afield to live in the main garrisons and found at least a measure of protection. Many, for instance, came from north Gloucestershire, south-east Worcestershire and south Warwickshire to Warwick in order to escape the depredations of the royalist garrison at Camden House in Gloucestershire.[88] Others came to Coventry from north Warwickshire; Richard Baxter wrote that 'thousands' of the godly lived in fear in their homes, 'and so they sought refuge in the parliament's garrisons'.[89] Following the royalist capture of Leicester in 1645, terrified inhabitants of Northamptonshire (probably from the east) fled to the parliamentarian garrison at Newport Pagnell.[90] Other people came in to the garrisons on a temporary basis, on the approach of enemy forces, or sheltered horses and goods in them to prevent theft.[91] This was a mutually beneficial relationship, as villagers were sometimes required to serve in garrison forces in emergencies.[92] Garrison administrations could be obsessive about security: in the late summer and autumn of 1643 for example, the Northampton Borough Assembly passed orders making assessments for the provisions of horses and equipping of men to act as scouts; money for the fortifications; orders for householders to work on the fortifications, and the creation of a select committee to appoint inhabitants 'of ability' to act as guards.[93] Although enemy forces were indeed sometimes able to approach close to the large garrisons, they were often beaten back, and the booty taken from the country people recaptured by the garrison forces.[94] Frequently, detachments were sent out from the garrisons into contested territory in order to drive off plundering enemy forces. Thus in August 1643, Banbury forces raiding in south Warwickshire were routed by a troop of horse from Northampton, whose forces also drove away royalists attempting to plunder Towcester. The Worcester garrison was able as late as August 1645 to drive away parliamentarians raiding in the Worcester-

88 *Mercurius Civicus*, (27 February–6 March 1645), B.L., E271(16), 481; S. Clarke, *The Lives of Sundry Eminent Persons in this later Age* (London, 1683), 48.
89 M. Sylvester (ed.), *Reliquiae Baxterianae* (London, 1696), 44–5.
90 *Letter books of Sir Samuel Luke*, 292.
91 See for example *ibid.*, 646–7; *The Kingdom's Weekly Intelligencer*, (21–28 May 1644), B.L., E49(26), 491.
92 See for example Northamptonshire Record Office (hereafter N.R.O.), Isham Correspondence, IC 3423.
93 N.R.O., Borough Records 3/2, Northampton Borough Second Assembly Book 1629–1714, 73–77.
94 For examples concerning the Warwick and Burley House garrisons, see *Letter Books of Sir Samuel Luke*, 521–2; *Certain Informations*, (15–22 January 1644), B.L., E29(20), 417.

shire countryside.[95] For many people, such protection clearly provided the *quid pro quo* for the otherwise burdensome presence of a nearby garrison.

In the more disputed areas such as south Northamptonshire and much of Leicestershire, the cumulative effect of being fought over resulted in a particularly bitter popular experience of the war. Even here garrisons and soldiers were sometimes close enough to offer at least the hope of protection. In Lutterworth, for example, the inhabitants still had sufficient faith in the Leicester garrison to co-operate with forces from there in driving off some of Hastings's men during an attempt at another raid in September 1644.[96] However this did not always apply in communities distant from the major garrisons. Such communities were sometimes too far away for garrison forces to save them from raiding parties. By the time word got to the garrison, and a detachment of horse was sent out to the village or town concerned, the plunderers had often come and gone. Thus in January 1644 the Leicester horse arrived too late to prevent the plunder of Lutterworth on its fair day by a party of Hastings's horse.[97] In Worcestershire, parliamentarian forces plundered successfully 'in all small villages', i.e. away from the reach of the permanent royalist garrisons.[98] The further from a garrison, the further from shelter or the chance of a counter-attack.

Garrisons were sometimes able to police nearby communities. From his small garrison at Edgbaston, for example, Colonel Fox ordered villagers to stay indoors when the royalists attempted to impress men and, when necessary, took recalcitrant villagers prisoner. On a number of occasions, the constable of Nether Whitacre in north Warwickshire was arrested for alleged misdemeanours and imprisoned in the Tamworth garrison; Hastings had similar power in west Leicestershire.[99] The comprehensiveness of such policing was of course enhanced by the proliferation of garrisons, and especially by the continued strength of the major parliamentarian garrisons.

The mere presence of the soldiery may also have provided a sense of authority. As we have seen from the demands made of communities

95 *A Continuation of Certain Special and Remarkable Passages*, (10–18 August 1643), B.L., E65(21), 7; Bodl., MS Eng. Hist. C53, fo. 65; *Mercurius Aulicus*, (10–17 August 1645), B.L., E298(23), 1699.
96 *Mercurius Civicus*, (11–19 September 1644), B.L., E9(7), 651.
97 *Mercurius Etc.*, (17 January 1644), B.L., E29(7), 5; *Certain Informations*, (22–29 January 1644), B.L., E30(13), 419.
98 *Mercurius Aulicus* (10–17 August 1645), B.L., E298(23), 1699.
99 Bodl., Firth MS C6, fo. 137; P.R.O., SP 28/187, Accounts of Chaddesley Corbett; Warwick County Record Office, DRB 27/5, Nether Whitacre Constables' Accounts, 1642–3, 1643–4, 1646 accounts; Bodl., MS Add. C132, fo. 50v; *C.S.P.D. 1644–5*, 544.

such as Brackley and Waltham-on-the-Wolds, such places were frequently full of soldiers of either side. In Northamptonshire, the traffic just of the parliamentarian forces was considerable. At various times, parishes were visited by soldiers under Waller, Grey, Manchester, Gell, Cromwell, Poyntz, Fairfax and the Scots, as well as a number of local officers. Soldiers passed through on their way to or from major conflicts such as Cropredy Bridge and Naseby, or more local actions such as those against Banbury.[100] Soldiers also came on errands such as collecting money for the 'house of correction' and escorting impressed men from outside the county.[101] Many of these parishes would also have hosted royalist troops on occasion. For such communities, martial authority was a palpable, almost everyday experience.

Indeed, it is notable that everywhere except Worcestershire, royalist and parliamentarian forces seem to have had little difficulty in maintaining troop levels without resorting to systematic conscription.[102] Of course, the mere absence of large-scale impressment does not necessarily mean that those who volunteered were committed to the cause of either side: pay, for example, may have been an important motivation for volunteers.[103] But it does mean that the military over much of the region were of sufficient influence to attract people into the local forces. This is certainly true of the parliamentarian forces. Parliamentarian muster rolls and accounts record strikingly consistent troop levels right across the region, even in the latter stages of the war.[104] The evidence for royalist forces is less conclusive, but Hastings built up a powerful army in the east without massive conscription, and popular support there generally seems not to have declined sharply until the military reversals of 1645 and 1646. Impressionistic evidence suggests that the royalist Compton family (governors of the Banbury garrison) had significant popular support in south Warwickshire and Northamptonshire.[105] It seems that in areas where there were strong garrisons, or where contested territory resulted in a strong cumulative military presence, neither side had serious manpower problems. The civilian population of these areas evidently maintained sufficient voluntary support to preclude the need for large-scale conscription. Impressment should

100 P.R.O., SP 28/173, Rothersthope, Scaldwell, Ravensthorpe and Teeton, Barnwell All Saints and Harringworth accounts.
101 N.R.O., 156P/105, Harringworth Constables' Accounts, 1645–6; P.R.O., SP 28/173, Scaldwell Accounts.
102 Osborne, 'Popular Religion, Politics and Culture in the Midlands', ch. 5 *passim*, esp. 218–67.
103 *Ibid.*, 264–7.
104 *Ibid.*, 228–36.
105 *Ibid.*, 236–49; Bennett, 'Leicestershire's Royalist Officers', 45 and *passim*.

therefore be regarded less as a cause of the Clubman outbreaks than as another symptom of the root cause, military weakness. It is significant that there were no Clubmen in east Worcestershire, where the people were to varying degrees pillaged, protected and policed by the competing garrisons.

In the hills of west Worcestershire, however, the situation was different. The civilian communities here were neither near the permanent garrisons, nor constantly fought over by rival forces. The parliamentarian garrisons were far too distant to offer an alternative source of protection or authority. Thus discontent generated by the demands and misdemeanours of the royalist horse regiments was able to ferment. Brereton wrote to the Committee of Both Kingdoms in March 1645 that if only the parliamentarian forces could make a strong showing 'in the remote parts of Salop, Herefordshire and Worcestershire', then they were sure to win support from the discontented populace.[106] But by the time parliament was able to make such a show in Worcestershire, the Clubmen were already active. With no-one else to turn to in the face of the collapse in royalist military authority and discipline, the west Worcestershire people armed themselves. Further east, even if the enemy seemed to offer an equally unattractive alternative, organising a neutralist movement under the noses of so many soldiers would have been extremely difficult. The Worcestershire Clubmen used parish churches as places for look-outs and rendezvous, and rang bells to communicate with neighbouring parishes.[107] With the roads, markets and alehouses elsewhere in the region so often full of soldiers, it is doubtful that such organization was possible there. In the Clubman areas, the military were strong enough to provoke discontent; but not strong enough to deter armed resistance.

Thus over much of the present region it may be that an effective military presence negated the growth of popular neutralism. It is not clear how far the arguments advanced here apply to areas outside the region which *did* see Clubman activity. Underdown has described much of the south-west as an area of intense military dispute.[108] Yet despite the apparent similarity to the present region, Clubman movements were widespread. However, the distinction between strong and weak garrisons may have been significant here, at least in some parts of the south-west. For example, Underdown believes that the inhabitants of the Wiltshire cheese country were inclined to support parliament; but

106   *Letter Books of Sir William Brereton*, I, 132.
107   *Kingdom's Weekley Intelligencer*, B.L., E274(24), 735–7.
108   D. Underdown, *Revel, Riot and Rebellion: Popular Politics and Culture in England 1603–1660* (Oxford, 1987, pbk. edn.), 146–8.

the Clubman erupted there because the parliamentarian garrison at Malmesbury failed to protect them from the enemy. Indeed, the spread of Clubman movements in the south-west was chiefly triggered by the arrival of Goring's rapacious army in Dorset early in 1645.[109] It seems therefore that until this intrusion the local garrisons had maintained a precarious balance in military–civilian relations.

However other Clubman areas, such as the Welsh borders and parts of the south-west, were not host to networks of rival garrisons, but were largely subject only to royalist garrisons.[110] Here, protection against enemy plundering would not have been such an important factor. In such areas, the association of Clubman movements with royalist territory may therefore partially be explained by other factors, for example by what some have seen as poorer levels of discipline amongst royalist troops, and the greater opportunities for the expression of discontent afforded by parliamentarian administrations.[111]

This may well have been the case in a number of areas – such as Shropshire, Herefordshire and east Somerset – where royalist garrisons became the direct target of the Clubmen. There was a more straight-forward relationship between military depredation and Clubman movements in these areas. But even here military weakness may have been a factor. The rapid spread of the Clubmen suggests a collapse in the ability of the local garrisons to police civilian communities. The importance of such activity is suggested by Sir William Russell's remark to Rupert that he needed a 'good strength' in the Worcester garrison to keep even the townsmen themselves in subjection.[112] It is unlikely that any one garrison prevented Clubman outbreaks by sheer repressive force alone; but given the lack of a *cumulative* military presence in royalist dominated areas, and the consequent lack of an alternative source of authority, any deterioration in conduct or weakening of power is likely to have been instrumental in the growth of Clubman movements.

Studies of the garrisons concerned are needed; but it is surely significant that the Clubman outbreaks were all late in the war, and largely in the context of royalist military reversal and a failing war effort. Royalist territory was especially prone to diminishing supply and temporary

---

109   *Ibid.*, 156–8; Underdown, 'Chalk and the Cheese', 39.
110   *Ibid.*, 46–7; Underdown, *Revel*, 157–8; Newman, *Atlas*, 78–9. But this did not include the Severn valley, where territory was bitterly contested: Roy, 'England Turned Germany?', 134.
111   Of course, this would not necessarily be inconsistent with the argument made here, that Clubmen may have been negated in *disputed* territory by the presence of effective garrisons. On conduct, see Underdown, *Revel*, 152–3. On the absorption of protest, see A. Hughes, 'The King, the Parliament, and the Localities during the English Civil War', *Jnl. of Brit. Studs.*, 24 (1985), 236–63.
112   B.L., Add. MS 18981, fo. 166.

influxes of defeated soldiers, leading to further plunder and provocation of war-weary civilians. In Bridgnorth, Shropshire for example, lack of supply was causing serious trouble by April 1644, whilst the arrival of Sir William Vaughan's defeated soldiers in this county, Herefordshire and Worcestershire in late October 1645, and their subsequent plundering, provoked the second rising of the Worcestershire Clubmen in December.[113] In this light, the Clubmen appear once again as a dramatic symptom of the absence of military authority in general, and the decline of royalist military power in particular.

Even a relatively cursory survey of the impact of the war on midland communities will show that many were heavily affected by the conflict. The war was so pervasive that any distinctions in the geographical distribution of its impact must be local rather than regional. It is not valid to assert that the east was less affected than the west. Much more helpful are distinctions based on the distribution of garrisons and extent of military authority. This allows the identification of communities largely within the control of one side, and thus offered a modicum of protection, and those in contested territory, and consequently taxed and plundered by both sides. It is these areas that were most heavily affected. Such distinctions are also important in considering the nature of military–civilian relations, and in accounting for the distribution of Clubmen in the region. Where the military were sufficiently strong they were able to offer a measure of protection to civilians, so negating the creation of neutralist movements, which where they did occur were undoubtedly linked to depredations by the soldiery. Even where the protection was poor, the ability of garrison forces to police local communities maintained military authority, and may have denied potential Clubmen the opportunity to organize. What distinguished the Clubman areas of west Worcestershire was not so much a different popular experience of the war as the inability of either side there to compensate, either through protection or repression, for the burdens and traumas of war.

---

113   Bodl., Firth MS C6, fos. 68, 140; Hutton, *War Effort*, 192–3.

11

England Turned Germany? The Aftermath of the Civil War in its European Context

Ian Roy

Originally appeared as Ian Roy, 'England Turned Germany? The Aftermath of the Civil War in its European Context' in *Transactions of the Royal Historical Society* 5th Series 28. Copyright © 1978 Royal Historical Society, London.

Many voices prophesied a destructive war for England on the eve of the Civil War. The miseries of the conflicts in Germany had been closely followed in the earliest newspapers published in England. With the outbreak of the Irish rebellion in 1641, and the consequent bloodshed, the wars were only a step away. In 1642 newsbooks and sermons vied with each other to paint the blackest picture possible of the evils in store for England, once it seemed that, at last, the nation was to be swallowed up in the general European conflagration.

Several pointed to the example of Germany. The principal apologist of the Parliamentary cause, Henry Parker, gave currency to horror stories from Germany, and predicted 'the manifold miseries of civil warre and discord' for his native country.[1] Some went further. Sir Benjamin Rudyerd told the Commons that when war came to England it would be more terrible than in Germany, for this country was a small island, and

This paper is based in part on research into the impact of the Civil Wars on Gloucester, Worcester and Oxford, currently supported by the Social Science Research Council, and I should like to thank the Council and my research assistant, Mr Stephen Porter, for their help. The study is not completed, and any conclusions reached here must be viewed as only tentative. I have benefited from discussing some of the topics dealt with in the paper with Dr John Broad, Mr Henry Reece, and Dr Joan Thirsk.

1 *The Manifold Miseries of Civil Warre and Discord in a Kingdome: By The Examples of Germany, France, Ireland, and other places*, by H. P. (London, 1642).

the war would be fought 'as in a Cock-pit'.[2] England should be warned by Holland, agreed a Welsh Royalist. The Dutch, in challenging their rightful sovereign, had made their country for almost a century 'the Cockpitt of Christendon'. If the English did the same, the kingdom would be embroiled 'in perpetuall warre'.[3] The danger was most graphically represented in the crude woodcuts and word pictures of the spectre which the wars on the continent had unleashed – the Plundering Soldier. 'The Grand Plunderer' was chillingly described as feeding on the entrails of the kingdom; the form of another monstrous apparition, the 'English-Irish soldier', was portrayed – in the manner of the contemporary attack on the monopolist – as composed of all the goods he had plundered.[4]

Once the Civil War had begun, Parliamentary propaganda had an easy task identifying the Plundering Soldier with the Royalist forces, led by the King's own German nephew, Prince Rupert. It was true that the Cavaliers – another term linking the King's party with the evils of continental warfare – were closely associated with military service abroad. The London press and pulpits highlighted atrocities committed by mercenaries trained, they believed, in a bloody school of war. The sack of West Country towns by Rupert, in an early campaign, was a case of 'England turned Ireland', according to one account.[5] It seemed certain that, as the war progressed, England would turn Germany.

The gloomy predictions of a damaging war in England and of parallels with the destructive wars on the continent made by some contemporaries have not been echoed by historians. On the whole, analogies between the Civil War and contemporaneous warfare on the continent have been rejected, if considered at all. Parliamentary propaganda has been discounted and the national experience of warfare in the 1640s has been viewed as distinctively English. Charles I's quick condemnation of Rupert's demand of money from Leicester has been widely accepted as indicating, at the very beginning of the war, that it was to be fought with restraint and mildness and without resort to deplorable continental practices.[6] The Civil War, in this version of events, was fought in a gentlemanly manner, the combatants being

2   Sir Benjamin Rudyerd His Speech . . . (London, 1643).
3   Sir Thomas Salusbury's view, cited N. Tucker, Denbighshire Officers in the Civil War (Denbigh, [1947]), p. 97.
4   The Grand Plunderer . . . ([London], 1643); The English Irish Souldier, who had rather eate than fight (London, 1642).
5   Marleborowes Miseries, Or, England turned Ireland, by T. B. et al. ([London], 1643).
6   The most recent biographer of Rupert treats this incident at length: see P. Morrah, Prince Rupert of the Rhine (London, 1976), pp. 76–8.

neighbours and brothers, who spared their non-combatant fellow countrymen. It was a 'war without an enemy'.[7] The winners were not mercenaries of foreign origin but Puritan squires-in-arms, like Oliver Cromwell himself, whose approach to warfare was contrasted favourably with that of continental soldiers of fortune.

The traditional view of the Thirty Years War aided in the reception of this analysis. The opinions of contemporary Englishmen, like Henry Parker, were accepted in this matter, and atrocity stories such as he retold provided some of the evidence on which the belief in the 'all-destructive fury' of the German wars was based.[8] According to this interpretation much of central Europe was the prey of warring powers, whose marauding armies laid waste whole regions; fire and sword, famine and pestilence, resulted in permanent population loss and economic destruction, which retarded the growth of Germany for generations. The wars were uniformly futile and destructive. By contrast, the Civil Wars had clearly proved no impediment to the remarkable rise of the English economy in the seventeenth century.

In the last twenty years, however, there has been a revision of the traditional view of the Thirty Years War. The conflict is no longer seen as uniformly disastrous; a more complex picture has been substituted, which stresses the varied effects of military activities in time and place. Some areas of Germany, in the path of armies throughout the wars, were devastated, and suffered severe population loss through high mortality and massive migration. Others remained immune from the conflict and even registered economic growth in the period. Losses were often short- or medium-term only, and the wars, though they lasted thirty years, were not continuous for most regions. The fact of regional variation, that Germany was not an economic unity, has prompted a growing number of local studies of the results.[9]

This substantial literature on the Thirty Years War has not been matched by work on the effects of the Civil War. Nearly fifty years ago Margaret James took a pessimistic view of the social and economic con-

7   Waller's celebrated letter to Hopton, containing this phrase, is often quoted: *e.g.*, M. Coate, *Cornwall in the Great Civil War* (London, 2nd edn, 1963), p. 77.
8   R. Ergang, *The Myth of the All-destructive Fury of the Thirty Years War* (Pocono Pines, Pa., 1956).
9   The raw material of the debate was first presented in G. Franz, *Der Dreissige Jährige Krieg und das Deutsche Volk* (Stuttgart, 3rd edn, 1961). See also T. K. Rabb, 'The Effects of the Thirty Years War on the German Economy', *Journal of Modern History*, xxxiv (1962), and *The Thirty Years War: Problems of Motive, Extent and Effect* (Boston, Mass., 1964); H. Kamen, 'The Economic and Social Consequences of the Thirty Years War', and J. V. Polisensky, 'The Thirty Years War and the Crises and Revolutions of Seventeenth Century Europe', *Past & Present*, 39 (1968). J. V. Polisensky, *The Thirty Years War* (London, 1974), is a study of devastation in Bohemia and Moravia.

sequences of the war, and recently new evidence on military disorder during and after the Civil War has thrown doubt on the view of the war as having little impact on society.[10] But there has not been to date a major revision of the old view. Standard economic histories of Stuart England, employing statistics which tend to reflect the dominance of London and the Southeast – where there was little actual fighting – agree that the wars had no dramatic effect, and did not reverse any long-term trend.

It seems clear, therefore, that there is room for a fresh attempt to measure the impact of the Civil War by reference to parallel developments on the continent, while allowing – where appropriate – for important differences. In this paper some examples of the war's effects in the West – particularly the towns on the Severn – will be looked at, in the light of both the national and the European experience of warfare.

The results of two different wars can only be usefully compared if the wars themselves can be shown to possess important features in common. At first sight they seem quite dissimilar. England had been at peace throughout the 1630s, when other powers were being drawn even further into the European coflict. Charles I possessed, in comparison to other monarchs, a puny military establishment. The many military developments produced by the long wars in the Low Countries and in Germany appeared to have passed England by: her own warlike traditions seemed at a low ebb. Her militia, chief armouries, coastal defences and town walls were all in decay.

When in the 1640s the British Isles did become embroiled in civil warfare, the nation was fortunate in that the preoccupation of the great continental powers with the Thirty Years War, and the command of the Narrow Seas by the Parliamentary navy, kept England free from foreign invasion. Conditions in England, where armies were composed, not of foreign, veteran, mercenary soldiers, but of native volunteers and conscripts, unused to war after a long period of internal peace, were not obviously identical with those in the Palatinate or Moravia.

But the differences are more apparent than real. The British wars could not be, and in the end were not, isolated from the continental struggle. If the King kept aloof from the wars of Europe before the Civil War, many of his subjects did not. Accounts of the wars, military manuals and drill books – often translated from the Dutch – had continued popular in the years of peace, and Dutch-trained veterans had

10   M. James, *Social Problems and Policy during the Puritan Revolution, 1640–1660* (London, 1930), pp. 35–66; J. S. Morrill, 'Mutiny and Discontent in English Provincial Armies, 1645–1647', *Past & Present*, 56 (1972); I. Roy, 'The English Civil War and English Society', *War and Society. A Yearbook of Military History*, ed. B. Bond and I. Roy (London, 1975).

taught 'the postures of the pike and musket',[11] to grammar-school boys like the later Colonel Hutchinson and General Ludlow, as well as the citizens of the capital. Perhaps as many as 20,000 of the subjects of Charles I had gone abroad to serve one or other of the warring powers, and on the outbreak of the wars in the British Isles – the Scots Wars and the Irish rebellion are as important as the war in England in this respect – hundred of volunteers flocked home again. After 1638 there was a constant, if not large-scale, two-way traffic in arms and men between all regions of the British conflict and the continent. The European powers continued to recruit for their armies in Britain, while allowing some of their own commanders, particularly the British among them, to return home, often with fellow-officers and followers.

Not only the Cavaliers, as the London press averred, but the Roundheads benefited from this influx of foreign or foreign-trained military talent. The extent of this penetration has been concealed by two developments. One was the device practised by both sides, of placing in titular command – of an army or a regiment – an important political figure or territorial magnate, and entrusting the real work to a professional second-in-command. Newcastle, the King's general in the North, had a Scots officer of great experience, James King, to advise him: Hampden's Foot was run by a soldier from French service, Joseph Wagstaffe: while the Royalist commander in the West Midlands in 1643, Lord Capel, was dependent on men like Michael Woodhouse, whose previous experience had been in the Irish wars.[12] The second was the later dominance of the New Model Army, and its previously untrained officers, such as Cromwell, which has overshadowed the professional content and approach of earlier armies, such as Essex's (whose commander, we may recall, had been 'the darling of the sword-men') and Waller's (over half of whose senior officers were Scots professionals). Rival provincial forces in 1645 were commanded by veteran continental-service generals, such as Massey and Poyntz.[13]

Men like these were influential in the more senior commands, the technical departments of armies, and in the fortification of strongholds. Many of the weapons used in the Civil War were imported at great cost.

11   C.Walker, *The History of Independency*, I (London, 1648), p. 117.
12   D[ictionary of] N[ational] B[iography] for King and Wagstaffe; for Woodhouse see J. and T. W. Webb, *Memorials of the Civil War . . . as it affected Herefordshire* (London, 1879), I, pp. 387–91, II, pp. 359–60.
13   Clarendon, *The History of the Rebellion*, ed. W. D. Macray (Oxford, 1888), I, p. 150; J, Adair, *Roundhead General. A Military Biography of Sir William Waller* (London, 1969), p. 106. Massey, though very young, had probably some Dutch as well as Scots Wars service before 1642; Sydenham Poyntz had served in the Imperial army in Germany (*D.N.B.*).

Parliament bought Dutch and Flemish arms and ammunition.[14] The Queen sent her husband, and brought with her in 1643, Spanish, Dutch and Danish cannon.[15] Alexander Leslie, commander of the Scots Covenanting army, had been paid his arrears by the Swedes in cannon and muskets; he brought them home for this new service.[16] Waller's general of artillery was a Scot, who employed leatherguns – which he had patented – on the Swedish model.[17] Essex's field train was supervised by French artillerymen.[18] Rupert's right-hand men were a Walloon engineer and a French fireworker.[19] Scarcely any theatre of war in Europe was not drawn upon for recruits, materials and methods in the Civil War, and it is hardly surprising that rival 'schools' of warfare made their appearance, as early as the first pitched battle, Edgehill, when Rupert and Lindsey quarrelled over whether the Royalist ranks should be deployed in the Swedish or Dutch fashion.[20]

Defences had to be as expensively brought up to date as gunnery, and there was a great rebuilding of town and country-house fortifications, under the eye of trained engineers, at the beginning of the war. Here the Dutch influence was predominant. The Welsh engineer whose waterworks transformed Oxford into an impregnable fortress, and who rebuilt the defences of Devizes in the latest style, had mapped the famous siege of Maastricht ten years before.[21] The great earthworks which now replaced or protected the old walls of many towns required not only heavy expenditure but the razing of suburbs beyond the walls. Only a city as wealthy as London could afford 'lines of communication' which enclosed her western suburbs.

The peculiar nature of the Civil War must however be kept in mind in any assessment of the role of these men. They did not have it all their own way, and there were drawbacks to their employment as well as benefits. Both Crown and Parliament were subject to conflicting pressures,

14 D. E. Lewis, 'The Parliamentarian Office of Ordnance, 1642–1648', Loughborough University Ph.D. thesis, 1976.
15 *The Royalist Ordnance Papers, 1642–1646*, ed. I. Roy, I (Oxfordshire Rec. Soc., xlii, 1964), pp. 40–1, 106–08, II (O.R.S., xlix, 1975), pp. 446–7.
16 F. Redlich, *The German Military Enterpriser and his Workforce*, I (Wiesbaden, 1964), p. 256.
17 Adair, *Roundhead General*, p. 125.
18 *The Army Lists of the Roundheads and Cavaliers*, ed. E. Peacock (London, 1863), p. 22.
19 *Royalist Ordnance Papers*, I, pp. 27, 32–3.
20 P. Young, *Edgehill 1642. The Campaign and the Battle* (Kineton, 1967), pp. 82–4, 289 and pl. 9.
21 Charles Lloyd, for whose career see *D.N.B.*, *D. Welsh B.*, *Royalist Ordnance Papers*, I, p. 187, II, pp. 469, 480, and H. Hexham and C. Lloyd, *A Iovrnall of the taking in of Venlo, Roermont, Strale, the Memorable Siege of Mastricht* (Delft, 1633).

and had to reconcile the demands of the military they employed with the stubborn localism of their own supporters. Some swordsmen were far from admirable, skilled though they were. As we shall see, many were concerned only to carve out a living for themselves, without regard for either local susceptibilities or national strategic considerations. They were often at odds with their fellow-officers, the local gentry, the civilian population, or their own soldiers. Those who considered themselves simply soldiers of fortune lacked loyalty to any cause, were able to change sides when convenient during the war, and returned to foreign employment at the end.[22] This was also a sign that, despite rivalries, the soldiers with continental experience shared a common body of knowledge, applicable equally – or almost so – in every theatre of war; and that forces in England, by 1646–7, when Rupert, Waller and even Cromwell offered their services to foreign powers, had been pulled up to the standard of, so to speak, the best reformed armies abroad.[23]

While the English materials with which they had to work continued intractable throughout, there are indications that trained soldiers played an increasingly important part as the Civil War both perpetuated itself and extended its reach to include Scots and Irish forces. The invasion of the Covenanters in 1644, and their campaigns in the North, the Welsh Marches and the Midlands until 1646, and the presence on the King's side of the regiments from Irish service, from 1643, in the West, reproduced there some of the conditions familiar to observers of the Thirty Years War. To these regions, too, came the soldiers of fortune from the fag-end of that conflict. French and Lorrainer troops fought alongside the Irish and Welsh for the King in 1645–6.[24]

The Severn valley was at the heart of this region. The towns on the river, if we include Bristol, formed the trading and communications centres for a wide area, stretching from North Wales to the West Country. It is in this area that we might expect to find the impact of the war at its greatest, for as a war zone it was vulnerable to the dislocation caused by armies. The river was navigable to Shrewsbury, and was, after the Maas, the busiest in Europe. The produce of the region – corn, coal and iron from the Upper Severn, apples and cider from Worcestershire and Herefordshire – was carried to the main outports, Bristol and Gloucester, by the shallow-draught and square-rigged trows, which

22   Among the better known examples of side-changers during the war are Sir Richard Grenville and Sir John Urry.
23   E. Warburton, *Memoirs of Prince Rupert and the Cavaliers* (London, 1849), III, pp. 236–7; Adair, *Roundhead General*, pp. 189–90; S. R. Gardiner, *History of the Great Civil War, 1642–1649* (London, 1893), III, pp. 222–3.
24   M. Toynbee and P. Young, *Strangers in Oxford. A Side Light on the First Civil War, 1642–1646* (London, 1973), pp. 47–8.

plied the river; and through all the towns from the mouth of the river to Shrewsbury came the imports marketed to the interior.[25] Apart from the north–south 'river line' the area possessed the main roads out of Wales, and along these passed the principal products of the region, to the rest of England. Much of the cattle of Wales and the cloth and woollen goods of the West were marketed at London.[26]

From the start of the war the whole region was militarily divided, and though the boundaries changed constantly as the war ebbed and flowed, it remained cut at several points until 1646. The flow of trade was severed between Shrewsbury and Oswestry, Worcester and Gloucester, Gloucester and Bristol, for most of the war. In 1644, only Gloucester remained in Parliament's hands, completely isolated between Royalist Wales and the King's main base area, which stretched in a crescent from Banbury in the north to Basing in the south, and which interdicted all the trade routes from the West to London. In late 1645 the position was reversed, and Worcester alone was a Royalist garrison, while Parliamentarian garrisons stopped the traffic between it and Oxford quarters. Strongly fortified towns like these could hold out against invading armies, but unwalled towns with small garrisons, like Tewkesbury and Malmesbury, changed hands frequently.

In a strategically vital area, hotly disputed, which contained important munitions industries and was a rich prize in itself, both sides quickly built up their occupying forces. Garrisons and camps proliferated as they competed for scarce resources. Characteristic of the Civil War in this region was the destructive raiding and skirmishing between them, which subjected the population to great hardship and was almost continuous throughout the year, as the troops sought to enlarge their winter quarters at the expense of the enemy's. Further, this mêlée was frequently interrupted by the invasion of the main armies of Crown and Parliament: Essex and the King in 1642, Waller and Maurice, the King and Essex in 1643, Rupert and the King in 1644, Rupert, Maurice, the King, the New Model Army and the Scots in 1645. If no region was more populated with warring troops throughout the year, none was more often overrun by field armies in the summers. Here, if anywhere, were the cockpit conditions to be found, of which Rudyerd had spoken.

25 T. S. Willan, 'The River Navigation and Trade of the Severn Valley, 1600–1750', *Economic History Review*, viii (1937); G. Farr, 'Severn Navigation and the Trow', *Mariner's Mirror*, 32 (1946); W. Court, *The Rise of the Midland Industries* (London, 1953).
26 T. C. Mendenhall, *The Shrewsbury Drapers and the Welsh Wool Trade in the XVI and XVII Centuries* (London, 1953); J. de L. Mann, *The Cloth Industry in the West of England from 1640 to 1880* (Oxford, 1971); G. D. Ramsay, *The Wiltshire Woollen Industry in the sixteenth and seventeenth centuries* (London, 2nd edn, 1965).

Not surprisingly, in these circumstances, the military element in the area became dominant. Arguments from military necessity, put by professional commanders, silenced the protests of civilian officials, which elsewhere often got a hearing. Quarter sessions, petty sessions and manorial courts were frequently suspended; town councils had to submit to high taxation, permanent garrisoning and the destruction of their suburbs. The governors of Gloucester appointed by Parliament, Massey and Morgan, were both career soldiers: the latter described himself and his men as soldiers of fortune.[27] During the war Worcester had nine governors, of whom only two could be said to be drawn from the local gentry.[28] The small but locally important stronghold of Berkeley Castle was commanded in rapid succession by a Scots soldier and an Irish soldier (for Parliament), a Scots soldier, a local gentleman and two English soldiers (for the King), until its final surrender in 1645. Each took what he could as quickly as possible out of the estate. The owner complained bitterly that their depredations among his goods and tenants had reduced his ancient seat to a wilderness.[29] A soldier of fortune, said another local landowner, cared nothing for the consequences of his actions, for he was 'here today and God knows where tomorrow'.[30]

Nor were local interests secure when their nominees obtained high commands. Untrained or half-trained gentlemen, promoted to governorships by local demand, were often only too anxious to imitate the worst of the swordsmen, and win the good opinions of the military. The two local appointees to the government of Worcester were both very quickly complained of by their fellow gentry for this reason.[31] Some of the gravest outrages against the inhabitants were committed not by professionals but by what might be termed enthusiastic amateurs, like the 'licentious governor' – and later destroyer – of Camden House, Gloucestershire, Henry Bard, Fellow of King's College, Cambridge, who 'exercised an illimited tyranny over the whole country'.[32]

27 H.M.C., *7th Report*, Appendix, p. 68.
28 *The Chamber Order Book of Worcester, 1602–1650*, ed. S. Bond (Worcestershire Hist. Soc. n.s., 8, 1974), p. 73.
29 *Lords' Journal*, vi, p. 69.
30 Warburton, *Prince Rupert*, III, p. 525.
31 Samuel Sandys led the attack on Sir William Russell, a previous governor, but being himself made governor 'he fell off from his good friends and Commissioners with him; he forgot his supporters, loved so much the soldier and his ranting ways' that he neglected his duty, according to a local Royalist (*Diary of Henry Townshend of Elmley Lovett, 1640–1663*, ed. J. W. Willis Bund (Worcs. Hist. Soc., 1915), I, pp. 134–5).
32 Clarendon, *History*, IV, pp. 37–8. For Bard, later Viscount Bellamont, see *D.N.B.*, and additional notes deposited in the Institute of Historical Research,

These men fought a war which was not distinctly different from that of the strategically important and fought-over regions of Germany and the Low Countries. They introduced continental practices, in order to mobilize the resources of the district for their own use, and prohibit, where possible, their use by the enemy. In doing so, in a region distant from Oxford and London, they were less restrained than commanders under the eye of the High Commands of either side. They handled a double-edged sword. As experienced commanders they borrowed from the Thirty Years War the devices developed there which permitted armies to live off the land without destroying civilian life and livelihood, such as Contribution treaties: but they also possessed an armoury of weapons of destruction, permitted by the rules of war, such as the taking of plunder. Implicit in the demands of the soldiers for Contribution payments, forced loans and even the church bells of captured towns was the threat of unlicensed pillage, and this threat might be carried out. The plundering soldier might be deliberately unleashed to punish, with fire and sword, a hostile or recalcitrant people, to lay waste territory on which enemy forces depended, or destroy vital mills and munitions works.

These actions took many forms, and that their presence in the Civil War has not been widely recognized may be due more to semantic than actual differences between English and continental practice. The Royalist taxation system which imitated the German bore the same name, the Contribution, and plunder was recognized for what it was, an age-old practice in a new German dress, 'a new name for an old Theft'.[33] But *Brandtschatzung*, or burning money, the payments made by towns to avoid firing by an army at the gates, was first disowned (by the King in the case of Leicester), and then disguised (Essex demanded a 'subsidy' from Tewkesbury), although it is clear that it was commonly exacted. A payment by Worcester to the Parliamentary governor at the start of the war was made to 'free this City from plundering'.[34] As the royal forces approached Worcester in 1644, the panic-stricken councillors voted first £100, then £200, and finally, as the size of the army surrounding the city became obvious, £1,000.[35] The term 'fire raid' was not used in the

London. Clarendon claimed that Camden House, burned down by Rupert and Bard in 1645, had cost £ 30,000 to build some years before.

33   *Angliae Ruina* . . . (London, 1647), p. 28. The word 'plunder' was first used in England in November 1642 (*O.E.D.*). On the German *Kontribution*, see F. Redlich, 'Contributions in the Thirty Years War', *Econ. Hist. Rev.*, xii (1959–60), and 'Military Entrepreneurship and the Credit System', *Kyklos*, x (Berne, 1957).

34   Worcester Guildhall, City Accounts, vol. 3 (1640–69), unpaged: £40 given to Colonel Thomas Essex.

35   *Chamber Order Book of Worcester*, pp. 580–1.

war, but the deliberate destruction by parties of Horse, sent out by neighbouring garrisons, of all resources within reach which might be useful to the enemy, was common, many years before French cavalry developed it as an instrument of policy to terrorize the Palatinate.[36]

Plunder was used as an instrument of policy where the populace was deemed to be hostile. As early as February 1643 Rupert, foremost in these practices, sacked Cirencester, a Puritan town in the Royalists' eyes. 'The value of the pillage was very great, to the utter ruine of many hundred families.' The victorious Cavaliers swept through the country, driving away 'all the horses, sheepe, oxen, and other cattle', before seizing 'cloth, wooll, and yarne, besides other goods from the clothiers, about Stroudwater, to the utter undoing . . . of thousands of poore people, whose very livelihood depends on that trade'.[37] The inhabitants lost 200–300 horses, with the result that they could not sow their crops that spring.[38] Communities in Worcestershire were deprived in the same manner of their essential draught animals, and others suffered the loss of their standing corn, deliberately trampled down by passing Horse, and the contents of their barns and stables. The forcible seizure by the military of carts, teams and drivers was frequent, with serious consequences for farmers and carriers.[39]

Destructive raiding was common in the congested war zone around Gloucester. Massey, the governor of the city, found that he could not collect the Contribution for his garrison, but he could do great damage with it. He stopped all trade, where he could, up the Severn, and within a radius of 20–30 miles around Gloucester engaged in mutually damaging warfare with Sir John Wintour at Lidney in the Forest of Dean. For two years this struggle continued, until in 1645, Massey having destroyed his rival's ironworks, Wintour 'deserted and fired his house at Lidney, having first spoyled the forest'.[40] A raid of a different kind was the punitive expedition launched by Rupert against the Clubmen in Herefordshire in March 1645. He took his cavalry through the county 'to refresh after the Dutch fashion', as he put it, by forcibly seizing men, money and supplies.[41] There was ample warrant for his action, in his view, from the German wars.

---

36 R. T. Ferguson, 'Blood and Fire: Contribution Policies of the French Armies in Germany, 1668–1715', University of Minnesota Ph.D. thesis, 1970.
37 *Bibliotheca Gloucestrensis: A Collection of Scarce and Curious Tracts, relating to the County and City of Gloucester* . . . , ed. J. Washbourn (Gloucester, 1825), pp. 184–5.
38 Petition of Royalist commissioners for Gloucestershire [March 1643] (British Library, Harl. MS. 6804, fo. 128).
39 *Ibid.*, fo. 140.
40 *Bibliotheca Gloucestrensis*, pp. 147, 329.
41 Warburton, *Prince Rupert*, III, p. 69.

The trade and industry of the region was, however, a rich prize, and too valuable to be merely plundered. Both sides had to weigh the pros and cons of permitting trade with enemy quarters, where the military division, as often happened, cut across the natural flow of commerce. Parliament decided from the start that the main danger was the carrying to the King of weapons of war. Newcastle and other ports, when they fell to the King, were blockaded; and a river guard was placed on the Thames to stop contraband goods being carried to Oxford.[42] Massey's action towards trade along the Severn was therefore authorized.

The Privy Council at Oxford, however, was more hesitant. The King's forces controlled the traffic on the Upper Thames and the main roads from Wales and the West to London, and could easily retaliate. But it was not until the summer of 1643, and after much debate, that trade with the capital was prohibited.[43]

Principally affected within the region by this restriction was the cloth industry of the West Country, and the cattle and cloth of Wales, both of which were marketed in areas under Parliament's control. Blackwell Hall in London was the principal outlet for the clothiers' products, although some wool, woollen goods and cloth were shipped through Bristol and Gloucester. For the North Wales drovers and clothiers the military divide between Oswestry and Shrewsbury was damaging, as was any prohibition of trade to the rest of England. With the capture of Bristol in the summer of 1643, and the Royalist domination of most of the western ports thereafter, a way seemed open to divert the trade of the West to the nearest entrepôts. This was all the more desirable after the introduction of a new tax, the excise, on the exchange of goods, borrowed from the continent and everywhere associated with rising military expenditure. A revival of trade within the King's quarters would yield substantial profits to the Crown. Bristol and Exeter were declared mart towns in 1644, excise offices were set up there, and reduced customs duties were offered.[44] The King's agents at the ports saw the possibility of having exports available which would help pay for the arms from the continent being landed there.[45]

42   J. Rushworth, *Historical Collections*, vi, pp. 193–202; *Calendar of State Papers Domestic, 1641–43*, p. 440.
43   Proclamation, 17 July 1643, *Tudor and Stuart Proclamations*, ed. R. Steele (Oxford, 1910), I, no. 2455; Clarendon, *History*, III, pp. 290–2.
44   Proclamations, 21 November 1643 and 9 April 1644 (Steele, *Proclamations*, I, nos. 2510, 2557); Commission of Excise and the Schedule, May 1644, *Oxford Books*, ed. F. Madan (Oxford, 1912), II, nos. 1638, 1639; Privy Council, 4 May 1644, Public Record Office, P.C. 2.53, fo. 226.
45   *Royalist Ordnance Papers*, II, pp. 393–4, 413–14.

Very little came of these hopes, however. Gloucester and Plymouth remained unreduced and, as centres of Parliamentary resistance in the West, continued to have a damaging effect – as did the naval blockade – on trade in Royalist quarters. The Irish and continental markets were depressed by war. The King's officials lacked sufficient cash and credit to sustain trade on a regular basis, and clothiers were too tied to the London market to be able to break free. The region generally was so impoverished by the war that there was little market for imported goods. All the evidence suggests that the cloth trade was not diverted from its usual channels, and that Bristol and Exeter continued to decline throughout the war.[46]

In these circumstances the King was forced to lift his prohibition in particular cases. Since the general embargo had been imposed, petitions had rained in from Welsh, Worcestershire and Gloucestershire clothiers, and the drovers of North Wales, complaining that without freedom to trade they could not subsist and could not pay their taxes to the King.[47] With the failure of new markets and outlets in the West their pleas became even more pressing. It was decided that, where the general restraint would be harmful, licences would be issued. In this way the trade could still be controlled, and the profits, from the sale of the licences, would still accrue to the King.

This move, however, reckoned without the independence – or indiscipline – of local commanders. The ensuing situation was well summarized by Clarendon.

> The disorder of the soldier was such, and so great a contempt of all acts of state, that it had not the effect designed, and in the end produced no other advantage than great gains to some particular governors, who, having garrisons near great roads, received large tolls for their safe conducts and protection, and sometimes very great seizures of such goods as thought to have escaped their notice, all which was converted to their own emolument.[48]

There are many examples of this happening. In 1644, when Worcester clothiers and chapmen set out with their wares for London,

---

46   *Ibid.*, I, pp. 42–3, II, pp. 416–18; W. B. Stephens, *Seventeenth-Century Exeter* (Exeter, 1958), pp. 60–4; J. de L. Mann, *Cloth Industry*, p. 3. In the summer of 1644 the excise revenue of Bristol was only £200 per week (B.L., Harl. MS. 6802, fo. 250).
47   *Calendar of Wynn Papers* (Aberystwyth, 1926), no. 1724. The original of this undated (but 1643) petition shows that it represented the case of the clothiers as well as drovers of the North Wales counties (National Library of Wales, MS. 467 E); *Oxford Books*, ed. Madan, II, no. 1438; *The Weekly Account . . .*, No. 44 (London, June–July 1644).
48   Clarendon, *History*, III, p. 292.

they were 'met withall by the Kings Forces upon the way', who seized their horses and cloth.[49] West Country clothiers, heading for London in March 1645 under Parliamentarian convoy and by country lanes, were still spotted by cavalry from the Banbury garrison and robbed of their seventy-two woolpacks 'of great value'.[50] Another group of clothiers from Wiltshire, taking the more southerly route to London, paid with great difficulty the tolls demanded by two governors whose garrisons they passed, but were still in the end plundered of every penny they possessed, 'Teems, Carts, Clothes and all', by a marauding troop sent out by the rapacious commander of Wallingford.[51]

These well-publicized losses deterred merchants from undertaking the hazardous journey to London, much as the seizure of shipping in the Channel led to a loss of confidence in those trading to Western ports. In both cases commerce did not cease completely but was reduced to a trickle. With the fall of some towns in the region to Parliament in 1645 – such as Shrewsbury and Evesham – more local trading and marketing became possible, and both Roundhead governors and Cavalier generals were accused of making profits from licences to trade, in the last year or so of the war.[52]

The picture otherwise for the agriculture and industries of the Severn and its hinterland was bleak. The drovers of North Wales had complained in their petition to the King in 1643 that the stop of the cattle trade threatened with ruin many thousand families in the mountainous parts of the six counties.[53] In 1645 Archbishop Williams, residing at Conway castle, reinforced their plea, describing the trade as 'the Spanish fleet . . . which brings hither that little gold and silver we have'.[54] The loss of the market at Shrewsbury for the coarse woollens of the same area spelt disaster for producers and the drapers of the town. Shrewsbury itself could no longer supply the surrounding district

---

49   *The Weekly Account* . . . , No. 44.
50   *Mercurius Belgicus* . . . (London, 1646); *Bibliotheca Gloucestrensis*, p. 138; J. de L. Mann, *Cloth Industry*, p. 3. The Royalist commander involved, the Earl of Northampton, was pursued through the courts later by twenty or more owners, *Cal. S. Papers Dom.*, *1652–53*, pp. 385–6, *ibid.*, *1653–54*, p. 62.
51   *Mercurius Veridicus* . . . , No. 5 (London, May 1645). This very circumstantial account by one of the clothiers involved, given immediately on his arrival in London, agrees with what we know of the character of all three governors, and may be accepted as accurate.
52   Order to Parliamentarian governors, December 1645, in *Cal. S. Papers Dom.*, *1645–47*, p. 258; complaints about the King's general in South Wales, August 1645, in B. L., Harl. MS. 6804, fos. 210–11.
53   *Calendar of Wynn Papers*, no. 1724.
54   *Ibid.*, no. 1748.

with the imported goods on which it depended.[55] The clothiers of Gloucestershire equally suffered. Cut off from the market at Blackwell Hall, they had no sale for their goods and no capital – tied up in London factors' hands – to set men to work.[56] There was severe depression and unemployment in West Country industrial towns and villages, and riots at the end of the war.[57]

The effects of high taxation, free quarter and plunder – particularly the seizure of livestock, seed corn, transport and labour – were severely felt by the farmers of the region. The interruption of normal farming and the marketing of produce led to a deterioration in land use with some land remaining untilled altogether. The tenants, forced to pay contribution, or accept free quartering, or both, could not afford to pay their rents in full. They expected compensation for war damage, in addition. The dislocation of the normal processes spread to the management of estates, and where records, such as court rolls, were lost or destroyed, or manorial courts were not held, because of the war, transfers of property and the negotiation of new terms for tenants could not take place. There was a drop of one third in landlords' incomes generally throughout England during the war, but there was wide variation from locality to locality.[58] The rental of a Gloucestershire M.P. fell by a fifth only, while in North Shropshire the Earl of Bridgewater's estates paid him no rent at all for four years. The Earl's stewards found that new leases could not be taken up, and the usual fines levied, until 1647.[59] 'The tenants of Merioneth-shire', reported a landlord there, 'are backwards of theire Rents for want of sale of cattel as they tell mee'.[60] In North Wales both landlords and tenants were in a miserable condition at the end of the war.[61]

In a region hard hit in these ways by the Civil War there were other miseries to be endured which were very comparable to those suffered

---

55   'The Civil Wars . . . were truly catastrophic' (Mendenhall, *Shrewsbury Drapers*, p. 206); H. Beaumont, 'Arthur, Lord Capel, The King's Lieutenant-General for Shropshire, 1643', *Trans. Shropshire Arch. and Nat. Hist. Soc.*, L (1939–1940), 80.
56   Gloucestershire petition of August 1643 (*Oxford Books*, ed. Madan, II, no. 1438).
57   Ramsay, *Wiltshire Woollen Industry*, p. 112.
58   J. Broad, 'Gentry Finances and the Civil War – the case of the Buckinghamshire Verneys', *Economic History Review* 2nd series, 32 (1979). I am grateful to Dr Broad for allowing me to read his article in advance of publication.
59   Gloucestershire Record Office, Stephens Collection: rent paid to Nathaniel Stephens, M.P., by Eastington and Frampton property; E. Hopkins. 'The Bridgewater Estates in North Shropshire in the Civil War', *Trans. Shropshire Arch. Soc.*, lvi (1957–60).
60   Nat. Lib. Wales, Dolfriog MS. 64 (letter of Kathrin Wynne, 3 February 1644).
61   G. Manley to his brother, July 1646 (*Cal. S Papers Dom.*, 1645–47, p. 454).

by the war zones in Germany. The armies brought fire and sword to many towns and villages, payment of burning money notwithstanding, and the risk of destruction by fire was much increased by the war. The most notable examples of firing by the military, for whatever reason, are Axminster, Beaminster, Bridgnorth, Bridgwater, Cirencester, Faringdon, Lyme Regis, Marlborough, Oswestry, Taunton and Wrexham, and the suburbs of Bristol, Exeter, Gloucester and Worcester.[62] The extent of loss varied. Beaminster, after French and Cornish Royalist troops had fought each other there in 1644, was 'the pitifullest spectacle that man can behold, hardly an house left not consumed with fire'.[63] Parliament later voted compensation to towns as severely damaged by fire or plunder as this.[64]

From 1644 to 1649 the population had also to suffer the ravages of plague, some forms of typhus, smallpox and other epidemics. The war created conditions in which they flourished, and it is not coincidental that the North and West suffered more than the South and East, Wiltshire, Somerset, Devon and Dorset being badly affected by plague.[65] The movement of armies spread disease, the fighting drove country people into the walled towns for protection, and there, in siege conditions – with gross overcrowding, interference, very often, with the water supply, a swollen garrison, and shortage of food – the death rate climbed.

In the towns on the Severn there was increased mortality, though its incidence varied. In Worcester, the four war years were not worse than one pre-war year of plague. Recorded deaths in Gloucester, however, increased by half in 1643 and doubled in 1645–6, and between autumn 1644 and the following autumn a quarter of the population of Bristol perished mostly from plague.[66] It is difficult to be precise, for the population of each was swollen by the presence of a large garrison – which usually accounted for a fifth of the total – and numerous refugees, and the records suffered equally in the general crisis. In St Nicholas parish, Bristol, the clerk and the sexton died in 1645 at the height of the sickness, 'by means whereof', the record runs, 'nott only they both butt many others are left outt of

62   I am grateful to Mr Stephen Porter for allowing me to consult his index of town fires for the early modern period.
63   J. Sprigge, *Anglia Rediviva;* . . . (London, 1647), p. 60.
64   Beaminster was granted £2,000 by Parliament in December 1646 (R. Hine, *The History of Beaminster* (Taunton, 1914), p. 120).
65   J. Shrewsbury, *A History of Bubonic Plague in the British Isles* (London, 1970), pp. 408–10.
66   Estimates based upon examination of five parish registers at Worcester, five at Gloucester, and six at Bristol.

this register'.[67] From being places of refuge for the surrounding countryside, well defended towns became at the end of the war, with overcrowding and pestilence, places to flee; and this had serious results on
their trade and industry. Bristol was almost a ghost town when it surrendered to Fairfax in 1645; wealthy citizens had departed, its markets
were deserted, and the garrison was demoralized. The city could not pay
its share of the agreed burning money to the New Model Army on its
capture.[68]

It can hardly be doubted that the region endured the 'manifold
miseries' predicted by Henry Parker during the Civil War. But if war
was the cause of the economic depression and social disruption of
the area, did the removal of the war bring recovery? The immediate
postwar period was one of harvest failure and high prices, limited
renewal of hostilities – culminating, for Worcester, in the worst
experience of all, the battle and occupation of the city in 1651 –
the continuation of garrisoning, and military disorders. Fighting
between soldiers and armed civilian bands, which had first occurred
in 1643 and reached a peak in the last year or so of the war, was
equally widespread in the two years following the peace, and affected
over thirty counties. Ex-Royalist highwaymen plagued some areas
after demobilization.[69]

In these conditions a sustained recovery would not be expected. The
gaps in the records caused by wartime disruption were not repaired in
the immediate postwar period, and detailed information on the extent
of revival is as scanty as in the war itself. But the figures we have, though
very incomplete, all point in the same direction. There was a sharp
but temporary recovery in economic activity in the towns of the West,
spurred, no doubt, by the removal of the obstacles to trade and marketing at the end of the war. A crude index to the health of the economy
of the towns is apprentice registration, and the graph (see p. 266),
though based on a limited sample, indicates the main trends.[70] In the
worst war years registration dropped to only a quarter of normal; at
the end of the war it immediately recovered; then fell back to the
prewar level by 1650.

67 Bristol Record Office, St Nicholas burial register, 1634–53, note at end of 1645
(o.s.).
68 H.M.C., *Portland*, I, pp. 283–6, 309.
69 See in addition to the articles referred to in n. 10, above, J. S. Morrill, *Cheshire,
1630–1660. County Government and Society during the 'English Revolution'* (London,
1974), pp. 194, 196; C. H. Firth, *Cromwell's Army* (London, 4th edn, 1962), pp.
270–1.
70 Gloucestershire Record Office, GBR 1458, 1458a; Mendenhall, *Shrewsbury
Drapers*, p. 234; Worcestershire Record Office, BA 5955/4.

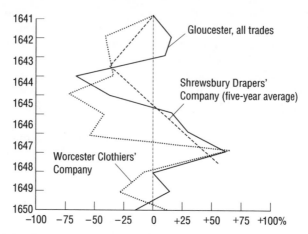

Figure 11.1 Apprentice registration in Gloucester, Shrewsbury and Worcester, 1640–50 (percentage change: annual average, 1636–40 = 0)

Other evidence appears to confirm these trends. Exeter benefited briefly from the collapse of London monopolies in 1646–7, and extended its trade once the sea and land passages were made secure.[71] Coastal trade at Gloucester, recorded in the only surviving port book for the city in the period, returned to somewhere near the pre-war level in 1647. As the majority of cargoes were going to Bristol – for which we have almost no trade records covering these years – the major port of the region may be presumed to have shared in this limited recovery.[72] Persistent problems, military and political uncertainty, permanent garrisoning and the privileges granted by the government to the soldiery in the late 1640s and the early 1650s – such as the suspension of apprentice regulations on their behalf – all contributed to the cutting short of this period of recovery. In other fields it continued longer. Landlord income rose sharply as rent collection resumed with more settled conditions, and in 1647, for instance, the administration of the Bridgewater estates in Shropshire was fully restored.[73] From 1646 most of the parish registers examined show a return to normal, with baptisms outnumbering burials.

War damage and dislocation in the Severn region had been severe for almost four years, and a short-lived revival in the immediate post-war period was insufficient to make good the losses suffered. A full recovery

71 Stephens, *Seventeenth-Century Exeter*, pp. 64–9.
72 Public Record Office, E 190.1248.14.
73 Hopkins, 'The Bridgewater Estates', pp. 311–12.

would be a work of time, and further research will, it is hoped, reveal if and when it occurred. It should also be possible to determine whether the war altered trends, in favour of less damaged regions. The lesson to be learned from studies of the Thirty Years War and the German economy is that there was wide variation in its effects. The same may be true of the Civil War. Some of the features of the war in the West – which it shared with the wars on the continent – were absent in the Southeast, for example. When the results of the Civil War in the regions are as well understood as those in Germany we will be able to test Clarendon's view, that London alone 'felt not the miseries of the war'.[74]

74   Clarendon, *History*, III, p. 291.

Part IV Consequences of the Civil War

Introduction to Part IV

Thirty months separated the end of the (main) civil war in summer 1646 from what might be termed the political 'revolution' of winter 1648–9 – the direct intervention of the parliamentary army in national politics, the trial and execution of the king, the abolition of monarchy and the House of Lords and the establishment of a commonwealth or republic. The latter were not the inevitable consequences of the civil war, though it is most unlikely that they would have occurred without the shattering and cathartic experience of a (civil) war. The bitter antagonism between royalists and parliamentarians which parliament's military victory had done nothing to resolve, the divisions within parliament over the essential elements of a future political, religious and constitutional settlement, the existence of a large and potent parliamentary army with views of its own, the uneasy alliance with the Scots which had given them a keen interest in any settlement south of the border, as well as the fragmentation of beliefs and ideas and the existence of a variety of often novel or radical views on religion, politics, government, society and the economy, all stemmed from the war years and the experience of civil war. The resulting breakdown and attempted resolution were undoubtedly shaped by the actions of individuals – the king's refusal sincerely to seek or accept a compromise settlement or the line adopted at key points by Sir Thomas Fairfax, Oliver Cromwell and a clutch of senior military commanders – and might be influenced by broader developments – most obviously, the social and economic distress caused by the bad weather and the resulting poor harvests of the latter half of the 1640s. However, in every case their roots can be found in the civil war itself.

Historians such as Robert Ashton, John Morrill, Ian Gentles and Austin Woolrych have explored the interplay between politics and the army, between attempts at settlement and growing or renewed divisions, in the years 1646–7.[1] There are differences of emphasis and some sharper divisions, which generally follow on from differing interpretations of the war and which were noted in the preceding section. For example, in keeping with his baronial interpretation of the 1640s, John Adamson has stressed the leading role taken by some of the titled aris-

---

1 R. Ashton, *Counter-Revolution: The Second Civil War and its Origins, 1646–8* (London, 1994); J. Morrill, *The Nature of the English Revolution* (Harlow, 1993), chapters 16–17; I. Gentles, *The New Model Army in England, Ireland and Scotland, 1645–53* (Oxford, 1991); A. H. Woolrych, *Soldiers and Statesmen. The General Council of the Army and its Debates, 1647–8* (Oxford, 1987).

tocracy in the negotiations and manoeuvring of these years,[2] an approach which has been received with some scepticism. In contrast, there has been broad acceptance of the now well-researched and detailed account of the post-war divisions, within the parliamentary cause as much as between parliamentarians and royalists. Historians have explored the religious divisions in parliament, between those who feared uncertainty, heresy and the social disorder which might result from the absence of clear religious leadership and control and who therefore favoured the restoration of a single, state church (whether upon the lines of a de-Arminianized Church of England or of a Scottish-style Presbyterianism) and those who welcomed the liberty of con-science and Protestant fragmentation of the war years and who bitterly opposed moves to restore a single church. Although historians might regret the religious labels which have been applied to the two parlia-mentary groupings, there is also broad agreement that these religious divisions were overlain by political and constitutional differences, between those who favoured the restoration of traditional, royal gov-ernment on minimal terms, perhaps merely turning the clock back to the position of autumn 1641 (the 'political' Presbyterians), and those who were more suspicious of the king and wanted to impose extensive new controls over the exercise of royal powers (the 'political' Independ-ents). The former tended to support, and the latter to oppose, the reim-position of a single state church, thus giving some credence to the religious labels. However, historians also stress that, as in the war years, opinion in both Houses could be fluid and influenced by a variety of per-sonal and policy issues and that, even though divisions undoubtedly sharpened during 1647, many MPs were not clearly or consistently aligned with either of the main groupings.

Recent work on the parliamentary armies, particularly the New Model Army, has explored the attempts of the political Presbyterians to reduce or remove the military presence, a vital precondition to reaching a settlement with the king and restoring traditional forms, and has shown how this attempted 'counter-revolution' brought them increas-ingly into conflict with the army during 1647. The growing fragmen-tation of the parliamentary cause itself reduced the likelihood of a firm and durable settlement and increased the possibility of renewed (armed) conflict, involving the armed forces. But while the main strands of this

2   J. Adamson, 'The English Nobility and the Projected Settlement of 1647', *The Historical Journal* 30 (1987); see also Adamson, 'Parliamentary Management, Men-of-Business and the House of Lords, 1640–9', in C. Jones (ed.), *A Pillar of the Con-stitution: The House of Lords in British Politics, 1640–1784* (London, 1989); Adamson, 'The Baronial Context of the English Civil War', *Transactions of the Royal Historical Society*, 5th series, 40 (1990).

story are clear enough, there are significant differences in assessments of the nature, timing and origins of military politicization, with historians such as Mark Kishlansky, Ian Gentles and Austin Woolrych disagreeing about precisely when, why and to what extent the New Model was politicized and became a radical force in the political process.[3] It is clear that by the spring and summer of 1647 elements within the army were expressing views on the future political and religious settlement of the country as well as seeking redress of purely military, material grievances, such as payment of arrears, and that during the latter half of the year many senior and junior officers and some members of the rank and file participated as active and ideologically informed players in the search for settlement. It is clear, too, that the rise in military disaffection and the overt involvement of the army in the religious, political and constitutional debates roughly coincided with the emergence of a London-based radical movement, the Levellers. Accordingly, a case could be made for a Leveller-inspired and Leveller-driven politicization of a hitherto largely apolitical parliamentary army during 1647, an interpretation which would stress the power and influence which Leveller ideas came to possess within and through the rank and file at least of the New Model Army. However, other historians have argued that the links between the Levellers and the army were weak and that the Leveller movement was not the catalyst which caused the New Model to become involved in the quest for settlement. Instead, some historians emphasize the deep faith and religious enthusiasm found within the New Model Army during the closing year of the civil war and argue that these religious beliefs and aspirations gave the army a political and constitutional as well as a religious awareness and ensured that from the outset it had a strong interest in the future settlement of the country. Once it became clear that the political Presbyterians were pursuing a settlement very different from that preferred by the army and that in the process they were seeking to exclude and neuter the army, to deny or ignore both its material and ideological aspirations, the New Model reacted. Thus began a power-struggle with the Long Parliament which, in physical terms at least, the army won through

3   M. Kishlansky, 'The Case of the Army Truly Stated: The Creation of the New Model Army', *Past & Present* 81 (1978); Kishlansky, *The Rise of the New Model Army* (Cambridge, 1979); Kishlansky, 'The Army and the Levellers: The Roads to Putney', *The Historical Journal* 22 (1979); Kishlansky, 'Consensus Politics and the Structure of Debate at Putney', *Journal of British Studies* 20 (1981); Kishlansky, 'Ideology and Politics in the Parliamentary Armes, 1645–9', in J. Morrill (ed.), *Reactions to the English Civil War* (Basingstoke, 1982); Kishlansky, 'What Happened at Ware?', *The Historical Journal* 25 (1982); I. Gentles, 'The Struggle for London in the Second Civil War', *The Historical Journal* 26 (1983); Gentles, *The New Model Army*; Woolrych, *Soldiers and Statesmen.*

direct military intervention in summer 1647, December 1648 and April 1653.

The Levellers have often been viewed as the most important and, through their connections with the New Model Army, potentially the most powerful of the political and religious radical groups which emerged in the wake of the civil war. As individuals and as a group or movement they have attracted a great deal of scholarly attention, though it is noticeable that no full-length study has appeared since the mid-1970s. The bulk of recent work, however, has tended to downplay the role and influence of the Levellers as a broad movement. The degree to which Leveller ideas really caught hold within the parliamentary armies has been questioned and it is emphasized that, on the few occasions when Levellerish unrest broke out in parts of the army, the senior officers were able swiftly and relatively easy to regain control. Many historians stress that, unlike most other radical groups of the period such as the Diggers, the Baptists and the Fifth Monarchists, the Leveller movement was geographically limited, tied very much to London, and that, like the Diggers, they enjoyed a brief lifespan, for they were in sharp decline and effectively broken and sidelined by summer 1649. Most recent work has also suggested that Levellerism had limited appeal outside the urban middling sort and did little to help women or the agrarian sector – though Brian Manning, for one, has argued that the Levellers did attempt to address rural issues – and that even the much vaunted support for broadening the franchise fell some way short of full manhood suffrage. On the other hand, the Levellers did tackle the question of the future settlement head on, setting out radical constitutional proposals which were designed greatly to enhance individual rights and liberties and to ensure that power was vested in a much broader section of the population. For a time, too, some Leveller ideas clearly did strike a chord within the New Model Army and were taken seriously by the senior army officers, who attempted not merely to crush rank and file unrest but also to weave some of the more acceptable Leveller ideas into their own constitutional proposals.[4] Without a doubt, the Leveller leaders were exceptionally skilful at presenting their wide ranging if varied ideas in print, at whipping up large-scale support in and around the capital on particular occasions and creating for a time a milieu which one historian has called 'radical chic'.[5]

---

4   See B. Taft, 'The Council of Officers' *Agreement of the People*, 1648/9', *The Historical Journal* 28 (1985).
5   Major studies of the Levellers include J. Frank, *The Levellers* (New York, 1955); H. N. Brailsford, *The Levellers and the English Revolution*, ed C. Hill (2nd edn, London, 1976); H. Shaw, *The Levellers* (London, 1968); G. E. Aylmer, *The Levellers in the English Revolution* (London, 1975); A. L. Morton, *Freedom in Arms: A Selection of*

In a paper first published in a 1973 collection (Chapter 12), Colin Davis focuses, not on the issue of Leveller links with the New Model Army, but on one of the less-explored facets of the Levellers, namely their links with religion. As Davis notes, although historians accept that religious beliefs and ideals played a part in shaping some individual Leveller writers, the movement as a whole and its objectives, most have argued that Levellerism was principally secular in its nature and programme. In exploring and laying an usually strong emphasis upon the religious basis of much Leveller ideology, Davis brings out the centrality to the movement of a small number of key writers and thinkers, the way in which some of their ideas changed and evolved during the mid and late 1640s and occasional divisions between them, highlighting how at one point Walwyn attacked his colleague Lilburne for an over-reliance upon legal precedence. Indeed, in developing an argument based upon equity, 'blending reason and religion, natural and divine law', Davis sees Walwyn in the van and Lilburne following. Linked with equity was the concept of 'practical Christianity', the stress upon the relief of suffering and want, a 'pragmatic' if 'vague' concept which provided 'a strong moral imperative'. Davis argues that the 'Christian pragmatism' underpinning the Levellers helps to explain their flexible approach to the form of government, willing at different times to support different constitutional arrangements. Like Cromwell (pointed to but not identified by name in the paper), they were principally concerned with the ends not the forms or means of government. Davis also highlights the Leveller belief in limited, inalienable and God-given self-propriety, which placed 'conscientious obligations' upon the individual, acting freely and enjoying religious liberty. In another parallel with Cromwell, Davis sees a firm belief in liberty of conscience as central to the origins and early writ-

Leveller Writings (London, 1975). Articles or chapters on specific themes include K. Thomas, 'The Levellers and the Franchise', in G. E. Aylmer (ed.), *The Interregnum: The Quest for Settlement, 1646–60* (London, 1972); A. L. Morton's study of 'Leveller Democracy – Fact or Myth?' in his *The World of the Ranters: Religious Radicalism in the English Revolution* (London, 1979); R. A. Gleissner, 'The Levellers and Natural Law: The Putney Debates of 1647', *Journal of British Studies* 20 (1980); R. B. Seaberg, 'The Norman Conquest and the Common Law: The Levellers and the Argument from Continuity', *The Historical Journal* 24 (1981). More recent work on the Levellers includes the closing chapters of B. Manning, *The English People and the English Revolution* (2nd edn, London, 1991); D. Wootton, 'Leveller Democracy and the Puritan Revolution', in J. H. Burns and M. Goldie (eds), *The Cambridge History of Political Thought, 1450–1700* (Cambridge 1991), ch. 14; A. Hughes,' Gender Politics in Leveller Literature', in S. D. Amussen & M. Kishlansky (eds), *Political Culture and Cultural Politics in Early Modern Europe* (Manchester, 1995); A. Sharp (ed.), *The English Levellers* (Cambridge, 1998), mainly reprinting Leveller writings but with a good, sharp introduction; the phrase 'radical chic' is Sharp's (p. xxix), noting that by June 1649 the Levellers' sea-green colours were 'no longer radical chic'.

ings of the Levellers and suggests that their legal, political and constitutional 'attitudes' grew out of this 'basic cause'. Even later on, as Levellerism developed, secular concerns were interlinked with, and in part sprang from, these religious foundations.

The stresses created by radical groups such as the Levellers exacerbated the growing divisions within and between both parliament and the parliamentary armies during 1647. This gave the king the opportunity to play a game of divide and rule. Entering into an uneasy alliance with the disgruntled Scots, he encouraged the series of risings and rebellions in parts of England and Wales during 1648 which, in tandem with an attempted Scottish-royalist invasion, are sometimes viewed as a second civil war. Some were well-organized, while others appear to have been spontaneous reactions to local circumstances. Some were triggered by the continuing presence of troops and garrisons, military-backed county committees and war-time levels of taxation, and may be seen as violent protests in favour of a return to traditional peace-time administrative, fiscal and religious forms. In a string of articles published during the 1980s, Brian Lyndon stressed that many of the risings were either overtly royalist from the outset, the actions of committed royalists, or were infiltrated and taken over by the king's men.[6] While that pattern works for many of the risings in southern and eastern England, especially the major action which came to focus on Colchester, it is not so convincing in some cases, most obviously in south and south-west Wales, where the initiative was taken by, and the leadership remained with, a group of disillusioned former parliamentarians.[7]

In the wake of renewed war and a second royalist defeat, the energized and reunited parliamentary army intervened directly in central politics to open the way for and to drive through the trial and execution of the king as well as the political and constitutional – though not a social and economic – 'revolution' of the winter of 1648–9. Regicide was not the result of any widespread ideological opposition to monarchy or support for republicanism. But it probably did result from more than just a pragmatic conclusion that in practice a secure peace and a durable settlement would be impossible so long as Charles lived. Many within the army, as well as some of their political and religious allies,

6 B. Lyndon, 'The South and the Start of the Second Civil War', *History* 71 (1986); Lyndon, 'Essex and the King's Cause in 1648', *The Historical Journal* 29 (1986); see also Lyndon, 'The Parliament's Army in Essex, 1648', *Journal of Army Historical Research* 58 (1980).

7 On Wales, P. Gaunt, *A Nation Under Siege. The Civil War in Wales, 1642—8* (London, 1991), ch. 7. For broader studies of the second civil war see Ashton, *Counter-Revolution: The Second Civil War and its Origins*; Morrill, *Revolt in the Provinces*, pp. 169–76, though in a final chapter added to the new edition Morrill supports Lyndon's reinterpretation, pp. 204–8.

came to believe that God had spoken against the king and against reaching a settlement with him. The divisions and renewed conflict of 1647–8 were seen as proof of divine displeasure at the attempts of parliamentary politicians and soldiers to settle with Charles. As Patricia Crawford shows in her 1977 article (Chapter 13), the stark biblical image of blood guilt had been deployed from time to time earlier in the war,[8] but during 1648 it was increasingly used in reference to the king. He was a man who had needlessly shed innocent blood, a defiler who in the process had become defiled, who had rendered himself polluted and impure, and against whom God demanded justice and retribution. As Crawford notes, 'a discussion of Charles I in terms of blood guilt avoided awkward constitutional issues' and might also serve to give a lofty, ideological veneer to more grubby, brutal, politically expedient actions. However, she also notes that by the latter half of 1648 many soldiers, politicians and ministers held a deep and genuine belief in the concept of blood guilt in general and its application to Charles I in particular, a belief which was to many officers and soldiers 'the decisive factor in the formation of policy'. For many, this belief drove them through the events of January 1649 and led them to seek further 'expiation of the nation's blood guilt', even after Charles's head had rolled. In contrast, some were not entirely convinced and remained hesitant – Crawford suggests here that Oliver Cromwell was one of them, a late and uncertain convert to regicide. In contrast, John Morrill has more recently argued that although he did not explicitly endorse the 'man of blood' imagery, from early 1648 Cromwell was convinced that God had spoken against Charles and that during the year his concern 'was not whether to remove the king but when and how'; Cromwell was not hesitant and wavering but 'was letting God's plan unfold at its own pace'.[9]

The final article in this collection is a piece by Christopher Hill first published in 1980 (Chapter 14). Hill was a – perhaps the – dominant figure in civil war studies for much of the 1950s, 1960s and 1970s; prolific and wide-ranging, he embraced the political, social, economic, religious, intellectual and cultural world of mid-seventeenth century English men and women and added enormously to our understanding of their world.[10] Although his emphasis upon socio-economic interpretations of the period is now (largely) out of fashion and his heavy reliance upon published and literary sources has drawn criticism, Hill's

8   Indeed, see also S. Baskerville, 'Blood Guilt in the English Revolution', *The Seventeenth Century* 8 (1993).

9   J. Morrill, 'King-Killing No Murder: Cromwell in 1648', *Cromwelliana* (1998).

10   See the comment of G. Burgess, 'how much have we lost in the reaction to Hill and Stone? For all of their many faults, both integrated into one picture economic, social, political, religious and intellectual history. Who does that any more?', quoted by Morrill, *Revolt in the Provinces*, p. 7, n. 24.

writings remain some of the richest and deepest on the seventeenth century in general and on the nature and essence of the mid-century in particular. The article reprinted here, by some way the broadest and in many ways the richest in this selection, encompasses the causes, nature and consequences of the civil war, though it focuses on the latter, and in the process it ranges well beyond 1649, often by several decades. Hill argues that, more often by accident than by design, the events of the mid-seventeenth century profoundly changed society and the economy as well as the political, constitutional and intellectual contexts, creating conditions favourable to the middle classes – 'the bourgeoisie' – and to the development of capitalism. He vigorously defends the concept of 'a bourgeois revolution', not as a revolution consciously willed by the bourgeoisie, but as one which proved to be 'a unique turning point', which broke for ever old constraints and thus fundamentally changed England, which during the 1650s and more so after the Restoration created a new climate with new opportunities from which the bourgeoisie benefited.

Sir John Oglander did not live to see this new world, for he died in the mid-1650s. But his spirit had been broken by 1650, sapped by the civil war, by the changes which it had brought to his beloved Isle of Wight and by the sufferings which he and his family had endured during the 1640s. Looking back in his commonplace book, Oglander wearily recorded the impact of the civil war and of what followed:

> What an Island we had from 1643 till 1650, how governed and by what means, it breaks my heart to tell you, or so much as to think of it . . . How is this poor Island altered in all things from better to worse! For our Captain we have now a Governor, as if we were slaves. And instead of our former joy, comfort & true liberty we have now as bad as Egyptian slavery. This Island was once a pleasant happy place, and men envied our happiness, but now we are slaves to mean soldiers, which formerly lived on our charity.

Depressed and embittered, by 1650 he was admitting that he hated the world and longed for death.[11] For Oglander, as for so many others, the 1640s had proved to be a searing experience, their world turned upside down, their way of life undermined, their comforts and certainties pulled away. The civil war created new potentials and opportunities, some realized, some dashed, and it can be viewed as a turning point in English (and British) history, a catalyst for change and innovation. But without doubt it also wrecked, destroyed and tore apart, creating a maelstrom of death, destruction and misery, and leaving a trail of blood and tears.

11   F. Bamford (ed.), *A Royalist Notebook. The Commonplace Book of Sir John Oglander, Kt, of Nunwell* (London, 1936), pp. 131–3.

12

The Levellers and Christianity

J. Colin Davis

Originally appeared as J. Colin Davis, 'The Levellers and Christianity' in
B. Manning (ed.), *Politics, Religion and the English Civil War*. Copyright
© 1973 Edward Arnold, London.

The relationship between religious and political thinking in the seventeenth century seems to grow more problematic rather than less, as time goes on. Not only are the traditional religious categories called in question[1] but what has been taken as the substance of specific political theories is shown never to have existed.[2] As interpretations of both the politics and the religion are challenged, relating the two becomes increasingly dangerous.

The influence of religious belief on the Levellers as a group of political thinkers has been seen in three main ways. Most commentators perhaps have followed William Haller in seeing religion as a secondary influence within the movement. 'Its leaders were animated by religious convictions and they were experienced in the organization of religious dissent, but the movement was not a religious but a secular one, aiming to secure certain positive rights and benefits by political action.'[3] Others, however, have seen religion as a primary influence either through the Christian liberty, individualism and egalitarianism professed within the

1   See, for example, C. H. George, 'Puritanism as History and Historiography', *Past and Present* No. 41 (1968), pp. 77–104.
2   For this process in relation to the Levellers see, C. B. Macpherson, *The Political Theory of Possessive Individualism* (Oxford, 1962), Ch. iii, 'The Levellers: Franchise and Freedom'.
3   W. Haller and G. Davies, *The Leveller Tracts, 1647–53* (Columbia, 1944), p. 7. *Cf.* D. M. Wolfe, *Leveller Manifestoes of the Puritan Revolution* (New York, 1944), P. 3; H. N. Brailsford, *The Levellers and the English Revolution* ed. C. Hill (London, 1961), pp. 549–51; H. Holorenshaw, *The Levellers and the English Revolution* (London, 1939), pp. 35–6; D. W. Petegorsky, *Left-Wing Democracy in the English Civil War* (London, 1940), pp. 25, 82; W. Schenk, *The Concern for Social Justice in the Puritan Revolution* (London, 1948), pp. 35, 36, 38; Gertrude Huehns, *Antinomianism in English History* (London, 1951), p. 115.

YALE COLLEGE
LEARNING RESOURCE CENTRE

sects or through the example of the voluntaristic and contractual organization of the sectarians' gathered churches.[4] Yet a third group see the influence of religion as varying over time or from one individual to another within the group.[5]

This essay attempts to show that religion was a primary influence on the Levellers but that the current way of describing that influence is unsatisfactory and produces an unwarranted emphasis on idealism in the political writings of the Levellers.

The main problem for those who have seen the Levellers as a religiously oriented group has been reconciling an apparently élitist religious position with their apparently democratic view of civil society and individual rights. A second problem, and one not so often attempted by historians, is that of explaining how the Levellers' extreme religious individualism did not lead to an anarchist political position as it did, for example, in the early writings of Gerrard Winstanley.[6] Both problems have been resolved in terms of the segregation of the sphere of 'nature', to which man *as man* belonged, from the sphere of 'grace', to which the saints as the elect of God belonged, in Leveller thought.[7] Across the gulf between the two the Levellers are seen as carrying, unconsciously or by analogy, equality, individuality and liberty but not the élitism of election. The rule of natural law over the sphere of nature imposed limits on the application of divine precepts within civil society, just as it was itself relative, conditioned in its performance by the imperfection of natural man. Unfortunately, there is very little real evidence for any process of segregation and analogy in Leveller

4   See, for example, P. Zagorin, *A History of Political Thought in the English Revolution* (London, 1954), pp. 12, 14; G. P. Gooch, *English Democratic Ideas in the Seventeenth Century* (Cambridge, 1927), Ch. III; T. C. Pease, *The Leveller Movement* (Washington, 1916), p. 363; D. M. Himbury, 'The Religious Beliefs of the Levellers', *The Baptist Quarterly* Vol. 33 (1954); R. M. Jones, *Mysticism and Democracy in the English Commonwealth* (New York, 1932), Ch. V; D. B. Robertson, *The Religious Foundations of Leveller Democracy* (New York, 1951); Howard Shaw, *The Levellers* (London, 1968), p. 4; A. D. Linday, *The Essentials of Democracy* (London, 1935), p. 11.
5   Joseph Frank (*The Levellers* (Cambridge, Mass., 1955)) appears to see religion as a diminishing influence on the Levellers and Richard Overton's 'secularized and pragmatic humanism' as increasingly important (p.129). Pauline Gregg (*Free-Born John: A Biography of John Lilburne* (London, 1961)) contrasts the religiously motivated Lilburne with Overton, 'the complete rationalist' (p. 113). On Overton as a rationalist see Keith Thomas, *Religion and the Decline of Magic* (London, 1971), p. 313.
6   See D. B. Robertson's discussion of this point, *The Religious Foundations of Leveller Democracy*, pp. 105–9.
7   A. S. P. Woodhouse, *Puritanism and Liberty* (London, 1950), Introduction.

thought[8] and even less direct evidence for the inspiration of congregational organization.

Those who see the Levellers as primarily a secular group do not, of course, have this problem of explaining the transference of values from grace to nature. Nevertheless, these historians insist that the Levellers segregated the two spheres and lay emphasis on the Levellers' argument from natural law. Here the difficulty can be the Levellers' preoccupation, especially in their early works, with religion and religious values in a social context. William Haller, for example, attempts to get round this by arguing that Lilburne confused natural and divine law and so was capable of being weaned from sectarian élitism by infusings of secularism.[9]

If the relationship between the Levellers' religious and political thinking is to be fully understood, however, it must be grasped that, in most important respects, the Levellers never distinguished between natural and divine law.[10] This essential point can be most clearly observed in their teaching on equity and in their inculcation of practical Christianity.

The concept of equity was used constantly throughout the Levellers' agitation and yet very little attention has been paid to it. They included it in their recurrent appeals to 'Justice, Equity and Conscience'.[11] 'I would have such a Government,' Lilburne proclaimed, 'that is founded upon the basis of Freedom, Reason, Justice and Common Equity. . . .'[12] 'Equity' seems to have meant two things to the Levellers. Less frequently and in their early days it was used in quasi-juridical sense as the spirit rather than the letter of the law, as those general principles of justice by which the execution of the law should be moderated. In this sense, while equity may be above the letter of the law, it is at least related to it: 'for the Law taken abstract from its originall reason and end, is made a shell without a kernel, a shadow without a substance and a body without a soul. It is the execution of Laws according to their equity and reason, which is the spirit that gives life to Authority the Letter kills.'[13]

---

8   See L. F. Solt, *Saints in Arms* (London, 1959), Ch. IV; Robertson, *The Religious Foundations of Leveller Democracy*, p. 92.

9   Haller and Davies, *Leveller Tracts*, pp. 41–4.

10   *Cf.* Ernst Troeltsch, *The Social Teaching of the Christian Churches* (New York, 1960), Vol. I, p. 344. 'The sects rejected compromise with the world, and therefore also relative Natural Law.' See also Robertson, *Religious Foundations*, pp. 50, 58–9, 71.

11   John Lilburne, *Englands Birth Right Justified* (1645), p. 8. See also, *Englands Freedom, Souldiers Rights* (1647), in Wolfe, *Leveller Manifestoes*, p. 254.

12   John Lilburne, *Strength our of Weaknesse* (1649), p. 14.

13   Lilburne, *Englands Birth Right*, p. 2. See also p. 5 for equity as the true sense or meaning or statute law. *Cf.* Richard Overton, *the Commoners Complaint* (1647), p. 8;

Elsewhere, however, and more typically, equity was visualized as something entirely independent of the letter of specific legal enactments or judicial decisions. 'Yea, if the Law should comptroule and overthrow the equity, it is to be comptrouled and overthrowne it selfe, and the equity to be preserved as the thing, only legally, obligatory and binding.'[14] John Wildman saw the equity and the letter of the law as by no means complementary and insisted accordingly that equity be expressed in the wording of statute law.[15] Richard Overton expressed much the same idea in *A Remonstrance of Many Thousand Citizens*. 'Yee know, the Lawes of this Nation are unworthy a Free-People, and deserve from first to last to be considered, and seriously debated and reduced to an agreement with Common equity. . . .'[16]

Clearly, the Levellers were here using the term 'equity' not in a juridical sense but in the general sense of what is fair and right. Once, for example, Overton defined it as 'Justice and plaine dealing', to be contrasted with 'Policies and Court Arts'.[17] In this way the vagueness of the term was increased but at the same time the Levellers endowed it with moral imperatives which are of great significance in understanding the relationship between divine and natural law in their thinking.

The principle of equity frequently finds expression for the Levellers through the golden rule: do unto others as you would be done by.[18] The golden rule was, however, a divine injunction: 'the scripture tells me, everyone ought to be fully persuaded in his own mind, and that whatsoever is not faith, is sin: it tells me I must doe as I would be done unto.'[19] In a highly significant phrase Lilburne declared that God had 'ingraved

Overton, *An Appeale from the Degenerate Representative Body* (1647), p. 159. Here Overton used almost exactly the same phrase, substituting 'Reason' for 'Equity' in the latter.

14   Overton, *An Appeale*, p. 161. *Cf.* the almost identical wording in Overton's *The Hunting of the Foxes or the Grandie Deceivers Unmasked* (1649) in Wolfe, *Leveller Manifestoes*, p. 362.

15   John Wildman, *Truths Triumph, or Treachery Anatomized* (1648), p. 11.

16   Richard Overton, *A Remonstrance of Many Thousand Citizens* (1646), p. 15.

17   *ibid.* p. 4.

18   See, for example, William Walwyn, *A Helpe to the right Understanding of a Discourse Concerning Independency* (1645), p. 3; Richard Overton, *The Araignement of Mr. Persecution* (1645), pp. 15, 22; Walwyn, *A Prediction of Mr. Edwards his Conversion and Recantation* (1646), p. 16; (?Walwyn), *No Papist Nor Presbyterian* (1648) in Wolfe, *Leveller Manifestoes*, p. 307. In reply to the Levellers an interesting conservative twist on the golden rule was used. '. . . justice is to render to everyone his owne, and not to do to another what you would not should be done to you'. *A Declaration of Some PROCEEDINGS of Lt. Col. John Lilburne, And his Associates* (1648), p. 39. The argument went on, 'The rich may be oppressed as well as the poor, property is to be preserved to all'.

19   William Walwyn, *A Whisper in the Eare of Mr. Thomas Edwards* (1646), p. 5.

by nature in the soule of Man, this golden and everlasting, principle, to doe to another, as he would have another do to him.'[20] In addition God had provided a model of equitable law-making: 'So likewise, when he came to give a Law to the Israelites, as a Nation in whom he tooke a special delight, he doth not only give them a Law in plaine words without ambiguous termes, short and in their own tongue, unto which they were required to give their consent and gave it: but he also declares it universally given to al men and woemen, rich and poore, without any exception. All which is evident; plain and cleare in Exod. . . .'[21] Consequently it was possible for the Levellers to see the pursuit of equity as a religious obligation and its attainment as a worthy offering. They offered their final Agreement in the name of God, 'desiring the equity thereof may be to his praise and glory. . . .'[22]

But equity and the golden rule were also identifiable with reason. 'Reason is demonstrable of it self, and every man (less or more) is endued with it; and it hath but one ballance to weigh it in, or one touchstone to try it by viz. To teach a man to do as he would be done to.'[23]

In a most important passage in *An Appeale*, Richard Overton argued that reason was above precedent and superior to law; 'severall are its degrees, but its perfection and fulnesse is only in God.' Law had to be based in reason in accordance with three rational principles: self-preservation is a law of reason; 'necessity is the law above all laws', the equity of the law is superior to the letter. 'Nothing which is against reason is lawfull, Reason being the very life of the Law of our Land: So that should the law be taken away from the Originall reason and end, it would be made a shell without a kernill, a shadow without a substance, a carkasse without life, which presently turns to putrifaction; and as Reason only gives it a legall Being and life, so it only makes it authoritative and binding.' Three pages later he restated the argument, substituting the term 'equity' for that of 'reason'.[24]

The moral imperatives behind equity in Leveller thinking are then both Christian and natural. Natural law is not made a clear concept and is never divorced from divine influence. As far as the notion of equity was concerned, there was no segregation between nature and grace, in

20   John Lilburne, *London's Liberty in Chains* (1646), quoted in Zagorin, *A History of Political Thought in the English Revolution*, p. 12. Forscripture and law as the twin sources of equity see Lilburne, *The Legall Fundamentall Liberties of the People of England Revived, Asserted, and Vindicated*, (1649), p. 20.
21   John Liburne, L. *Colonel John Liburne His Apologeticall Narration* (1652), pp. 17–18.
22   John Lilburne, Richard Overton, Thomas Prince, William Walwyn, *An Agreement of the Free People of England* (May 1649), p. 3.
23   Lilburne, *Strength out of Weaknesse*, p. 14.
24   Overton, *An Appeale*, pp. 158–61.

fact the two are seen as complementary. 'I say no Power on earth is absolute but God alone, and all other Powers are dependants on him, and those Principles of Reason and Righteousnesse that hee hath indowed man with, upon the true Bassis of which all earthly power or Majestracy ought to be founded, and when a power of Majestracy degenerates from that Rule, by which it is to bee Ruled, and betakes it selfe to its crooked and innovating will, it is to be no more a Power or Majestracy, but an obnoxious Tyranny, to be resisted by all those that would not willingly have man to usurp the soveraigntie of God to Rule by his will and pleasure.'[25]

The explanation of how the Levellers could fail to distinguish between nature and grace and still avoid both secularism and also the political élitism of the presbyterians or Fifth Monarchists, is to be found in the influence of the doctrines of antinomianism and universal salvation on their writing and thinking. This is not to suggest that all of the Levellers were antinomians, but some of them were and their influence is paramount in this respect.[26]

The idea that salvation was provided fully and freely for all men is a marked and consistent feature of Walwyn's writing. In an early tract he argued that the work of redemption was already perfected in Christ's death and that there was nothing more to do. '. . . we are all justified freely by his grace through the redemption that is in Jesus Christ.' '. . . neither infidelity, nor impenitency, nor unthankfulnesse, nor sinne, nor anything whatsoever can make void his purpose.' It was 'a worke perfected, depending on no condition, no performance at all', not even belief.[27]

Walwyn restated this theme in a later work, *The Vanitie of the Present Churches* (February 1649). He believed that the law had been replaced

---

25 Lilburne, *Strength Out of Weaknesse*, pp. 21–2.
26 Lilburne shows evidence of antinomianism: see, for example, *A Copie of a Letter to Mr. William Prinne Esq.* (1645), p. 3. His protestations are usually of salvation rather than of élitist election. See, for example, *A Work of the Beast* (1638); *Come Out of Her my People* (1638), pp. 5–6; *A Coppy of a letter written by J. Lilburne, close prisoner in the wards of the Fleet, which he sent to Iames Ingram and Henry Hopkins* (1640?), p. 6. The influence of Walwyn on him was, as I shall argue, considerable. For Lilburne as rejecting the idea of the elect and tending in the direction of comprehensive grace see D. B. Robertson, *Religious Foundations*, pp. 15–16. Overton also shows traces of antinomianism, see for example, *Mans Mortallitie* (1644), p. 5: '. . . none can be condemned into Hell, but such as are actually guilty of refusing of Christ.' Gertrude Huehns emphasized the influence of antinomianism in Leveller thought, *Antinomianism in English History*, pp. 109, 114. Leo F. Solt, on the other hand, believed that although Walwyn was an antinomian and a believer in universal salvation, he was untypical of the Levellers in these respects, *Saints in Arms*, p. 67.
27 William Walwyn, *The Power of Love* (1643), pp. 24, 30–2.

by the gospel and that 'the same Jesus whom the Jewes crucified, was Lord and Christ: That he is the propitiation for our sins, and not only for ours, but for the sins of the whole world, That it is the bloud of Christ which cleanseth us from all our sinne, That his love is so exceeding towards us, that even when we were enemies Christ died for us.'[28]

In April 1649 his enemies charged that 'he did not beleive [sic] that God would punish men for ever for a little time of sinning'.[29] In reply Walwyn proclaimed the importance of antinomianism to him, describing it as 'that *unum necessarium*, that pearl in the field, free justification by Christ alone'.[30]

For those like Walwyn, antinomians and believers in universal salvation, natural and divine law became indistinguishable. Since all men were saved, divine law, God's law made known to the elect, became the universal prescript. Thus natural law and divine law had to be seen as complementary, or rather as mutually inclusive, since both applied to all men.

The development of Lilburne's use of natural law argument illustrates well the influence of Walwyn's ideas, and the antinomian, free-grace views behind them, upon the general course of Leveller thinking. In 1638 Lilburne very sharply attacked the use of 'Philosophy and Logick' as being 'not the inventions or Institutions of Jesus Christ nor his Apostles, but of the Divell and Antichrist, with which they mainly and principally have upheld and maintained their black, darke, and wicked Kingdome: for Christ nor his Apostles in all their Disputes that ever they had with their Enemies ever made use neither of Logicke nor Philosophy but only of the Authority of the Scripture.'[31]

The problem here is how did Lilburne develop from this position to one where he could argue in terms of natural law and reason? William Haller saw Lilburne's progress to natural law, to an appeal to reason, as passing via the tuition of the legal theorists – St Germain, Henry Parker and above all Coke.[32] There are certainly signs of this in, for example, *Englands Birth Right Justified*, but the problem obviously still bothered Lilburne in that work for he appended to it a discussion of the relationship between natural and divine law. In this, divine law was described as superseding natural law, which was a minimal requirement.[33] Again,

28   William Walwyn, *The Vanitie of the Present Churches*, p. 30; see pp. 29–31.
29   (?John Price), *Walwins Wiles or the Manifestators Manifested* (1649), p. 9.
30   William Walwyn, *Walwyns Just Defence* (1649), p. 10; see also p. 8.
31   John Lilburne, *An Answer to Nine Arguments Written by T. B.* (1645), pp. 2–3. Although published in 1645, this tract was written in 1638.
32   Haller and Davies, *The Leveller Tracts*, pp. 42–5.
33   Lilburne, *Englands Birth Right Justified* Postscript.

where he had ventured to use natural law argument in the body of the tract he had made it subservient always to divine law.[34]

In fact, however, it does not appear to have been the legal theorists who taught Lilburne to use natural law argument, but rather William Walwyn. In *Englands Lamentable Slavery* (which according to Thomason appeared only a few days after *Englands Birth Right Justified*) Walwyn urged Lilburne to drop his arguments from legal precedent and to appeal to natural law. He specifically attacked Lilburne's reliance on Magna Charta as interpreted by Coke. Magna Charta was a dupe, a 'messe of pottage', and 'when so choice a people . . . shall insist upon such inferiour things, neglecting greater matters, and be so unskilfull in the nature of common and just freedom as to call bondage libertie, and the rights of Conquerours their Birth rights, no marvaille such a people make so little use of the greatest advantages; and when they might have made a newer and better Charter, have falne to patching the old.'[35] Instead Walwyn urged Lilburne to appeal to equity '. . . for any man to be imprisoned without cause declared and witnessed (by more than one appearing face to face) is not only unjust, because expresslie against Magna Carta, but also against all reason, sense, and the Common Law of equitie and justice.'[36]

Although the legal theorists were important in the development of Lilburne's thought it appears to be Walwyn, with his identification of nature and grace, who pushed Lilburne in the direction of appeal to natural law. In January 1647 Lilburne published an attack on English law in the name of reason and nature. 'Observe from hence,' he wrote, 'from what a pure fountain our inslaving Laws, Judges, and Practices in Westminster Hall had their originall; namely from the will of a Conqueror and Tyrant. . . .' Nature taught man to defend himself, reason to do so in accordance with the golden rule of equity. '. . . nature tells me there is a God, reason dictates unto me, that I should speak honourably and reverently of Him.'[37]

Thus the Levellers' recurrent emphasis on equity illustrates a fusion of divine and natural law taking place in their thinking under the influence of antinomianism and in particular under William Walwyn's expo-

---

34 *ibid.* p. 7. The argument here was that examination on interrogatories was condemned by natural law but also by the conduct of Christ. The same argument had been used by Lilburne in an earlier work, *A Work of the Beast* (1638), p. 13.
35 William Walwyn, *Englands Lamentable Slavery* (1645), pp. 4–5. Thomason dated *Englands Birth Right Justified* 8 October 1645 and *Englands Lamentable Slavery* 11 October 1645. For a contemporary caricature of Lilburne's dependence on Magna Carta see *The Recantation of Lieutenant Collonel John Lilburne* (1647), p. 5.
36 Walwyn, *Englands Lamentable Slavery*, p. 5.
37 John Liburne, *Regall Tyrannie discovered* (1647), pp. 10, 16.

sition of it. No doubt these ideas were transmitted with a great deal of vagueness and no small confusion. Nevertheless it is essential to be aware of them if one is to understand the Levellers' political pragmatism and their view of the individual.

The adoption of the idea of universal free grace meant that there could be no segregation between nature and grace in human affairs. Society became, as it were , the invisible church made visible. In Walwyn this produced a political concern with society as a whole and as a sum of individuals. '. . . love makes you no longer your owne but Gods servants, and prompts you to doe his will in the punishment of all kind of exorbitances, whether it be a breach of oaths, breach of trust or any kinde of injustice in whomsoever, and to be no respecter of persons; nor will any ones greatnesse oversway or daunt your resolutions, but you will be bold as Lions not fearing the forces of men, you will when need requires, that is, when tyrants and oppressors endeavour by might and force to pervert all Lawes, and compacts amongst men, and to pervert the truth of God into a lie. . . .'[38] Richard Overton was in fact suggesting much the same thing when he wrote, 'it is against the Law of Charity, not to doe as we would be done unto.'[39]

This emphasis on equity, blending reason and religion, natural and divine law, is paralleled by and related to another main theme of the Levellers, the theme of practical Christianity: 'were we all busied onely in those short necessary truths,' wrote Walwyn, 'we should soon become practical Christians; and take more pleasure in Feeding the hungry, Cloathing the naked, visiting and comforting the sicke, releeving the aged, weake and impotent; in delivering of prisoners, supporting of poore families or in freeing a Common wealth from all Tyrants, oppressors and deceivers, thereby manifesting our universal love to all mankind, without respect of persons, Opinions, Societies or Churches.'[40]

Like the other Leveller leaders, Walwyn believed that 'the essence of true religion is located in conduct.'[41] St James's definition of pure religion, with its injunction to be not only hearers but doers of the word, was repeated on numerous occasions by Walwyn.[42] But the Levellers as

---

38 Walwyn, *The Power of Love*, p. 39.
39 Overton, *The Araignement of Mr. Persecution*, p. 15.
40 Walwyn, *The Vanitie of the Present Churches*, p. 43.
41 Zagorin, *A History of Political Thought*, p. 25
42 James 1, 27, see also Matthew 25, 35–9. *Cf.* Walwyn, *A Prediction of Mr. Edwards his Conversion*, p. 18; *A Whisper in the Eare of Mr. Thomas Edwards*, p. 9; *A Still and Soft Voice* (1647), pp. 7–9; *The Vanitie of the Present Churches*, p. 23; *The Compassionate Samaritane* (1645), p. 37. Note also the reporting of Walwyn's holding this view in (?Price), *Walwins Wiles*, p. 7.

a whole were always 'earnestly desirous to make a right use of that opportunity God hath given us to make this Nation Free and Happy.'[43] Together they endorsed the primacy of practical religion. 'Though we were not so strict upon the formall and ceremoniall part of his service, the method, manner and personall injunction being not so clearly made out unto us, nor the necessary requisites which his Officers and Ministers ought to be furnished withall as yet appearing to us in any that pretended thereunto: yet for the manifestation of God's love in Christ, it is clearly assented unto by us; and the practicall and most reall part of Religion is as readily submitted unto by us, as being, in our apprehensions, the most eminent and the most excellent in the world as proceeding from no other but that God who is Goodnesse it self.'[44]

The sanction of practical Christianity was both a standard for criticism of those already in power and a spur to renewed political concern and activity. Lilburne's denouncement of the apostasy of the parliamentary party is typical in its critical use of that standard. 'When I seriously consider how many men in the Parliament and else-where of their associates (that judge themselves the onely Saints and godly men upon earth) that have considerable (and some of them vast) estates of their own inheritance, and yet take five hundred, one, two, three, four, five, six thousand pounds per annum salaries, and other comings in by their places . . . when thousands, not onely of the people of the world, as they call them, but also of the precious and redeemed Lambs of Christ, are ready to starve for want of bread, I cannot but wonder with my self, whether they have any conscience at all within them or no, and what they think of that saying of the Spirit of God: that whoso hath this worlds good, and seeth his brother hath need, and shutteth up his bowels of compassion from him . . . how dwelleth the love of God in him?'[45]

In *The Power of Love* Walwyn attacked the lack of charity of the clergy; 'the wants and distresses of the poor will testify that the love of God they have not.' He found that, 'True Christians are of all men the most valiant defenders of the just liberties of their countrye.'[46] He explained his own involvement in politics in terms of 'true religion', '. . . there is no man weake, but I would strengthen; nor ignorant, but I

---

43   Lilburne, Overton, Prince, Walwyn, *An Agreement of the Free People of England*, p. 2.
44   John Lilburne, Richard Overton, Thomas Prince, William Walwyn, *A Manifestation* (1649), p. 6.
45   Lilburne, *Legall Fundamentall Liberties*, p. 59.
46   Walwyn, *The Power of Love* 'To the Reader', see also p. 37 and *Walwyns Just Defence*, pp. 22–4. Lilburne was of the same opinion, see for example, *The Just Defence of John Lilburne* (1653), p. 2.

would informe: nor erronious but I would rectifie, nor vicious but I would reclaim, nor cruel, but I would moderate and reduce to Clemency: I am as much grieved that any man should be so unhappy as to be cruel and unjust, as that any man should suffer by cruelty or injustice . . . it is from this disposition in me, that I have engaged myself in publick affairs.' 'I esteeme it a high part of true religion to promote common justice. . . .'[47]

Lilburne saw the spread of practical Christianity as a way of reducing litigation,[48] and the Levellers generally sought in their specific proposals to practise 'true religion'. In the petition of March 1647, for example, they asked for 'powerful means to keep men, women, and children from begging and wickednesse that this nation may be no longer a shame to Christianity therein', and also for a 'just, speedy, plaine and unburthensome way for deciding controversies and suits in Law, and reduce all Lawes to the nearest agreement with Christianity'.[49]

Here, of course, one is very close to the relationship between the Levellers' views of practical Christianity and the religious sanction implicit in their view of equity. On occasion this relationship becomes explicit. In his narration in *A Picture of the Council of State*, Richard Overton urged that his piety should not be judged by his 'personal infirmities' but by 'my Integrity and Uprightness to the Commonwealth, to whatsoever my understanding tells me is for the good of mankind, for the safety, freedom, and tranquillity of my Country, happinesse and prosperity of my Neighbours, to do to my neighbour as I would be done by, and for the freedom and protection of Religious people. . . .'[50]

The important point about practical Christianity was that, like the Levellers' notion of equity to which it was related, it was a vague and pragmatic concept, providing a strong moral imperative but no precise means of defining forms and procedures: '. . . wherefore,' asked John Wildman, 'have God united people into a body or Society, or Nation? is't not for this that everyone should be helpful each to other and endeav-

---

47   Walwyn, *A Whisper in the Eare of Mr. Thomas Edwards*, pp. 3, 5. On occasion, Walwyn visualized socially radical effects arising from the practice of practical Christianity: '. . . it will empty the fullest Baggs: and pluck downe the highest plumes.' *A Still and Soft Voice*, pp. 8–9
48   Lilburne, *Englands Birth Right Justified*, p. 37.
49   *To the Right Honourable and Supreme Authority of this Nation, the Commons in Parliament Assembled* (March 1647), p. 6 clause 12, p. 5 clause 7.
50   John Lilburne, Richard Overton, Thomas Prince, *A Picture of the Councel of State* (1649), p. 43. See also Walwyn, *Walwyns Just Defence*, pp. 10–12. Walwyn here quotes Montaigne on the need for a practised Christianity and justifies himself by saying, 'I recite these passages, because I am in love with them [his adversaries], wishing them also of the same mind, for I wish them no worse then I wish to my self. . . .'

our one anothers good mutually.'[51] The constitutional theorist might be forgiven for thinking that this answer was no answer. But it was precisely the type of answer that the Levellers kept on giving and its vague generality is indicative of their pragmatism.

The Levellers were true pragmatists in the sense that they were concerned about consequences rather than about forms in themselves.[52] Despite all that has been written about them as constitutional idealists and innovators, forms always remained secondary to them. They held with Henry Parker, John Goodwin and Roger Williams that God had endorsed government in general but not any particular form of government.[53]

This naturally had the effect of freeing them from adherence to traditional forms: 'now unto things in themselves disputable and uncertaine,' wrote Walwyn, 'as there is no reason why any man should be bound expressly to any one forme, further than his judgement and conscience doe agree thereunto, even so ought the whole Nation to be free therein to alter and change the publique forme, as may best stand with the safety and freedome of the people. For the Parliament is ever at libertie to make the people more free from burthens and oppressions of any nature but in things appertaining to the universall Rules of common equitie and justice, all men and all Authority in the world are bound.'[54] Here the limitation on pragmatism appears to be equity, which was itself, as applied by the Levellers, a pragmatic concept.

In *Strength Out of Weaknesse*, Lilburne asserted that 'the People may by a common consent alter their Government (for no Form of Civil Government is *Iure Divino*).'[55] Elsewhere the Levellers suggested that the life of all things was in their right use and application, not in the forms they took;[56] 'the just freedom and happiness of a Nation, being above all constitutions, whether of Kings, Parliaments or any other'.[57] This was felt to be so too in relation to church government. They repeat-

51 Wildman, *Truths Triumph*, p. 4.
52 See Frank, *The Levellers*, Ch. X; Zagorin, *A History of Political Thought*, p. 27.
53 John Wildman at the Putney debates declared 'we cannot find anything in the word of God of what is fit to be done in civil matters', but he added significantly that justice, mercy, peace and meekness are of God. Woodhouse, *Puritanism and Liberty*, p. 108. *Cf.* Henry Parker, *Observations Upon Some of his Majesties late Answers and Expresses* (1642), p. 1; John Goodwin, *Anti-Cavalierisme* (1642), pp. 7–8; Roger Williams, *The Bloudy Tenent* (1644), p. 196.
54 Walwyn, *Englands Lamentable Slavery*, p. 6.
55 Lilburne, *Strength out of Weaknesse*, p. 12.
56 Lilburne, Overton, Prince, Walwyn, *An Agreement of the Free People of England* (1649), p. 2.
57 Walwyn, *The Bloody Project*, p. 13.

edly pronounced themselves prepared to accept an unspecified form of state-sponsored church provided that there was no coercion of individuals.[58]

Walwyn adopted the same pragmatic approach in his search for true doctrine. 'I carry with me in all places,' he wrote, 'a Touchstone that tryeth all things and labours to hold nothing but what upon plain grounds appeareth good and usefull: I abandon all niceties and useless things: my manner is in all disputes reasonings and discourses, to enquire what is the use: and if I find it not very materiall, I abandon it, there are plain usefull doctrines sufficient to give peace to my mind: direction and comfort to my life: and to draw all men to a consideration of things evidently usefull, hath been a speciall cause that I have applyed my selfe in a friendly manner unto all.'[59]

Many of the utterances of the Levellers appear obviously question-begging, expressive of the confused, good intentions of the apolitical: 'That as the Laws ought to be equal, so they must be good, and not evidently destructive to the safety and well being of the people.'[60] In A Manifestation, the Leveller leaders justified the efforts of their dying campaign on the grounds that 'if it produces not so good a settlement as ought to be, yet certainly it will prevent its being so bad as otherwise it would be.'[61] These rather callow statements become more readily understood if the essential Christian pragmatism which stands behind them be remembered.

This can also help to explain the Levellers' willingness to chop and change the details of their programmatic statements, their little analysed but remarkable constitutional inconsistence.[62] It was possible for them to appear as republicans and as constitutional monarchists,[63] to take a democratic stance and then advocate a severely limited

58   See, for example, Lilburne, *A Copie of a Letter to Mr. William Prynne*, p. 7. As D. B. Robertson points out, 'Establishment *per se* was not the question', *Religious Foundations*, p. 8.
59   Walwyn, *A Whisper in the Eare of Mr. Thomas Edwards*, p. 10.
60   *An Agreement of the People for a firme and present Peace, upon grounds of common-right and freedome* (November 1647) clause IV, reserve 5, in Wolfe, *Leveller Manifestoes*, p. 228.
61   Lilburne, Overton, Prince, Walwyn, *A Manifestation*, p. 4.
62   See J. C. Davis, 'The Levellers and Democracy', *Past and Present* No. 40 (1968), p. 180.
63   For examples of the Levellers as republicans, see John Wildman, *Putney Projects or the Old Serpent in a new Forme* (1647), pp. 15–22; John Lilburne, *Englands New Chains Discovered* (1649), p. 159; as monarchists, John Lilburne, *An Impeachment of High Treason against Oliver Cromwel, and his son in Law Henry Ireton Esquires* (1649), p. 8; Lilburne, *Strength Out of Weaknesse*, p. 12; Lilburne, *Come Out of her my People*, p. 14.

franchise,[64] or to say nothing about the franchise at all,[65] because these, while important, were not the essence. They were more concerned with the quality of administration than with constitutional forms, although they recognized that the former could be influenced by the latter: 'give us but Common Right, some foundations, some boundaries, some certainty of Law, and a good Government; that now when there is so high discourse of Freedom, we may be delivered from will, power, and meere arbitrary discretion, and we shall be satisfied.'[66] Like others, they were not 'wedded and glued to forms of government'.

Even the proposal of an Agreement of the People was only a device, never an article of faith with them. They might assert the correct way of introducing such an Agreement but, in itself, it was never a cardinal feature of their activity. The fact that they produced three different versions within a year and a half is indicative of their pragmatic attitude to it.

The importance of the Agreements in Leveller strategy and thinking has been generally overrated. The Levellers never suggested that an Agreement of the People was the only means by which a national settlement could be attained. They appear to have seen the device in a more limited way, as a medium for joint action with the army and in fact the army was indispensable to the strategy of the Agreement because it offered the only feasible means of popular subscription on a national basis. The third Agreement of 1 May 1649 is the only Leveller Agreement addressed directly to the nation and even here the document appeals over the heads of the officers to the mutinous regiments of the army. Lilburne and Wildman, the main exponents of the Agreement idea among the civilian Levellers, had also the strongest military connections and background. The idea itself may have originated in the example of the army's Solemn Engagement of June 1647, rather than in covenant theology. Rainborough asked significantly, at the Putney debates, that the Levellers' first Agreement be judged by the standard of

---

64 For examples of the Levellers as democrats, see John Lilburne, *Rash Oaths Unwarrantable* (1647), p. 50; as exponents of a limited franchise, *To the Supream Authority of England, the Commons assembled in Parliament. The Earnest Petition of many Free-born People of this Nation* (January 1648), in Wolfe, *Leveller Manifestoes*, p. 269. See also the discussion in Keith Thomas, 'The Levellers and the Franchise', in G. E. Aylmer (ed.), *The Interregnum: The Quest For Settlement 1646–1660* (London, 1972), pp. 57–78.

65 *To the Right Honourable the Commons of England in Parliament Assembled. The humble Petition of divers wel affected Persons* (September 1648) in Wolfe, *Leveller Manifestoes*, pp. 283–90. (Henceforth referred to as the petition of 11 September 1648.) This called for annual elections but said nothing on the franchise although it was subsequently considered by the Levellers to be a most important statement.

66 Walwyn, *Walwyn's Just Defence*, p. 5.

the Solemn Engagement.[67] The idea of an Agreement appears to have had no independent appeal to the Levellers. As early as April 1645, Overton had suggested a national covenant to engage everyone in public freedom,[68] but during the next two and a half years there was no response from his colleagues.

The Agreement then was a compromise device used when the Levellers wished to work with the army. Their flexibility in relation to its details and implementation can best be illustrated by their changing attitude to the officers' Agreement, presented to the House of Commons in January 1649. In June 1649 Lilburne roundly condemned it and its presentation to parliament, as contrary to the whole spirit of an Agreement.[69] Yet two months earlier, in April, Lilburne and Overton had offered to be satisfied with the officers' Agreement, subject to some amendment of the clauses concerning religious liberty.[70] In A Manifestation, also published in April, the Leveller leaders had proclaimed that they would have accepted the officers' Agreement had it been put in execution.[71] As late as May 1652 Lilburne was still urging the Grandees to go back to it.[72] Indeed the Levellers' rejection of the officers' Agreement of January 1649, and the breach with the Independent and Baptist congregations that this apparently resulted in, has never been satisfactorily explained.

The use of Agreements remained an extraordinary device, and the Levellers went on petitioning. After each of their failures to negotiate an Agreement with the army they reverted to petitions. Moreover, it was in their petitions that the Levellers advanced their original constitutional ideas, as they did, for example, in The Case of the Army and the great petitions of November 1647, January 1648 and September 1648. The last of these, the petition of 11 September 1648, has been rightly described as 'the most important of the Levellers' proposals'.[73] The point here is that, although it said nothing about the franchise, the Levellers appear to have regarded it as in many ways

67   Woodhouse, Puritanism and Liberty, p. 47. The whole issue involved in the preliminary dispute over engagements has to be seen against this background.
68   Overton, The Araignement of Mr. Persecution, p. 30.
69   Lilburne, Legall Fundamentall Liberties, pp. 35–41. See also Lilburne's detailed criticisms in Englands New Chains Discovered.
70   Lilburne, Overton, Prince, A Picture of the Councel of State, pp. 22, 37.
71   Lilburne, Overton, Prince, Walwyn, A Manifestation, p. 7.
72   Lilburne, As You Were (1652) cited in Haller and Davies, Leveller Tracts, p. 32.
73   Brailsford, The Levellers, p. 350. See also Haller and Davies, Leveller Tracts, p. 147. Thomas May described it as the petition 'which broke the Ice' with regard to demands for justice against Charles I and the fomentors of the second civil war. Thomas May, A Breviary of the History of the Parliament of England (1655) in Maseres, Select Tracts (1815), Vol. I, p. 127.

more important than their second (December 1648) and third (May 1649) Agreements.

In their petition of January 1649 they described themselves as 'Presenters and Promoters of the late Large Petition of September 11 MDCXLVIII' rather than as promoters of the Second Agreement.[74] Again in March 1649 Lilburne, Overton and Prince described themselves as 'presenters and approvers of the later large Petition of the Eleventh of September 1648'.[75] Against the charge of economic levelling readers were referred to the September petition rather than the second Agreement, although such a purpose was disavowed in both documents.[76] Even later, after the publication of their third Agreement (1 May 1649), the Leveller leaders were still appealing back to the petition of 11 September 1648 as the full and crucial statement.[77]

This process of appealing, beyond the second and third Agreements, back to the September petition may indicate that, in negotiating with the army, the Leveller leaders had risked alienating their London support and that in their breach with the Grandees they sought to appeal to a platform which had united that support. More important in this context, however, the willingness to shift tactics, the flexibility in relation to forms that the Levellers reveal, is symptomatic of their fundamental pragmatism.

That pragmatism, however, was conditioned by a morality basically Christian, expressed in terms of equity and practical Christianity. It was modified by a view of man which gave them their one element of formal consistency.

It has been rightly insisted by Macpherson that the Levellers' theory of possessive individualism or human self-propriety forms a key feature of their thought.[78] What has not been sufficiently emphasized is that the

---

74 *To the Right Honourable, the Supreme Authority of this Nation, The Commons of England in Parliament Assembled. The humble Petition of firm and constant Friends to the Parliament and Common-wealth, Presenters and Promotors of the late Large Petition of September 11 MDCXLVIII* (19 January 1649). Lilburne similarly described his followers on the title page of *Englands New Chains Discovered*, a petition presented to the Rump on 26 February 1649.
75 John Lilburne, Richard Overton, Thomas Prince, *The Second Part of Englands New Chains Discovered* (March 1649) title page.
76 Lilburne, Overton, Prince, Walwyn, *A Manifestation*, p. 4. See the Petition of 11 September 1648 p. 6; *Foundations of Freedom; or an Agreement of the People* (December 1648) in Wolfe, *Leveller Manifestoes*, p. 301.
77 Walwyn, *Walwyn's Just Defence* (May/June? 1649), p. 27; Richard Overton, *The Baiting of the Great Bull of Bashan Unfolded and Presented to the Affecters and approvers of the PETITION of the 11 Sept. 1648* (July 1649), p. 42; Lilburne, *An Impeachment of High Treason* (August 1649), pp. 1, 5; Lilburne, *Strength Out of Weaknesse* (October 1649), p. 2.
78 Macpherson, *The Political Theory of Possessive Individualism*, Ch. III and pp. 3, 265–7.

Levellers saw man primarily as a moral entity or agency and that their view of self-propriety was conditioned by this. It is true that, while a writer like Henry Robinson saw self-propriety only by analogy,[79] the Levellers saw it as rooted in the nature of man.[80] Nevertheless, for them a man's property in himself was a limited property, over which he could exercise only a limited control, the function of which was a moral and religious stewardship.[81]

The Levellers did not conceive man's right of possession in his own person and capacities as absolute. Man, in relation to himself, had, as it were, a leasehold rather than freehold. His property was limited since in certain respects he could not alienate it. The most important of these inalienable prerogatives was his capacity for religious belief. Moreover, this was not only inalienable, but the individual himself was seen as having little control over it. In *A Compassionate Samaritane* Walwyn argued that man must *necessarily* follow his own reason and arrive at his own conclusions regarding religious belief.[82] Elsewhere, he wrote, 'I have no quarrell to any man, either for unbeleefe or misbeleefe because I judge no man beleeveth any thing but what he cannot choose but beleeve.'[83] Since 'whatsoever is not of faith is sin' man's property in his conscience was both naturally and morally inalienable.[84] It followed that 'no man can refer matters of religion to any other regulation. And what cannot be given cannot be received. . . .' Therefore the civil magistrate had no authority in matters of religion.[85]

Overton reached the same conclusion in a very similar way. There could be no compulsion in religion, 'for wee could not conferre a Power that was not in ourselves, there being none of us, that can without wilfull sinne binde ourselves to worship God after any other way, then what (to a tittle) in our owne particular understandings, wee approve to be just.'[86]

79   See, for example, Henry Robinson, *Liberty of Conscience* (1644), pp. 19, 38, 40.
80   See, for example, Richard Overton, *An Arrow Against All Tyrants and Tyranny* (1646), p. 3: 'To every individual in nature is given an individuall property by nature . . .'; p. 5 'For by nature we are the sons of Adam, and from him have legitimately derived a naturall propriety, right and freedome. . . .'
81   *Cf.* Macpherson, *Possessive Individualism*, p. 158. 'They can claim the distinction of being the first political theorists to assert a natural right to property for which the individual owes nothing to society and which entails none of those duties entailed in the earlier doctrine of stewardship.'
82   Walwyn, *Compassionate Samaritane*, p. 7.
83   Walwyn, *A Still and Soft Voice*, p. 15.
84   Walwyn, *A Prediction of Mr. Edwards his Conversion*, p. 4; *Compassionate Samaritane*, p. 43.
85   Walwyn, *A helpe to the right understanding of a Discourse concerning Independency*, p. 4. See Macpherson, *Possessive Individualism*, p. 145.
86   Overton, *A Remonstrance*, p. 12.

The limitations on one's rights to exploit one's capacity, to alienate aspects of one's property in oneself, also extended to man's capacity to injure himself and to injure others.[87] It was this inalienable and limited quality of self-propriety, that enabled Sexby at Putney to distinguish between it and real property: 'We have had little propriety in the kingdom as to our estates, yet we have had a birthright.'[88]

Most important, it was from this concept of limited self-propriety that the notion of limited government so characteristic of the Levellers was derived. Richard Overton demonstrated the link between the two most clearly. '. . . all iust humaine powers,' he argued, 'are but betrusted, confer'd and conveyed by ioynt and common consent, for to every individual in nature, is given an individuall propriety by nature, not to be invaded or usurped by any (as in mine Arrow against tyranny is proved and discovered more at large) for every one as he is himselfe hath a selfe propriety, else could not be himselfe, and on this no second may presume without consent.' But at the same time governments were impowered by men only 'for their severall weales, safeties and freedomes, and no otherwise: for as by nature, no man may abuse, beat, torment or afflict himself; so by nature, no man may give that power to another, seeing he may not doe it himselfe, for no more can be communicated from the generall then is included in the particulars, whereof the generall is compounded.'[89] This was what Overton called, on occasion, the 'defensive principle'. Against it 'no degrees, orders or titles amongst men can or may prevaill, all degrees, orders and titles, all Lawes, Customs and manners amongst men must be subject to give place and yeeld thereunto, and it unto none, for all degrees and titles Magisteriall, whether emperiall, regall, Parliamentarie, or otherwise are all subservient to popular safety . . . for without it can be no humane society, cohabitation or being, which above all earthly things must be maintained, as the earthly soveraigne good of mankind, let what or who will perish, or be confounded, for mankind must be preserved upon the earth and to this preservation, all the Children of men have an equall title by Birth, *none to be deprived thereof*, but such as are enemies thereto, and this is the groundwork that God in nature hath laid for all commonwealths, for all Governours and Governments amongst men, for all their laws executions and administrations.'[90]

87   See, for example, Walwyn, *The Bloody Project*, pp. 1–4; Overton, *An Arrow Against All Tyrants*, p. 4.
88   Woodhouse, *Puritanism and Liberty*, p. 69.
89   Overton, *An Appeale*, in Wolfe, *Leveller Manifestoes*, p. 162. *Cf.* Overton, *An Arrow Against All Tyrants*, p. 4.
90   Overton, *An Appeale*, in Wolfe, *Leveller Manifestoes*, p. 178. (My italics.)

This last point brings out the third aspect of self-propriety as the Levellers saw it. Not only was it limited and in part inalienable. It was also God-given, a trust to be exercised with traditional Christian stewardship. 'From this fountain or root,' wrote Overton of self-propriety, 'all just humaine powers take their original; not immediately from God (as Kings usually plead their prerogative) but mediatly by the hand of nature, as from the represented to the representors; for originally, God hath implanted them in the creature, and from the creature those powers immediately proceed; and no further: and no more may be communicated then stands for the better being, weale, or safety thereof: and this is mans prerogative and no further, so much and no more may be given or received thereof: even so much as is conducent to a better being, more safety and freedome, and no more; he that gives more, sins against his owne flesh. . . .'[91] Walwyn believed that the right, the equitable exercise of a man's self-propriety would 'empty the fullest Baggs: and pluck downe the highest plumes'.[92]

The Levellers' recurrent emphasis on practical Christianity is itself illustrative of their belief that it was only as stewards that men held their own persons. '. . . no man is born for himself only,' they declared in 1648, 'but obliged by the Laws of Nature (which reaches all) of Christianity (which engages us as Christians) and of Publick Societie and Government, to employ our endeavours for the advancement of a communitative Happinesse, of equall concernment to others as ourselves. . . .'[93]

In consequence of this the individual had definite conscientious obligations which could not be delegated. Walwyn believed that those who sought true religion must try all faiths: ''tis your selfe must doe it, you are not to trust to the authority of any man, or to any man's relation: you will finde upon tryall that scarcely any opinion hath been truly reported to you.'[94] Or again, 'Whatsoever is not founded on faith is sin, and . . . every man ought to be fully persuaded of the trueness of that way wherein he serveth the Lord.'[95]

Similarly Lilburne argued that one of the two great evils facing those who professed religion was 'living upon other mens light, takeing all for Gospel which Learned men say without tryall'. 'Carnal Professours'

---

91   Overton, *An Arrow Against All Tyrants*, p. 4.
92   Walwyn, *A Still and Soft Voice*, pp. 8–9.
93   Lilburne, Overton, Prince, Walwyn, *A Manifestation*, p. 3. See also Walwyn, *Power of Love*, p. 39.
94   Walwyn, *Power of Love*, p. 97.
95   Walwyn, *A Compassionate Samaritane*, p. 43; *Cf.* Walwyn, *A whisper in the Eare of Mr. Thomas Edwards*, p. 5; *A Prediction of Mr. Thomas Edwards his Conversion*, p. 40; *The Vanitie of the Present Churches*, p. 50.

such as these were satisfied with forms only.[96] This attitude spilled over into Lilburne's political activity. He was reported by his enemies as insisting with his agents on the necessity 'to inform the people of their Liberties and Privileges; and not only to get their hands to the Petition, for (said he) I would not give three pence for ten thousand hands.'[97] Because of the commission with which he was entrusted man's activity had to be conscientious.

If this were to be so, however, if men were to act conscientiously in their relations with God and with other men, if they were to exercise their self-propriety as real stewards, then they must be free from compulsion or restraint in matters of conscience. The Levellers' demand for toleration thus sprang from their assumptions about self-propriety and its limited nature. Moreover, not only was this essential demand for freedom of belief and practice the most consistent feature of the Leveller programme, it was also the basis upon which were built in pragmatic fashion, all their further constitutional demands.

The consistency of the Levellers in demanding liberty of conscience is generally recognized. All three of their Agreements of the People set down as the first power withheld from government that of compulsion in religious observance. They were all equally clear against military impressment.[98] The fact that some of the Levellers seem to have believed that the fight for liberty of conscience was the primary purpose of the movement is not so frequently commented upon by historians.

'Of all liberty,' wrote Walwyn, 'liberty of conscience is the greatest; and where that is not a true Christian findeth none.'[99] In 1646 he believed that this was the main issue at stake. He held the same view three years later.[100] Captain Clarke, at the Whitehall debates, saw the important petition of 11 September 1648 as principally concerned with freedom of conscience.[101] Lilburne himself believed the same issue to have been the stumbling block in negotiations between the army, the Independents and the Levellers in late 1648.[102]

Even a superficial review of the early history of the Levellers reveals how their political programme grew out of their anxiety over freedom

96   Lilburne, *An Answer to Nine Arguments* 'To the Reader'; *Come Out of Her my People*, p. 4. *Cf.* Walwyn's 'morall Christians', *A Still and Soft Voice*, pp. 2–3.
97   *A Declaration of Some Proceedings*, p. 14. See also Walwyn's, *The Bloody Project*, for instance, on this in relation to war service.
98   Wolfe, *Leveller Manifestoes*, pp. 227, 300, 405.
99   Walwyn, *A Word More*, p. 5, quoted in Schenk, *The Concern for Social Justice*, p. 48.
100   Walwyn, *A Whisper in the Eare of Mr. Thomas Edwards*, p. 12; *Walwyn's Just Defence*, pp. 3–4.
101   Woodhouse, *Puritanism and Liberty*, p. 141.
102   Lilburne, *Legall Fundamentall Liberties*, pp. 34–5.

of conscience. The polemical careers of Lilburne, Walwyn and Overton all began, in the late 1630s and early 1640s, with demands for religious freedom and assaults on the pursuit of heresy by the established authorities. In 1645 the renewed threat from the Presbyterians and the imprisonment of John Lilburne drew those three together. In the first four months of that year, Walwyn produced *The Compassionate Samaritane* and *A helpe to the right understanding of a Discourse concerning Independency*; Lilburne published *A Copie of a letter to Mr. William Prinne, Esquire*,[103] and Overton, *The Araignement of Mr. Persecution*. All these tracts were concerned with religious liberty and the Presbyterian threat to it.

In May and June 1645, Lilburne was before the Committee of Examinations concerning his part in the controversy with Prynne, and more particularly for his remarks on the power of magistrates in religious matters. At this time, he and Walwyn appear to have been in direct association.[104] They were both involved in the action against Lenthall which led to Lilburne's arrest on 19 July.

From July to October 1645, Lilburne was in prison and this provided the second focus around which a 'coherent and purposeful' group developed.[105] When he published *Englands Birth Right Justified* in October, Lilburne still presented freedom of conscience as the central issue.[106] In order to defend it, however, he felt obliged to deal with the distinction between the equity and the letter of the law, with the logic of parliament's fight for freedom, the danger of vested interests, foremost among which was the monopoly of preaching, and the injustice of the Solemn League and Covenant. Thus an accretion of political and legal attitudes was building around the basic cause of liberty of conscience.

Similarly, in *Englands Lamentable Slavery* (October 1645) Walwyn argued that liberty of conscience was the main issue but that in order to secure it the authorities must be made accountable. His attitude to forms remained pragmatic. They were to be judged by the liberty they secured.[107]

In 1646 while the fight for liberty of conscience was still to the fore,[108] the imprisonment of Lilburne by the House of Lords in June, followed

103   Haller suggested that this was printed by Richard Overton or someone associated with him. *Tracts on Liberty in the Puritan Revolution*, Vol. III, p. 179.
104   Gregg, *Free-Born John*, pp. 116–19.
105   *ibid.* p. 134.
106   Lilburne, *Englands Birth Right Justified* Preamble.
107   Walwyn, *Englands Lamentable Slavery*, pp. 6–7.
108   Walwyn wrote seven tracts on liberty of conscience between January and October 1646.

by that of Overton in August, renewed the Levellers' awareness that the issue of that fight was bound up with legal and constitutional problems. The relevance of these constitutional concerns to those of religious freedom and the Levellers' view of man's limited self-propriety is well illustrated in Overton's *A Remonstrance of Many Thousand Citizens* (July 1646). Here, after protesting against Lilburne's imprisonment, Overton argued that parliament was merely a convenience, chosen by the people for their welfare and endowed by them with a strictly limited trust. It followed that their powers in relation to church government must be limited too. 'Yee may propose what Forme yee conceive best, and most available for Information and well-being of the Nation, and may perswade and invite thereunto, but compell, yee cannot justly; for ye have no Power from Us to doe, nor could you have; for wee could not conferre a Power that was not in our selves, there being none of us that can without wilfull sinne bind our selves to worship God after any other way, then what (to a tittle) in our owne particular understandings we approve to be just.'[109]

An Arrow Against All Tyrants (October 1646) was directed by Overton against the twin threats from the House of Lords' illegal claim to jurisdiction over commoners and from 'the most unnaturall, tyrannical, bloodthirsty desires and continuall endevour of the Clergy, against the contrary minded in matters of conscience'.[110] Although the tract was concerned primarily with the constitutional and legal threat emanating from the House of Lords, Overton thought it appropriate to begin with his fullest exposition of the concept of self-propriety.

This was merely carried a stage further in the Levellers' petition of March 1647. Here again the two most important areas of concern, religious freedom and legal rights, were seen as interconnected,[111] but specific constitutional reforms were now proposed. The burning of this petition by order of the House of Commons in May 1647 sealed the emergence of the Levellers as a movement of constitutional reform. They could now visualize England as returned to a state of nature and consequently accept as necessary the strategy of appealing to the army and through it to the people at large.

The constitutional proposals of the Levellers were thus in part derived from their fear that, without some such arrangements, freedom of conscience could not be guaranteed. At the Whitehall debates Clarke argued that, since the magistrate had always usurped power

109   Overton, *A Remonstrance*, p. 12.
110   Overton, *An Arrow Against All Tyrants*, pp. 6, 12.
111   *To the Right Honourable and Supreme Authority of this Nation, the Commons in Parliament assembled* (March 1647), in Wolfe, *Leveller Manifestoes*, p. 136.

over conscience, they ought now to reserve it.[112] What D. B. Robertson has said of the third Agreement may be applied to the whole Leveller effort to find an acceptable constitution: it was 'an attempt . . . to prevent men from getting into a position to molest their neighbours.'[113]

That men in power would be tempted to excess, to violation of the self-propriety of others, was something that the Leveller leaders recognized early in their activity: 'standing water will speedily corrupt, if it have not fresh running springs to feed it, though it were never so pure at first'.[114] At Whitehall, Wildman argued that the magistrate was 'more probable to err than the people that have no power in their hands, the probability is greater that he will destroy what is good than prevent what is evil.'[115] 'We have proposed such an Establishment,' professed the Leveller leaders in one of their last joint statements, 'as supposing men to be too flexible and yeelding to world Temptations, they should not yet have a means or opportunity either to injure particulars, or prejudice the Publick, without extreme hazard and apparent danger to themselves.'[116]

In this respect, the third Agreement only epitomizes what is to be found elsewhere. The concern there shown for the details of representation, legislative quorums, the ineligibility of public officials for election, the restriction against the election of the same people to successive Representatives; the fundamental provisions against compulsion or interference in religion, against impressment, self-incrimination, legal injustice, trade restrictions and more besides; all these things stem from the fear that those in authority, if unchecked, would not leave individuals free to exercise their stewardship in their own persons: 'having by wofull experience found the prevalence of corrupt interests powerfully inclining most men once entrusted with authority, to pervert the same to their own domination and to the prejudice of our Peace and Liberties. . . .'[117]

William Haller once wrote that for the Levellers, 'there could be no liberty without toleration. . . .'[118] It would be truer to say that for them there could be no toleration without civil liberty. The distinction is more than a marginal one for without it one fails to appreciate the fact that

112 Woodhouse, *Puritanism and Liberty*, pp. 141–2.
113 Robertson, *Religious Foundations*, p. 104.
114 Lilburne, *Englands Birth Right Justified*, p. 33.
115 Woodhouse, *Puritanism and Liberty*, p. 161.
116 Lilburne, Overton, Prince, Walwyn, *A Manifestation*, p. 7.
117 Lilburne, Overton, Prince, Walwyn, *An Agreement of the Free People of England*, p. 5.
118 Haller, *Tracts on Liberty*, Vol. I, p. 87. *Cf.* Zagorin, *A History of Political thought*, p. 7.

their programmatic statements were pragmatically conceived; that their pragmatism was modified by Christian values expressed in their doctrines of equity and practical Christianity, and by their concept of man's limited self-propriety, that is to say by the fundamental place of traditional Christian stewardship in their social thinking.

13

Charles Stuart, That Man of Blood

Patricia Crawford

Originally appeared as Patricia Crawford, 'Charles Stuart, That Man of Blood' in *Journal of British Studies* 16 (1977): 41–61. © Copyright by The North American Conference on British Studies. All rights reserved. Reproduced by permission of The University of Chicago Press.

I

By 1648 in England many of parliament's supporters believed that peace was as far away as ever. The members of parliament who had declared they were fighting to rescue the king from the hands of his evil counsellors may have rethought their views about the personal responsibility of the king, but they still believed that the only viable settlement would be one based upon agreement between king and parliament. Consequently they had dispatched, with wearisome monotony, negotiators and messengers with propositions for peace to the king. Their initiatives were always destroyed in the last resort because Charles refused the terms offered, but apart from governing without him for the time being, the members of parliament could think of nothing else but a settlement based on agreement with Charles. The political thinking of the majorities in both Houses was bound by convention: a king was essential. Outside parliament, pamphleteers had questioned the importance of the king, but parliament's view was not seriously threatened until 1647 when it showed itself incapable of settling the kingdom and the Army showed a willingness to intervene in politics. The outbreak of the second Civil War in 1648 convinced the soldiers that parliament's policies of either seeking terms with the king or of ignoring him were alike futile and dangerous. So long as Charles remained alive, at the center of roy-

I wish to thank my friends who have helped with this article, especially Dr. D. E. Kennedy who first introduced me to the idea of blood guilt.

alist hopes, so long would wars continue and lives be lost. At this point the Army spoke of the king in a new way. No longer was he King Charles, but Charles Stuart, a man of blood. Convinced that Charles was one against whom the Lord had set his face, the Army considered it imperative that he be brought to justice.

A man of blood was one who shed innocent blood, and with whom the Lord would have no peace. To speak of Charles I in this way swept aside the sacredness of his person. For King Charles I was a partly sacred person.[1] Anointed at his coronation, the Lord's powerful protection encompassed him: 'Touch not mine anointed' was the Lord's command. Charles claimed the ancient mystical power to heal the disease known as the King's Evil, as his predecessors had done, and he continued during the Civil Wars, to touch those afflicted, although the parliamentarians tried to brand this as superstitious by a declaration in April 1647.[2] More effective in destroying Charles's sacredness was the belief, of equally ancient pedigree, that the shedding of blood polluted him who shed it. Blood guilt could render null the discharge of a sacred function: a king polluted by blood could be a king no more. Operating on another level from rational political argument, discussion of blood guilt effectively diminished the aura around King Charles. How could Charles, demanded Milton, 'think to scape unquestionable, as a thing divine, in respect of whom so many thousand Christians destroy'd, should lie unaccounted for, polluting with their slaughtered carcasses all the land over, and crying for vengeance against the living that should have righted them.'[3]

Ideas about blood guilt and retribution for the shedding of blood have a long history in many societies. From Anglo-Saxon times there were laws governing bloodshed in England. By the Norman Conquest rules had been established so that murder did not necessarily lead to a blood vendetta but could be expiated by a money payment. Gradually the king claimed jurisdiction over homicide, and by the seventeenth century the practice of the law had been modified to take account of motive, so that the unintentional shedding of blood would lead the courts to recommend the king's pardon.[4] Blood guilt still tarnished the innocent slayer.

1 For a discussion of this see M. Bloch, *The Royal Touch*, trans. J. E. Armstrong (London, 1973), and especially pp. 207–10.
2 *Journals of the House of Commons*, II, 151.
3 John Milton, *The Tenure of Kings and Magistrates*, in *The Works of John Milton* (New York, 1931–38), V, 20.
4 F. L. Attenborough (ed.), *The Laws of the Earliest English Kings*, (Cambridge, 1922). J. E. A. Jolliffe (ed.), *The Constitutional History of Medieval England from the English Settlement to 1485* (4th edn.; London, 1961), pp. 3–5. D. Whitelock (ed.), *English Historical Documents c. 500–1042* (London, 1955), pp. 391–92. F. Pollock and F. W. Maitland, *The History of English Law* (2nd ed.; Cambridge, 1923), II, 448–88.

Blood was a pollutant which, while it might no longer incite revenge, could exclude a man from certain rites. If, for example, a man were unintentionally guilty of shedding blood, it could debar him from ordination in the Church.[5] The implications of blood guilt for one already a priest were investigated in 1621 in the case of the Archbishop of Canterbury who accidentally shot a keeper while hunting. John Williams, Bishop elect of Lincoln, drew to James I's attention the scandal of leaving 'a man of blood, Primate and Patriarch of all his Churches.'[6] Although bloodshed in a church might demand that the church be reconsecrated, ordination had been deemed an indelible rite since the fifth century, and a priest's shedding of blood did not necessitate his reordination.[7] Blood guilt could thus involve moral guilt but not necessarily punishment.

Although blood guilt could be a pollutant which was not punished, a series of Biblical texts could be marshalled to present an argument which demonstrated that blood guilt was a moral offence which someone had a duty to punish. Basically it was blood for blood. According to Scripture, any man who slew another unjustly was guilty of blood, and for this innocent blood the Lord demanded expiation: 'Whoso sheddeth man's blood, by man shall his blood be shed.' (*Genesis*, ix, 6.) If men made no expiation for innocent blood then they too would suffer the Lord's vengeance. A whole land could be defiled by unexpiated blood: 'for blood it defileth the land: and the land cannot be cleansed of the blood that is shed therein, but by the blood of him that shed it.' (*Numbers*, xxxv, 33.) According to the marginal gloss in the Genevan Bible, this duty of expiating innocent blood belonged to the duly consti-

---

5   Salisbury Constitutions of 1236 quoted in *The Canon Law of The Church of England* (London, 1947), p. 60. The seventh-century Council of Toledo had debarred clergy involved in blood judgments from handling the sacraments and from further advancing in holy orders. J. W. Baldwin, *Masters, Princes and Merchants: The Social Views of Peter the Chanter & his Circle* (Princeton, 1970), I, 178. In some instances, blood *per se* could be a pollutant, even for menstruating women. A seventh-century penitential excluded women from the church and from communion during menstruation, and even in the seventeenth century one minister was said to have refused the sacrament to a menstruating woman. J. T. McNeill and H. M. Gamer (eds.), *Medieval Handbooks of Penance* (New York, 1938), p. 197; K. Thomas, *Religion and the Decline of Magic* (London, 1971), p. 38.

6   *Cabala sive scrinia sacra* (London, 1663), p. 260. Williams refused to be consecrated by Archbishop Abbot. Abbot was suspended from his duties while a royal commission investigated his offence. Subsequently a special release was issued under the Great Seal and he was reinstated. S. R. Gardiner, *History of England 1603–1642* (London, 1883–84), IV, 139–40; *Dictionary of National Biography*, articles on George Abbot (1562–1633) and John Williams (1582–1650).

7   *New Catholic Encyclopaedia* (Washington, 1967), Reordination; Churches, dedication of.

tuted civil authority, and 'The exercising of the sworde is forbide to priuate persones.' (*Matthew*, xxvi, 52.)

God had entrusted the duty of enforcing His command against murder to the civil authority – that is, to the law – but in the Civil Wars there were conflicting views of the law. Since all law went in the name of the king, it was legally impossible to prosecute or to sue him. But although the civil authority might fail to avenge the innocent blood shed in the wars, the matter did not end there: innocent blood cried to Heaven for vengeance. While some might argue that this could be left to God – 'Vengeance is mine . . . saith the Lord' – to others it was imperative that somebody should act lest the whole land be defiled and the Lord's terrible wrath fall upon the whole nation. Innocent blood could not be left unavenged.

Themes of the inevitability of punishment for sin and of the Lord's determination that evil doers should be cast out pervade English thought in the sixteenth and seventeenth centuries. People examined events as testimonies of the Lord's purposes, and they thought that a civil war was so serious a national calamity that it must be the divine retribution for national sins. In seeking the causes of the Civil War in 1642, both parliamentarians and royalists looked for the sins which had provoked the Lord. Luxury and debauchery during the years of peace had led God 'to punish us (as we may fear) by a civil war, to make us executioners of Divine vengeance upon ourselves', declared Bulstrode Whitelocke to the House of Commons in July 1642.[8] Clarendon wrote of the inevitable 'castigation of Heaven' for their kingdom 'swoln with long plenty, pride, and excess.'[9]

This is not the place for a lengthy discussion of the role of the theme of divine retribution, nor more specifically of the extent of that of blood guilt, but a few examples from the plays of Shakespeare and from the work of Thomas Beard may illustrate something of the range and variety of the notion of blood guilt. Henry V, on the eve of Agincourt, prayed that God would not think of his father's fault in coming to the throne:

Five hundered poor I have in yearly pay,
Who twice a day their wither'd hands hold up
Toward heaven, to pardon blood;[10]

There might be appeals to the civil magistrate for vengeance, as Lady Capulet appealed to her kinsman, the Prince of Verona:

8   Bulstrode Whitelocke, *Memorials of the English Affairs* (Oxford, 1853), I, 176.
9   Edward Hyde, Earl of Clarendon, *The History of the Rebellion and Civil Wars in England*, ed. W. Dunn Macray (Oxford, 1888), I, 1–4.
10   *King Henry V*, IV, i.

O, the blood is spill'd
Of my dear kinsman! – Prince, as thou art true,
For blood of ours shed blood of Montague.[11]

An individual might take upon himself the responsibility for vengeance, as Bolingbroke did for the blood of his uncle, the Duke of Gloucester:

Which blood, like sacrificing Abels, cries,
Even from the tongueless caverns of the earth;
To me for justice and rough chastisement.[12]

Thomas Beard, Cromwell's schoolmaster, argued in 1597 in *The Theatre of Gods Judgments* that God was determined that murder would be punished 'by those who are in his stead upon the earth, and have the sword of vengeance committed unto them.' Beard showed that the massacre of St. Bartholomew led to the punishment of not just its authors but the whole of France:

> they also felt the severe scourge of Gods justice, partly by civile wars and bloudshed, and partly by famine and other plagues; so that the Lord hath plainly made knowne to the world, how precious in the sight of his most Holy Majestie is the death of innocents, and how impossible it is for cruell murderers to escape unpunished.

Those to whom the sword of justice had been committed had a great responsibility, but should they use their power against those whom they were appointed to defend, 'it must needs follow . . . [they] must receive a greater measure of punishment.'[13] Beard's work was reprinted several times during the seventeenth century, including the year 1648, when it did indeed seem that the land was suffering from 'the severe scourge of Gods justice.'

In discussing usages of the concept of blood guilt during the 1640s it is often impossible to determine whether the idea is being used literally or figuratively. In some instances it may appear to be figurative, but to seventeenth-century Englishmen accustomed to look to Scripture for binding precedents to guide them in practical matters, scriptural language had real meaning. Furthermore, scriptural language offered a respectable way of talking about the king to those who were, for other reasons, convinced that he was an obstacle to the peaceful settlement of the kingdom. Parliament's language, which began and

11   *Romeo and Juliet*, III, i.
12   *Richard II*, I, i.
13   Thomas Beard, *The Theatre of Gods Judgements* (4th edn.; London, 1648), esp. pp. 208, 200, 226.

ended with the premise that the government should be by King, Lords, and Commons, led to a political stalemate. The language of blood guilt offered a new set of arguments for dealing with the king and breaking the deadlock. The question was no longer one of how to compel the king to assent to the peace terms; it was what should be done about the Lord's evident wrath for the nation's blood guiltiness. Thus blood guilt could be used both as a moral imperative to compel people to action, and as an excuse for action, as a respectable device in propaganda for convincing people that something had to be done about Charles.

The following discussion seeks to illustrate the general usage of the concept of blood guilt in the Civil Wars, to show its application to the royalists, and finally its extension to Charles himself. It is beyond the scope of the article to attempt to assess the relative importance of blood guilt in bringing about the king's death,[14] but it will be argued that blood guilt was no mere figure of speech but an inherited complex of notions which played a part in countering the divinity that hedged about the king.

II

Ideas about blood guilt were so much a part of the common cultural heritage for both sides during the Civil Wars that they had to be taken into account in persuading men to take up arms. The casuists on both sides sought to demonstrate that it was their opponents, fighting in an unjust cause, who were guilty of shedding innocent blood. The king told parliament in August 1642 that if it rejected his overtures for peace, 'We have done Our Duty so amply, that God will absolve Us from the Guilt of any of that Blood which must be spilt.' In November 1642, when the Commons considered breaking off peace negotiations with the king, they justified their decision to ignore the king's provocations on the grounds that they did not wish to incur the sin of blood guilt: 'the Guilt of any blood that shall be split may not lie on their Consciences.'[15] John Goodwin, a London minister, attempted to reassure supporters of par-

---

14   For which see P. Crawford, 'A Study of the Attitudes of the Parliamentary Opposition to the Crown, 1642–1649' (M.A. thesis, University of Western Australia, 1964).
15   *Commons Journals*, II, 741, 841. Peace negotiations were renewed because there was a strong group in the House of Commons desperately anxious for peace. J. H. Hexter, *The Reign of King Pym* (Cambridge, Mass., 1941), p. 17.

liament who feared the sin of blood guilt if they fought in an unjust war. The royalists had provoked the quarrel and 'their blood is upon their owne heads.'[16]

Although the parliamentarians blamed the royalists for the war, a civil war seemed a sign of the Lord's resentment against the nation as a whole. In addition to the widespread belief that the war was a punishment sent by God for the nation's sins in general, some searched for the specific sins for which God might be scourging them. Interestingly, one of these was blood guilt, dating from the previous century. A petition of the citizens of London in November 1642 complained that there had been no expiation for the blood of the Marian martyrs.[17] Edmund Calamy's earlier plea to the Commons in a fast sermon before the war to 'Doe something, To purge the land more and more of innocent blood of the Martyrs shed in Queene Marys dayes' had gone unregarded,[18] but in February 1643 the two Houses passed an ordinance for 'an Earnest Confession, and deepe Humiliation for all particular and Nationall Sins.' Listed among the sins was the 'crying and cruell Sin of Bloodshed, that calls aloud for Vengeance,' dating from the time of Mary and her predecessors under whom 'many hundreds of the deare Martyrs and Saints of God lost their precious Lives.' Although the acts by which their innocent blood had been shed were repealed, 'yet to this very day, was never ordained such a solemne Publique and Nationall acknowledgement of this Sin, as might appease the wrath of that Jealous God.'[19] The interesting point is that by taking action parliament accepted the idea that the civil magistrate had a duty to avert the Lord's wrath.

Parliament considered blood guilt in fairly general terms and made no attempt to brand the king or his supporters as men of blood. This restraint is not surprising, since parliament's official policy was that the king could do no wrong and all faults were to be attributed to his evil counsellors. The guilt of these evil counsellors was assessed in a legalistic fashion, as can be seen from the careful calculation in the royalist

16   John Goodwin, *Anti Cavalierisme*, [21 Oct.] 1642, printed in W. Haller (ed.), *Tracts on Liberty in the Puritan Revolution, 1638–1647* (New York, 1934), II, 260, 234; I, 30–32.

17   *Commons Journals*, II, 847.

18   Edmund Calamy, *Gods free Mercy to England*, 23 Feb. 1642, p. 49 (Cornmarket reprint, *Fast Sermons*, 2, p. 191).

19   C. H. Firth and R. S. Rait (eds.), *Acts and Ordinances of the Interregnum, 1642–1660* (London, 1911), I, 80–82. The unexpiated blood of the Marian martyrs was one of the sins listed by Henry Scudder in his fast sermon to the House of Commons on October 30, 1644; Henry Scudder, *Gods warning to England by the Voyce of his Rod*, 1644, p. 19 (Cornmarket reprint, *Fast Sermons*, 13, p. 307).

composition fines.[20] Besides, parliament preferred to use the law when the law would serve rather than enlist more primitive notions of justice. Outside parliament there was a different climate of opinion, and ideas about the royalists and the king as men of blood were taken up in pamphlets and sermons. Edward Bowles, a minister and later Presbyterian, argued against the peace negotiations with the king in January 1643 because they made no expiation for blood guilt:

> how can the Land by this Accomodation be cleansed from bloud, that crying sin, which hath been contracted by this quarrell . . . God will not prosper an Accomodation without the execution of justice upon these bloudthirsty men . . . If the people, especially the Parliament does not their utmost to wash their hands, & cleanse the Land from this innocent & pretious bloud that hath been shed; I feare that bloud . . . will be avenged upon them, which they will believe, when they see their Accomodation turned into an Assassination.[21]

In 1644 *The Souldiers Catechisme*, published unofficially for the parliamentary armies, taught the soldiers that the royalists were enemies of God who fought for the Antichrist, and therefore 'all the blood that hath been shed lies upon their score.' *The Catechisme* called the soldiers to action: 'God now calls upon us to avenge the blood of his Saints that hath been shed in the Land.'[22] Some thought that parliament's declaration blaming the royalists for the war implied a charge of blood guilt which they were prepared to make explicit.[23]

H. R. Trevor-Roper has drawn attention to the bloodthirsty fast sermons preached to the Lords and Commons in October 1644 which he argues announced the imminent death of Archbishop Laud.[24] The ministers assumed that the signs around them showed clearly that the Lord was angry and they sought the cause in an examination of the nation's sins. Blood guilt was one of these and the ministers urged par-

20 M. A. E. Green (ed.), *Calendar of the Proceedings of the Committee for Compounding &c., 1643–1660* (London, 1889). The degrees of guilt were set forth in the propositions which parliament submitted to the king from the Nineteen Propositions onward. For which, see S. R. Gardiner (ed.), *The Constitutional Documents of the Puritan Revolution, 1625–1660* (3rd edn.; Oxford, 1906).
21 [Edward Bowles], *Plaine English*, 12 Jan. 1643, Thomason Tract, (hereafter, T.T.), E. 84. 32, p. 18.
22 [Robert Ram], *The Souldiers Catechisme: Composed for the Parliaments Army* (London, 1644), pp. 7, 8, 14. [Not in Thomason].
23 'So that to sum up all, the Parliament told him plainly in their late letter sent to him at Oxford, That he was guilty of all the innocent blood shed in England, Scotland, & Ireland'; John Lilburne, *Regall Tyrannie Discovered*, 6 Jan. 1647, p. 57.
24 H. R. Trevor-Roper, 'The Fast Sermons of the Long Parliament' in *Religion, the Reformation and Social Change* (New York, 1968), pp. 317–19.

liament to expiate this by punishing the guilty. Edmund Calamy told the Commons that 'all the guilty bloud that God requires you in justice to shed, and you spare; God will require the bloud at your hands.'[25] Henry Scudder listed the sins for which the Lord was now smiting them, among which was the provoking sin of blood guiltiness:

> It cannot go well with a Kingdom where the guilt of innocent blood is not put away by the hand of the Magistrate [Deut., xix., 13] God will not pardon a Land polluted with Innocent blood: he will sooner or later be avenged of it [2 Kings, xxiv, 4.][26]

Francis Woodcock and Edmund Staunton preached in a similar vein.[27] In the context of these sermons the execution of the old Archbishop appears less of a political gesture designed to appease the Scots or to counter the conciliatory effect of the peace negotiations at Uxbridge than a parliamentary attempt to cleanse the land of blood guilt. King Charles also commented upon Laud's death in terms of the Lord's reckoning for blood guilt. The Earl of Strafford's innocent blood, Charles argued, had been a cause of the Lord's judgment against both sides, "but now, this last crying blood being totally theirs, I believe it is no presumption hereafter to hope, that his hand of justice must be heavier upon them, and lighter upon us, looking now upon our cause, having passed by our faults.'[28]

Parliament's reaction to its supporters' discussion of the royalists' blood guilt seems dictated by political circumstances. Parliament disavowed the association when it seemed impolitic and tacitly acquiesced in its use as damaging propaganda at other times. When the commissioners for the king and for parliament met at Uxbridge in January 1645 to negotiate terms for peace, a sermon by Christopher Love scandalised the king's commissioners. Love declared that:

> men who lye under the guilt of much innocent blood are not meet persons to be at peace with, till all the guilt of blood be expiated and avenged, either by the Sword of the Law, or law of the Sword, else a peace can neither be safe nor just.[29]

25   Edmund Calamy, *Englands Antidote against the Plague of Civil Warre*, 22 Oct. 1644, p. 27 (Cornmarket reprint, *Fast Sermons*, 13, p. 153).
26   Scudder, *Gods Warning to England*, p. 23 (Cornmarket, *ibid.*, p. 311).
27   Francis Woodcock, *Christ's Warning-piece*, 30 Oct., 1644, pp. 30–31 (Cornmarket, *ibid.*, pp. 360–61); Edmund Staunton, *Pheneas's Zeal in Execution of Judgement*, 30 Oct. 1644, p. 24 (Cornmarket, *ibid.*, p. 270).
28   Charles I to Henriette Marie, 14 Jan. 1645, *The King's Cabinet opened* in T. Park (ed.), *Harleian Miscellany* (London, 1808–13), V, 533.
29   Christopher Love, *Englands Distemper. A sermon preacht at Uxbridge*, 30 Jan. 1645, T.T.E., 274.15, p. 37.

The parliamentary commissioners dissociated themselves from Love, and parliament sent for Love and imprisoned him. A month later, after the peace negotiations had broken down, parliament released him, which suggests that his detention was dictated by reasons of policy rather than abhorrence of his sentiments.[30] Edmund Ludlow, thinking back in later years, bluntly spelt out the implications of Love's ideas, which the minister had avoided:

> Mr. Love . . . averred, that the King was a man of blood, and that it was a vain thing to hope for the blessing of God upon any peace to be made with him, till satisfaction should be made for the blood that had been shed.[31]

The most serious association of the king with blood guilt during the first Civil War was in the admonition of the General Assembly of the Kirk of Scotland of June 1645. The Assembly publicly warned Charles to repent of blood guilt:

> we make bold to warn your Majesty That the Guilt which cleaveth fast to your Throne is such, as . . . if not timely repented, cannot but involove your self and your Posterity under the Wrath of the Everliving God: For your being guilty of shedding of the Blood of many Thousands of your Majesty's best Subjects.[32]

The tone the Kirk adopted towards Charles in 1645 – grave and righteous indignation towards a guilty sinner rather than the accustomed and expected reverence for the monarch – showed the significance of blood guilt as a levelling idea. The Kirk's statement was at variance with some other discussions of blood guilt in that it implied that a 'timely repentance' would be adequate satisfaction. Although the blood guilt was specific to the king and his followers, and was not said to pollute the whole land, the Scottish ministers had no intention of being – or of directing anyone else to be – an agent of punishment. The ministers' view did not prevent the Scots from making terms with the king in 1647 – much to the disgust of former allies such as Ludlow and Marten: 'You do not remember us with what Horror the Assembly of your Church did look upon his [the king's] Misdoings.'[33] The Scottish ministers who

---

30 Commons Journals, IV, 40, 49. Sir William Dugdale, A short view of the late troubles . . . [with a] narrative of the treaty of Uxbridge (Oxford, 1681), pp. 764–65.
31 C. H. Firth (ed.), The Memoirs of Edmund Ludlow (Oxford, 1894), I, 118.
32 The Remonstrance of the General Assembly of the Kirk of Scotland to his Majesty, July 5, 1645, printed in Rushworth, Historical Collections, Pt. 4 (1), 229–30.
33 Ludlow, Memoirs, I, 136; Henry Marten, The Independency of England endeavoured to be maintained (1648), in Old Parliamentary History (London, 1751–62), XVII, 61.

protested at the execution of the king in 1649 were reminded by Milton of their earlier preaching against Charles as 'an enemie to God and Saints, lad'n with all the innocent blood spilt in three Kingdoms.' Milton was scornful of such backsliders who spoke of the unrepentant Charles as 'a Sovran Lord, the Lords anointed, not to be touch'd.'[34] But although the ministers would not accept the whole apparent logic of arguments about blood guilt, that blood had to be avenged, their warning to Charles contributed to undermining his prestige and sacred character. The Scottish commissioners published this admonition in 1645 so 'that the candor and integrity of our Church and Kingdome may appear,'[35] and later references in English sources suggest that it made an impression. Thomas May justified publishing it in full in his *History* 'because the admonition of a National Church may seem a thing of some moment.'[36]

Although there is some evidence to suggest that a sympathy with millenarian ideas may have made an individual sensitive to the sin of blood guilt,[37] neither religious nor political radicalism was a precondition for applying ideas about blood guilt to the king and the royalists. Presbyterian clergy were prominent in the discussion. Christopher Love, the minister who referred publicly to Charles as a man of blood, later lost his life for plotting to restore Charles II to the throne in 1651. Blood guilt was a respectable argument which appealed to conservatives even more than to radicals. Radicals had, after all, other ways of resolving the problems posed by a king who seemed obstinately bent against his parliament. Vengeance for blood guilt was not just a part of a general cultural heritage, it was divinely authorized by Scripture. Scripture was an unimpeachable directive for human action, and as such acceptable to conservatives. A discussion of Charles I in terms of blood guilt avoided awkward constitutional issues. Thus it is not surprising to find that the members of parliament in the 1640s appealed to the concept of innocent blood unavenged to justify their actions. After they read the King's correspondence captured at Naseby in 1645, the majority had little doubt as to the use to which further personal negotiations with the king for peace might be put, but one of the arguments in which

34   Milton, *Tenure of Kings, Works*, V, 6.
35   *Correspondence of the Scots Commissioners in London, 1644–46*, ed. H. W. Meikle [Roxburghe Club] (London, 1917), p. 86.
36   Thomas May, *A Breviary of the History of the Parliament of England* (1655), reprinted in F. Maseres (ed.), *Select Tracts relating to the Civil Wars in England* (London, 1815), I, 72.
37   Many of those who discussed blood guilt appear in Capp's lists of Fifth Monarchists; Bernard Capp, *The Fifth Monarchy Men. A Study in Seventeenth Century English Millenarianism* (London, 1972).

they expressed their refusal of the king's request for a personal treaty was that 'there having been so much innocent Blood of Your good Subjects shed in this war by Your Majesty's Commands and Commissions; . . . We conceive, that, until Satisfaction and Security be first given to both Your Kingdoms, Your Majesty's coming hither cannot be convenient, nor be assented unto.'[38] While this was a generally acceptalbe reason, it was not merely useful propaganda. The 'innocent Blood' provided a real obstacle to communication until some satisfaction should be made.

III

Blood guilt was used by the conservatives to justify an action deemed politically expedient: radicals appealed to the idea to urge a new course of action. John Lilburne discussed blood guilt incidentally in his pamphlet *The Just Mans Justification*, published in August 1647. He rehearsed the standard arguments, that God required satisfaction for blood, that this must be by the blood of the guilty, that unless parliament expiated the innocent blood the wrath of God would descend upon the whole kingdom; and he backed these ideas with over thirty scriptural texts. What was new was Lilburne's passionate fusion of belief in both justice and social equality. The Lords and Commons, he argued, should: '*thinke upon the grand murtherers of England* (for by this impericall Law of God there is no exemption of *Kings, Princes, Dukes* . . . more then of *Fisher-men, Cobblers, Tinkers* and *Chimney-Sweepers*.)' There could be no peace in England until parliament had expiated the nation's blood guilt: 'it is but a folly and a madnesse, for the *King, Parliament,* or *People,* to talke of peace until inquisition be made for Englands innocent blood, and Justice done upon the guilty.'[39] The Levellers appealed explicitly to the Army to intervene in the political settlement of the nation. In *A Cal to all the Soldiers of the Army by the Free People of England,* one author, possibly John Wildman, repeated the argument that there could be no peace with Charles while there was no expiation for the soldiers' innocent blood. He attacked the Army officers who negotiated with the king for peace: 'Why doe themselves kneele, and kisse, and fawne upon him? . . . Oh shame of men! Oh sin against God! What, to doe thus to a man of blood, over head and eares in the blood of your dearest friends and fellow commoners?' The soldiers should show Cromwell that as they loved him when he 'hated the King as a man of

---

38 *Journals of the House of Lords*, VIII, 99.
39 John Lilburne, *The Just Mans Justification*, Aug., 1647, pp. 10–11.

blood,' so he ceased to be an object of affection when he negotiated for peace.[40]

At Putney the officers and soldiers debated the Army's role in the political settlement. Some accepted the idea that the unsettled state of the nation was due to its pollution by blood, and urged political action to cleanse the land. Lieutenant Colonel John Jubbes questioned whether a purged parliament might satisfy the Army's just desires 'and declare the king guilty of all the bloodshed.' Captain Bishop discovered, 'after many inquiries in my spirit' for the reasons for the dying state of the kingdom, that it was 'a compliance to preserve that man of blood, and those principles of tyranny, which God from heaven by his many successes hath manifestly declared against.'[41] Colonel Thomas Harrison spoke even more bluntly at a meeting of the Council of Officers on November 11, 1647: 'That the Kinge was a Man of Bloud, and therefore the Engagement taken off, and that they were to prosecute him.'[42] The Agitators wanted to dissociate the soldiers from any further propositions that might be sent to the king, especially from the propositions which asked indemnity for fighting against him, for 'so the guilt of innocent blood taken upon your own heads.'[43] On November 5, such a letter was actually written.[44]

The belief that Charles was a man of blood had thus begun to play a part in forming Army policy, although the officers subsequently disavowed the letter to parliament which withdrew Army support from further peace negotiations. Cromwell was not convinced at that date that Charles was a man of blood and questioned whether the murders of which Charles was guilty were punishable.[45] The officers restored Army discipline by force, but at the price of alienating the soldiers.[46] Subsequent pamphlets expressed the soldiers' disquiet. By depending on the king for peace 'the invaluable price of all the precious English blood . . . shal be imbezlled or lost; and certainly, God the

40   [John Wildman], *A Cal to all the Souldiers of the Armie by the free people of England*, [29 Oct.] 1647, T.T.,E. 412.10 p. 2.
41   A. S. P. Woodhouse (ed.), *Puritanism and Liberty Being the Army Debates (1647–49)*, (2nd ed.; London, 1951), pp. 100, 107.
42   C. H. Firth (ed.), *Clarke Papers* [Camden Soc., new ser.] (London, 1891–1901), I, 417.
43   Woodhouse, *Puritanism and Liberty*, p. 452.
44   *Clarke Papers*, I, 440–41.
45   Cromwell answered Harrison 'by putting severall cases in which merther was nott to bee punished.' *Ibid.*, p. 417.
46   S. R. Gardiner, *History of the Great Civil War 1642–1649* (London, 1894), IV, 22–23. One of the soldiers was shot, an act incurring blood guilt according to Richard Overton. D. M. Wolfe (ed.), *Leveller Manifestoes of the Puritan Revolution* (New York, 1944), p. 363.

avenger of blood, wil require it of the obstructors of justice and freedom. *Judges* 9.24.'[47]

The rift between officers and soldiers was partly bridged in December 1647 when the Army Council withdrew Army support from further negotiations with the king and pardoned the offences of some of the radicals, including Rainsborough. In the Commons' debates on future policy towards the king early in January 1648, Cromwell was prominent in opposing any further overtures to him. Nevertheless, the outbreak of the second Civil War seemed a sign that the Lord was angry, and the Army held a prayer meeting at Windsor on April 29, 1648. According to the account of William Allen,[48] published in 1659, the officers sought the Lord in prayer, and He led them to see that their sin had been in 'those cursed carnal conferences' with the king. Consequently they resolved 'that it was our duty, if ever the Lord brought us back again in peace, to call Charles Stuart, that man of blood, to an account for that blood he had shed.'[49] The second Civil War thus became a test for the Army. If the Lord did indeed view Charles as a man of blood, He would vindicate His cause and give victory to the Army. The soldiers had struck a bargain with the Lord: if they were victorious, they would bring Charles to justice. The identification of Charles as a man of blood was thus a serious threat to the king's future.

Although the events of the subsequent months would show that not all the officers or soldiers regarded this bargain with the Lord as of binding force, the Army's willingness to identify the king as a man of blood was an important alteration of policy towards Charles. This was particularly significant because parliament had no new policies to launch when war was renewed. Instead, the two Houses fell back on their old idea of negotiated settlement and repealed the Vote of No Further Addresses on August 24, 1648. They came closer to negotiating a peace at the Isle of Wight than they had done on any previous occasion, but without the threatening stance of the Army it seems unlikely that a majority in the Commons would have accepted the king's concessions as a satisfactory basis for settlement on December 5, since Charles had conceded only personal powers, not the prerogatives of the crown.

47　'The earnest Petition of many Free-born People of this Nation' in *A Declaration of Some Proceedings*, 14 Feb. 1648 in W. Haller and G. Davies (eds.), *The Leveller Tracts, 1647–1653* (New York, 1944), p. 107. See also J. Lilburne, *The People's Prerogative*, 17 Feb. 1648, quoted by Wolfe, *Leveller Manifestoes*, p. 69.

48　Firth suggests that the author, Adjutant-General William Allen, was the same William Allen who was an agitator in 1647, a trooper in Cromwell's horse. *Clarke Papers*, II, 432–33.

49　William Allen, *A faithful Memorial of that remarkable Meeting of many Officers of the Army* (1659), in Sir W. Scott (ed.), *Somers Tracts* (London, 1809–15), V, 501. For the dating of the meeting see Gardiner, *Civil War*, IV, 117, n. 2.

It is clear from the subsequent hesitations of Oliver Cromwell that he was not yet persuaded that if the king were a man of blood he should be brought to justice. He was unconvinced by the dispensations which other men claimed to have received from the Lord. Over the months after parliament's victory in the second War, Cromwell's mind ran upon the 'outward dispensations,' 'the mind of God in all that chain of Providence,' on the zeal of officers 'to have impartial justice done upon Offenders,' and 'they that are implacable and will not leave troubling the Land.'[50] C. V. Wedgwood accepted Cromwell's November statement about the king as 'a man against whom the Lord hath witnessed' as evidence that he was determined to bring Charles to justice,[51] but Cromwell's subsequent conduct casts some doubt upon this. The most recent interpretation by D. Underdown follows that of S. R. Gardiner in arguing that during December Cromwell was secretly trying to save Charles's life, while outwardly he supported the radicals, officers, and soldiers.[52] On December 19, the Earl of Denbigh visited Fairfax before going to Windsor, where Charles was a prisoner, with a final ultimatum.[53] On December 25 Charles refused to see Denbigh, while Cromwell was arguing in the Council of Officers that 'there was no policy in taking away his life.'[54] Cromwell's attempts at compromise were defeated even before Charles's intransigence was known, Underdown argues, by the radicals' determination not to spare him. Possibly the soldiers' attitudes were part of the testimony of events for Cromwell, because by January 1649 he claimed that 'the Providence of God' had cast the Commons upon the trial of the king, and he signed the death warrant.[55] In later years he wrote of the king's death as 'an eminent witness of the Lord for blood-guiltiness.'[56] This is not the place for a lengthy discussion of Cromwell's relationship with the Army – leader or follower? – but it should be noted that Cromwell's hesitations need not invalidate the argument that for many in the Army the fate of 'that man of blood' was to be decided by the Lord's verdict on their forces in the war.

The second Civil War was fought with greater fierceness and brutality than the first had been. The Army was exasperated and angry at the unnecessary shedding of blood. The condemnation of three royalist offi-

---

50   W. C. Abbott (ed.), *The Writings and Speeches of Oliver Cromwell* (Cambridge, Mass., 1937–47), I, 644, 696, 690, 638.

51   C. V. Wedgwood, *The Trial of Charles I* (London, 1964), p. 77 and n. 30.

52   D. Underdown, *Pride's Purge, Politics in the Puritan Revolution* (Oxford, 1971), pp. 163–72. Gardiner, *Civil War*, IV, 281–87.

53   Wedgwood, *Trial of Charles I*, p. 77 and n. 30, does not accept the pro-Royalist sources' interpretation of the purpose of Denbigh's mission.

54   *Clarke Papers*, II, xxx.

55   Gardiner, *Civil War*, IV, 288.

56   Abbott, *Writings and Speeches*, I, 756.

cers and the execution of two of them after the siege of Colchester reveals the Army's new mood of vengeance. Sir Thomas Fairfax justified the executions to the House of Lords as 'some satisfaction to military Justice, and in part of Avenge for the innocent Blood they have caused to be spilt.'[57]

In October 1648 Ireton's regiment petitioned for justice upon 'all criminal persons,' and requested that any who spoke on the king's behalf should be treated as traitors 'till he shall be acquited of the guilt of shedding innocent blood.'[58] Sir William Constable's regiment petitioned that the kingdom's destroyers be punished without delay, 'That God may be glorified, the Cause and honour of the Parliament affected and vindicated, the land cleansed from blood, and rendered capable of some happie establishment.'[59] Ingoldsby's regiment also petitioned for justice.[60] Finally, in November 1648 the Army Council presented a *Remonstrance* to parliament demanding' That the capital and grand Author of our Troubles, the Person of the King . . . may be speedily brought to justice.' Justice would deter tyrants, settle the nation in peace, and expiate blood guilt.[61] Later in 1650 the Army minimized the importance of the first two arguments about tyranny and settlement, and explained their actions solely in terms of their desire to expiate blood guilt. Victory in the second Civil War, the soldiers claimed, was 'a second testimony given from heaven to justify the proceedings of his poor servants against that bloody Anti-christian brood' and after that:

> we were then powerfully convinced that the Lord's purpose was to deal with the late King as a man of blood. And being persuaded in our consciences that he and his monarchy was one of the ten horns of the Beast . . . and being witnesses to so much of the innocent blood of the Saints that he had shed in supporting the Beast, and considering the loud cries of the souls of the Saints . . . we were extraordinarily carried forth to desire justice upon the King, that man of blood.[62]

---

57   Rushworth, *Historical Collections*, Pt. IV (2), 1243. While it appeared that the execution of these two soldiers of fortune fell within the rules of war, the execution of officers after a siege was exceptional in England at this time.
58   *The True Copy of a Petition promoted in the Army*, 18 Oct. 1648, T.T.,E. 468.18.
59   *The Moderate*, 10–17 Oct. 1648, *ibid.*, E. 468.2, p. 17.
60   Rushworth, *Historical Collections*, VII, 1311–12.
61   *Remonstrance*, 16 Nov. 1648, in *Old Parliamentary History*, XVIII, 228.
62   *A Declaration of the English Army Now in Scotland*, 1 Aug. 1650, in Woodhouse, *Puritanism and Liberty*, p. 477. The Declaration, under the Imprimatur of Rushworth, was in answer to a paper directed by the Scots, 'To the Under-Officers and Soldiers.'

Such language captures the intensity of emotional force generated by the identification of Charles as a man of blood. Parliament tried to ignore the *Remonstrance*, so by November 26, 1648 the General Council of Officers was 'seeking God by prayer' to direct them how they might 'bee instruments that justice may bee done uppon those who have caused soe much bloud to bee shed.[63] During December, while the purged House of Commons instituted a court for the trial of the king, the Army divided over what should happen to Charles.[64] Cromwell was working for a compromise and a royalist newsletter of December 1648 suggested that some of the officers wanted to murder Charles quietly while the soldiers and Levellers wanted to bring him to trial.[65] Both groups were prepared to discuss the king's fate assuming that the Lord would give guidance in the matter. The Army Council listened to Elizabeth Poole on January 5, 1648, who claimed she had a command from God to deliver a message: the king should be brought to trial but his life should be spared. The text 'Vengeance is mine, I will repay, saith the Lord' was cited to justify non-intervention.[66]

Many sermons after the second Civil War swelled the chorus demanding satisfaction for blood. The ministers contributed to the king's death by arguing that blood guilt must be expiated, irrespective of the high estate of the guilty: 'no Murderer shall then plead Prerogative to exempt him from Trial before this Iudge; When poor souls cry to God to avenge their blood, he will do it. . . .' The members of the House of Commons should depend on God alone, who would judge the earth through the agency of his Saints.[67] Thomas Brooks reminded the Commons at their monthly fast in December 1648 of the zeal of Phineas in executing judgment: 'when men doe execute their just judgement, then God will divert and turne away his judgement from a Nation.' If they should fail to punish the guilty, 'that shall be charged on your skore. When justice is not executed, a Land is defiled. *Num*. 35, 33.34.'[68]

Thus in 1648 blood guilt was a political issue of some importance. Individual attitudes differed. To many of the officers and soldiers blood guilt was the decisive factor in the formation of policy. Convinced that

---

63   *Clarke Papers*, II, 58.
64   For discussion of Army division over policies generally, see Underdown, *Pride's Purge*, pp. 182 ff.
65   Bodleian Library, Clarendon MS 34, f. 7.
66   *Clarke Papers*, II, 163–70 and notes.
67   George Cokayn, *Flesh Expiring, and the Spirit Inspiring*, 29 Nov. 1648, pp. 11, 16–17. (Cornmarket reprint, *Fast Sermons*, 32, pp. 27, 32–33).
68   Thomas Brooks, *Gods Delight in the Progresse of the Upright*, 26 Dec. 1648, pp. 15, 17 (Cormarket, *ibid.*, pp. 101, 103).

Charles was a man of blood, they demanded his trial and execution. To others it was a justifying argument. Political necessity demanded the trial of the king and arguments about blood guilt reinforced this. Public discussion of the issue helped to create the atmosphere in which Charles could be attacked.

The Act establishing the High Court for the king's trial made no mention of blood guilt. The Army's desire that Charles should be brought to *justice* meant that there was an attempt to judge him within a legal framework. Nevertheless, the speeches and writings of individuals associated with the trial show that blood guilt was in their minds. John Bradshaw, the President of the Court, told Charles they intended 'to make inquisition for Blood.' The charge that Charles was a murderer implied that he was guilty of shedding innocent blood, and before he was sentenced, Bradshaw made this explicit: 'Sir, I will presume that you are so well read in Scripture as to know what God him-selfe hath said concerning the shedding of mans bloud. *Gen.9.Num.35.* will tell you what the punishment is.' Bradshaw went on to recite the familiar theme: the land was defiled with blood, Scripture directed it could be cleansed only with the blood of the guilty, and there was no dispensation from blood guilt because the commandment against murder 'extends to Kings, as well as the meanest Peasants, the meanest of the People.' God was before their eyes, he continued, 'that God with whom there is no respect of persons, that God that is the avenger of innocent blood,' and he would curse them if they failed to shed the blood of the guilty malefactor.[69] In the speech John Cook had prepared to deliver if Charles had entered a plea, he concluded with an emotional appeal for justice:

> I do humbly demand and pray the justice of this high court, and yet not I, but the innocent blood that hath been shed in the three kingdoms, demands justice against him . . . This blood hath long cried, How long, parliament, how long, army, will ye forbear to avenge our blood?[70]

Colonel Hutchinson, one of the signatories of the death warrant, believed 'that if they did not execute justice upon him, God would require at their hands all the blood and desolation which should ensue by their suffering him to escape, when God had brought him into their hands.'[71] Ludlow, another of the regicides, betrayed his obsession with the notion of blood guilt in his account of the events leading up to the

69   *King Charls his tryal* (1649), pp. 4, 41–43.
70   John Cook, *King Charles his Case* (1649), in *Somers Tracts*, V, 233.
71   Lucy Hutchinson, *Memoirs of the Life of Colonel Hutchinson* (London, 1908), p. 266.

trial and execution of the king. The negotiations of the Isle of Wight were, he believed, unsafe to the people of England, and unjust and wicked, drawing down 'the just vengeance of God upon us all.' Charles should be brought to justice because he 'was guilty of all the blood shed in the first and second war.' Blood guilty for Ludlow was more than a moral justification for action. It was an incentive to action. Hugh Peter was not actually a regicide, but he was tried in 1660 for his part in promoting the king's death. He was charged with preaching sermons and assuring the soldiers that the Bible directed that blood was required for blood, 'and that neither the King nor any other person are excepted from this general rule.'[72]

Charles shared the parliamentarians' view that innocent blood defiled the land and that some civil power had a duty to remove this pollution. His own willing self-sacrifice would, he hoped, assuage the Lord. On the scaffold he denied his guilt of all the blood shed in the wars, blaming some 'ill Instruments' between him and his parliament. He recognized the unjust sentence upon himself as a retribution for his having allowed an unjust sentence upon the Earl of Strafford in 1641.[73] Strafford's blood had been on Charles's conscience for many years: 'Nothing can be more evident,' he wrote in 1645, 'than that Strafford's innocent blood hath been one of the great causes of God's just judgments upon this nation, by a furious civil war.'[74]

The royalists saw the king's death as a terrible act which made the parliamentarians guilty of blood, and even some of parliament's supporters in 1649 shared this view.[75] In 1650, six royalists murdered parliament's representative in Spain, and their deed was admired as an attempt 'to revenge the blood of their King.'[76] The royalists' decision of 1657 that all but the actual regicides should be pardoned suggests that expiation for the king's blood was in their minds,[77] but when pardons came to be debated in 1660, it was unnecessary for them to use extralegal arguments about blood guilt because the law was on their side. The 'severe and full justice' of which the royalists spoke would have been enough to convict not just all those who had signed the death warrant, but also those who had 'compassed the death of the King' by levying war

72   Ludlow, Memoirs, I, 207, 205; II, 331.
73   King Charles his speech made upon the scaffold (1649), pp. 4–5.
74   The King's Cabinet Opened (1645), in Harleian Miscellany, V, 533. See also J. Bruce (ed.), Charles I in 1646 [Camden Soc., LXIII] (London, 1856), 19, 80.
75   H. Cary (ed.), Memorials of the Great Civil War, 1642–1652 (London, 1842), II, 117–19; The Moderate, 23 Jan. 1649.
76   Clarendon, History, V, 142.
77   W. D. Macray (ed.), Calendar of the Clarendon State Papers (Oxford, 1876), III, 286.

against him.[78] Although thirteen men were executed, the king's blood still seemed unexpiated. 'God forbid the blood-guiltinesse, especially of our King, should go unpunisht' wrote one royalist in 1662;[79] and a royal mandate of the same year added to the Book of Common Prayer a service for King Charles the martyr with prayers imploring the Lord not to punish the whole nation for 'the Guilt of that sacred and innocent Blood.'[80] Over twenty years after the king's death a deprived minister who had actually witnessed the execution was still praying on its anniversary 'deliver ye nation from bloud-guiltines o: God.'[81]

In 1649 not all of parliament's supporters believed that the king's death was sufficient expiation of the nation's blood guilt. Two Army officers, Goffe and Carter, both argued against mediating with parliament for the lives of any of the royalists condemned to death in 1649. 'Godly and conscientious men,' argued Goffe, 'are satisfied in judgement and conscience that these men ought to die as such as are guilty of that innocent bloud that bath defiled this land.'[82] Others pointed out that the Lord did not demand a total blood bath to cleanse the polluted land.[83] The subsequent conduct of Oliver Cromwell in Ireland in 1649 was also influenced by ideas of blood guilt. In addition to arguments based on military necessity, Cromwell justified his infamous slaughter at Drogheda as satisfaction for the bloodshed by the Irish in 1641: 'a righteous judgment of God upon these barbarous wretches, who have imbrued their hands in so much innocent blood.'[84]

The intensity of emotion generated in the discussion of blood guilt varied. The arguments were basically the same, and were supported with similar selections from the same Biblical texts. Sometimes there was a sense of the Lord as simply an accountant in this matter: 'It pleaseth the Lord many times to seal up, as in his treasury, the sins of a Land, and to keep them as in a Bag.'[85] At the other extreme, strict accountancy was swamped in emotionalism and near hysteria:

78 Kent Archives Office, Diary of Sir Edward Dering, May 14, 1660. The regicides denied that they had acted unjustly, and accused the royalists of seeking blood and revenge. Hutchinson, *Memoirs*, pp. 321–33; Ludlow, *Memoirs*, II, 291–92. Pepys described Harrison's execution as 'the first blood shed in revenge for the blood of the King.' R. Latham and W. Matthews (eds.), *The Diary of Samuel Pepys* (London, 1970), I, 265.
79 *The Royal Martyr, or King Charles the first no Man of Blood but a Martyr for his people* (London, [1662]), preface.
80 This service was continued in the prayer book until 1859.
81 M. H. Lee (ed.), *Diaries and Letters of Philip Henry* (London, 1882), p. 236.
82 John Goodwin, *The Obstructours of Justice*, [30 May] 1649, T.T.,E. 557.2, p. 61
83 *Clarke Papers*, II, 191–98.
84 Abbott, *Writings and Speeches*, II, 127.
85 Scudder, *Gods Warning to England*, p. 19 (Cornmarket reprint, *Fast Sermons*, 13, p. 307).

Cursed be he that holdeth back his Sword from blood; yea, Cursed be he that maketh not his Sword starke drunk with *Irish* blood, that doth not recompence them double for their hellish treachery to the English, that maketh them not heaps upon heaps, and their Country a dwelling place for Dragons, an Astonishment to Nations: Let not that eye look for pity, nor that hand be spared, that pities or spares them, and let him be accursed, that curseth not them bitterly.[86]

Just as the emotional level of the appeal to the concept of blood guilt varied, so too did the purpose of the appeal. Some, such as the Presbyterian ministers and the Scots, used the argument but did not want Charles executed. Others adopted blood guilt as a justification for a course of action after they had concluded that a negotiated settlement with Charles was impossible. In both these cases the discussion of the king's blood guilt undermined his divinity and set him apart from the peace negotiations as a polluted person. Recognition of the role of blood guilt thus adds a dimension to the conventional accounts of the king's death. The greatest significance of the concept of blood guilt is in explaining the Army's intervention: at the prayer meeting in April 1648 the soldiers espoused the view that Charles was a man of blood, and the logic of the demand of blood for blood directed their actions over the following months. Charles's blood guilt was a crying scandal both directing them to demand his death and justifying their actions to that end.

---

86   [Nathaniel Ward], *The Simple Cobler of Aggavvum in America* [29 Jan.] 1647, T.T.,E. 372.21, p. 73.

14

A Bourgeois Revolution?

Christopher Hill

Originally appeared as Christopher Hill, 'A Bourgeois Revolution?' in
J. G. A. Pocock (ed.), *Three British Revolutions*. Copyright © 1980 by
Princeton University Press.

This kind of government [of the church] God doth not manage
according to the wisdom and thoughts, no not of his very people, but
wholly according to the counsel of his own will and the thoughts of his
own heart: doing things that they must not know yet, but must know
afterwards; yea, such things as for the present seem absurd and absolutely
destructive. – William Dell, *The Way of True Peace and Unity in the True
Church of Christ* (1651), in *Several Sermons and Discourses* (1709), p. 225.

The ends of the actions are intended, but the results which actually follow
from these actions are not intended. . . .

The final result always arises from conflicts between many individual
wills, of which each again has been made what it is by a host of particular conditions of life. Thus there are innumerable intersecting forces
which give rise to one resultant – the historical event. – F. Engels, *Ludwig
Feuerbach*, in Karl Marx, *Selected Works* (Moscow, 1935), 1, 457; *Selected
Correspondence of Marx and Engels* (ed. Dona Torr, 1934), p. 476.

The cultural consequences of the Reformation were to a great extent . . .
unseen and even *unwished-for* results of the labours of the reformers.
They were often far removed from or even in contradiction to all that they
themselves thought to attain. – Max Weber, *The Protestant Ethic and the
Spirit of Capitalism* (London, 1930), p. 90.

It is impossible to discuss this subject without first clearing away some
stereotypes. Many non-Marxists, even non-Marxist scholars, attribute
to Marxists fixed positions of the 'all Cretans are liars' type, which by
definition cannot be challenged. I have learnt from long and painful

I am deeply grateful to Eric Hobsbawm and Edward Thompson for reading a draft of
this chapter and making helpful comments and criticisms. They are not responsible
for what has resulted. In the following notes, the place of publication is London
unless otherwise stated.

experience that if I am asked the question 'Are you a Marxist?' I must answer (however much it goes against the grain) 'It all depends what you mean by Marxist.' For if I answer 'Yes,' with however many scholarly qualifications, the next question is bound to be 'What do you do when you meet a fact which does not fit in with your Marxist assumptions?' It is too late then to plead that I have no more assumptions than the next historian, or that – like him – my ideas are being modified all the time by fresh information. For my interlocutor *knows* both that Marxists have dogmatic preconceptions and that all Cretans are liars. Nothing I can say will shake him: he only becomes progressively more convinced of my dishonesty as I attempt to deny what he knows to be true.

So in discussing whether the English Revolution was a bourgeois revolution or not we must begin by defining terms. As I have argued at length elsewhere, the phrase in Marxist usage does *not* mean a revolution made by or consciously willed by the bourgeoisie.[1] Yet when I so argued, even a relatively friendly reviewer supposed that I was recognizing 'a difficulty . . . in the Marxist conception of a bourgeois revolution,' and that I hoped 'to solve it by adopting an interpretation of this term which Isaac Deutscher put forward, . . . *contrary to the traditional view that the bourgeoisie . . . played the leading part in it.*'[2] If this is 'the traditional view' of what Marxists hold, it is held only by ill-informed non-Marxists. I quoted Deutscher as a respected and representative Marxist, not as an innovator. Lenin, who may perhaps be allowed to know something about the subject, argued at one stage in favor of bringing about a bourgeois revolution against the wishes of the Russian bourgeoisie.[3]

The English Revolution, like all revolutions, was caused by the breakdown of the old society; it was brought about neither by the wishes of the bourgeoisie, nor by the leaders of the Long Parliament. But its *outcome* was the establishment of conditions far more favorable to the development of capitalism than those which prevailed before 1640. The hypothesis is that this outcome, and the Revolution itself, were made possible by the fact that there had already been a considerable development of capitalist relations in England, but that it was the structures, fractures, and pressures of the society, rather than the wishes of leaders, which dictated the outbreak of revolution and shaped the state which emerged from it. In our society businessmen and politicians do not will

1 See my *Change and Continuity in Seventeenth-Century England* (1974), pp. 278–82.
2 Review by R. H. Nidditch in *Isis*, 68 (1977), 153–54.
3 For Lenin's views see V. I. Lenin, *Selected Works* (1934–38), I, 492–93, III, 135–37.

a slump, though after the event we may conclude that their attempts to avert it helped to bring it on. In the 1640s peasants revolted against enclosure, clothiers against poverty resulting from depression, the godly against Antichrist in order to bring about Christ's kingdom on earth. As a New England supporter of Parliament summed up in 1648, 'Saith one, I fought and engaged for the removing evil councillors from the King; . . . saith another, I engaged for the establishment of preaching; . . . saith another, I fought against the King, as conceiving him rather to act than be acted of any evil councillors whatsoever; another, he fought against oppression in general.' Gerrard Winstanley thought that all strove for land – gentry, clergy, Commons.[4] Few indeed of the rank and file of the New Model Army fought to create a world safe for capitalist farmers and merchants to make profits in; they protested loudly when Commissary-General Ireton hinted at such a possibility. As the Revolution developed, men with ideas of what was politically desirable tried to control it, none of them very successfully. The outcome of the Revolution was something which none of the activists had willed. Once the old constraints had broken down, or been broken, the shape of the new order was determined in the long run by the needs of a society in which large numbers of unideological men minded their own business.[5]

In England by 1640 the Stuart monarchy was unable to continue governing in the traditional way. Its foreign policy was deplorably weak, partly because of lack of money; the financial measures to which it was forced to resort alienated its potential supporters no less than its enemies. To say that this situation was the ultimate consequence of stresses and strains produced by the rise of the capitalist mode of production is not to say that Charles I's government was overthrown by a gang of capitalists – it was not – nor that a more skillful policy could not have enabled it to survive longer – it could. But by 1640 the social forces let loose by or accompanying the rise of capitalism, especially in agriculture, could no longer be contained within the old political framework except by means of a violent repression of which Charles's government proved incapable. Among 'the social forces accompanying the rise of

4   George Downing to John Winthrop, 8 March 1647–48, in *Collections of the Massachusetts Historical Soc.*, VI, 541; ed. G. H. Sabine, *The Works of Gerrard Winstanley* (Ithaca, N.Y., 1941), 373–74; cf. ed. J. T. Rutt, *The Parliamentary Diary of Thomas Burton* (1828), III, 145, 186–88.
5   The reader interested in what Marx and Engels actually said on these questions is referred to Marx, *Selected Works* (Moscow, 1935), I, 210–11, 241, 456–68, II, 175, 315, 344–45; Marx, *Selected Essays* (New York, 1926), pp. 69–70, 201–6; Marx-Engels, *Gesamtausgabe* (Moscow, 1927–), Abt. I, VII, 493; Engels, *Socialism, Utopian and Scientific* (1936), pp. xix–xxii; *Anti-Dühring* (1954), pp. 226–29; *Selected Correspondence of Marx and Engels*, pp. 310–11, 475–77, 517–18. What they find here may surprise holders of 'the traditional view.'

capitalism' we must include not only the individualism of those who wished to make money by doing what they would with their own but also the individualism of those who wished to follow their own consciences in worshiping God, and whose consciences led them to challenge the institutions of a stratified hierarchical society. Similar stresses and strains produced analogous conflicts in other European countries,[6] and were no doubt related to the population upsurge as well as to the rise of capitalism. But the outcome in England was different from that in any other European country except the Netherlands. In Spain, France, and elsewhere the absolute monarchy survived the mid-century crisis; in England this crisis put an end to the monarchy's aspirations to build up an absolutism based on a standing army and a bureaucracy.

As Marx pointed out, one of the essential differences between the English Revolution and the French Revolution of 1789 was 'the continuous alliance which [in England] united the middle class with the largest section of the great landowners,' an alliance which he associated with sheep farming and dated from the sixteenth century.[7] The rural nature of capitalism in England differentiates it from that of most continental countries, and creates difficulties for purists who regard 'rural bourgeoisie' as a contradiction in terms. Linguistic arguments apart, it is difficult to deny that a section of the English gentry and yeomanry, especially in the South and East, from the sixteenth century onward took part in production for the market, notably through the woolen and extractive industries; and that this is a main difference between England and those continental countries in which absolute monarchies survived.[8]

The landed ruling class in sixteenth-century England was a narrow one, secure only so long as united. In the two generations before 1640 it was no longer united by fear, whether of Spain, of dynastic civil war, or of peasant revolt: it was split over economic questions, notably monopolies, and over religion. After 1618 it was divided in attitudes toward foreign policy, so closely linked with religion. The clothing depression of the 1620s and the battle for the forests alienated the common people and a section of the gentry from the Crown and the

---

6   P. B. Merriman, *Six Contemporaneous Revolutions* (Oxford, 1938), *passim*; E. J. Hobsbawm, 'The Crisis of the Seventeenth Century,' *Past & Present*, 5 and 6 (1954); H. R. Trevor-Roper, 'The General Crisis of the Seventeenth Century,' *Past & Present*, 16 (1959), and a discussion in 18 (1960).

7   Marx, *Selected Essays*, pp. 204–6; Marx, *Capital*, I (ed. Dona Torr, 1946), 430, III (ed. F. Engels, Chicago, 1909), 928–46.

8   On the 'mutual dependence' of the absolutist state and 'strong peasant property' in France, see R. Brenner, 'Agrarian Class Structure and Economic Development in pre-Industrial Europe, *Past & Present*, 70 (1976), 68–73.

great aristocrats who were enclosing forests and common lands.[9] From at least the 1620s conflicts over the parliamentary franchise in boroughs revealed a split between the oligarchic tendencies of the Crown and some of the gentry, and a willingness of gentlemen less closely associated with the Court to support a wide borough franchise.[10] The gentry excluded from office, and those whose long-established control of local government was interfered with, resented the attempt to create a stronger central government and bureaucracy. Laud's policy in the Church alienated middle-of-the-road traditionalists hardly less than it infuriated Puritans; it led to disaster in Scotland. Strafford's success in Ireland was as disastrous as Laud's Scottish failure, because Ireland was seen as the base for building up an army – the other component necessary to any attempt to create an absolute government.

The Scottish war of 1639–40 revealed the government's inability to rule, to raise taxes or an army that would fight, and allowed plotters among the gentry to visualize a return to power by means of popular support. So when Parliament at last met, some of its leaders were prepared to use or accept pressure by London mobs to force concessions from the government. They were ready to connive at religious toleration as the price of popular support against bishops, to connive at enclosure riots directed especially against the Crown and big landlords, to connive at riots against papists. London mobs made possible the execution of Strafford, the exclusion of bishops from Parliament and the safety of the Five Members when Charles I tried to arrest them in January 1642; yeomen from many of the home counties marched up to London in a demonstration of support.[11]

Henceforth, as Mr. Manning has shown, the popular party in the Commons was to some extent trapped, was no longer in control of events. The publication of the Grand Remonstrance is rightly seen as a parting of the ways between those like Hyde and Falkland whose opposition to the Crown did not extend to continued reliance on popular support, and those who had no qualms about pressing on – like Oliver Cromwell, with his experience as leader of the fenmen in the 1630s, or Bulstrode Whitelocke, the popular candidate in a class-divided election in 1640. Religious toleration was a similarly polarizing question. The breakdown of ecclesiastical authority in 1640 saw the emergence from underground of lower-class heretical groups who had long been beyond

9   Brian Manning, *The English People and the English Revolution* (1976), chs. 1 and 7. For forests see n. 18 below.
10   Derek Hirst, *The Representative of the People?* (Cambridge, 1975), especially chs. 3, 4, and 10; P. Clark and P. Slack, *English Towns in Transition* (Oxford, 1976), pp. 134–40.
11   Manning, *The English People*, chs. 1, 4, p. 104.

the pale of respectable Protestantism. Whether or not there was a continuing underground from Lollards via Anabaptists and Familists to the sectaries of the 1640s,[12] the emergence of the latter did much to scare away aristocratic reformers like Sir Edward Dering. Few indeed were those who, like Milton, had a friendly word for Familists in 1642;[13] but under pressure of military necessity and London radicalism leaders like Oliver Cromwell opted for religious liberty and promotion by merit rather than by birth (the Self-Denying Ordinance).

When Civil War broke out it was not the gentry but the clothiers of the West Riding who forced the pace in Yorkshire; and Fairfax followed. In Lancashire it was the common people who insisted on fighting, whilst the gentry havered until Brereton put himself at their head. Neutralism was popular among the gentry of very many counties. Whatever the original intentions of Parliament, other wills took over from 1642–43.[14] The waverings of the 'peace party' and the 'middle group' among MPs were overcome by pressures from outside Parliament – first from the London populace, then from the Scottish army, then from the English army. The war was won by artillery (which money alone could buy) and by the disciplined morale of Cromwell's yeomen cavalry. The real crisis came when the fighting was over, when the Leveller democratic organization gave a dangerous political significance to what had hitherto been spontaneous activities, like those of London mobs, of antipapist and antienclosure rioters, just as the more extreme sectaries made dangerous sense of radical religious ideas, some of which – like those of Ranters, Diggers, and early Quakers – had political as well as theological significance and struck conservatives as simply irreligious.[15] In the end the social anxieties to which Levellers and radical sectaries gave rise were to reunite the propertied classes. Thanks largely to the skill with which in 1649 Charles I played the only card left to him, acting out the role of royal martyr, and to the great propaganda success of *Eikon Basilike*, this reunion focused on the monarchy. But the reunion was based on strong material links between the two sections of the propertied classes as well as on the magic of monarchy.

By 1660 transformations in the English political and social scene had occurred which – whatever the intentions of those who brought them about – had the consequence of facilitating the development of capital-

---

12   See my 'From Lollards to Levellers,' in *Rebels and their Causes: Essays in English History published in Honour of A. L. Morton* (ed. M. Cornforth, 1978); read at the Folger conference.
13   See my *Milton and the English Revolution* (1977), pp. 95–97.
14   Manning, *The English People*, ch. 7.
15   *Ibid.*, chs. 9 and 10; cf. my *Irreligion in the 'Puritan' Revolution* (Barnett Shine Foundation Lecture, 1974), *passim*.

ism. Abolition of feudal tenures and the Court of Wards (1646, 1656, confirmed 1661) 'turned lordship into absolute ownership,' as Professor Perkin put it. Landowners were set free from the incidence of arbitrary death duties, and their land became a commodity which could be bought, sold, and mortgaged; thus, long-term capital investment in agriculture was facilitated. This was 'the decisive change in English history, which made it different from the continent.' 'From it every other difference in English society stemmed.'[16] The abolition of feudal tenures also removed a great lever of royal control and finance, and so gravely weakened the independent position of the monarchy.

In the late forties and fifties the radical demand for equivalent security of tenure for copyholders was defeated. The confirmatory act of 1661, which was the first business Parliament took up after recalling the King, specifically excluded copyholders from the advantages which their betters were voting themselves. So far from copyholders winning security of tenure, an act of 1677 extended their insecurity to small freeholders except in the unlikely event of the latter being able to produce written title to their estates. So most obstacles to enclosure were removed. This set the stage for a rapid expansion of capitalist agriculture, employing the new techniques popularized by the agricultural reformers of the Interregnum. Food prices steadied, and there were no more famines in England, though there still were in France. Parliament positively encouraged enclosure and cultivation of the waste, protected farmers against imports, authorized corn hoarding and established the bounty on exports. The struggle for forests and commons before 1640, to which Mr. Manning rightly attaches so much importance,[17] had aimed at cultivating them more profitably. The King and the great landlords were trying to use their political power to increase their share of the surplus. Pressure to cultivate fens and wastes came from the expanding market – for food and clothing for a growing population, for cloth exports. By 1660 this battle had been lost by King and commoners alike. Oliver Cromwell, who as Lord of the Fens had led opposition to the draining of the Great Level, was responsible for the defeat of the Levellers which made possible the resumption of drainage under his patronage, on terms more advantageous to the drainers than to the Fenmen.[18] To quote Professor Perkin again, 'the provision of land for agricultural improvement, mining, transport, factories and towns was so little of a problem in the British Industrial Revolution that it is often

16   H. J. Perkin, 'The Social Causes of the British Industrial Revolution,' *Trans. Royal Historical Soc.* (1968), p. 135; cf. Daniel Defoe, *The Compleat English Gentleman* (1890), pp. 60–63 (written 1728–29).
17   Manning, *The English People*, ch. 6.
18   H. C. Darby, *The Draining of the Fens* (Cambridge, 1956), p. 80.

forgotten what an obstacle feudal, tribal or fragmented peasant land tenure can be in underdeveloped countries.' This was another great difference between England and the continent.[19] After 1688 Parliament encouraged the development of mineral resources, and a series of judicial pronouncements against restraints on trade completed the pattern.

The Navigation Acts (1650, 1651, confirmed 1660, 1661), made possible the closed colonial system, which could now be enforced thanks to the vast navy inherited by the Commonwealth government and the new system of taxation evolved to pay for fighting the Civil War. The Dutch War of 1652–54 was the first state-backed imperialist adventure in English history; it was followed by Cromwell's Spanish War, England's first state-backed grab for colonies in the New World. The new taxes which financed this government expenditure were doubly advantageous to businessmen, since the excise on consumption fell especially on the ostentatious expenditure of the very rich and the necessities of the poor;[20] and the land tax was based on a new assessment which hit big landowners far harder than the pre-1640 subsidy had done.

The confirmation in 1660 of legislation against monopolies and against nonparliamentary taxation, together with abolition of the prerogative courts, made any government control over economic life impossible except in agreement with Parliament. There were to be no more Cokayne Projects, no more economic interference by the Privy Council. In the late sixteenth and early seventeenth centuries, as agriculture was being commercialized, so the common law was being adapted to the needs of capitalist society and the protection of property. After 1640 arbitrary government interference with due legal process was made impossible; and due legal process now meant the law as developed by Sir Edward Coke. Parts II, III and IV of his *Institutes* could not be printed before 1640; in 1641 Parliament ordered their publication, and henceforth Coke's works, in Blackstone's delicate phrase, had 'an intrinsic authority in courts of justice, and do not entirely depend on the strength of his quotations from older authorities.'[21] Monopoly ended in industry though not in foreign trade, where organization and state naval backing were still required. The defeat of the Leveller-led democratic movement in the guilds, and the wartime breakdown of apprentice regulations, seriously undermined the security of small masters in industry. The period after 1660 saw both machine-breaking and the beginning of

19 Perkin, *The Social Causes*, pp. 137–38.
20 As Marx noted in 1847 (*The Poverty of Philosophy*, 1941), p. 129). Charles II received compensation for feudal tenures from the excise.
21 Quoted in my *Intellectual Origins of the English Revolution* (1965), pp. 255–56; see also p. 227, and ch. 5 *passim*.

trade union organization. The liberty and mobility of the revolutionary decades also facilitated a great expansion of the class of middlemen, traveling traders, whose activities were as much encouraged by post-Restoration legislation as they had been harassed by pre-1640 governments. In 1663 Pepys observed that it was cheaper for small men to buy agricultural products than to try to grow them themselves. Sixty years later Defoe said there was 'hardly a parish of all the 10,000 but has some of these retailers in them, and not a few have many hundreds.' We are on the way to Adam Smith's nation of shopkeepers. The revolutionary decades also saw an expansion of urban professional classes, catering in the open market for the needs of those with money, rather than relying on aristocratic patronage.[22]

After 1660, as before, the gentry dominated English society and the state. But now the social context was different. The land confiscations and sales of the Revolution, short-lived though many of them were, and the redistribution of wealth by taxation, together with the defeat of the radicals, all expedited the breakdown of traditional patriarchal relations between landlords and tenants. Royalist landlords were forced by the economic pressures of the Revolution, and by the absence of the Court as a source of windfall revenue, to turn to improving their estate management. These habits survived the Restoration. When Sir Edward Dering lost Court office in 1673, he drew up elaborate plans for reorganizing his estate management so as to increase production for the market.[23] Enclosure, which as recently as the 1630s had been officially denounced by Archbishop Laud, was defended in the pamphlet warfare of the 1650s and became a patriotic duty. General Monck, his biographer tells us,

> very well knew . . . how unable the nobility are to support their own esteem and order, or to assist the crown, whilst they make themselves contemptible and weak by the number and weight of their debts and the continual decay of their estates. And if the wealth of the nation come to centre most among the lower and trading part of the people, at one time or other it will certainly be in their power, and probably in their desires,

22   Ed. H. T. Heath, *The Letters of Samuel Pepys and his Family Circle* (Oxford, 1956), p. 3; D. Defoe, *The Complete English Tradesman* (1841), II, 209; cf. I, 241–53 (first published 1727); A. Everitt. 'Social Mobility in Early Modern England,' *Past & Present*, 33 (1966); *Change in the Provinces* (Dept. of English Local History, Leicester University, Occasional Papers, 2nd Series, No. 1, 1969), pp. 43–46; D. Davis, *A History of Shopping* (1966), especially ch. 6, p. 181; G. W. Chalklin, *Seventeenth-Century Kent* (1975), p. 160; cf. my *Change and Continuity in Seventeenth-Century England*, ch. 7.
23   Ed. M. F. Bond, *The Diaries and Papers of Sir Edward Dering, Second Baronet, 1644 to 1684* (H.M.S.O., 1976), p. 14; cf. *A Royalist's Notebook* (ed. F. Bamford, 1936), p. 231; *The Moore Rental* (ed. T. Heywood, Chetham Soc., 1874), p. 119.

to invade the government. These and the like considerations had moved the Duke of Albemarle to become as great an example to the nobility of honourable husbandry as he had been before of loyalty and allegiance.[24]

Who better? The Royal Society, to membership of which all peers were welcome, propagandized actively on behalf of improved agricultural production. The agrarian revolution of the later seventeenth and eighteenth centuries contributed to the accumulation of capital which was to make possible the Industrial Revolution, and to a significant increase in the domestic market for its products. A smaller labor force produced enough food to maintain a landless class as superfluous labor left the land for industry.[25]

After 1660 the republican and Cromwellian foreign policy of active support for English trade and navigation was continued. Charles II may have had antirepublican interests in leading England into the second and third Dutch Wars; but for most propertied Englishmen the Dutch were the main commercial rivals. Once their competitive power had been broken, their Protestantism was remembered again, and they were welcomed as allies against Louis XIV's France. The navy and the system of taxation which had made possible the Navigation Act and the first Dutch War were taken over by post-Restoration governments: the second and third Dutch Wars would have been impossible without them.[26] In 1694 the Bank of England was established. A bank could not have been set up in England earlier, nor in Louis XIV's France, because 'the merchants feared . . . the King would get his hands on the deposits.'[27]

After 1660 no doubt Charles II (from time to time) and James II (more seriously) dreamed of building up the absolute monarchy that their father had failed to achieve. But, thanks to the Revolution, there was never any chance that they could succeed. Without an army, without an independent bureaucracy, absolutism was impossible.[28] The post-Restoration state, and especially the post-1688 state, was strong in external relations, weak at home. The cheapest way to rule and to keep the lower orders under control was to make use of the willing but unpaid services of the natural rulers of the country, the gentry and merchant oligarchies. It had the additional advantage of maintaining habits of deference and of easing the acceptability to landowners of an expensive foreign policy.

24 T. Skinner, *Life of Monck* (2nd ed., 1724), p. 384.
25 Cf. Brenner, 'Agrarian Class Structure,' pp. 67–71.
26 See p. 127 below.
27 F. Braudel, *Civilisation materielle et capitalisme* (Paris, 1967), I, 396.
28 I owe this point to an unpublished paper by Professor J. R. Jones.

So 1660 saw a reunion of Roundheads and Cavaliers against religious, political, and social radicalism. Although formally no legislation not accepted by Charles I was valid after 1660, enough concessions had been forced from the monarchy in 1640–41 for this not to matter. There was 'a king with plenty of holy oil about him' but no risk of absolutism, bishops but no High Commission, so that Church courts could be effective only against those thought to be socially dangerous – dissenters and the lower classes. With the abolition of the prerogative courts, the triumph of Coke's common law, and later the independence of the judiciary from the executive, institutional restrictions on the development of capitalism had been removed. Whether they wanted to or not, peers and gentry had to come to terms with it. Society could not be put back into the hierarchical straitjacket of the 1630s: the Earl Marshal's Court, which used to fine and imprison commoners for speaking impolitely of their betters, was not restored.[29] Henceforth deference was paid to money, not just to land.

Peers and other great landowners still had enormous assets which could be employed in capitalist development: land, prestige, access to Court office. Marx anticipated Professor Stone in stressing 'the wonderful vitality of the class of great landlords' in England. 'No other class piles debt upon debt as lightheartedly as it. And yet it always lands on its feet.'[30] The strict settlement ensured accumulation of capital at a time when the expansion of foreign trade, navy, and bureaucracy (under parliamentary control) offered new jobs for younger sons, when the agricultural boom made the Church once more an acceptable profession, and made available richer portions for daughters. Everything combined to reconcile the aristocracy to the victory of the new social order in which they had a secure position. By the end of the century, participating in or benefiting from England's greatest capitalist industry, its money invested in the Bank of England, the peerage was sociologically a very different class from the hangers-on of James I's Court. Marx and Engels were both careful to date 'the political supremacy' of the English bourgeoisie, and its acceptance by the aristocracy, from after 1688.[31] Mr. Thompson speaks of the eighteenth-century gentry as 'a superbly successful and self-confident capitalist class.'[32]

29 *The Life of Edward Earl of Clarendon* (Oxford, 1759), I, 72–73, 76–77.
30 Marx, *Capital*, III, 841.
31 *Marx, Germany, Revolution and Counter-Revolution, in Selected Works*, II, 44; Marx, *Capital*, I, 746–47; Engels, *Socialism, Utopian and Scientific*, pp. xxiii–iv.
32 E. P. Thompson, 'The Peculiarities of the English,' *The Socialist Register*, 2 (1965), 317–18.

Between 1660 and 1688 there was an uneasy balance. As Professor Trevor-Roper has observed, there were no problems before the Civil War which could not have been solved by sensible men sitting round a table. But before the settlement was achieved, Kings and archbishops had to be taught that they had a joint in their necks, the navy and the new system of taxation had to be built up, and the country had twenty years' experience of very successful rule by parliamentary committees. These results could not have been achieved without unleashing religious, social, and political radicalism. In the forties, censorship and the control of Church courts broke down, and a wild revolutionary ferment ensued in which every heresy under the sun was preached and printed. Mechanics and their womenfolk freely met together and publicly denied the existence of heaven and hell, of the devil, of a historical Christ, of the afterlife. They treated the Bible as a collection of myths, to be used for current political purposes. They rejected a state Church, its clergy and its tithes. They claimed that all mankind would be saved, and that all men should have the vote. Some rejected the Ten Commandments and monogamy, others called for the abolition of landlordism and private property. Groups formed to achieve some of these ends. The deferences and decencies of all social order seemed to be crumbling.[33]

This unprecedented radicalism was slowly and painfully suppressed in the fifties, but it left a searing memory. In 1660 MPs were so afraid of its revival, so anxious to disband the dangerous army as quickly as possible, to reestablish control over lower-class sectaries, that they failed to impose precise enough terms on the monarchy. When the events of 1678–81 revived memories of the forties Charles II could get away for a short time with nonparliamentary rule in alliance with the Tory gentry and the Church of England. He could pack corporations – the parliamentary electorate – and James II profited by this in 1685. But Charles knew the social limits within which he could safely operate. When James II, after routing the Monmouthite radicals in 1685, really tried to put the clock back, and in particular when he abandoned the Tory-Anglican alliance and tried to use the social forces which the parliamentarians had employed against his father twenty years earlier, then the ranks closed against him – and against the radicals. The failure to impose precise terms on the monarchy was put right in 1688–89.

The obsessive fear of radicalism which led to the overkill of 1660 had regrettable social and political consequences. After the victory of the liberalized common law, demands for further legal reform and codification had come especially from the radicals. In the postrevolutionary panic

---

33   I have discussed these matters in *The World Turned Upside Down.*

they were jettisoned; apart from the Habeas Corpus Act of 1679, the establishment of the independence of juries from dictation by the judge, and, after 1701, of the judiciary from the executive (all of which benefited the propertied classes), legal reform, like franchise reform, was forgotten by 'responsible' politicians until the nineteenth century. The modest educational advances of the revolutionary decades were also abandoned. The ending of schemes for more equal educational opportunity meant that the talents of the poorer three-quarters of the population were inadequately mobilized for the Industrial Revolution which England pioneered. The exclusion of dissenters from universities as well as from political life brought about a disastrous split in the English educational system (whose consequences are still with us) between classically educated amateurs who govern, and socially inferior scientists and technologists who work.[34] Lower-class mobility was restricted by the Act of Settlement of 1662 and the poor were accepted as a permanent part of the population. The steam engine was invented but not developed. Monarchy, peerage, and the Established Church survive in England till this day.

The Marxist concept of bourgeois revolution is thus not refuted by demonstrating that the House of Commons of the Long Parliament, like its predecessors, contained a cross-section of the natural rulers of the countryside, any more than the concept of bourgeois revolution would be established if it could be shown that every MP was a factory owner. To say that there was a division between Court and Country, though true, does not get us much further than saying that the French Revolution started with a revolt of the nobility.[35] What mattered in the English Revolution was that the ruling class was deeply divided at a time when there was much combustible material among the lower classes normally excluded from politics. 'The parliament men of the early 17th century were sometimes acutely aware of the political forces operating outside Westminster,' Dr. Hirst has demonstrated, 'and on occasion attempted to present the aspirations of those forces.' To win support against the Court they were prepared to enlarge the electorate. But by now, as Dr. Manning has pointed out, 'This enlarged electorate was less easy for the gentry to control and more capable of asserting its own opinions.'[36]

34   See C. Webster, 'Science and the challenge to the scholastic curriculum, 1640–1660,' in *The Changing Curriculum* (History of Education Soc., 1971), pp. 32–34; and my *The World Turned Upside Down* (Penguin ed., 1975), p. 305.
35   For the conventional view see P. Zagorin, *The Court and the Country: The Beginning of the English Revolution* (1969).
36   Hirst, *The Representative*, p. 158; Manning, *The English People*, p. 2. In his *The Debate on the English Revolution* (1977), Dr. R. C. Richardson shrewdly pointed out that, though quite fortuitously, the argument of Dr. Meaning's *The English People and the English Revolution* 'followed on from where Hirst's book left off' (p. 143).

Though normal in composition, the Long Parliament was elected in conditions of abnormal political excitement. It is not enough to say that an MP was a gentleman or a lawyer. We must ask how he was elected. Some represented their counties, and others pocket boroughs; others again were returned as a result of conflict within an urban electorate, in which the successful candidate was the nominee of one particular group. For instance, at Great Marlow the richer citizens wanted the local land-lord, who was also a courtier; 'bargemen of the town' and 'the ordinary sort of townsmen' wanted Bulstrode Whitelocke. In an atmosphere of fierce conflict Whitelocke was returned. We classify him as a gentleman and a lawyer; but his defeated opponent was also a gentleman, son-in-law of Attorney-General Bankes, and had himself been educated at the Inner Temple.[37] A sociological analysis which cannot differentiate between the two is not very helpful. When Civil War was forced upon reluctant MPs each individual took decisions in the light of his religious beliefs, of the location of his estates, of individual hopes, fears, ambitions, hatreds, loyalties, temperaments. Counting and classifying MPs will never explain the origins of the Civil War, any more than counting and classifying Fellows of the Royal Society will explain the scientific revolution, useful though each activity may be in itself.

In every county there were long-standing rivalries within the ruling gentry, which often meant that if one family chose to support Parliament, another almost automatically chose to support the King. If we restrict our gaze to a single county, this creates the impression that the Civil War was either something external, forcing would-be neutralists unwillingly to choose sides, or an accidental conflict on to which local rivalries latched. But the national alignments in the Civil War were the sum of alignments in individual counties: it was because the traditional structures and the traditional consensus had broken down in the local-ities that Civil War could not be avoided.

The Long Parliament did not make the Revolution. MPs coped as best they could with the breakdown of the old system of government. They had to balance the pressures of the popular forces whose hostility was directed (or came to be directed) against aristocracy, gentry, and the rich generally, against their fear of these forces. Winning the war forced actions upon the parliamentarian leaders about which they were less than happy. If victory was to be consolidated, the army could not be disbanded; but the army itself became a greater liability to a stable propertied social order than even the Stuart monarchy had been. Cromwell wrestled with these problems. In the last resort it was fear –

---

37   M. R. Frear, 'The Election at Great Marlow in 1640,' *Journal of Modern History*, 14 (1942), 433–48; M. F. Keeler, *The Long Parliament, 1640–1641* (American Philosophical Soc., Philadelphia, 1954), p. 111.

fear of social radicalism, of religious radicalism, of political radicalism leading to 'anarchy' – that allowed the reemergence of the successors of the 'party of order' of the forties. They first returned to local government, and finally brought down the government of the republic by the same measures as had brought down Charles I's government – a tax strike covered by an invasion from Scotland.

Nor does the Marxist concept of bourgeois revolution, as I understand it, demand that the rulers of England in 1649 (or 1646, or 1658) should have had specific policies of 'free trade,' colonial imperialism, and the like. There had been pressure for a Navigation Act from the 1620s; the logic of the economic situation demanded it. It became politically possible because the Civil War had forced a reconstruction of the country's tax system and the creation of a great navy. It is no doubt true, as the Venetian Ambassador in Madrid observed, that the rulers of republican England were more amenable to merchant pressures than their predecessors in the twenties and thirties.[38] The Dutch War of 1652–54 avenged the Amboyna massacre of 1623 to which James I had failed to react. There is a difference between his attempts to balance between English and Dutch merchants, both rather distasteful to him,[39] and the truculent attitude of the Commonwealth government.

Similarly the export of the lighter New Draperies to the Mediterranean area suggested the desirability of a naval presence there. James in 1620 sent an expedition against the Tangier pirates, but it was not until the 1650s that Blake's fleet ruled the Mediterranean waves. Charles I had wished to build a navy, but his attempt at the financial reorganization necessary to pay for it (Ship Money) led to Civil War, which was in part a revolt against the ineffective foreign policy of a government that could not protect merchants from pirates, even in British waters. In 1588 the Spanish Armada had been defeated by private enterprise as much as by the efforts of the government; by the 1650s only the state could raise fleets adequate to the demands of English merchants. There was continuity between the power structure and the financial structure of England in 1649–53 and the 1660s; there was much less continuity between prerevolutionary and postrevolutionary England. But in the consciousness of the rules of the Commonwealth, dreams of a powerful Protestant coalition, which the Dutch could be forced if not persuaded to join and which could then be used for an anti-Catholic crusade, may have loomed as large as merely economic considerations; though things get very complicated when we recall that the

38   *Calendar of State Papers, Venetian, 1647–1652*, p. 188.
39   G. N. Clark and W. J. M. Eysinga, *The Colonial Conferences between England and the Netherlands in 1613 and 1615* (Bibl. Visseriana, tomes 15 and 17, Lugd, Bat., 1940).

most enthusiastic supporters both of the first Dutch War and of an international crusade, the Fifth Monarchists, drew their main support from clothiers and their employees.[40]

Cromwell's conquest of Ireland took place because it was strategically and financially imperative for the young republic. Yet behind it was the pressure of investors who had speculated in Irish land futures, and the recollections of City merchants whom Charles I's government had swindled over the Londonderry plantation. Such men no doubt appreciated the significance of the colonization of Ireland for the development of English capitalism; so did a William Petty or a Benjamin Worsley; but there is no evidence that economic considerations played a part in the calculations of the rulers of England in 1649. Nevertheless, in the 1660s, the Cromwellian settlement was confirmed in essentials, at the expense of the Irish and of English Cavaliers; and Ireland remained a colony to be exploited by England. The imports of sheep, cattle, butter, and cheese to England were prohibited. After the second suppression of Ireland in 1689–91 Parliament gave great weight to economic considerations in imposing restrictions on Irish trade, backed up by the penal code. The Irish clothing industry was killed.

Similar considerations applied to the war against Spain in 1655. Cromwell gave as his reasons (a) that there was a fleet in being, which it was safer and cheaper to use than to pay off; (b) that Spaniards were idolators and did not allow free trade to Protestants; (c) that the Lord had brought his English people thus far in order to achieve something great 'in the world as well as at home' – probably a hint at an anti-Catholic crusade.[41] I believe him. But there had been economic thinkers, from John Dee and Richard Hakluyt onward, who dreamed of a British empire across the Atlantic which would bring economic benefits to the mother country. Between them the pragmatists and the imperialists laid the basis for the Commercial Revolution which Professor Davis has seen as the necessary condition of England's priority in the Industrial Revolution.[42] The confirmation in 1661 of Cromwell's conquests of Jamaica and Dunkirk 'had the most universal consent and approbation from the whole nation that ever any bill could be attended with.' Sir Josiah Child in 1672 thought the Navigation Act had trebled 'the building and employing . . . of ships and seamen.'[43]

40   B. S. Capp, *The Fifth Monarchy Men* (1972), pp. 82–89, 152–54.
41   Ed. C. H. Firth, *The Clarke Papers*, III (Royal Historical Soc., 1899), 203–8.
42   R. Davis, *A Commercial Revolution* (Historical Association Pamphlet, 1967), *passim*.
43   C. M. Andrews, *The Colonial Period of American History* (New Haven, 1964), III, 32; R. Davis, *The Rise of the English Shipping Industry* (1962), ch. 18; Sir Josiah Child, *New Discourses on Trade* (1751), pp. 87, xxi (first published 1672).

Nor is the concept of bourgeois revolution, on this interpretation, refuted by the observation that rich businessmen scrambled to win privileges and monopolies under the pre-1640 regime, and that some of the richest merchants supported Charles I during the Civil War. Businessmen naturally always want the greatest possible profits: such profits were best obtained in Charles I's England by establishing close links with the government in return for monopoly privileges. Professor Ashton has described the symbiosis of Crown and customs-farmers in London, which operated to the great advantage of both parties until the crash came in 1640.[44] The oligarchies of the great merchant companies were alternately 'burdened and protected' by the Crown, but on balance protection in their privileges against interlopers outweighed resentment of the plundering.[45] It was the price to be paid for working an unsatisfactory system. By the same token, merchants and industrialists *excluded* from monopoly privileges were always potential enemies of the Crown that gave privileges to their rivals, though they might be open to offers. What was new in the early 1640s was that the royal government could no longer protect the privileges of its favorites; that customs farmers and monopolists were isolated from the rest of the business community and wide open to attack from London citizens who protected the Five Members from Charles I's attempted coup. But this was in a revolutionary situation.

Similarly in local government, where oligarchies came increasingly to dominate in the decades before the Revolution. These oligarchies were ready to cooperate with the government so long as it supported their monopoly of local power and therefore of local perquisites: the Crown preferred to have local government in the hands of small groups, which were easy to deal with, depended on the Crown for protection, and were therefore likely to support its policies. Rank-and-file craftsmen, and merchants excluded from the oligarchy, often opposed the rulers of their town; local politics became increasingly merged with national politics because of the Crown's support for oligarchy.

The House of Commons came to favor a wider electorate in most boroughs; conversely the 'outs' in boroughs used elections to Parliament as part of their struggle against their local rivals. So some gentlemen tended to put themselves at the head of the 'outs' against the 'ins' in order to get elected to Parliament.[46] The two conflicts fused, and though there

44   R. Ashton, *The Crown and the Money Market* (Oxford, 1960), *passim*.
45   See the shrewd analysis by the Venetian Ambassador in 1622 (*Calendar of State Papers, Venetian, 1621–1623*, pp. 434–35).
46   Hirst, *The Representative*, especially ch. 3; Paul Slack, 'Poverty and Politics in Salisbury, 1597–1666,' in *Crisis and Order in English Towns, 1500–1700* (ed. P. Clark and P. Slack, 1972).

were occasional exceptions, the natural result was for oligarchies to support and be supported by the Crown (or, if they did not support it satisfactorily, to be purged and reconstituted by the Crown), and for the middling sort of merchants and craftsmen, and craftsmen outside boroughs, to look to Parliament.[47] But we should not think of 'the bourgeoisie' as a self-conscious class. Any individual merchant or industrialist was naturally prepared at any time to accept privileges for himself from the Crown and to abandon support of the 'outs.' But in England before 1640 the numbers of those small masters and small merchants who formed the 'outs' increased steadily, so that individual defections made little difference to the class alignments. They do, however, confuse those historians who suppose that a class must necessarily be conscious of itself as a class. I think of a class as defined by the objective position of its members in relation to the productive process and to other classes. Men become conscious of shared interests in the process of struggling against common enemies; but this struggle can go a long way before anything emerges which we can call 'class consciousness.' Otherwise the activity of Marx, Lenin, and other Marxists in trying to stimulate 'class consciousness' in the proletariat becomes inexplicable.

To classify the English and French Revolutions, and the Russian Revolution of 1905, as bourgeois revolutions does not mean that they are to be forced into one mold. There are, it seems to me, interesting analogies, but the English gentry and merchants of the seventeenth century were very different from the leaders of the French *Tiers Etat*, faced by a highly privileged *noblesse* and a state machine permeated by the purchase of office; and both were very different from the timid Russian merchants and manufacturers, dependent on foreigners for ideas no less than for capital. As Marx recognized, the English gentry became a bourgeoisie of its own particular kind.[48] It continued to exploit its tenantry through manor courts, to use money as a source of political power as well as of capital. To recognize its dependence on capitalist relations of production is not to deny the specific way in which it adapted the institutions of the old society, from Parliament and common law downward, to its own needs.

Maurice Dobb long ago spelled out the reasons why in pre-1640 England many capitalists supported the old regime. He analyzed the

---

47 Any government, including those of the Commonwealth and Protectorate, preferred oligarchies in local government because they were easier to control. The House of Commons lost its enthusiasm for wide electorates after 1660, since popular support against the government was no longer necessary.

48 Marx, *Economic and Philosophical Manuscripts of 1844* (ed. D. Struik, 1970), pp. 100–104, 125–26. I owe this reference and some of what follows to the kindness of Edward Thompson.

difference between the 'two paths' for bourgeois revolution, the 'really revolutionary way' in which radical groups representing the middling sort drive the revolution further than the moderates wish to see it go, and so clear the decks for more radical capitalist development, and on the other hand the 'Prussian path,' in which such popular 'excesses' are avoided.[49] In its ultimate outcome the English Revolution was closer to the Prussian model than to the French, though in the 1640s the radicals played a part which hints at that of the French Jacobins. The point of stabilization under the bonapartism of Oliver Cromwell was less radical than the point of stabilization under the bonapartism of Bonaparte.

In no capitalist state in the world today, so far as I am aware, is state power exercised directly by big businessmen. There are close links between government and business, but a Henry Ford or a J. D. Rockefeller have better things to do than attend to the details of administration. So it was in the years after 1649. Many observers noted that merchants had more political influence than previously; and that members of the government came from a slightly lower social class than their predecessors; but there was no direct takeover of power by 'the bourgeoisie.'

At all points, then, I wish to disclaim the imputation of conscious will, which the opponents, but not the proponents, of the idea of bourgeois revolution attribute to it. Bourgeois revolution is not possible until capitalist relations of production have developed within a country; it comes on the agenda only when the traditional government cannot go on ruling in the old way. This inability is itself the indirect consequence of social developments, as James Harrington realized was the case for England in the 1650s.

'Bourgeois revolution' is an unfortunate phrase if it suggests a revolution *willed* by the bourgeoisie, as 'the Puritan Revolution' suggests a revolution made by Puritans to achieve Puritan ends. Perhaps a better analogy is the scientific revolution, to which contributions were made by many who were most 'unscientific' by the standards of the science which emerged from the revolution. Boyle and Newton took alchemy seriously, Locke and Newton were millenarians.

In this chapter my emphasis had been principally on the economic transformations brought about by the Revolution, because this is a point which traditional critics of a Marxist interpretation usually stress. But a revolution embraces all aspects of social life and activity. Cromwell thought that religion was 'not the thing at first contested for, but God

49   M. H. Dobb, *Studies in the Development of Capitalism* (1946), especially ch. 4.

brought it to that issue at last.' Control of the Church, the main opinion-forming body in the country, was as politically important as control of radio or TV today. In England, Puritanism had flourished in the economically advanced South and East, and in the industrial areas and ports of the North and West. Professor Collinson has shown that Puritan demands under Elizabeth raised social no less than religious issues. A Puritan settlement then would have meant an earlier subordination of the Church to the natural rulers, whether or not contemporaries saw it in that light.[50] In the 1640s all institutions and ideas were called in question in England, and though the Episcopal Church came back with the monarchy and House of Lords, and the sects ultimately decided that Christ's kingdom was not of this world, the apparent continuity was illusory. The Church of England could never again be used as a propaganda agency outside parliamentary control. Bishops had been Charles I's most reliable tools; it was bishops who first refused obedience to James II. Radical hostility to the Church had been motivated, among other things, by hatred of tithes, whose economic pressure notoriously bore especially on the middling and poorer sort; it was also caused by the activities of Church courts against sabbatarianism and working on saints' days, to mention only the most obvious economic connections.[51] The 'Latitudinarians' carried over into the post-Restoration Church Puritan attitudes toward sabbatarianism, preaching, science, and business ethics: there were no claims to the divine right of bishops or of tithes after 1660. By the 1680s Church courts had ceased to matter: parsons helped squires to maintain control of their villages, but dissent had established itself in the towns.

One test of a revolution is that those who live through it feel it as a unique turning point. The widespread millenarianism of the forties and early fifties is one example of this. But detached observers like Aubrey and Hobbes, and relatively detached observers like Marvell and Harrington, no less than eager participants like Levellers, Diggers, Quakers, preachers of Fast Sermons, all believed that they were passing through an unprecedented crisis. Milton described the achievements of the English Revolution as 'the most heroic and exemplary since the beginning of the world' – not excluding, apparently, the life and death of Christ.

Some will think that I overemphasize the importance of the defeated radicals at the expense of the mainstream achievements of the English

50   P. Collinson, *The Elizabethan Puritan Movement* (1967), passim.
51   See my *Society and Puritanism in Pre-Revolutionary England* (Panther ed.), especially chs. 4 and 5.

Revolution. Yet without the pressure of the radicals the Civil War might not have been transformed into a revolution: some compromise could have been botched up between the gentry on the two sides – a 'Prussian path.' Regicide and republic were no part of the intentions of the original leaders of the Long Parliament; they were forced on the men of 1649 by the logic of the revolution which they were trying to control.

The ferment of discussion which Milton had welcomed in *Areopagitica*, some of it highly sophisticated, some not, bubbled on for eight years or so before conservatives managed to get the lid back on again. The memory of it faded – more slowly and less completely perhaps than the books usually suggest. Blake remembered it, and so did Catherine Macaulay and the Wilkesites, Paine and the American rebels, Thomas Spence, William Godwin, the Corresponding Society, and the Chartists. The young Wordsworth recalled Milton the libertarian, Shelley recalled Milton the defender of regicide. The Revolution had shown that the old order was not eternal: the possibility of establishing God's kingdom on earth had been envisaged, especially by those normally excluded from politics. The Long Parliament itself had argued that 'reason hath no precedent, for reason is the fountain of all just precedents'; Levellers, Hobbes, Locke, and many others evolved systems of rational and utilitarian politics. By 1742 David Hume could assume that no one took claims to divine right seriously.

It is difficult for us to appreciate how great the intellectual revolution was, to think ourselves back into a hierarchical universe dominated by precedents and authorities, where God and the devil intervened in daily life. There was, of course, no sudden break in popular acceptance of magic. Many early Fellows of the Royal Society regarded belief in witchcraft as necessary if belief in God was to survive. But after 1685 no more old women were burnt as witches. Aubrey among many others spotted the revolutionary decades as the period in which traditional superstitions yielded to freedom of discussion and enquiry. Parliamentary sovereignty and the rule of law made late seventeenth-century England a freer country than any in Europe, except possibly the bourgeois Netherlands. The land had 'enfranchised itself from this impertinent yoke of prelaty, under whose inquisitorious and tyrannical duncery no free and splendid wit can flourish' – not as completely as Milton would have wished, but enough to allow Petty, Newton, and Locke to speculate freely. From 1695 the censorship could be lifted, not in the interests of freedom of thought, but of the right to buy and sell. By now the consensus among the men of property was accepted; they could be trusted to censor themselves, and the number of those who did not conform was negligible.

Nobody, then, willed the English Revolution: it happened. But if we look at its outcome, when the idealists, the men of conscious will on either side, had been defeated, what emerged was a state in which the administrative organs that most impeded capitalist development had been abolished: Star Chamber, High Commission, Court of Wards, and feudal tenures; in which the executive was subordinated to the men of property, deprived of control over the judiciary, and yet strengthened in external relations by a powerful navy and the Navigation Act; in which local government was safely and cheaply in the hands of the natural rulers, and discipline was imposed on the lower orders by a Church safely subordinated to Parliament. This Church was as different from the Church which Archbishop Laud had wished to see as the state of William III was from the state of Charles I and Strafford, as the culture of Pope, Defoe, and Hogarth was from the culture of Beaumont and Fletcher, Lancelot Andrewes, and Vandyke. Two ways of life had been in conflict and the outcome had transformed life styles and intellectual assumptions at all levels of society. With Hume and Adam Smith we are in the modern world. Before 1640 the English ruling class aped Spanish, French, and Italian fashions and ideas; after 1688 Britain was to give the lead to Europe. The novel, the bourgeois literary form *par excellence*, developed from the spiritual autobiographies of the sectaries and from Bunyan's epics of the poor: Defoe, Richardson, and Fielding could not have written as they did without the heritage of the seventeenth-century Revolution. But they produced a new art form for the whole of Europe.

If the Revolution of 1640 was unwilled, the coup d'état of 1688–89 and the peaceful Hanoverian succession were very much willed. The self-confident landed class had now consciously taken its destiny into its own hands. So, as George Wither put it in 1653:

He that would, and he that would not too,
Shall help effect what God intends to do.
. . .
Yea, they who pull down and they who do erect
Shall in the close concur in one effect.[52]

Andrew Marvell gave this theological conclusion a Harringtonian twist when he wrote, ironically, 'Men may spare their pains when Nature is at work, and the world will not go the faster for our driving.' The wise will 'make their destiny their choice.' But destiny, the historical forces, worked through the 'industrious valour' of Oliver Cromwell and his like which had ruined the great work of time:

52   G. Wither, *The Dark Lantern* (1653), pp. 10–11.

'Tis madness to resist or blame
The force of angry heaven's flame.[53]

The Revolution was God's work, both because it was unwilled by men and because it was a turning point in human history.

53   A. Marvell, *The Rehearsal Transpros'd* (ed. D. I. B. Smith, Oxford, 1971), p. 135; *Upon Appleton House*, line 744; cf. *On Blake's Victory over the Spaniards*, lines 141–42; *An Horatian Ode*, lines 25–26, 33–34.

Select Bibliography

The best general studies of the early and mid-seventeenth century are parts one, two and three of B. Coward, *The Stuart Age. England 1603–1714* (2nd edn, Harlow, 1994), R. Lockyer, *The Early Stuarts. Political History of England 1603–42* (2nd edn, Harlow, 1998) and D. Hirst, *England in Conflict, 1603–60* (London, 1999). On the mid-seventeenth century see I. Roots, *The Great Rebellion* (London, 1966) and G. Aylmer, *Rebellion or Revolution? England from Civil War to Restoration* (Oxford, 1986).

The reign of James VI and I is best approached via C. Durston, *James I* (London, 1993), S. Houston, *James I* (2nd edn, Harlow, 1995) and R. Lockyer, *James VI and I* (Harlow, 1998). Similarly, there have recently appeared three good, concise studies of the reign of Charles I: B. Quintrell, *Charles I, 1625–40* (Harlow, 1993), C. Durston, *Charles I* (London, 1998) and M. Young, *Charles I* (London, 1997), which takes a more historiographical approach. For both kings, this trio of overlapping but complementary short studies offers a sharper and more up to date picture of the monarch and his reign than any of the older, full-length biographies.

There are four good, wide-ranging collections of articles covering the pre-war decades: C. Russell (ed.), *The Origins of the English Civil War* (Basingstoke, 1973), now a little dated but still useful; H. Tomlinson (ed.), *Before the English Civil War: Essays in Early Stuart Politics and Government* (Basingstoke, 1983); R. Cust and A. Hughes (eds), *Conflict in Early Stuart England* (Harlow, 1989), reflecting an anti- or post-revisionist stance; and, on religion, K. Fincham (ed.), *The Early Stuart Church, 1603–42* (Basingstoke, 1993).

Although their revisionist tone has been criticized and is now out of fashion, C. Russell, *Parliaments and English Politics, 1621–29* (Oxford, 1979) and K. Sharpe, *The Personal Rule of Charles I* (London, 1992) remain important studies of the 1620s and 1630s respectively. T. Cogswell, *The Blessed Revolution: English Politics and the Coming of War, 1621–4* (Cambridge, 1989), R. Cust, *The Forced Loan and English Politics, 1626–8* (Oxford, 1987) L. J. Reeve, *Charles I and the Road to Personal Rule* (Cambridge, 1989) and E. S. Cope, *Politics Without Parliaments, 1629–40* (London, 1987) provide alternative viewpoints, with a greater stress upon conflict and mismanagement.

The descent into war in the late 1630s and early 1640s is viewed in different ways by A. Fletcher, *The Outbreak of the English Civil War* (London, 1981) and C. Russell, *The Fall of the British Monarchies, 1637–42* (Oxford, 1991). The latter should be read with Russell's broader study of *The Causes of the English Civil War* (Oxford, 1990).

The causes of the civil war have recently been reviewed by A. Hughes, *The Causes of the English Civil War* (2nd edn, Basingstoke, 1998) and N. Carlin, *The Causes of the English Civil War* (Oxford, 1999). R. C. Richardson, *The Debate on the English Revolution* (3rd edn, Manchester, 1998) is a historiographical review of the continuing debate. J. Morrill, *The Nature of the English Revolution* (Harlow, 1993) is a wide-ranging collection of Morrill's articles with new introductory chapters, encompassing the causes, nature and consequences of the 'revolution'.

Sound, mainly military accounts of the civil war are legion. M. Ashley, *The English Civil War* (Stroud, 1990) is a traditionally-based account: M. Bennett, *The Civil Wars in Britain and Ireland, 1638–51* (London, 1997) is more detailed and takes a three kingdoms approach; C. Carlton, *Going to Wars: The Experience of the British Civil Wars, 1638–51* (London, 1992) emphasizes the heavy and destructive impact of the wars; I. Gentles, *The New Model Army in England, Ireland and Scotland, 1645–53* (Oxford, 1991) focuses on the main parliamentary army formed towards the end of the first civil war; J. P. Kenyon, *The Civil Wars of England* (London, 1988) seeks to blend the military and political history of the war years; J. P. Kenyon and J. Ohlmeyer (eds), *The Civil Wars. A Military History of England, Scotland and Ireland, 1638–60* (Oxford, 1998) is another three kingdoms study, thematic rather than chronological in structure; and S. Reid, *All the King's Armies. A Military History of the English Civil War, 1642–51* (London, 1998) focuses upon the military history of England and Wales.

Some of the most interesting work on the civil war over the last two or three decades has taken the form of local studies. J. Morrill, *Revolt in the Provinces. The People of England and the Tragedies of War, 1630–48* (2nd edn, Harlow, 1999) focuses on the impact of, and reaction to, the civil war in the provinces of England and Wales. R. C. Richardson has edited two valuable collections on local themes: *Town and Countryside in the English Revolution* (Manchester, 1992) and *The English Civil War: Local Aspects* (Stroud, 1997). Amongst the best town studies are D. Underdown, *Fire From Heaven. Life in an English Town in the Seventeenth Century* (London, 1992) on Dorchester; S. Porter (ed.), *London and the Civil War* (Basingstoke, 1996); P. Tennant, *The Civil War in Stratford upon Avon* (Stroud, 1996); M. Stoyle, *From Deliverance to Destruction: Rebellion and Civil War in an English City* (Exeter, 1996) on Exeter; and J. Lynch, *For King and Parliament: Bristol and the Civil War* (Stroud, 1999). Amongst the best county studies are J. Morrill, *Cheshire, 1630–60. County Government and Society during the English Revolution* (Oxford, 1974); A. Fletcher, *A County Community in Peace and War: Sussex 1600–60* (Harlow, 1975); A. Hughes, *Politics, Society and Civil War: Warwickshire, 1620–60* (Cambridge, 1987); and M. Stoyle, *Loyalty and Locality: Popular Allegiances in Devon during the English Civil War* (Exeter, 1994), which attempts to show how and why the allegiances of the Devonian non-elite divided. Amongst the best regional studies are C. Holmes, *The Eastern Association in the English Civil War* (Cambridge, 1974), which focuses upon East Anglia and the East Midlands; D. Underdown, *Revel, Riot and Rebellion. Popular Politics and Culture in England, 1603–60* (Oxford, 1985), which explores divisions and allegiances in Somerset, Dorset and Wiltshire; R. Sherwood, *Civil War in the Midlands* (Stroud, 1992); P. Tennant, *Edgehill and Beyond. The People's War in the South Midlands, 1642–45* (Stroud, 1992); and R. Hutton, *The Royalist War Effort, 1642–46* (2nd edn, London, 1999), which assesses the royalist war machine in Wales and the Marches.

The impact and the direct consequences of the civil war of 1642–6 are explored in J. Morrill (ed.), *Reactions to the English Civil War* (Basingstoke, 1982), Morrill (ed.), *The Impact of the English Civil War* (London, 1991) and S. Porter, *Destruction in the English Civil Wars* (Stroud, 1994), as well as in Carlton's *Going to Wars*.

The outburst of political and religious radicalism unleashed by the civil war is assessed in C. Hill, *The World Turned Upside Down* (London, 1972), J. McGregor and B. Reay (eds), *Radical Religion in the English Revolution* (London, 1984) and F. D. Dow, *Radicalism in the English Revolution* (London, 1985). Puritanism has been examined by W. Lamont, *Puritanism and Historical Controversy* (London, 1996) and J. Spurr, *English Puritanism* (Basingstoke, 1998).

M. Kishlansky has explored *The Rise of the New Model Army* (Cambridge, 1979), though many historians favour the interpretation of Gentles, *The New Model Army in England, Ireland and Scotland* and of A. H. Woolrych, *Soldiers and Statesmen. The General Council of the Army and its Debates, 1647–8* (Oxford, 1987), a masterly account of the role of the army in politics. From a less military perspective, R. Ashton, *Counter-Revolution: The Second Civil War and its Origins, 1646–8* (London, 1994) provides a very detailed study of those years. D. Underdown, *Pride's Purge. Politics in the Puritan Revolution* (Oxford, 1971) is the definitive account of the political prelude to and context of the trial and execution of the king. Despite the burst of new studies thrown up by the 350th anniversary of the regicide, the classic account of the episode with which this volume closes remains that of C. V. Wedgwood, *The Trial of Charles I* (London, 1964).

Index

76992

Wellingborough, 231
Wentworth, Sir Thomas *see* Strafford
Westminster Assembly, 194, 204
Wharton, Philip, lord, 79–80
Whigs and Whig history, 10–11, 35–6,
    38–9, 43, 44, 49, 59–60, 63, 73
White, Peter, 45
Whitehall debates, 300–1
Whitelocke, Bulstrode, 2–3, 4, 197–8,
    306, 328, 337
Whortley, Sir Francis, 174
Widdrington, Sir William, 94, 136
Wight, Isle of, 1–2, 219, 278, 316, 321
Wilby, 111
Wildman, John, 282, 289–90, 292, 301,
    314
William III, 345
Williams, John, 262, 305
Williams, Roger, 290
Wilson, Thomas, 210, 215, 219
Wiltshire, 29, 52, 154, 160, 161, 246–7,
    262, 264
Windebank, Francis, 90, 132, 133
Windsor, 316, 317
Winstanley, Gerrard, 280, 326
Winter or Wintour, Sir John, 159, 259
Wither, George, 345
Wolstenhome, Sir John, 114

Wolverhampton, 174
Wood, Andrew, 158
wood-pasture, 52, 160
Woodbury, 239
Woodcock, Francis, 311
Woodford, Hannah, 104, 108, 110,
    111
Woodford, Robert, 55–6, 104–27, 155
Woodhouse, Michael, 253
Woolrych, Austen, 148, 271, 272
Worcester, 228, 230, 235, 241, 243,
    247, 256, 257, 258, 261–2, 264,
    265
Worcestershire, 160, 162–3, 178,
    226–48, 255, 261
Worsley, Benjamin, 339
Wray, John, 20
Wren, Matthew, 117, 126, 189
Wrexham, 264
Wyllys, George, 129

yeomen, 19, 28, 71, 160, 180, 182, 327,
    328, 329
York, 79, 120, 130, 133, 134, 140
Yorkshire, 208, 329
Young, Michael, 42

Zagorin, Perez, 51